943
J267
v.12

THE GERMAN PEOPLE

VOL. XII.

HISTORY OF THE GERMAN PEOPLE at the
Close of the Middle Ages. By Johannes Janssen.

Vols. I. and II. Translated by M. A. Mitchell and
A. M. Christie.

Vols. III.—XVI. Translated by A. M. Christie.

HISTORY OF THE GERMAN PEOPLE AT THE CLOSE OF THE MIDDLE AGES

By JOHANNES JANSSEN

VOL. XII.

ART AND POPULAR LITERATURE TO THE BEGINNING OF THE THIRTY YEARS' WAR

TRANSLATED BY A. M. CHRISTIE

LONDON

KEGAN PAUL, TRENCH, TRUBNER & CO. LTD.

BROADWAY HOUSE, CARTER LANE, E.C.

B. HERDER BOOK CO.

15-17 SOUTH BROADWAY, ST. LOUIS, MO.

1907

TRANSLATOR'S NOTE.

These Volumes (XI. and XII.) are translated from
Vol. VI. of the German [Fifteenth and Sixteenth Editions,
improved and added to by Ludwig Pastor].

CONTENTS

OF

THE TWELFTH VOLUME

BOOK III

DRAMATIC LITERATURE

HISTORY

OF

THE GERMAN PEOPLE

AT THE CLOSE OF THE MIDDLE AGES

—◦◦◦—

BOOK III

DRAMATIC LITERATURE

CHAPTER I

RELIGIOUS DRAMA

THE national religious drama which had grown up out of the depths of the religious life of the people, in close connection with the Church liturgy, was at the height of its glory in the middle of the fifteenth century.[1] It did not indeed attain to the artistic finish which characterised the Spanish *autos*, but by the ideal nature of its contents and the noble pomp of its representations, it acquired an influence and a signifi-

---

[1] ** This opinion has been newly confirmed by Wackernell's researches concerning the oldest Passion plays in Tyrol. Vienna, 1887. For the origin of the religious drama in the Catholic Liturgy see also Wetzer and Welte's *Kirchenlexikon*, ii. (2nd edition), 1457 ff.

cance which may well stand comparison with the power of ancient Greek tragedy.[1]

The most elevated and profound subjects of these plays were the symbolic representations of the divine revelations to mankind;[2] the performance of these constituted also the most edifying of the popular festivals.[3]

---

[1] See our remarks, vol. i. pp. 296–305. A few later dramas of a religious nature, notably the Oberammergau Passion-play, have made it possible for us in the present day to form an idea of the powerful effect of this religious drama of the people, and to measure the benefit which further harmonious development of this art would have conferred on the whole spiritual life of the nation. 'The popular tone, the good-humoured pleasantry which were prominent in the old religious representations,' says Weinhold (p. 79), ' did not injuriously affect the reverence of the people ; they were indeed more impressed by these performances than by dry, dogmatic dissertations, or by endless polemics.' That there were not wanting here and there cases of deep desecration of holy things is shown by a Tyrolese peasant-comedy, a so-called *Bruderspiel*, on the meeting of Jesus with the disciples at Emmaus. See A. Pichler, *Über das Drama des Mittelalters in Tyrol*, Innsbruck, 1850. On the whole, however, in Germany, says Devrient (i. 30–31), ' the sanctity of religious matters was very seldom violated.' ' The German plays resemble the Spanish in one particular, viz. that the burlesque element in them is used more as a vulgar counterfoil to enhance the sacred elements, than with the intention of dragging these down.' The devil who appears in the religious dramas of the Middle Ages does not, as in those of the sixteenth and seventeenth centuries, play a terrifying and triumphant part, but is always obliged, against his will, to figure in ludicrous guise as an over-wise, or poor, or stupid devil, and to represent grotesque, laughable characters.

[2] Devrient, i. 73. ** Concerning the Latin Easter solemnities, and Easter and Passion-plays, cf. G. Milchsack, *Oster- und Passionsspiele*, i. Wolfenbüttel, 1880 ; K. Lange, *Die Latein. Osterfeiern*, Munich, 1887 ; M. Wirth, *Oster- und Passionsspiele bis zum 16. Jahrhundert.* Halle, 1889. This last-named work deals also with the inner development of the German Passion-play ; cf. also in this connection R. Froning, *Das Drama des Mittelalters* (Stuttgart, 1889), 3. Teil (in Kürschner's *Nationallittera-tur*, pp. 174, 175 and 178). W. Creizenach, *Gesch. d. neueren Dramas*, i. (Halle, 1893), and Wackernell, *Altdeutsche Passionsspiele aus Tirol* (Graz, 1897).

[3] ** In Tyrol we can trace these back in nearly all the towns for

Very imposing, for instance, must have been ' the solemn plays ' acted in the last years before the out-break of religious and political storms, on the three Whitsuntide festivals of 1516, in the public market-place at Freiberg in Saxony. The first day's per-formance was ' the story of the fall of the angels, of the creation and fall of man, of the expulsion from Paradise, and of the two unlike children of Adam and Eve ' ; on the second and third days scenes from the New Testament and the Day of Judgment were represented.[1] The impressive subject-matter comprehends in its scope the sublimest ideas of the poetry of a Dante and a Milton, treated not in cold sermonising fashion, but in living and dramatic form. Duke George of Saxony attended the performances with his wife and his whole court retinue, and the play was regarded not merely as a religious function, but as a distinguished municipal affair, so that the council appointed as actors Hans Rudolf, the then town sheriff, and Hans Pfeffer, who later on was town bailiff. In an Easter Passion-play, acted at Frankfort-on-the-Main in 1506, which lasted four days and in which 267 persons performed, William Stein, pastor of the Dreikönigskirche at Sachsenhausen, played the part of Christ ; the leaders of the play were two curates of the Liebfrauenkirche. The piece ended with the Ascension of Christ, and an after-play celebrated the triumph of the Church.[2] At Alsfeld, in 1517, an Easter Passion-play lasted three days ;[3] at Botzen, three years earlier, a seven

a whole century ; cf. Wackernagel, *Die ältesten Passionsspiele in Tirol,* p. 154 ff.

[1] Goedeke, *Grundriss,* ii. 332, No. 5.
[2] Fichard, *Frankfort Archives,* iii. 131–158.
[3] Wilken, *Gesch. der geistlichen Spiele in Deutschland,* p. 110.

days' 'Passion' was performed, its representation
being spread over different festivals between Palm
Sunday and Ascension Day.[1]

A Heidelberg Passion-play, written in 1514, treats
all those events in Old Testament history which are
regarded as divine revelations, predicting and preparing
for the work of redemption, with the same detail as the
incidents in the life and passion of the Saviour. Among
these are the very same Old Testament types which
later on, dealt with singly, formed the favourite dramatic subjects, especially with the Protestant poets :
Joseph in Egypt, David and Goliath, Susanna, and
others.[2] The story of Susanna here,[3] as also in a
Viennese ' Susanna ' of the fifteenth century, is treated
in a strikingly chaste manner,[4] as compared with many of
these plays of later times. At Munich in 1510, besides
the representation of a play of the Day of Judgment,
in which the end of the world, the advent of the Judge,
the separation of the good and the bad, were depicted
on a large scale, there was a performance of an impressive tragedy ' Vom sterbenden Menschen ' (' Dying
Man '). In this last we note the development of the
same idea which, a few decades later, acquired such
great importance in the numerous allegorical Homulus
and Hekastus tragedies.[5]

Large towns and small villages, religious and secular

---

[1] Pichler, *Dramen des Mittelalters in Tirol*, p. 64.

[2] *Das Heidelberger Passionsspiel*, published by G. Milchsack in the
Bibl. des litterarischen Vereins at Stuttgart, vol. 150 (Tübingen, 1880).
Milchsack, pp. 296–297, refers to the ' prefigurations.'

[3] Milchsack, p. 80 ff.

[4] Cf. Pilger, *Die Dramatisierungen der Susanna*, p. 139.

[5] K. Trautmann in the *Jahrbuch für Münchener Gesch.* i. 196–202.
Fuller details concerning the allegorical plays occur in Goedeke's article,
' Everyman,' &c.

corporations vied with each other in getting up performances of this kind, and everybody took part in
them either as player or onlooker.[1] At Frankfort-on-
the-Main, in 1515, a special fraternity was formed for
the representation of religious plays.[2]

When, then, the new religious movement broke out,
when Sickingen set going his plans for the overthrow
of the imperial constitution, and, soon afterwards,
the social revolution flooded a large part of Germany,
leaving frightful ravages behind, it was naturally
no longer possible to keep up the old festival plays,
which not only required a peaceful, joyous state of
mind, but also involved great sacrifice of time and
money. Wherever iconoclasm raged, there fanaticism swept away the sacred drama, as well as the
glories of the plastic arts. On the other hand ' plays '
of a different kind were acted in many places. As in
the wild uproar of iconoclasm altars and images had
been smashed up, so, too, vestments intended for divine
service were seized by the desecrators of churches, and
used in public processions for the most unworthy pan-
tomimes. It pleased the coarse taste of the mob to
see all the solemnities of the Catholic worship dragged
down into carnival farces and low comic mummery.
Burlesque dialogues, like libellous pamphlets and lampoons, had been, from the first, among the most potent
means for stirring up sedition.

The old religious popular drama received a fresh
vital impulse in the Catholic cantons of Switzerland
after the middle of the sixteenth century—earlier.

---

[1] See *Neues Archiv für sächsische Geschichte und Altertumskunde*, iv.
104 ff. C. Meyer, *Geistliches Schauspielkunst*, p. 2.
[2] Mentzel, *Gesch. der Schauspielkunst*, p. 2.

indeed, than in those districts of Germany which had remained Catholic.[1] At Lucerne, in 1549, an imposing drama 'Das Jüngste Gericht' ('The Last Judgment') was put on the stage.[2] Passion- or Easter-plays were performed there very frequently,[3] and indeed with such splendour that the costs of a representation sometimes amounted to 1000 or even 2000 crowns.[4]

In the year 1583 'The Old and the New Testament' was played, the performance lasting two days, with 290 actors on the first day, and 204 on the second. The parts were sold to the players, for forty, thirty, or eight shillings according to their importance ; the performers had to provide their own stage dresses, and also the scenery ; as sole compensation they received free board and drink.[5]

In the year 1599 the burghers, 'For the praise and glory of God Almighty, for the extension of the Catholic faith, for the instruction of the people and the increase of their piety,' arranged for the performance of 'Die

[1] See Gall Morel 'Das geistliche Drama vom zwölften bis neunzehnten Jahrhundert in den fünf Orten und besonders in Einsiedeln' in the *Geschichtsfreund* (Einsiedeln, 1860), xvii. 75–144, and also *Nachträge* (1868), xxiii. 219–234.

[2] Gall Morel, in the *Geschichtsfreund*, xvii. 83.

[3] See the catalogue of the plays of 1545–1597 in Mone, *Schauspiele*, ii. 420–422.

[4] Goedeke, *Grundriss*, ii. 353, No. 95.

[5] See G. Kinkel's contributions in Pick's *Monatschrift für die Gesch. Westdeutschlands*, 1881. pp. 301–334. For the *mise en scène* of the Easter-play of 1583 see Genée, pp. 12–14. A performance of 1584 appears to have given very little satisfaction to the abbot Ulrich von Einsiedeln. He wrote in his account-book : 'Six crowns against Lucerne for the play. They might well have been saved' (Gall Morel, xxiii. 221). ** Cf. Vogt-Koch, *Deutsche Litteraturgeschichte*, p. 262 (where there is a picture of the wine-market at Lucerne as the theatre of the Easter-play of 1583 after F. Leibing): 'Über die Inscenierung des zweitägigen Luzerner Osterspieles vom Jahre 1583 durch Renwart Cysat, 1869'

Histori der heiligen Apostel' in the open market-place, and paid the whole costs of it themselves.[1] At Zug, also in 1598, the leading burghers took part in a representation of the 'Erfindung und Erhöhung des heiligen Kreuzes'[2] ('Invention and Exaltation of the Holy Cross').

The tragedy 'Johannes der Täufer' ('John the Baptist') written in 1549 by Johannes Al, preacher at the Dom in Solothurn, and performed by the burghers there, may be reckoned among the best dramatic writings of the century.[3]

At Freiburg-in-the-Breisgau Passion-plays were acted in the years 1555 and 1557, and not unfrequently —as for instance in 1599—the Passion was played in connection with the Corpus Christi procession performed by the guilds. Several of the martyrs also, who had given their lives for the Saviour, were introduced into the play. At the end 'the four last things' were represented, after 'Mary with the little mantle' had first admonished the hearers as follows :

> While I, Mary, ready wait,
> A mother of misericord,
> From my Son, the Lord,
> Grace and mercy manifold
> To obtain, let young and old
> Who would be God's children dear,
> Flock beneath my mantle here.
> Let them all their lives amend
> While there's still time to repent,
> Ere has come the judgment hour,
> And I no more to help have power.

---

[1] Gall Morel, xxiii. 221–222. At Beromünster in 1560 there was a performance of 'eine heilige, katholische und apostolische Tragedi uss den Geschichten der Aposteln' ('a holy, Catholic and apostolic tragedy out of the histories of the Apostles'), l.c. p. 224.

[2] Gall Morel, xvii. 85–86.

[3] The complete title is in Goedeke, *Grundriss*, ii. 348, No. 68.

The whole moral of the play was summed up at the
end as follows :

> Now be not harder than hard stones,
> And give thanks that His blood atones.
> Behold and see the saints of God
> Who suffering's path so gladly trod,
> And for Christ's sake endured death's pain,
> They now will honour Him again,
> By their blood His witnesses,
> His grace and love have done all this.[1]

Up to shortly before the outbreak of the Thirty
Years' War representations of an imposing nature still
occasionally took place at Freiburg. For instance,
Thomas Mallinger records in his diary : ' In the year
1615, June 18, the comedy or commemoration of our
Redeemer and Saviour Jesus Christ's holy life and
bitter passion and death was performed here in Freiburg
by several hundred actors, burghers and their children,
young and old, men and women. Many thousand
spectators, not from this place only, but from the
country many miles around, witnessed the performance; it began in the morning and went on into the
night.' [2]

The burghers of Munich took ' great pleasure and
delight in comedies.' When the Emperor Charles V.
and his brother Ferdinand made their entry there in
1530, three plays were got up in their honour, ' very
artistically and wonderfully ' ; one of these was the
' History of Esther,' which, according to the statement
of Sebastian Franck, was ' so charming, artistic, and

---

[1] Schreiber, p. 54 ff. The Passion-play of 1599, published by E. Martin
in the *Zeitschr. der Gesellschaft für Beförderung der Geschichtskunde von
Freiburg*, iii. 3–95.

[2] Mone, *Quellensammlung der badischen Landesgeschichte*, ii. 529.

well managed that everybody was astonished, and it would not have been easy to improve it.'[1] The Corpus Christi plays assumed the most important form in Munich. They exhibited all the leading events in the Old and the New Testament in an infinite number of *tableaux vivants* ; even the mystic prophecies of Holy Writ concerning the future of the human race were represented in this manner. The clergy and all the town guilds took part in these performances ; each different guild contributed its own share towards the pageant, which aimed at the glorification of the Holy Sacrament.[2] Daniel Holzmann gave a ' true and exact account ' of the Corpus Christi play of 1574, in which ' nearly fifty-six figures from the Old and New Testament were drawn, and all the people, lay or clerical, of whom there were as many as 1439, were designated by their baptismal names and their surnames, and over every figure there was an explanation in German rhyme according to the Bible text.'[3]

Religious comedies for schools, which in Bavaria, as elsewhere, had been in vogue long before the outbreak of the religious revolution, found a zealous promoter at Munich in the middle of the sixteenth century in Jerome Ziegler, rector of the town gymnasium. As a student at Ingolstadt he had taken a lively part in the representation of such plays, and he now himself composed several dramas of a religious nature, which were acted by his pupils in Latin and German : as, for instance, ' The Sacrifice of Isaac,' ' The Three Holy

[1] K. Trautmann in the *Jahrbuch für Münchener Gesch.* i. 202–203.

[2] Cf. Westenrieder, *Beiträge*, v. 83–181 ; Von Winterfeld, *Zur Gesch. heiliger Tonkunst*, ii. 299–308 ; Bäumker, *Orlandus de Lassus*, pp. 40–43.

[3] Goedeke, *Grundriss*, ii. 384, No. 285.

Kings and King Herod,' ' The Wise and the Foolish Virgins,' and others.[1]

Four Christmas plays by an unknown Bavarian poet, at the beginning of the seventeenth century, are distinguished by fitness of arrangement, by the pathos and poetic warmth of many passages, and by general facility of language.   One of the shepherds sings :

> Joy fills our field, joy upon joy,
>   Delight in brimming measure,
> Vales, woods and mountains skip, and I
>   Go shepherding with pleasure !
>
> The meadows are with blossoms bright
>   As though for Spring bedecked,
> The roses' purple is in sight,
>   All earth has newly waked.
>
> Richly the sweet honey-juice
>   Exudes from hollow oaken ;
> No natural force can this produce,
>   'Tis sure a heavenly token.

His wife then tells him what had happened in Bethlehem : three shepherds, surprised and enraptured by the smiles of the Child, had presented their humble gifts with admiration, and on departing had sung a hymn of eight verses, the first of which ended with the words :

> Sinners to save, the young Child hastes:
> Love his chariot is.

To the soul longing for the Saviour the angel says that ' its yearnings will be put to rest, the manger will become its school of virtue ' :

> 'Tis not enough with passing thought
>   On Christ His birth to meditate,
> In your heart and mind it must be wrought,
>   His love your soul must permeate.

As at the Bavarian court, so also at the court of

[1] Cf. *Jahrbuch für Münchener Gesch.* i. 204 ff.

Archduke Ferdinand II. at Innsbruck, religious dramas
were performed, and the Archduke himself, in 1584,
was the author of ' a fine comedy,' ' Speculum Humanae
Vitae,' or ' A Mirror of Human Life,' in which, without
any special poetic endowment, he administered all sorts
of good lessons and admonitions.[1]

A like aim was pursued by the halberdier and marker
Benedict Edelpöck in a ' Komödie von der freuden-
reichen Geburt unseres einigen Trostes und Heilandes
Jesu Christi,' which he dedicated to the Archduke
in 1568. ' Many a pious heart,' Edelpöck hoped, might
derive no small consolation from this play ; young
people inclined to all sorts of sin and vice would
recognise in it a mirror of their defects, and the old
would learn from it their neglect in the education of
the young. ' Further, the common people would be
instructed by representations of this kind in a sight-
knowledge of Holy Writ ; for what is seen by the eye
is much more strongly impressed on the hearts and
minds of simple lay folk than what is only heard by
the ear.' But the well-meant aim and the pious ideas
of the author were not supported by any exalted
treatment of his material. The sacred personages were
handled like common people of the soil. On their
departure for Egypt Joseph says to the Holy Virgin :

> Since we must go and have no cart,
> To carry the luggage shall be my part :
> Spoons, pans, dishes, platters, candles,
> Lanterns and clothes I'll tie in bundles ;
> Take bread and cheese, and fill the flask.

---

[1] Hirn, i. 366–367. ** See the new edition of the *Speculum* by J.
Minor (Halle, 1889), and H. Kluibenschedl, *Erzherzog Ferdinand II. von
Tirol als Schauspieldichter*, *Programm des Gymnasiums zu Görz*, 1891.
See also Nagl-Zeidler, *Deutsch-österr. Litteraturgesch.* p. 580 ff.

And when Mary will have nothing to do with the
' flask,' he says :

> . . . I'll not leave behind me the flask,
> However heavy should be my task.

On the way he offers the Holy Virgin a drink, which,
however, she refuses, exclaiming :

> It is not seemly, it looks most ill
> When young women drink their fill.
> I have read in Scripture text
> That wine is poison to our sex.
> It's not respectable or proper
> For a woman to be a toper ;
> All sense of decency is over
> When a wife comes home unsober.[1]

The same criticism applies to the dialogues which the
Vienna schoolmaster Wolfgang Schmeltzl, in his ' Aus-
sendung der Zwölf Boten,' in 1542, puts into the mouths
of the Apostles before they start on their journey ' into
all the world ' : their talk shows no high conception of
these sacred personages, and it was certainly not in
accord with the character of the men to whom the charge
was given by the Son of God to divide the globe between
them, and conquer it for Christendom, that James,
in spite of the wonders of the day of Pentecost, should
scarcely be able to speak for sorrow at leaving : ' For
grief my heart might almost break.' Bartholomew
says :

> . . . Dearest brother mine, I pray
> Thou would'st not be so sad to-day,
> Because we now must tramp the roads,
> Leaving our children, wives and goods.
> God will reward us, well I know :
> Keep a good heart ; away I go.

---

[1] The comedy printed by Weinhold, pp. 193–288. In a German

Philip, however, asks Andrew for another 'farewell drink' out of his flask, which the poet reckons among the natural equipment of the Apostles :

> Andrew, lend me that flask of thine,
> And let me lave this heart of mine.

And Andrew, the herald of the Cross, answers :

> Oh, dear Philip, with all my heart,
> I'll give thee a drink before we start,
> For thou my dearest brother art.

Such words as these suggest the leave-takings of honest artisans on departure from the common work-shop, and from their lips they would come with natural warmth and heartiness.[1]

And yet Schmeltzl was by no means wanting in higher sentiment. His best piece, 'David and Goliath,' written in 1545, breathes lofty enthusiasm for the war against the Turks, and this same enthusiasm kindles him to warm language in other places also.

Schmeltzl, with the help of his pupils, represented his Biblical dramas, seven in number, on the stage, and it deserves special notice that, in contradistinction to so many school dramatisers, he kept all vulgarity and coarseness out of his pieces.[2] Other German school plays—such, for instance, as those frequently performed at Nuremberg—were of a very different nature. The

Christmas play of the fifteenth century a poet had already made St. Joseph say to Mary :

> Now up and follow me, don't fear ;
> We'll go and swallow some good beer.

Meyer, *Geist. Schauspiel*, pp. 172–173. Let the reader compare with this, at vol. xi. p. 208, the manner in which Dürer once represented St. Joseph.

[1] Spengler (p. 47) considers that these farewell scenes represent 'Schmeltzl in his most touching vein.'

[2] Fuller details in Spengler, pp. 21 ff., 66 ff., 79, 81–83.

Protestant schoolman, Paul Praetorius, rector of the
school of St. Sebald at Nuremberg, apprehended from
these latter great danger to the moral culture of the
young ; he thought they would still further feed the
loose tendencies already too strongly developed in
them.[1]

[1] Holstein, pp. 41–42 ; cf. Nagl-Zeidler, p. 570 ff. Concerning the
Latin school comedies and the Jesuit drama, see vol. vii. pp. 106 ff., 118 ff.
of the present work (see the German original which is not yet translated
into English), and Nagl-Zeidler, p. 655 ff. ' So much has already been
written,' says K. Trautmann in the *Jahrbuch für Münchener Gesch.* i.
209–210, ' about the tasteless and senseless pomp of the Jesuit plays,
that one may well wonder how princes who understood and encouraged
art so well as did the Wittelsbachers should have taken any pleasure in
these performances. One thing, however, the writers on the subject
have forgotten to lay stress on, namely, that in the sixteenth century at
any rate, the *mise en scène* was always managed by genuine artists ;
that leading representatives of Munich art, then already at such a high
pitch of development, a Hans Müelich, a Christopher Schwarz, a Hubert
Gerhard, busied themselves, with unstinted expenditure of money, to
realise the scenic intentions of the poets ; that one of the accessory means,
for instance, by which many of these plays were helped, the choruses
sung by hundreds of well-trained voices, had no less a director than
Orlando di Lasso, the much-famed musician. What the Jesuits contributed to the field of stage technique can only be described as grandiose.
We may form some conception of the sort of poetical impression produced
on the crowds on the occasions of these representations, if we picture
to ourselves one of these gala days with the whole decorated town for the
stage—as, for instance, the performance of *Constantinus* in 1574, in
which over 1000 people took part, and the victor of Maxentius made
his entry through garlanded portals, on glittering triumphal cars, surrounded by 400 riders in shimmering antique armour and equipment ;
or the powerful drama of *Esther*, or the still more imposing pageant in
honour of the archangel Michael, held in an open space in 1597 at the
consecration of the newly built church of St. Michael, with its tremendous
concluding scene of 300 devils cast into the blazing, soaring flames
of hell. In the midst of all this splendour there were not wanting
homely, pathetic interludes, as when the Jesuit pupils all filed out to the
lonely Grosshesselohe, to act there Balde's dialogue, *The Battle of the
Giant with the Dwarf*, there in the silent forest glade, under wide-spreading
primeval trees.' The plays acted in Protestant towns may well have
been of a less influential nature than those which Felix Platter of Basle
calls up from the recollections of his youth : ' There was a play acted in

The question which most exercised the minds of the Protestants, namely, the overthrow of the old Church system, occupied also a prominent place in their dramatic literature. From the lowest carnival farce up to Biblical and religious plays, almost the whole of their drama is of a controversial character, or at least it is full of didactic allusions to the controversies of the day, of complaints about the Catholic Church and of its doctrines and institutions, about the papacy, the priest-hood, celibacy, monastic life, good works, the mass and purgatory, the veneration of Mary and the saints.

It was inevitable that such a tendency as this

the college, *The Resurrection of Christ*; my father's boarders made a number of fools, and there were also devils' clothes among the stage properties. . . . On June 6, 1546, the play, *Paulus Bekehrung* (" The Conversion of Paul "), made by Valentin Boltz, was performed in the corn-market. The burgomaster of Brun was Saul, Balthasar Han was the Lord God in a round heaven, hanging over the stage, out of which there flashed a furious rocket, which, as Saul fell from his horse, set fire to his hose. Rudolf Fry was the captain; he had about 100 burghers under his banner, all wearing his colours. The thunder was made in heaven with barrels filled with stones and rolled over. Long before Ulrich Coccius had played the *Susanna* in the fish-market. The wooden platform was on the fountain, to which a tin case, in which Susanna washed herself, had been adapted.' ' My father' (the schoolmaster Thomas Platter) ' played in the school the *Hippocrisis*, in which I was one of the Graces. They dressed me in Herwagen's daughter Gertrude's clothes, which were too long for me, and in going about through the town I could not hold them up, so they were greatly damaged. The affair went off very well, but the rain came at last and spoilt the play.' They often held plays in the crypt of the Augustinians' churches. When-ever the new rector gave the meal, the students invited him with fifes and drums into the hostel, with the Regent, and a comedy was acted. Those which I saw in this manner were, first, the *Resurrection of Christ*, secondly *Zacchaeus*, a comedy which Dr. Pantaleon wrote and acted, thirdly, the comedy of *Haman* ; when the executioner was going to hang the son of Haman, the latter made a false step and so remained sus-pended, and if the hangman had not at once cut the rope he would have been strangled : he had a red mark round his neck in consequence (Boos, pp. 143-144).

should maim all truly creative force, and should also cause the outward technique of the drama—taste, language, and presentation—to sink lower and lower. The impartial attitude of mind and the peaceful joy in creativeness which are necessary to bring art to greatness had been uprooted. In the noise and turmoil of party strife these conditions were not likely to regain ground. The men of greater genius, in their striving after higher ideals, were perpetually torn away into the dismal whirl of strife, whilst talentless controversialists pushed themselves to the fore and sought to convert any poetic matter which still lived in their memories into a mere motive for their rhymed tendency-prose.[1]

While among Protestant preachers there were not wanting those who wished to put down all plays, Luther again and again expressed himself in favour of dramatic representations. ' The acting of comedies,'

---

[1] ' The didactic ebullitions which begin to invade the German drama ' are described by Pilger (p. 155) as one of the ' damaging influences which resulted from the Reformation.' ' In the hands—hands as unskilled and unqualified as they were zealous—of the majority of those who produced this " tendency " or " problem " poetry, those elements which, with the most skilful treatment, could at the outside have served only as accessory matter, became such an important and essential part of the whole, that most of the writers thought themselves justified in introducing them whenever and wherever they liked.' Scherer (*Deutsche Studien*, p. 185) says : ' Germany cannot be said to have produced any really great dramatist in the sixteenth century ; only a few noteworthy ones, together with many mediocre and still more bad ones.' W. Wackernagel (*Drama*, p. 142) speaks of a ' great, hundred-year-long, confused hurly-burly of the German drama ' ; and in his *Gesch. der deutschen Litteratur*, p. 462, of an ' unfruitful, mongrel mixture of homegrown and foreign.' Chrysander (ii. 319) says : ' Song-book rhymes, or the forms of religious and secular songs, impede free dramatic language. This was a symptom, and the root-defect of the whole range of our dramatic poetry at that period, a defect so self-evident that even the English noticed it.' ' The Germans exhibit on the stage things which the preacher ought to deal with in the pulpit,' writes Whetstone in 1578, in his dedication of the *Historye of Promus and Cassandra*.

he says, 'must not be forbidden to boys at school, but allowed and encouraged ; first because it is a good exercise for them in the Latin language, and secondly because in comedies which are artistically constructed, written and represented, those persons by whom the world is instructed, and indeed every individual in turn, will be reminded of the duties of his office and station, and of what is becoming for a servant, a gentleman, for young fellows, and for the old, and what they all ought to do.' ' Besides which in these plays we find written down and described the cunning tricks and the frauds of bad people ; also what are the duties of parents and children ; how children and young people are to be attracted to matrimony when they are of a suitable age, and kept faithful to it; how children are to be obedient to their parents, and how they are to carry on courtship.' ' And Christians must not altogether shun plays, because there are sometimes coarseness and adulteries in them; for that reason they would have to give up the Bible also. Therefore this is no argument against the plays, and no reason for forbidding Christians to read and act them.' [1]

Luther considered Bible matter especially adapted to religious plays ; indeed, he said, ' the books of Judith and Tobias were nothing more than fine poems and dramas ; the Jews had a great many such, and performed them for the instruction and edification of the people.' ' The text of Susanna, of Bel, Habakkuk, and the Dragon was like beautiful, religious poetry, as were Judith and Tobias.' On the other hand, he was opposed to representations of the Passion of Christ, because it was not

---

[1] Luther's *Table-Talk*, published by Förstemann, iv. 592–593. Cf. Holstein, pp. 19–20.

right to pity and weep over Christ on account of His being an innocent man. Melanchthon also set himself against Passion-plays, because four men had lost their lives at one of these plays : [1] ' this was a judgment of God to show His anger against the despisers of the veritable Passion of Christ, which He did not wish to have represented on the stage any more.' In the Brandenburg district the Passion-plays remained still a good long while in vogue, but they were abolished in 1598 by the Elector Joachim Frederic as survivals of ' papism.' [2]

After Luther had spoken out decisively in favour of dramatising Bible matter, an immense quantity of Biblical plays with a didactic or polemical tendency were produced. But the principal motives of religious drama had disappeared : with the old eucharistic faith it had lost its vital, central point ; with the old liturgy, its sacred character disappeared, and with the organic cohesion of the old dogmas, its deeper meaning. However many New Testament subjects may have been handled by the preaching dramatists, their predilections were essentially on the side of Old Testament subjects. Nevertheless the attitude towards the New Testament had also changed. The typical significance of the Old Covenant with its sacrifices, priests, ceremonies, its visible means of grace and its hierarchical organisation, which found its fulfilment and completion in the Catholic Church, was greatly diluted by the doctrines of faith without works

---

[1] At Bahn, a small town in Pomerania ; cf. Kantzow, *Pommerania,* ii. 463.

[2] Holstein, pp. 20 ff., 25, 131. In Marburg a Passion-play was performed as late as the year 1561 (Bechstein, *Kalendertagebuch,* p. 9).

and universal priesthood, and the inner connection
between the two Testaments was severed. The histories
of the patriarchs, judges, kings and prophets were in
general treated merely as mirrors of domestic and political life ; in the hands of the poets as well as in those of
plastic artists of that epoch, the grandiose figures of
the Bible [1] received a more or less commonplace, bourgeois character. The kingdom of God became chiefly
confined to the narrow circle of the affections and the
family.

One of the most prolific fashioners of Biblical
dramas, in this narrow bourgeois sense, was Hans
Sachs. With the same facility of language and rhyming
with which he treated his secular material he set to
work also at the sacred books, and turned half the Bible
into dramas. The piety and devoutness of his intention
is unmistakable in these productions ; the good feeling
which permeates them not seldom makes up for his
didactic jejuneness. But he is entirely wanting in power
of artistic dramatic development and motive. His
energies are chiefly confined to reducing his materials to
rhyme, whereby the force both of the original Biblical
text and of Luther's translation loses considerably.
The poet Sachs is generally far more prosaic than
the prose writer Luther. In how mechanical a manner
he adapted the Bible to the stage is shown very palpably
by the twofold arrangement of his ' Saul ' of the year
1557 : ' Tragedie König Sauls mit Verfolgung König
Davids, ganz vom Authore selbst mit zweyen Actis und
sieben Personen gemehret, und hat jetzt sieben Actus
und einundzwanzig Personen ' (' Tragedy of King Saul,
with his persecution of King David, enlarged by the

[1] See vol. xi. p. 207 ff.]]

author himself with two acts and seven persons, and has
now seven acts and twenty-one persons ') ; ' Tragedi,
mit vierzehn Personen die Verfolgung König Davids
von dem Könige Saul, hat fünf Actus ' (' Tragedy with
fourteen persons, the persecution of King David by King
Saul, has five acts '). The first was written in August,
the second in September, 1557, and these two months
also produced a ' Komedia, der Daniel ' and a ' Tragedie, der hörnen Sewfriedt,' in seven acts, and works
of other kinds besides : ' Drei Kleger ob einem bösen
alten verstorbenen Weib,' ' Zwei schöne Gesprech,' a
farce ' das Ay mit den achtzehn Schanden,' ' Die halb
Rossdeck,' ' Der Kolb im Kasten,' a ' Gesprech St.
Peter mit den faulen Bauernknecht,' a farce ' der
Pfarrherr mit den Ehebrecher Bauren,' a farce ' der
Bauren Aderlass,' a farce ' der Teufel hat die Geiss
erschaffen,' and ' Der Teufel nahm ein alt Weib zu der
Ehe.' Then followed, on October 2, another carnival
play ' Das Narrenschneiden,' on the following day a
' Tragedie, der gottloss König Ahab mit dem frommen
Nabot,' on October 6, a farce ' der Bauernknecht mit
dem zerschnittenen Kittel,' and on the same day a
' Komedia des Mephiboset ' from the Second Book of
Kings.[1] Such rapidity is in itself enough to determine
the artistic value of the Biblical dramas of Sachs, the
number of which amounts to more than forty.

Luther and Melanchthon had objected to the
dramatic representation of the Passion, but notwithstanding this Sachs composed in 1558 a ' Tragedia, der
ganz Passio nach dem Text der vier Evangelisten vor

---

[1] Cf. Goedeke, *Grundriss*, ii. 431, Nos. 334–350. ' Hans Sachs was not
only the indefatigable actor poet who himself took part in the performances, but he was actually the stage-director ' (Genée, pp. 126–127).

einer christlichen Versammlung zu spielen' ('A Tragedy of the whole Passion after the Text of the four Evangelists to be played before a Christian Audience'). The Saviour is crucified on the stage, His sides are pierced, the arms and legs of the thieves are broken with clubs; and the poet gives directions that this linen club is to be dipped in red colour.[1] In other pieces also Sachs introduced bloody actions into some of the scenes. In his 'King Saul' for instance, 'Goliath takes off his helmet, goes up to David, who flings a stone at his forehead; Goliath falls, David draws out his sword and cuts off his head,' and so forth.

Just as Meister singing required no higher qualification than a facility for rhyming, so too the 'religious drama' as Hans Sachs handled it was a species of art which anybody could practise. Classic culture and a knowledge of foreign languages were indeed necessary for other branches of the drama, as they comprised much ancient and foreign matter within their scope; but for the Biblical drama everything which the author needed was contained in Luther's translation of the Bible: materials, persons, characters, motives, and a rich, pithy, vernacular language equally adapted to blunt coarseness and to pious sentiment. Biblical poets sprang up in great multitudes at that epoch; preachers,

---

[1] Cholevius (i. 299) makes the following criticism on the poet's Biblical dramas: 'He is careful at no single moment to be guilty of dramatic development, but adheres rigidly to the text, never stopping to ask whether the presentation of any particular incident is advisable, or even possible.' 'Throughout the whole range of his work all dramatic requirements are as good as wholly ignored. Each separate character is only recognisable in the roughest outlines, and the unfolding of a psychological process is never even attempted.' W. Wackernagel (*Drama*, p. 137) says: 'Hans Sachs with his dramas is not only a representative of dramatists; we must see in him their leader, the chief who towers over all the rest.'

schoolmasters, clerks, councillors, artisans, wandering
minstrels : all courted the dramatic muse.   Most of them
gave very little thought to construction.   Even Hans
Sachs dragged his pieces out to the length of five or ten
acts ; the ' Fine new Play of King Saul and the Shepherd
David ' which the Rappoltsweiler town-clerk Matthias
Holzwart dedicated to the Basle council and which was
performed there in 1571, lasted two days and employed
100 speaking and 500 mute actors.[1]   A dull, insipid
drama of the history of the Apostles, which the Latin
schoolmaster John Brummer got up in 1592 and
which was performed by the burghers of Kaufbeuren,
contained nearly 9200 verses ; ' the number of *dramatis
personæ* in this comedy ' was meant to be 246.[2]   John
Schlayss, by the introduction of all manner of episodes
adapted to the coarse taste of the audience, spun out
his comedy ' vom frommen und keuschen Joseph ' (' The
pious and chaste Joseph ') to twelve acts, which in print
covered 310 octavo pages.[3]   James Ruof's ' Neu und
lustig Spiel von der Erschaffung Adams and Hevä '
(1500) (' New and merry Play of the Creation of Adam
and Eve '), covering 240 pages of print, took two days to
perform.   James Funckelin, preacher at Biel, wrote in
1551 a ' ganz lustige und nützliche Tragödia von dem
rychen Mann und armen Lazaro ' (' A quite merry and
useful Play of the Rich Man and poor Lazarus '),
and for the embellishment of his Biblical treatment
introduced a mythological episode as interlude, ' ein
Streit Veneris und Palladis ' (' Contest between Venus

---

[1] Goedeke, *Grundriss*, ii. 351, No. 85.

[2] Several parts, however, were put into one hand ; cf. K. Trautmann
in the *Archiv für Litteraturgesch.* xiv. 234–235.

[3] Tübingen, 1593.

and Pallas '), to which he devoted three acts.[1]   John
Rasser, pastor at Ensisheim in Upper Alsatia, who
worked at the same time for the Catholics and the Protestants, published at Basle in 1575 a comedy ' Vom
König, der seinem Sohne Hochzeit macht' (' Of the King
who makes a Marriage for his Son '), which contained
fifteen acts and took three days to perform. It had
162 characters ; two angels, two court-councillors, one
fool, a number of halberdiers, courtiers and peasants,
two allegorical figures, three patriarchs, three prophets,
three Jews, a Roman senate of twenty-three persons,
drummers and fifers, three apostles and one bailiff,
lictors, advocates, hangmen and cripples, and lastly
Lucifer and ' Death.' [2] A strangely confused medley
was also produced by the Protestant theologian Andrew
Hartmann of Saxony in his ninety-six pages entitled
' Neuen ausbündigen, sehr schönen und durchaus
christlichen Komödia vom Zustande im Himmel und in
der Höllen' (' A new, uncommon, very fine and altogether
Christian Comedy of the Conditions in Heaven and in
Hell ').   In company with John the Baptist, Martha, and
Mary Magdalen, he places the Elector John Frederic
of Saxony, Luther and Melanchthon, David, Elias and
Benjamin.   In the last act Lucifer and his devils are
dancing in hell, and the author gives instructions that,
' During the dancing, rockets are to be let off and
made to fall from heaven on the devil and the damned
souls, especially hitting the dancing devils.' [3]   In the
Old Testament pieces of the Zurich painter and poet

[1] Goedeke, *Grundriss*, ii. 347, No. 8ᵃ and 349, No. 71. Genée, pp.
73–75. ** Baechtold, *Deutsche Litteratur*, Anmerkungen, p. 91 ff.
[2] Goedeke, *Grundriss*, ii. 390, No. 321. Genée, pp. 186–187. ** Concerning Rasser cf. *Zeitschrift für deutsche Philologie*, xxvi. (1893), 480–493.
[3] Magdeburg, 1600. Goedeke, ii. 369, No. 201. Genée, p. 214

Josias Murer, campaigns, battles, trumpets and war alarms play an important part. His siege of the town of Babylon, described from the prophets Isaiah, Jeremiah and Daniel, was divided over two days; the first prologue was recited by the fool, the second by the devil.[1]

Learned culture and unusual dramatic endowment were possessed by Paul Rebhun, Protestant schoolmaster at Kahla, Zwickau and Plauen. His ' Geistlich Spiel von der gottesfürchtigen und keuschen Frauen Su-sannen ' (' Religious Play of the God-fearing and modest Dame Susanna '), which was first performed in 1535 by some of the burghers at Kahla, is among the best dramas of the period.[2]   In the edition of 1544 the poet says that he thinks it very important that good moral teaching should be inculcated into the young in their amusements and that they should be stimulated to what is good by entertaining plays.[3]

He set to work with the purest intentions, but he does not always fully master the objectionable elements in his material.   The passion of the two judges is too strongly painted, and the representation lapses occasionally into lowness, especially where the judges come to an under-standing about their concerted crime :

> Eh, dear Sir, what's this I hear,
> If this be so I will not fear ;
> For though according to the saw,
> ' When at one bone two dogs do gnaw,

---

[1] Genée, p. 184.

[2] Rebhun, *Dramen* (Palm's edition), pp. 1–88 ; cf. p. 180 ff., where there are also fuller details concerning Rebhun's imitators. Tittmann, *Schauspiele*, i. 19–106. Cf. Pilger, pp. 156–169, ** and Vogt-Koch, *Deutsche Litteraturgesch.* p. 295.

[3] Rebhun, *Dramen*, pp. 87–88.

They do not long at peace remain,
But only fight the prize to gain,'
Yet I hope we sha'n't dispute thus
But the spoil divide betwixt us ;
Chiefly because in this affair
The one alone too feeble were
To carry out his heart's desire.
And so I trust it will not tire
You a helping hand to lend
To lift the cart from out the mire
And bring this matter to an end.

To what depths dramatic taste sank later on is plainly seen by comparing Rebhun's drama with the ' Susanna' of Duke Henry Julius of Brunswick. The conversation of the two old men in Susanna's garden and before the court of justice is here beyond measure obscene and full of the lowest terms of abuse, and yet this piece was performed in the presence of the court.[1]

Another dramatist worthy of mention for his psychological treatment of his material is the Catholic, Thiebolt Gart, burgher of Schlettstadt, who in the year 1540, in imitation of Cornelius Crocus, also a Catholic poet, worked up the story of Joseph into a ' Schöne und fruchtbare Komedia,' and had it performed.[2] This

---

[1] *Schauspiele des Herzogs Heinrich Julius von Braunschweig*, p. 43 ff. Pilger (p. 189 ff.) says concerning this much belauded play : ' It is nothing more than a rearrangement, partly free, partly literal, of Frischlin's drama of the same name, but it is so badly done that in almost all essential points it is far behind the original.'

[2] Fuller details in E. Schmidt in the introduction to his reprint of the piece (Strassburg, 1880). ** See, now, concerning the statements of Gény, *Die Reichsstadt Schlettstadt und ihr Antheil an den socialpolitischen und religiösen Bewegungen der Jahre 1490–1536*, p. 97 note. Concerning Gart's model, the *Comoedia sacra cui titulus Joseph* of the Dutchman, Cornelius Crocus, published in 1536, which had an immense circulation and was used to a great extent by later dramatists, von Weilen (p. 25 ff.) remarks : ' There are few dramatists in the sixteenth century who work so well and with such originality as Crocus. He thoroughly understands how to explain the Bible by subtle psychological treatment.' The *Joseph*

subject also, like the story of Susanna, was among
the favourite themes of the German drama, and the
treatment of many of the writers, in the scene where
Joseph's chastity is put to the test, was by no means
such as to make vice repulsive to the onlookers. Even
with Gart the burning passion of Potiphar's wife is
painted in far too seductive colours.[1]

In the play of ' Joseph ' by the dean, John Schlayss,
two devils take part in the coarsely depicted seduction
scene. Satan says exultingly :

> It cannot fail, I'm sure,
> The game is quite secure,
> Fine and smooth it is,
> Naught will go amiss.

He means to appear to Potiphar's wife in her sleep
in the guise of Joseph; Potiphera concocts a magic
potion for Joseph.[2] Balthasar Voigt, Lutheran pastor at
Drubeck, who insisted that his ' Aegyptischer Joseph '
should be acted as a religious play both in large and
small schools and that ' one or two days should be
devoted to the proper performance of it,' clothed the
adulterous love of Potiphar's wife, whom he named
Medea, in the lowest language ; the scene between her
and Joseph is not fit to quote.

of the Bernese poet Hans von Rüte (1538) is in part only a literal translation from Crocus (pp. 30–39). The drama of the same name by the
Catholic poet George Macropedius, ' the most important new-latin
dramatist ' (Holstein, p. 57), is discussed by von Weilen, pp. 77–85.

[1] ' The poet appears to have been seized with a certain sympathy and
love for this poetic figure, and when later dramatists speak of one who
painted the temptation in too attractive colours, they appear to have
Gart's work in their minds. But the fatal transition to psychological
drama had taken place in the play, and few of Gart's successors have been
able to make a purely moral example of this love episode' (Von Weilen,
p. 61).

[2] Schlayss, Act iv. scenes 1 and 2.

In general, indeed, the poets were too often guilty of coarseness and vulgarity and lapsed into buffoonery unworthy of religious plays. In Voigt's 'Joseph' Potiphar sets about to avenge his wife on the 'adulterous villain' and orders the executioner Urian to put Joseph to torture and apply the thumbscrew to him. Medea's request that he shall be placed in the 'Owl or Beansack prison' Urian is unable to grant.

> Lady, he cannot enter at this hour,
> Enchantresses fill each tower,
> And I shall not let them come out
> Until I've made them fat and stout,
> That on St. Vitus' day
> Relish them I may.

Then a band of drinking peasants come on the scene; they belabour a sacristan, and knock down the innkeeper, and the poet thunders fiercely against 'the swinish living' of the peasants and the workmen. Finally the fool advises the spectators to betake themselves to the tavern if they have any money to spend on drink.[1]

In the comedy of Schlayss Joseph denounces his brothers to his father as 'the most wicked, shameless flatterers.' Jacob calls Reuben a 'great big ass, a boorish, bloated blockhead.' The brothers' abuse of Joseph is much worse. Simeon says :

> I know we shall yet be the devil's stool
> If we do not break the yoke of this fool.

He means to wash his hands in his brother's blood :

[1] Von Weilen. This comedy was dedicated to the burgomaster and council of Halberstadt ; it was printed in 1618, but the author had already worked at it in his youth. It also contains polemical thrusts at the Catholics, 'according to whose teaching the saints must suppress and strangle all their human nature.'

Now, now thou must die, thou arrant rogue,
Stab him valiantly on the helmet.

Later he regrets that he did not 'joyfully pierce his
brother's throat.' [1]

In the 'Comedy of the Patriarch Joseph' which
Andrew Gasmann, school-rector at Rochlitz, dedicated
to the Duchess Sophia of Saxony in 1610, Joseph is
flogged by his brethren, and the 'chief villain,' Levi,
eggs them on with the words : 'Now quickly strike
his throat in two !' Potiphar is rated by his wife as a
'lazy fool' who 'swills himself full.' Levi complains
of a stomach-ache because he has drunk too much beer
and wine, and Simeon is so dead drunk that he can
scarcely get to the door; and so on in the same
style.[2]

The 'Great Comedy of the pious old father and
patriarch Jacob and his dear son Joseph, together
with Joseph's brethren,' which the shoemaker Adam
Puschmann, of Görlitz, a pupil of Hans Sachs, wanted
to have performed in Breslau, was interdicted by the
pastor of the place because it was 'both bad and silly,'
and contained certain obscene words and gestures which
'were not fit for modest ears and eyes.' None the less,

[1] Schlayss, Act i. scenes 1, 4 ; Act ii. scene 2.
[2] Von Weilen, pp. 151–157 ; cf. Goedeke, *Grundriss*, ii. 376, No. 245.
Von Weilen (p. 131) finds 'the complete deterioration of the religious drama'
already exemplified in the *Comedy of Joseph*, written in 1586 by Aegidius
Hunnius, then professor of theology at Marburg. 'The superabundance
of episodes which have nothing to do with the development of the plot,
but which often minister in an objectionable manner to the love of laughter,
is here in full force, whereas formerly the comic element only ventured
to show itself timidly now and then.' 'How amusing the episodes in
Hunnius are ! I am convinced that even at that period these formed
the principal charm of the piece,' as indeed is evident from the frequency
of its representation and the number of translations and imitations
which were made of it.

however, it was represented on the stage in 1583 with music and song.[1]

In many other religious plays also, the requirements of morality and decency, as well as dramatic form and all good taste, were not seldom seriously violated. James Ruof's 'Neu und lustig Spiel von der Erschaffung Adams und Heva' ('New and merry Play of the Creation of Adam and Eve') performed by the burghers of Zurich in 1550, puts into rhyme the story of the creation and propagation of man till the Flood; it represents how Adam knew his wife and begat a son and a daughter; and in the same act another pair of twins is procreated.[2] In a 'Christian and useful Play,' written by John Römoldt in 1564 and directed against the vice of pride, the chief character King Balenicus appears on the stage naked.[3]

The preacher Ambrose Pape, in the first of his 'Zwo christlichen Spiele vom Laster des Ehebruchs' ('Two Christian Plays on the Vice of Adultery') treats David's adultery with Bathsheba in a manner anything but suitable for the young people whose welfare he pretends to have so much at heart.[4]

Still more objectionable is a play by John Baumgart, pastor of the 'heiliger Geist' at Magdeburg, 'The Judgment of Solomon,' written in 1561 'for the benefit and pious edification of the young,' and performed before the town council. The abominable terms of abuse which the two disputing women hurl at each other, the indecent gestures of one of the women

[1] Holstein, p. 87; cf. Goedeke, *Grundriss*, ii. 407, No. 396.
[2] From Gervinus, pp. 3, 101.
[3] Goedeke, *Römoldt*, pp. 368–369.
[4] Magdeburg, 1602. The complete title is in Goedeke, *Grundriss*, ii. 367, No. 187.

in the presence of King Solomon, the vices with which another woman charges an usurer, and the language used by a hangman who comes on the scene make the concluding words, 'A youthful band of young lads and students acted this,' seem truly appalling.

From the mouth of King David the audience were treated to the following words concerning David's son Adonias :

> Because my crown he's tried to seize
> The devil shall him well chastise . . .
> He's also called himself the king,
> For this the devil shall . . .[1]

What sort of nutriment John Baumgart considered suitable 'for parents and children for Christian education, &c.' is plainly shown in his publication based on a popular tale and entitled 'Wunderliche und überaus ganz lustige Figur, wie unser Herr Gott Even Kinder nach Schöpfung der Welt den hl. Katechismus selbst überhöret' ('Strange and amusing Description of how our Lord God after the Creation of the World himself heard Eve's Children repeat the Holy Catechism'). Cain behaves very stupidly in words and gestures, whereupon God the Lord says to him : 'You stupid ass, you clown, you're a great big ruffian and a filthy beast of a peasant. See how you're standing there like a great gawk ; see how you're hanging your head like a thief, scratching your hands ; your eyes, your nose, your mouth are full of filth. Yea verily, you're a Romanist, and a perverted Christian, a Papist and Antichrist, an epicure, a godless wretch, who believes

---

[1] Baumgart, Act i. scene 2 ; Act ii. scene 6 ; Act iii. scene 1, and so forth. Gervinus (iii. 94) says respecting this play : 'It is incredible, what the young were then allowed to say and to act.' 'Even the lowest cast of actors would not dare to perform such things nowadays.'

neither in God nor in His Word. . . . Yes, like a true
Romanist and Papist you do not believe, either, whether
there is any eternal life, you godless rascal ; off to the
gallows with you, you good-for-nothing wretch.' [1]

All this sort of thing could not possibly tend to
improve the ways of the young, who according to
general complaint were in such a demoralised condition ; nor indeed could any good influence be expected
from the comedy 'Hans Pfriem or Meister Kecks,'
which Martin Hayneccius, rector of the *Fürstenschule* at
Grimma, ' published for the benefit of Christian schools
and laity' and had printed again and again.[2] In

[1] In the appendix to the catechism published by Baumgart in 1559. In
Baumgart's hands, says his co-religionist Löschke (61 ff.), ' the angry God
becomes a regular scold ; his judgment becomes vulgar abuse.' ' It is
disgraceful that he should put into the mouth of God all the dirty heap
of abusive words which he has raked together, and then that he should
lightly hurl all this filth, after it has served its turn on Cain, at his religious
opponents ; thus in their earliest years filling the minds of evangelical
boys and girls with hatred and disgust towards persons of a different
faith.' ' What sort of an idea must the children have formed of a God
who could scold in such a low fashion ! We may excuse the coarseness of
language in general by the coarseness of the age. But this does not exonerate
the century.' ' When such a God as this is presented to the young, how can
they be filled with reverence for him ! And if reverence to God is wanting,
all the bands of discipline are at once loosened.' Pastor Baumgart also did
not shrink from putting ' quite obscene words and scenes before children.'
** John Bussleb, teacher at the school at Egeln in the Magdeburg
district, composed in 1568 an ' amusing and very useful ' comedy entitled
' *Ein Spiegel, bereit wie die Eltern ihre Kinder auferziehen, auch die
Kinder gegen die Eltern sich verhalten sollen*' (' A Mirror to show how
Parents should bring up their Children and how Children should behave
to their Parents '). Ed. Jacobs, in the *Zeitschr. des Harzvereins*, i. 351, is
almost inclined to deny that this piece was performed ' by and in the
presence of young people.' ' We cannot believe,' he says, ' that an honourable council, tenacious of strict discipline and credited with Christian respect
for domestic chastity, could be capable of allowing a " merry comedy " of
this sort, full of filth and indecency, to be performed before their children.'

[2] Reprint of the first edition (1582) by Theobald Raehse. Halle-on-
the-Saale, 1882.

this comedy it was made known to the youthful spectators, according to a 'beautiful legend,' how once in the absence of St. Peter his wife Petrona had let the waggoner Hans Pfriem into heaven. Peter complains furiously of his 'old hag' who had 'dragged him into a mire.' Hans Pfriem behaved throughout 'impudently and defiantly.' To Mary Magdalen, who tries to soften him and refers him to the help of the saints, he answers: 'What do I care for the saints? I'll have nothing to do with the saints.' He goes on to her:

> Thou . . .
> Thou . . .
> Thou . . .
> No longer, I am sure, in thee
> The seven wicked devils reign
> Which thou before didst entertain,
> But many, many more, yea even
> As many as seventy times seven.
>
> .   .   .   .
>
> And in the lapse of time
> Each has grown seventy times worse.
> That is my strong belief:
> By them art thou now possessed.

To St. Peter he says: 'Holy Father Pope, as you are called, are you not the man whom Christ the Lord called a devil?'

> Apostate mameluke, hell's jaw
> Will gulp thee down into hell's maw,
> Thou threefold cursed, perjured one,
> Had justice unto thee been done,
> Long ages in the pit of hell
> Thou would'st have groaned with Judas fell,
> Yea ten times more than he thou dost
> Deserve the gallows, wretch, accursed,
> Thou art an evil-doer greater
> A thousand times than Judas traitor.

When Peter was asked by Paul what Christ the Lord

said about Hans Pfriem having been let into heaven,
he answered : Christ said ' nothing much,'

> . . . now as before
> And at all times, he keeps his way ;
> As long as he likes, he here may stay,
> May Paradise with us divide
> And mid heavenly joys abide ;

only he must keep the peace and do no harm to anybody.

Even in a Christmas play, 'Weihnachtsfreund
und gute neue Mähr,' by the poet laureate John
Seger of Greifswald (1613) one comes upon scarcely
credible coarsenesses. Lucifer, for instance, speaks
concerning the Holy Virgin :

> Pfui, thou wanton witch and H . . .
> On thee fall hell's worst plagues galore,
> Pfui, thou cursed seed of woman,
> Now must I suffer woe inhuman . . .

whereupon the archangel Gabriel replied ; ' You must
have your shameless lying and blaspheming jaw stopped
a little, if you slander the Virgin Mary so infamously —
you're a godless liar lost to all honour. . . .' [1]

The spectators could not possibly behave in a serious
and suitable manner at such ' religious comedies ' and
representations of Bible stories. Well-meaning contemporary writers complained that all that the audience
cared for in the performance of religious pieces was
' outward effect, the dresses of the actors, the jokes
and buffoonery of fools and peasants, excitement,
fighting, scuffling and laughter.' Thus spoke Joseph
Goetze, rector of the town gymnasium at Halle in 1612,

---

[1] Gottsched, i. 171–173. ' Lucifer and Beelzebub talk a great deal
of Latin and French ; the first-named wants to encounter the Saviour
with all the monsters of the pagan hell.'

VOL. XII.

in the preface to his ' Tragico-Comödia von dem heiligen Patriarchen Joseph.' [1] Earlier even than this George Rollenhagen, pro-rector of the school at Magdeburg had said in his preface to a play, ' Vom reichen Mann und armen Lazarus ' : ' It often happens at such performances that all the common people among the audience behave in a rowdy manner, disturb the more respectable and distinguished spectators, and even upset the actors, who cannot play their parts properly under such circumstances, and who are filled with distress because the expectations of their masters are disappointed, and all the time and trouble they have expended thrown away, because on account of the great commotion nobody can see properly what is going on. The greater part of the audience is only on the look-out for benches and tables to smash, for scuffles on the stage or anything that may raise a complaint or a laugh. The actors are also obliged to put up with insults and abusive threats if they will not allow any amount of noise and rioting to go on.' [2] Jörg Wickram, in the year 1551, before the commencement of his play of ' Tobias ' allowed the turbulent mob to bring a devil on the stage and to read a letter from Lucifer in which the hearers were admonished as follows :

> Let not one of you keep quiet,
> Make much tumult and much riot,
> My messenger obedient will
> Help you these orders to fulfil ;
> Let me hear you roaring, raving,
> All like lunatics behaving . . .

---

[1] Von Weilen, p. 158. ** At Spandau in 1571, ' 22 quarts of Bernau beer were drunk in the church while the schoolboys (under the rector, John Buchner) were acting a comedy there ' (J. Bolte, pp. 203–204).

[2] Ackermann's und Voith's *Dramen, Einleitung*, pp. 146–147.

John Schlayss put this letter into his comedy of ' Joseph ' (1593) word for word, and added also a speech of the fool who is angry because

> There are many fools without their cap
> And many young good-for-nothings
> Who roar and stamp, laugh and talk
> Tread on, push and pinch one another ;
> They grin like the dog of St. Vitus,
> Laugh with their ears, see through their mouths.[1]

In a play by James Ayrer, Lucifer says :

> I do not think that even in
> Hell, there could be such noise and din,
> As these people here are making,
> I went in with fear and quaking.
> Are these called Christians brought up well ?
> Off with you all to the devil in hell.

Satan threatens that he will bind up the jaws of these rioters, or gag their throats, or sew up their tongues.[2]

The devil, began, indeed, to play a very important part on the stage.

[1] Schlayss, Bl. A 7–8.   Cf. Von Weilen, p. 144.

[2] Cf. Prölss, pp. 138–140. As regards the representation of these plays, Gervinus, iii. 103, says : ' When the schoolmasters and pastors conducted serious pieces it may be that the pedantic pathos served at least to maintain decency in the proceedings ; when uneducated artisans carried their performances round the country, everything lapsed into absurdity and vulgarity.' ' Rist had seen (as late then as the seventeenth century) a *Judith* performed by linen-weavers ; the heroine cut off the head of a live calf which represented Holofernes in bed ! Harsdörfer saw *Lazarus* performed outside a tavern ; the " rich man " sat with his friends at table and said nothing but : " Pour out, drink on, that's right, I'm getting drunk ; " at the same time they devoured pork and roast calves without knives and forks, and Abraham, dressed in a pastor's coat, looked out of the tavern window ! '

CHAPTER II

POLEMICAL-SATIRIC DRAMA — THE DEVIL ON THE STAGE

BEFORE the treatment of Biblical matter came into vogue among Protestant dramatists, there had already grown up what may be called a drama of creed and controversy, which soon gained the widest footing. Here and there Catholic writers cultivated this particular art, and these, though few in number, helped to convert the drama, like every other branch of literature, into a faithful mirror of the violent religious strife of the day.

In the very first years of the religious revolution, two men, natives of Switzerland, Pamphilus Gengenbach, burgher and printer at Basle, and Nicholas Manuel, painter at Bern, figured as leaders of the polemical drama.[1]

The first-named, who had already composed several carnival plays, wrote at the beginning of the twenties a dramatic poem called ' Eine jämmerliche Klage über die Totenfresser,' that is to say, over the clergy who had invented masses for the dead in order to fleece the people. On an accompanying woodcut which represents a company of people feasting, the Pope is carving a dished-up corpse, and at the beginning of

---

[1] Concerning Manuel as painter of nudities see vol. xi. pp. 53, 235, note.
** Fresh documentary information concerning Pamphilus Gengenbach is given by Baechtold, *Deutsche Litteratur, Anmerkungen zum Text,* p. 63 ff.

the poem he summons his followers to banquet and carouse :

> God for our sins enough has done,
> As written in St. Paul I find,
> Therefore Luther must be blind
> Who bids us live in penitence,
> Since we can earn no recompense,
> And God takes all our sins away,
> As John the Baptist well doth say.

Thus, then, the Lutheran doctrine that ' we can acquire no merits ' is introduced here as Catholic teaching :

> Since God, then, by his suffering
> Has wiped all our misdeeds away,
> What further need we ask ?

God had given him, the Pope, authority by the power of binding and loosing to ' fleece the simple Christians ' who, impelled by the doctrine of purgatory,

> Found many anniversaries and masses,
> And so we batten on the dead
> While here on earth we're living,
> Although the soul is to go to the devil.

A bishop, a secular priest, a Bernardine monk, a friar, a nun, a priest's maid make merry over the profits of the masses for the dead ; they complain, however, that these are lost through Luther's teaching ; the devil has taken possession of the peasants, so that they will not hear anything more about purgatory. ' Eating the dead makes us fat,' says the priest's maid, and the nun says :

> The bones of the dead have a right good taste,
> And day and night on them we feast.

The devil with the fiddle says exultingly :

> These are all my children choice,
> None on earth me more rejoice,

> Therefore my fiddle to them I play
> That they may have a pastime gay,
> That they may dance and fife and sing,
> And then with me *ad infernum* spring.

While, moreover, it had been made a reproach against the convents that they encouraged begging by their almsgiving, the beggars are made to lament that they cannot get any food because everything is consumed by the monks and priests ; the peasant also complains of the monks and priests :

> Early and late they eat my sweat
> And I my bread can scarcely get,
> Scarcely can I earn the sums
> That I must give monks, priests, and nuns.[1]

An earlier carnival play written by Gengenbach and described as follows: ' Der Nollhart : diss sind die Prophetien sancti Methodii, gespielt im 1517. Jor uf der Herren Fastnacht von etlichen ehrsamen und geschickten Burgeren einer löblichen Stadt Basel ' [2] was rearranged at Strassburg in 1545, and described in the title as the old play ' played by a young company of burghers at Basle.' It bubbles over with indignation against the Pope and the spiritual and temporal princes. ' We are all of us calumniated in Germany,' exclaims the Pope, but

> We'll avenge such scandalous shame
> With drowning, burning, hanging dead,
> Greater tortures I'll not name
> Of which we daily still shall think,

---

[1] Goedeke, *Pamphilus Gengenbach*, pp. 153–159. Cf. 505, No. 9, pp. 619–620. ** See also Baechtold, *Deutsche Litteratur*, p. 281, and *Anmerkungen*, p. 73.

[2] ' The Nollhart : these are the Prophecies of St. Methodius, played in the year 1517, at our Lord's Carnival by some of the honourable and skilful Burghers of the laudable Town of Basel.'

> And sour wine give you to drink.
> Whate'er we list, that shall we do,
> And we mean to be obeyed by you.
> Then leave your Scripture talk alone
> Or I will flay you skin and bone,
> As many other scamps I've flayed,
> And thus will you be rightly paid.[1]

The first dramatist who used the papacy as a motive for carnival farces was Nicholas Manuel. He wrote two plays in 1522 which were acted at Bern, in which ' the truth about the Pope and his priests was set forth in jest,' and in which ' the great difference between the Pope and Christ Jesus our Saviour is shown.'

This was the same year in which the poet attached himself, as military clerk, to the confederate soldiers who were attempting to win back for the French king, Francis I., the German imperial fief of Milan. Novara was taken by storm by the Swiss, ' churches and convents were pillaged, the cruelty of the confederates called for vengeance,' and Nicholas Manuel belonged to the number of those concerning whom, when the atrocities were complained of, ' a pious town, Bern, instituted special inquiries, in order to punish the stealers of chalices and perpetrators of other crimes.' [2]

Manuel's claim to be called a reformer is scarcely consistent with this conduct.

The first of his two dramatic pieces transplants the

---

[1] Goedeke, *Pamphilus Gengenbach*, pp. 462–502. The original play of the year 1517, pp. 77–116. Holstein, in *Die Reformation im Spiegelbilde der dramatischen Literatur des sechzehnten Jahrhunderts* (Halle, 1886), writes, p. 169: ' The *Endechrist* [Antichrist] appears as early as in this piece; it is the Pope whose dominion will soon come to an end.' This is erroneous. The Antichrist in this piece is introduced only in the same way as in the old play, *Vom Aufgang und Untergang des Antichristes*, written at Tegernsee; see our remarks, vol. i. p. 270.

[2] Baechtold, *N. Manuel*, p. xxviii

spectators to Rome, where the Pope, Entchristelo, and all his court are ' assembled in great magnificence ' just as a corpse is being carried out of a house. The priests and their wenches are exulting over their booty :

> Death is good venison to me,

says the Pope.

> The whole world we'll punish, plague and scold,
> And rob them of food, goods, money and gold.

The cardinal Anselm von Hochmuth (Haughtiness) thirsts for war and blood.

> Mightily I have enjoyed it,
> For Christian blood to me is dear,
> And that's why a red hat I wear.

Bishop Chrysostom Wolfsmagen (wolf's stomach) explains how he flays his flock and is not really a shepherd, but ' in plain German, a brothel-keeper.' Dean Schinddenpuren (peasant-flayer) cries out :

> What care I what Christ may be
> If it brings not so much as a farthing to me ?
> What want I with Bible and prophets ?
> Oh had I a book of Elsie and Greta !

A young monk complains that the devil has stuck him in a cowl, and that he is undergoing a life-long martyrdom ; a Beguin nun, on the other hand, tells with delight how well she has learnt the trade of pandering, and that she has made a good living by it for a long time. Peasants complain of the fraud of indulgences, and a nobleman is so incensed against the clergy that he exclaims :

> Yea, you're the devil's fatted swine,
> Although you're princes with titles fine !
> We must brush you up a bit,
> Thunder blast your bellies,
> You greasy, shaven crew !

A Knight of Rhodes, who implores help from the Pope against the Turks, is scornfully dismissed; for a war against the Turks, says the Pope, would add 'no bacon to the turnips'; not against them, but against the Christians, he intended, with his good friend the Emperor Charles V., to go to war.

As a friend of the French and the hireling of the French King, the poet directed his shafts also against the German Emperor, Charles V., who, he makes the knight say, was, like the Pope, to blame for the blood that had been shed by the Turks. He cursed the bloodhounds.

> Your scarlet hats and tonsured priests,
> Have bloody teeth like savage beasts!
> Good sausage-makers you'd have made
> Since thus in blood you love to wade,
> And butchering people is your trade! . . .
> May you and all your friends galore
> Burn in hell-fire for evermore.

Then a preacher gets up and says the Pope was not worthy to be the very least of all swineherds. On his asking the 'pious country-people' who are present if nothing is known to them of the popish 'infamy,' the peasants answer unanimously:

> Neighbour, God smite the Pope with the 'Rangen.' [1]

The Pope proceeds to enlist troops for fresh bloodshed, while Peter and Paul step forth from the background, and in their wrath against the Pope's criminal deeds call down God's judgment upon him:

> What have we to do at Rhodes?
> God grant he by the Turks be toasted
> As he the Christians would see roasted,
> But we have other work on hand
> That we may conquer still more land.

---

[1] A disease of pigs.

Finally the preacher announces the approach of the day of truth.[1]

In the second piece there appears on the one side Christ, riding on a young donkey, with the crown of thorns on His head, and behind Him a long train of people, blind, lame, palsied, and poor ; while on the other side the Pope is riding ' in armour and with a great military retinue on horse and on foot, with great banners and standards, trumpets . . . large pieces of ordnance, culverins, harlots and villains.' Two peasants, Claiwe Pflug and Rüde Vogelnest, talk together about the contrast, and

> By God, for painful beastly wounds !
> How these priests have scraped and skinned us !
> By God, for dirty, filthy sweat—
> How smooth the rascals are and fat !
> We have had to fatten them up.
> ' May the devil reward the priests and break their necks.'

The peasants also get on the subject of indulgences, and one of them takes the opportunity of declaring his faith in Christ :

> If then from Christ my pardon I get,
> The pope's pardons and bans I reject,
> Which only for money are made,
> And written on dogskin in Rome.
> Should ever their filth fall on me again,
> They themselves shall take it away. . . .
> Thereto I have pledged my word,
> And am ready to draw my sword.

With utterances of this sort this piece, admired as ' a good, honest play,' concludes.[2]

[1] Baechtold, *N. Manuel*, pp. 31–102.

[2] Baechtold, pp. 103–111. Tittmann, *Schauspiele*, i. 9–18. ' How heartily and at the same time powerfully these peasants talk ! ' says Baechtold, p. cxxxviii. Tittmann (p. 8) also considers that ' the poetic

In a third piece written in 1525, 'Der Ablasskrämer'
('The Indulgence Merchant'), the author was not content with all manner of coarse, indecent utterances,
but he gave instructions that the peasant-women who
appeared on the scene were to seize 'Richard Hinter-
list' by main force. 'They all took hold of him together
and threw him down on the ground, belabouring him
with ladles, distaffs and logs, and a wicked old hussy
hobbled up with a rusty old halberd, bound him hand
and foot, and hung him high up in the very way,
form and shape in which a murderer is stretched out';
and then he was made to confess all sorts of enormities
which Manuel attributed to him.

His torturers wring from him the words :

> The devil has carried me amongst the women :
> By them I've been pummelled, trodden on, beaten,
> Stretched out till I'm nearly broken.
> Is there in hell any pain like this ?
> If the devils are as bad as these women there is
> Torture and anguish enough methinks.[1]

Manuel followed up this play the next year with an
'Amusing Dialogue,' in 1940 verses, under the title
'Barbali,' in which, with appeal to all sorts of Bible
passages, and in opposition to her mother and several
clerical persons, a girl of eleven, destined to enter a

merit of the piece lies in its lifelike presentation and adaptation to the
needs of the people, and in the popular treatment of the dialogues, which,
if not free from harshness and clumsiness, at any rate speak to the heart
of the people.'   Holstein (p. 173) considers both pieces vivacious, intensely
witty and pungent.

[1] Baechtold, pp. 112–132. This play also won the warm approval of the
editor. 'It is worked out,' he says, ' with such daring, such irresistible
humour and such lifelike naturalness, that like the small carnival farces,
among the most excellent productions of Reformation satire it has no
counterpart.'

nunnery, expresses her disgust and horror of convent life.[1]

The language put into the mouths of several clergymen in this 'Dialogue' is amongst the worst specimens of vulgarity and indecency which the century has to show.[2]   The eleven-year-old girl says she has 'no nun's flesh,' and looks forward to the joys of a mother :

> A simple stuff gown, thick and coarse,
> And a linen apron over it,
> That must be the coat and kit
> That for me will be most fit.
> At the Mass *Drute Ninne* I sing,
> And if it's God's will that children I bear,
> And if in the morning they will not cease crying,
> I'll sing ' Hensli uf der Schiterbigen.' [3]

Barbali converts a priest with her teaching, and the mother exclaims :

> How wonderful
> That the great and learned men
> Should be so hard put to 't, and then
> That you, my child, should be so knowing—
> It must be the Holy Spirit's doing.

In May 1526 the Council of Bern had enjoined the Catholic cantons to persist in the old faith, but the very next year the religious innovators gained the upper hand in both the colleges of councillors, and in February 1528 the council issued a mandate concerning 'general reform and improvement.'   There followed a

[1] Baechtold, pp. 133–202.   The eleven-year-old Barbali does indeed appear to the publisher 'an unchildlike Rabelaisian, but for the rest there is an immense deal that is admirable.'   'With what assurance the little chit confronts the learned men, how ready she is with her answers as though she had come straight from a disputation with Eck and Faber in Baden ; how excellent are the descriptions of convent life, of a poor marriage, of the vexation of the clerical band ! '

[2] Cf. for instance what the pastor ' Stulgang ' says, pp. 156, 166, 178.

[3] Baechtold, pp. 137, 171.

raging storm of iconoclasm, in which the most beautiful art treasures of the Middle Ages were plundered and destroyed. Unconditional adoption of Zwingli's teaching was most strictly enjoined on everybody ; every priest who after the first punishment dared to say a Holy Mass again was to be pronounced an outlaw.[1]

Manuel had taken a prominent part in the introduction of Zwinglianism, and he now wrote a burlesque dialogue, 'Krankheit und Testament der Messe' ('Illness and the Testament of the Mass'), which far surpassed his earlier productions. The Pope receives from a cardinal the news that the Mass has been denounced as blasphemy of God and grossest idolatry, and that it has fallen ill in consequence. In vain attempts had been made to bring the moribund patient back to life with strong Roman declamations, and the powerful voice of the Fathers and the Councils. Its throat rattled, its feet began to grow cold. The fire of purgatory at which they wanted to warm them had been extinguished with holy water by the peasants, 'and some of them were so wicked that they used the stoup for vile purposes.' They thought to carry the patient to a picture of our dear Lady, but the peasants had destroyed the chapel, the house and the courtyard ; the holy oil could not be administered, because the sexton had greased his shoes with it ! '[2]

[1] See our remarks, vol. v. p. 134 ff.
[2] Baechtold, pp. 216–236. Even Gervinus (ii. 404) found satire of the wittiest kind in this play. Grüneisen (p. 221) praises in it ' not only the rich poetic gift of humour, but also the fine artistic taste of which none but a distinguished genius in the happiest moment of inspiration could be capable.' ** Vogt-Koch (*Deutsche Litteraturgesch.* p. 293) praises ' the choice humour of this prose dialogue.' Baechtold says (clxxv.) ' I do not hesitate to pronounce Manuel's *Krankheit der Messe* to be the finest and most trenchant satire of the Reformation period.' According

This lampoon also met with great approval. As
a painter, the poet, it appears, experienced a certain
amount of pain at the vandalic destruction of the
cathedral at Bern, in the decoration of which he had
once co-operated. He wrote a ' Klagred der armen
Götzen ' ('Lament of the poor Idols ') in which the latter
give themselves up to their fate, but are of opinion
that they were not so bad as many other idols that are
worshipped in life. The poet then depicts the growing
depravity of the people in lifelike colours. ' The idols,'
i.e. the sacred pictures, say, at any rate they have
not killed anybody, nor their substance

> Squandered in a drinking-house
> Where men gather to carouse,
> Nor made another man so drunk
> That 'neath the table he has sunk ;
> We've never led a villain's life
> Nor been unfaithful to a wife,
> We've never been adulterous :
> These crimes no one can lay on us.
> Yet many of those who us condemn
> Forget how it has been with them.
> That all their lives they've never given
> Aught to God, nor for Him striven,
> And they who now our judges are
> Have more and greater idols far.

There must be a campaign against idols of other
sorts :

> Of idols there are such a host,
> Everyone has some, almost :
> Much lust and profligacy,
> Scandal, vice and villainy,
> To gorge, to drink, and to blaspheme
> To old and young all fitting seem ;
> Freely they all shed guiltless blood,
> And are reckless about others' goods.

---

to Schaffroth (p. 38) also, ' it is the most brilliant satire of the whole
Reformation period,' ' it is Manuel's masterwork.'

Adultery 's so common grown,
Nobody loves his wife alone ;
Everybody skins and flays, . . .
The world 's so artful in its ways,
No other creed they seem to hold
Than how to take their neighbour's gold.
There is no discipline of youth,
What the young say is all untruth ;
Wantonness is their delight,
Father and mother think it right. . . .

The extraordinary popularity of Manuel's plays
is shown by the quantities of editions which were
printed. Of his first carnival plays there are still
eleven extant, of ' Barbali ' eight, of the ' Krankheit
und Testament der Messe ' (the ' Illness and Testament
of the Mass ') sixteen editions and adaptations.[1]

An imitator of Manuel, the Bernese councillor,
Hans von Rüte, wrote a carnival play called ' Ursprung,
Haltung und Ende beider, heidnischer und päpstlicher
Abgöttereien ' (' Origin, Duration and End of both
Pagan and Popish Idolatries '), which was acted by the
young burghers of Bern on March 19, 1531.[2] The
actual aim of the piece is to excite hatred against the
Catholic clergy, ' who ought to be expelled ' :

You cursed priests, you idle slobberers,
You devil-seekers, greedy dish-lickers,
Deceivers of men, dealers in God, lazy chaps,

---

[1] Goedeke, *Grundriss*, ii. 338–341. Concerning the character of his
own writings Manuel himself was perfectly clear. In a letter to Zwingli
of August 12, 1529, he calls them ' libellous writings put into rhyme.'
He had sent Zwingli a few of them to look through, *Ein Gougler vom
Ablass sprechend*, *Ein Ablasskrämer*, and others, and he wanted them
back to distribute them in Baden ' among some well-meaning Christian
people of St. Gall ' (Baechtold, p. li. note 2).

[2] Basle, 1532. Cf. Goedeke, ii. 344, No. 52. This burlesque does
not, as Crecelius maintains in Birlinger's *Alemannia*, iii. 53, give ' an
interesting account of the influence ' of the saints ; it is merely a popular
skit on the veneration of saints.

> I have a mind to cover you with wounds ;
> I would I saw you all dispersed,
> By the devil chased about. . . .
> Be off, you greedy rascals !
> Be off and away, far and wide,
> You blasphemous, lazy dirt paunches,
> Or my anger shall be on you ! [1]

The Pope ' had robbed God of His honour ' :

> Inasmuch as in God's place he's dared
> To put himself, so he must be declared
> A living devil, for he is no whit
> Better than Lucifer, who thought it fit
> Himself next God to sit. [2]

The worship of saints had introduced all sorts of scandals and devil's tricks. The author compares the veneration of St. Mary to the worship of the goddesses Juno and Venus, while that of St. Catherine is compared to the worship of Minerva. By the worship of saints ' the papists have acquired all sorts of vices.'

> By worship of false gods and saints they learnt
> To lie and cheat, their faith and oaths forsake,
> To wrong their neighbours and shed blood.
> Is it not gross sin and shame,
> That they should invoke the name
> Of God and saints to fornicate
> And all that's wanton perpetrate ? . . . [3]

To this end the worship of St. Afra was specially adapted.[4] Pamphilus had spoken differently about the veneration of saints. Christians, he said, must ' at all times hold Mary in honour,'

> She to her Child for us will pray
> That all our sins forgive he may,
> And drive our enemies away,

---

[1] Bl. L 4, M.   [2] Bl. L 1b.
[3] Bl. M 2–3.   [4] See the disgraceful rhymes (Bl. H. 3c.)

And leave us not at our last end.
On her alone for comfort we depend,
Pardon for sinners she can well obtain . . .
I, Pamphilus, have pondered long
And in her honour made this song.[1]

While the Swiss in their dramatic lampoons said openly what they meant, the former monk, Burchard Waldis, at Riga, took the ‘ evangel,’ *i.e.* a parable from it, as a cloak for his polemics. In 1527 his carnival play, ‘ Der verlorene Sohn,’ written in Low German dialect, was performed at Riga.[2]

[1] Goedeke, *Pamphilus Gengenbach*, p. 53.

[2] Reprint by G. Milchsack (Halle, 1882). This carnival play deserves close attention, for it is held in the highest esteem by nearly all historians of literature. Goedeke criticises it first in his pamphlet on Waldis (p. 22 ff.), where he bestows the most effusive praise on it. In his *Grundriss* (ii. 449) he says : ‘ Waldis began his literary career with the dramatisation of the parable of the Prodigal Son, which is not only his most important work, but one of the most important in the whole range of dramatic literature in Germany in the sixteenth century. Considered from the point of view of the poet’s own personal development, this play gives a vivid and profound insight into the zeal with which he promoted reform work in Riga ; it reveals a depth of conception which no other play on the same subject has shown. From the local standpoint it opens up an unexpected view into an unexpected world. How advanced must have been the stage of culture, moral and intellectual, in general in Riga at that time, if we presuppose only a tolerably adequate understanding of this mystery which soars up to the Godhead ! It had no precursor, it had no successor equal to it in the same line.’ According to Holstein (pp. 150–153) this piece stands ‘ at the head of the German drama of the sixteenth century not only relatively to the epoch, but also from its intrinsic merit ’ ; it is distinguished, he says, ‘ by its grandiose conception of a grand subject.’ Milchsack also speaks in the same strain (p. vi.) : ‘ From the most diverse aspects this play produces the impression of a work of supreme significance.’ ** G. Buchenau, *Burchard Waldis* (p. 15), praises the *Prodigal Son* as a ‘ splendid carnival play ’ ; the author, he says, ‘ makes both Churches confront each other in the sublimest manner ; the old Church with its doctrine of outward righteousness through the works of the law, personified in the son who stayed at home with his father, the new one with its belief in righteousness through faith alone, personified in the prodigal son.’ Buchenau then refers to the ‘ two admirable criticisms of the piece by Mittler and Goedeke, and adds : ‘ It is the most important work of our

This play travesties the Catholic doctrine of the
merits of works done in faith for the attainment of
salvation, and distorts it in the usual way into hypocritical and damnable sanctity through works, and
represents the Lutheran doctrine of faith alone as the
only one leading to salvation. At the opening of the
piece the ' Aktor,' or stage director, says that Christ
has redeemed us ' by His own grace and favour alone,
without any works or efforts of our own.' The devil,
enraged at this, sent the Pope, ' the Antichrist ' who,
breaking out into angry words, declared that ' such a
faith was of no use : he knew a better way ; mankind
must prize good works, and get into heaven by their
means.' Then the Pope, ' to revile and mock at God,'
had come to Germany with his cardinals and his
Romish thieves and indulgences :

> From thee, O God, he's us divided
> And with his sophistry has blinded,
> Has brought us to disgrace and scandal,
> Our wives and children led to whoredom,
> Our honour ruined and our goods,
> And on our souls inflicted wounds.
> With his ban he's coerced us
> And into hell with might us forced,
> From life he brought us to the grave,
> And body and soul to the devil gave.

But now that God had revived His Word, the empire
of the Pope, the Antichrist, had been destroyed, the
great city had fallen in which the scarlet whore was
seated.

> With its chalice of abomination
> Murder it sowed and desolation,

---

poet.' Spengler, *Der verlorene Sohn* (v.), is of a similar opinion ; he says :
' Unquestionably Waldis's maiden work belongs to the grandest productions of Reformation polemics.'

With its shameless tonsured brood
Was worshipped as though itself God.[1]

The whole structure of the piece, outward and inward, shows little artistic sense. The play begins with the ' Aktor ' repeating his polemical prologue of 196 verses, after which the Gospel parable is read out from the New Testament ; then the ' Aktor ' comes forward again and declaims twenty-two verses, by which the spectators are informed that it is not a secular burlesque, like those of Rome, that they are about to witness, and they must not grumble if the style is not in accordance with Terence and Plautus, for it is no fable, but sacred truth, which is going to be represented. After the song of praise, ' nun bitten wir den heiligen Geist,' has been sung, the first act begins with the appearance of the prodigal son. He addresses the audience and his brother in a dull, commonplace manner, and tells his brother that he wishes to leave the paternal roof. The father then comes on the scene and the son asks him for his inheritance. In vain the father remonstrates with the purblind youth, reminding him, not exactly in elevated style, that :

> The donkey had fed to his satisfaction,
> And thought himself fit for mighty action ;
> He went a dancing on the ice,
> He broke a leg, and then grew wise.

Even the pagan poet Horace had lamented over disobedient youngsters. As, however, the son persists in his resolve, the father orders the servant to unlock

---

[1] Holstein (pp. 150–151) modifies as follows the speech of the ' Aktor ' : ' The devil sent the Anti-Christ, who promised to show a better way ; He, with his gang, incited the Pope to spread the doctrine that works could help to procure salvation. This led to a great deal of evil. But God revived His Word which had long lain hidden.'

the money chest in which there were all sorts of moneys and coins and 500,000 Rhenish florins. Half of the contents are given to the son, and the father dismisses him with the words : 'Now go and make yourself merry with this.' The son speaks his thanks and goes off. This is the first scene.

The second scene is enacted in a brothel ; the *dramatis personae* are the host of the brothel, the 'sharper,' the prodigal son, and the harlots Elsie and Grethe. The sharper finds the host greatly cast down on account of the bad times which Luther has occasioned by his sanction of marriage in the church, and his prohibition of unchastity. The sharper comforts him and brings in the prodigal son. What follows is in character with the scene of action ; the two women pay their court to the prodigal son, and a couple of score verses of the drinking song ' Wo soll ich mich ernähren, ich armes Brüderlein ' are sung. We quote a few specimen verses :

> Had I the empire for mine,
> And all the tolls upon the Rhine,
> And Venice likewise, it
> Would all be lost, I swear,
> Squandered every bit.
> A card and three good dice,
> That's the shield I bear,
> Six pretty maidens nice,
> Three on either side,
> Come hither, my lovely bride. . . .

After the prodigal son has given part of his money to Elsie, he loses the rest in a game of cards, pawns his jerkin and hose to the host, with the help of the sharper is further stripped down to his shirt, and in this piteous plight turns to the audience with the words

> Now stand I naked before the folk . . .

To the two wenches saying:

> See, Elsie, what's befallen me!
> Some mercy, show me, I pray thee,
> And give me an old cloak.

But by both the women and also by the host he is repulsed with lewd abuse and driven off 'in the devil's name.'

The proceedings in the brothel fill over 500 verses, nearly a quarter of the whole piece. The characters are all of the lowest type of lowness, and the scenes are tacked together without any attempt at inward psychological development. Without the slightest inward struggle the young man surrenders at once, while the women say out boldly that all they care for is money, and they turn their backs on their victim as soon as they have sucked him dry.[1]

---

[1] Holstein (p. 152) passes over the brothel scene, only saying: 'After the prodigal son had squandered all his money he began to repent of his riotous life'; on the other hand, he puts into the mouth of the host fourteen verses of complaint against Luther, 'because he forbade and condemned unchastity.' ** How Vogt-Koch, *Deutsche Litteraturgesch.* (p. 294) can maintain that this play of Waldis 'was performed in a serious spirit' is difficult to understand. In his preface Waldis says that in this piece his intention was to turn the idolatry of the Shrove Tuesday festival 'initiated by the pagans' and celebrated annually by the masqueraders at Rome into a 'spiritual Shrove Tuesday.' Holstein evidently did not think the brothel scene suitable to this 'spiritual' Shrove Tuesday, and therefore was silent on the subject. In an incomparably more worthy manner this same subject was treated by Hans Ackermann, burgher of Zwickau, in his play of *The Prodigal Son* (1536 and 1540), without admixture of polemics and without offending the delicacy of the spectators. Ackermann's *Dramen*, pp. 6–139; the *Beschluss*, pp. 135–139, is extremely fine. Even the English comedians in their *Prodigal Son*, of which Goedeke says (*Grundriss*, ii. 544, No. 1), 'the Biblical matter is here degraded to coarseness and vulgarity,' did not go so far as Waldis. In this English play the prodigal is also stripped of his clothes, but the host, at any rate, throws him 'some old hose and an old jerkin' (see Tittmann, *Die Schauspiele der englischen Komödianten*, p. 66). The conclusion of this piece is also more dignified than in Waldis's. 'With a broken, contrite and believing heart'

Not less superficial and coarsely realistic is the treatment of the after misery of the prodigal. He appeals first to a burgher, who spurns the ' naked fellow ' who has ' no shoes and stockings '; then to a bailiff, who says :

> I will not feed your belly here,
> You may go and beg elsewhere.

The dialogue then ceases, and the ' Aktor,' in 225 verses, in which there are incessant references to Bible texts and numerous hits at the papacy, uses the first part of the parable to exemplify the opposition between faith and works. Then a psalm is sung, and another act begins.

This second act has only two *bona-fide* scenes : the father's welcome to his penitent son, and the complaint of the envious elder brother. After a dialogue of 236 verses the 'Aktor ' appears again, and in a sermon of 270 verses expounds the second part of the parable as typical of the doctrine of faith alone.

This sermon is such a thoroughgoing success that, quite independently of the stage action, the keeper of the brothel comes forward and says he intends to become a reformed character; and after another sermon by the stage manager he declares himself reformed, but without any thought of restoring the stolen money. Then the 129th Psalm is sung in five parts, and here the piece might conclude. But the poet's polemical soul is not yet satisfied. The eldest son now appears as a hermit with a crucifix in one hand and a long Pater-

---

the prodigal son returns home, and the elder brother is reconciled to him : ' Beloved Father, you have now put me right ; I heartily rejoice at my brother's conversion that with us he may gain the Kingdom of Heaven. I go to make merry with you ' (Tittmann, pp. 70–73).

noster in the other, and the seam of his garment covered with memorial pictures; he stretches out his arms and speaks with a loud voice in the character of the self-righteous Pharisee, making feeble allusions to the Catholic monastic orders. In opposition to him the converted brothel-keeper plays the part of the publican, who ' standing afar off would not lift up so much as his eyes unto heaven. . . .' The manager then, in a concluding speech of thirty-eight verses, compares the hermit with the host, as follows :

> This hypocrite remaineth just the same,
> Because before his God he plays a game ;
> The other leaves the temple full of glee,
> And home returneth from his sins set free.[1]

---

[1] Ludwig Geiger in the *Beil. zur Allegmein. Zeitung*, 1882, No. 204, pronounces a true and unprejudiced judgment on this piece, which has been so much praised by other literary critics (see above, p. 49, n. 2). ' The application of the parable to the religious battles of that period is an egregious mistake. What could be more gratifying to the Catholics than an admission of this sort from the Protestants themselves, that they had forsaken their Father's house taking its treasures with them, had disported themselves in low company, and had only returned to their Father for their belly's sake ? Again, where do we find in this play any dramatic effects, any delineation of character, any depth of treatment ? The characters come and go at the author's will ; without any notice, the paternal house changes to the street, the tavern, the open place, the paternal acres. The characters have no individuality . . . and if by chance the author does attempt to show moral improvement, as for instance when the brothel-keeper is changed from a person of degraded aims and action into a man trusting in the grace of God, he does it so suddenly and without any transition, that at the utmost he forces a smile from his readers, but not the conviction that he is representing the truth. Finally, how material is his treatment of the son ! Greed drives him out of the house, and hunger drives him back again ; we are told nothing of a gradual transformation of the inner man ; it is no picture of domestic peace and the thought of the forfeited father's blessing which come to him as admonition, but the recollection of the " plenty " in his father's house ; there is no recognition that he has acted wrongly and that it is only by true inward reform that he can become a new man, but only the convenient assurance, which the author, in order to make his meaning quite plain, repeats again and again in large print :

Ten years later, in 1537, the Lucerne actuary, Hans Salat, who was also decidedly gifted as a dramatist, published his ' Parabel oder Gleichnus von dem verlorenen Sohn,' in order to hold up to his contemporaries a mirror of the moral corruption of the day.[1] The devil, who appears in the play as ' Tempter,' rejoices that

> Vice, sin and shame so fast are growing,
> They fill all lands to overflowing ;
> The whole world lives so wickedly,
> Crime has so got the upper hand,
> That woe is over all the land ;
> The folk fly to us, all out of breath,
> As though outside hell they'd freeze to death.

For the people

> A bulwark for their sins had found,
> On Jesu's cross all sins were bound,
> And this could cancel them alone.
> No works availed from any one,
> No penitence or absolution . . .
> No doctrine e'er pleased me better than that.
> We devils were always aristocrats.[2]

The conversion of the Prodigal is not the result of the efficacy of works, but is in accordance with the old Catholic teaching : the sinner must be ' filled with

---

" We can only stand acquitted before God through the grace and favour of God, without any human co-operation, without works or effort." ' As on the stage so also in the pulpit this parable was used for the purpose of heaping all sorts of calumny on the papists and the Catholic clergy. Let the reader, for instance, compare the four sermons *Acolastus* by D. Hänichen (Leipzig, 1604), and the five sermons on the Prodigal Son by N. Cornopöus (Hamburg, 1616).

[1] Newly published by J. Baechtold in the *Geschichtsfreund* (Einsiedeln, 1881), xxxvi. 1–80. Also, pp. 81–90, verbal explanations and a criticism of the play and the use made of it by Protestant poets. ** Cf. (now) also Spengler, *Der verlorene Sohn*, p. 12 ff., and Baechtold, *Deutsche Litteratur, Anmerkungen zum Text*, p. 80.

[2] Verse 835 ff.

abhorrence for his guilt,' and like the penitent on the cross 'must believe in Christ with all his heart' :

> The grace divine it is which leads
> The sinner to repent his deeds,
> To think how our Father, in his house,
> The bread of grace so richly gives.
> His labourers here on earth do know
> That from his hands it all doth flow.
> God's pity to himself he takes ;
> To receive it, himself he ready makes.

The whole process of conversion is then described : ' The sinner, relying on God's mercy, repents, confesses, accepts his penance, resolves not to sin again. The first step is to cry to the Father of mercy in repentance and sorrow ; the next is to confess with the mouth and sincerely—as the Prodigal did ; then to do penance : the Prodigal Son was willing to work as a labourer on his father's farm. Thus the parable shows the qualities of true repentance : sorrow in the heart, confession in the mouth, satisfaction through good works wrought in faith.' [1]

With regard to those who have apostatised from the Catholic grace the poet makes one of the hermits say :

> On us poor grieving creatures, Lord,
> Look down in thy misericord ;
> Grant us our sinful state to see
> And thus be reconciled to thee !
> Confound us not in the ruin dread
> Which now o'er all the earth is spread.
> Lead back the erring from their fall,
> Give us a shepherd and a stall. [2]

At the very beginning of the play the Holy Trinity is invoked :

> All that we sinners need, supply,
> Now and in all futurity,

---

[1] Verse 2323 ff.   [2] Verse 1670 ff.

> Peace, rest, help, comfort, unity,
> To us and to all Christianity.
> Unto the true faith lead thou back
> All who have erred from the right track.[1]

Language of this sort contrasts pleasantly with the insults and abuse which Burchard Waldis and so many other writers of 'religious plays' showered on the holders of another creed. The self-same spirit of Christian tolerance and love is also found in the explanation of the parable : God the Lord is 'a Father of all men upon earth,'

> And none's excluded from His kirk,
> Pagan, Tartar, Jew, or Turk.[2]

Among the personal satires in the form of comedies which Luther's teaching called forth, the 'Lutherische Strebkatz' ('Luther's Tug of War') of the year 1524 or 1525 deserves special notice. It is taken from a play in which two parties are tugging from opposite sides at one object, a cord or cable. The characters in the play who have to pull the 'Strebkatz' against Luther, Eck, Emser, Lemp, Murner, Cochläus and others are described in the prologue as the chief enemies of the cross of Christ and the general Christian welfare, as more like devils than men, menials of the Antichrist, sunk in fornication, adultery, sodomy and all sorts of vices, bloodthirsty, godless beasts. Luther implores the Saviour for help ; he has found out in the Holy Scriptures that the Pope is the abominable Antichrist :

> Truth has brought me to the fight,
> 'Gainst him the *Strebkatz* I must pull with might.
> On my side I have no support
> Beyond thy Passion, dearest Lord ;
> But he of devils has a host :
> For me to pull much pain will cost.

---

[1] Verse 97 ff.   [2] Verse 457 ff.

But Christ instils courage into him : He will be with him in the battle against the Pope, who has set himself above God, and is leading the people to the devil. Luther then begins the game with the Pope, and pulls his head down to the ground so that his triple crown falls off. The Pope turns to his followers, addressing himself first to Emser, the ram, and cries ' Help, help ! '

> I declare my A . . . is stinking,
> My head is tottering, and sinking.
> Ah, help me ; give it a poke, and jam
> My head on tightly, my dear ram.

The helpers come up singly one after another, but they can do nothing, they are overpowered by the ' genius '—that is to say, says the prologue, ' their own conscience, nature, in short *themselves*,' and made to betray what they are really by words and actions. Murner, for instance, who addresses the Pope as ' my God and Lord,' is forced to hear from the ' genius ' that ' he blasphemes God and sanctions scandal and vice by his writings ' :

> We know this Murner who 's just spoken,
> Soon as his money bags are broken,
> He knows how to get back his hoard—
> Like Judas he betrays the Lord.[1]

The play ends with the words :

> Praised be thou, my Lord,
> Through whom we have been released
> From the seven-headed dragon's poison,
> As the Holy Scripture calls him.[2]

In allusion to a popular game at cards called ' Bock ' a Catholic satirist wrote a piece called a ' Bockspiel Martini Luthers, darinnen fast alle Stände der Men-

---

[1] See on such accusations against Murner, vol. xi. p. 342, note 1.
[2] In Schade, iii. 112–135 ; cf. ii. 364, *die Strebkatz ziehen.*

schen begriffen, und wie sich ein jeder beklaget der jetzt laufigen schweren Zeit, ganz kurzweilig und lustig zu lesen ' ('A game of Bock with Martin Luther, in which almost all classes of men are included, and how each of them complains of the present hard times ; quite amusing and merry to read '). It was performed in the Castle at Rämbach on June 25, 1531, and printed at Mayence the same year. It is intended to show how the game begun by Luther ' corrupts all classes ' and ' destroys love and peace ' :

> Great fraud, tricks, craft on earth we see,
> But no more faith and honesty ;
> The fleshly teaching is to blame
> Which many years ago first came,
> Which pious hearts has disconcerted,
> And many consciences perverted.

Each of the characters comes forward only once. Luther appears first, and says :

> I began the game, so I
> Will be the first to cast the die ;
> And I myself the cards will deal
> According as inclined I feel.

He goes on to say that whosoever stands by him, and contradicts him in nothing, will not go unrewarded : he has the power to fill all the pastorates and pulpits in Germany. The imperial cities and many princes and lords are on friendly terms with him :

> Their grace and favour I've obtained,
> And I'm a pope in the German land.

He no longer fears anybody, and his actual intention is to root the clerical estate out of Germany :

> To this end all my teaching tends ;
> Who doubts this knows not me, my friends.

John Cochläus then says: 'Yes, Luther, you're right;' everybody must diligently attend to Luther's game, and he will then see if he (Luther) has the spirit of God: he is the enemy of all good works, which nevertheless are the fruits of faith; he slanders, reviles, mocks and ridicules all who do not give in to his will— Duke George of Saxony, King Henry VIII. of England, even the pious Emperor Charles V., who in all gentleness of spirit is trying to promote unity; he excites tumult and sedition:

> Therefore, good Christians all, do ye
> Take him as warning, and keep free
> From Luther's sect and Luther's lore,
> Which has occasioned such uproar:
> What good 's come from it anywhere,
> O pious Christian, note with care!
> It's only from envy and hate, I vow,
> That Martin Luther's striving now.

John Eck also refers to Luther's libellous books in which he does nothing but slander; in the Peasants' War he ordered all the peasants to be slaughtered, although there was many an honest citizen among them who had only been compelled by necessity to join in the rising. John Eck laments that Germany will go to ruin if the Emperor does not come to the rescue:

> My nobly ordered Fatherland,
>   So grievously by Luther's cant
> In short years is laid waste;
>   Nor seems the misery like to end,
> And if to work we do not haste
>   I fear things will not mend.
> Therefore this counsel true is mine,
>   That his Imperial Majesty,
> With help of providence divine,
>   Should re-establish unity.

John Faber devotes himself especially to attacking

Luther's writings, which were full of libellous words and contradictions. In his dissolute life Luther was not aware of these contradictions ; but he, John Faber, would point them out to him in due season :

> With scolding, sland'ring, and so forth,
> With monstrous arrogance and wrath
> To protect himself he tries,
> And then, what he has said denies.
> Contradicts himself, quite flat,
> In all the publications that
> He 's written, as I'll show unmistakably
> At fitting opportunity ;
> Now it would all be lost on him,
> For he tears all up in anger grim,
> As he's now doing in this game.
> I've picked up therefore many a scrap
> Which he all heedlessly did drop,
> When early and late he 's sat and sopped,
> Drinking, swilling, night and day
> In thorough Epicurean way,
> Indulging all the lusts of flesh,
> Yielding to every impulse fresh :
> Yea, all with care I have collected,
> As Luther not one whit suspected,
> But thought they all forgotten were.
> So mad he grows with Saxon beer,
> He never thinks what he indites,
> And that's why he so strangely writes.
> Writes to-day, to-morrow denies ;
> But I'll show it all, before his eyes,
> From his own books which, carefully,
> I've read right through, so much that I
> Can show each one who wants to know
> How Luther is his own arch-foe,
> And oft none but himself doth fight,
> Yet always will be in the right,
> And to no one will submit,
> Nor be advised in the least bit.
> Persists for ever in his way
> Of hatred, and himself doth say
> With spite and hatred the affair began,
> And must wind up on the same plan.

Then follow in succession, each and all complaining

of their present condition and of the general chaos
in affairs, an apostate monk, an apostate nun, an
apostate priest, a nobleman, a merchant, the imperial
cities, a burgher, an artisan, an apprentice, a soldier,
a peasant, and an old man.

The worst complainant is the peasant, who says
that Luther dealt in tricks and lies ; he had first of all
goaded the peasants to war, and then, when he saw
that he had lost the game, he had slipped his neck out
of the collar, turned upon the peasants, brought them
to misery and death, and summoned the princes to
massacre them :

> That anyone puts up with such
> Deceitful play, I wonder much,
> As in the revolt he showed,
> To which he did us peasants goad :
> He wrote unto the princes all
> That they should slay us great and small,
> Whether we guilty were or not,
> Though he himself the rising did plot.

The peasants had not yet recovered from the
injuries :

> Nor shall recover evermore,
> For castle and cloister, where great store
> Of good provisions was of late,
> Have been ransacked by Luther's hate.
> The cloisters were well filled of old,
> Abbeys and castles plenty did hold.
> If then a famine came in the land,
> Help for the poor was close at hand.
> What to these convents now is sent,
> Be it tithes, or be it rent,
> By lords and towns on themselves is spent—
> They take it by force violent.

> Of old, things were quite different :
> When tithes to the monks and priests we brought,
> In times of scarceness of us they thought,
> They lent us corn, they lent us wine ;
> But now with their ' evangel ' fine,

> They never give the poor a drink.
> I've had enough of this game, I think.
> If God will let the lords bear sway
> And keep me in the olden way,
> As from my father good I learnt,
> Whose opinion you now shall hear.

This peasant, an old man, wonders that the world has grown so mad and so blind :

> I am nigh a century old,
> Wonders I've witnessed manifold,
> But the greatest wonder seems
> That everybody vice esteems ;
> *That* man is now the properest
> Who can curse and swear the best.

Profligacy, adultery and other vices were on the increase :

> All has changed in a few short years,
> Nor faith, nor truth on earth appears.

The artisan says he had thought that Luther had begun his work for the furtherance of love and peace, but

> Now first I see what is his aim,
> From envy then he plays his game ;
> This Luther seeks his gain and glory,
> That's plainly traced in all the lore he
> For many years the world has taught,
> Which industry's to ruin brought.
> Trade was in good repute of old,
> The goods at proper prices sold ;
> But all things now are over-priced,
> And he who has not others fleeced
> Is little thought of nowadays,
> And in the background stands always ;
> He's no use in great merchandise,
> Nor e'en in law courts deemed a prize,
> But those who at deceit are apt :
> Monks and priests who have escaped
> Though they try to keep it secret.
>
> These now are all brought to the fore,
> While we must stand behind the door ;

> There is no trade how small soever
> But makes use of these villains clever.

In every branch of handicraft also these apostate monks and priests are employed : without any sense of shame or honour, they decamp like thieves when they have incurred great debts ; in this way business is dishonoured, and even honest men are no longer trusted :

> The poor are left to suffer hunger :
> Be it artisan or burgher.
> Who, in need, for help applies,
> The lenders must have their money's price,
> And so a rate of interest they charge
> Which in course of years becomes so large
> A sum, the mortgage they cannot recover,
> And must needs let it stand over.
>
> All this our Luther organised
> When he the common chest devised.
> At first a fair outside it had
> To all in need : they would be glad
> To give assistance—yes, but when
> They've pledged their goods, and then
> Money on these goods is lent ;
>   This is the plan of the common chest,
> But those who have the management
>   Grow rich and fare the best.

The ' merchant ' in like manner complains that faith and honesty have disappeared :

> Cheating gains the upper hand,
> Faith is nowhere in the land ;
> He who best can gull another
> He's the clever man and brother.
> Whereby all trade is brought to ruin,
> And this is all good Luther's doing,
> In that he carnal freedom taught,
> Which many a one to ruin 's brought,
> And those who faith and truth once held
> Have now grown dissolute and wild.

No less bitter are the complaints of an apostate

monk, an apostate nun, an apostate priest.   The first
of them says :

> Hunger is growing worse and worse ;
> My house full of children empty my purse,
> Roof and clothing scant and bare,
> Want and misery everywhere.
> In labour I do not succeed,
> Therefore I am full of need,
> And know not how life to support,
> And yet escape the hangman's cord. . . .

Finally Thomas Murner represents to the audience
that at the very beginning, when Luther started his
game, he had warned people to beware of his deceitfulness : if they had listened to him they would not need
to be making all these complaints. But instead of
listening to him they had accused him of sinning
against God.

> They slandered me and scolded too,
> And when the peasants drunken grew
> 'Twas Murner who had caused it all—
> A blockhead they did Murner call.
> His life was not safe anywhere ;
> But 'twas the ' evangel ' I declare
> Which gave the peasants liberty
> To practise every villainy.
> Who best slandered, abused and blamed,
> ' Good Christian ' instantly was named.
> The ' evangel ' Luther chanced to bring
> To light was everywhere in swing.
> From the dust he dragged his gospel lore,
> And it was painted up on wall and door,
> On coat and sleeves too it was sewn ;
> Now first it properly was known,
> The Church's creeds were foolishness,
> Christian truth now comes to bless—
> And no one will submissive be,
> Churches and castles sacked we see.
> Such were the right fruits of the ' truth,'
> Report said everywhere, forsooth. . . .

Whosoever nowadays wishes to lead a pious life is

looked upon as a nincompoop : ' that's what has come of evangelical living.'

The people have been blinded to such an extent by the devil and his enchantments, that they no longer know themselves : all trouble is wasted on them.

To the ' gracious lords ' in whose castles the performance took place the concluding words are addressed :

This, gracious lords, is the affair
Which thus has brought us to despair
With famine, pestilence, and strife,
Through Luther's enviousness grown rife,
Who turned the world all upside down
(As to your lordships we've made known),
Encouraged it in wantonness,
Rebellion and all lawlessness,
Till neighbour love quite disappeared.
And still the world's eyes are so bleared,
All this as Christian truth they count ;
You'll find it hard to turn them round.
Before our God we guilty were.
If now with patience we could bear
Our heavenly Father's punishment,
The storm would soon be overspent,
And the Christian faith our hearts long for
Would grow and increase more and more.[1]

---

[1] Extracts in Riederer, *Nachrichten*, ii. 226-239. In a dedicatory letter ' given at Rämbach on June 26, 1531,' to ' Herr Georg von N., captain at N.,' the poet signs himself ' Hanns will Keller,' and Goedeke (*Grundriss*, ii. 227, No. 58) affixes this name to John Cochläus. In spite of much trouble that I have taken I have been unable to procure a complete copy of this play at any library. ** Through the exertions of his friend Francis Falk, who was ready with his help, Janssen obtained later on information concerning a complete copy of this play at the Scheur library at Nuremberg, and he sent extracts from it to the *Katholik*, 1889 i. 184 ff., to supplement his earlier contributions, which extracts are used above. With regard to the author, Janssen expresses himself *loc. cit.* against the assumption of Goedeke. ' Is it not probable,' he writes, ' that the composition of the play performed at Rämbach in 1531 and printed in the same year belongs to an earlier date, and proceeds from Jerome Emser ? Emser generally had his family arms—a goat's head on the shield and the helmet—printed on the title-page of his writings, for which

In reference to a tragedy published by Agricola of Eisleben about John Hus there appeared in 1538 a publication entitled ' Ein heimlich Gespräch zwischen Dr. Martin Luther und seinen guten Freunden

reason he was called mockingly by Luther the ' he-goat of Leipzig.' Well, on the title-page of this play there are a ram and a goat with the inscription :

> Thou haughty ram, lay down thy pride,
> If thou losest the fight thou'lt be despised ;
> The noble goat is strong enough
> To give thy pride a lesson rough.

If Cochläus had written the play, would he not, seeing that he introduced Luther's chief opponents, have brought in Emser also, who played a leading part among the latter ? On the other hand, the omission is quite natural on the assumption that the author was Emser, for he would not have wished to put himself on the stage. And further, is it possible, to judge from his other German writings, to credit Cochläus with so much facility in German versifying as the author of the *Bockspiel* possessed ? Emser, on the contrary, did possess this ease. To prove this we need only point to the rhymes in his ' Answer ' to the ' Warning to the he-goat Emser,' and to the poem which he wrote against Luther's pamphlet on the ' murderous and pillaging peasants,' *Der Bock tritt frei auf diesen Plan— hat wider Ehre nye gethan—wie sehr sie ihn gescholten han.* I have quoted long extracts from both poems in vol. ii. pp. 120–121 and pp. 611–613 (German original ; these are not in the English translation). Much in these has the ring of the *Bockspiel* versification. In the last of them it says, word for word as in the *Bockspiel*, that Luther first of all stirred up the peasants to revolt and then slipped his neck out of the collar. Like the author of the *Bockspiel*, Emser says, in the ' Answer to the Warning,' that he wants no bloodshed, but that for the good of all German lands

> For peace and brotherly union
> He's written with good intention, &c. &c.

The words attacking Luther, which the poet puts into the mouth of John Faber at the end of the above-quoted passage, remind one to a certain extent of what Emser said against Luther in his pamphlet *An den Stier zu Wittenberg* (to the Bull at Wittenberg) Bl. A². ' I have thrice warned you in a brotherly manner, and implored you for God's sake to spare the poor people who are most especially sufferers in this matter. You answered me at last with these words : " The devil take you ; the matter was not begun for the sake of God, and it will not end for the sake of God." The author of the *Bockspiel* hopes that the pious and soft-hearted Emperor Charles will, with the help of divine providence, restore to order the

auf die Weise einer Komödie, durch Johann Vogel-
gesang' (A Secret Conversation between Dr. Martin
Luther and his good friends in the manner of a
Comedy ').[1]

The author is Cochläus,[2] not, as has been hitherto

universal chaos which has set in. In the poem, *Der Bock tritt frey auf
diesen Plan*, Emser begs the princes to show mercy to the misled peasants
and to give their help in restoring orderly conditions, so that everything

> Back to peace may be restored,
> And each and all contented be
> With rights assured, and no deceit or fraud.

Of late years M. Spahn, in the *Katholik* (1897, ii. 360 ff.), has tried
to establish that ' Luther's *Bockspiel* ' is to be ascribed to Cochläus ;
Spahn's reasons, however, do not appear convincing either to my honoured
friend N. Paulus or to myself. A much more likely author than Cochläus
would be John Hasenberg. This Leipzig *magister* brought out in 1530,
in the Latin tongue, a play in four acts, in which the ' playing Luther was
played ' : *Ludus ludentem Luderum ludens.* In the first act Luderus and
his wife Catherine come on the stage. Luderus in a festive song glorifies
card-playing, laughter, tricking and rioting ; Catherine, however, who
has been frightened by a remarkable dream, withdraws herself from his
caresses and contends vivaciously in favour of vows and virginity. In
the second act the Christian religion, once the queen of Europe, complains of its banishment and misery, and is comforted by a ' Christian
orator.' In the third act ' Heresy ' appears as the new empress of Europe,
with her companions ' Uproar ' and ' Corruption of Scripture,' boasting
proudly of her successes. In the fourth act, Luderus and the Christian
orator dispute together about the prevalent condition of things, and, as
they cannot come to an understanding, they appoint an arbiter in the
person of ' Philochristus,' who hears both parties in turn and condemns
Luderus, charged and convicted with numerous crimes, to the dreadful
punishment for heresy, death by fire. See Holstein, pp. 189-190, and
J. Soffner, *Ein Lutherspiel aus alter Zeit : Ludus ludentem Luderum
ludens, quo Joannes Hasenbergius Bohemus in Bacchanalib. Lypsiae,
omnes ludificantem Ludionem, omnibus ludendum exhibuit.* Breslau, 1889.

[1] *Ein heimlich Gesprech*, &c. A copy in the library at Freiburg-in-the-
Breisgau has the date of the year MDXXXVIII. Goedeke (*Grundriss*,
ii. 360, No. 139ᵃᵃ) cites an edition of 1539. ** Cf. Holstein, in the
Zeitschrift für deutsche Philologie, pp. 20, 484 ff. Concerning Lemnius,
see also the clever treatise of Höfler in the reports of the sessions of the
Königl. böhmischen Gesellschaft der Wissenschaften, 1892, p. 79 ff.

[2] ** See Paulus in the *Katholik*, 1895, i. 571 ff. See also Spahn,
J. Cochläus (Berlin, 1898), pp. 264, 266.

thought, Simon Lemnius, favoured by Melanchthon, at enmity with Luther, who in his Latin drama ' Monachopornomachia ' collected together the worst things that had ever been written against Luther, his wife, several of his closest friends and their wives.[1] The ' Heimlich Gespräch ' (' Secret Conversation '), conceived in the same spirit, contains a trenchant satire on the manner of conduct and the married life of the Wittenberg celebrities. It is divided into five acts and a variety of scenes, but it is in reality only a conversation between Luther, Melanchthon, Justus Jonas, Spalatin, Agricola, and their respective wives, Käthe, Prisca, Elsa, Gutta, and Martha, and Agricola's daughter Ortha. Melanchthon's wife Prisca says of Käthe : ' She is a wanton beast, because she has some noble blood in her,' and with regard to her and to the other women who appear on the scene she says : ' Oh, the helpless paunches ! oh, the stinking concubines of monks and priests ! how high they hold their heads, and what a lot they think of themselves ! I alone among all these women have a lawful husband, honourably mine in the sight of God, and the haughty minxes regard me as the meanest of them all.'[2] Agricola's wife says to her daughter : ' Your father is a drunkard and a gambler into the bargain, and worse still which I will not tell you ; for weeks together he has

---

[1] See Holstein, pp. 220–221.

[2] ' It is noteworthy,' says Holstein, p. 224, ' that Melanchthon's wife, in sharp contrast to the other women, is described as the one " who honourably and in the sight of God has a lawful husband," because her husband had never abjured the vow of celibacy ; for this reason also she is treated by the other women, " the concubines of monks and priests," with a certain amount of contempt, and she feels herself at every turn set aside ; but she comforts herself with the proud consciousness that she is the only one whose husband is not suspicious concerning the faithfulness of his wife.'

not given me two groschen for cooking, and has done nothing but drink and swill day and night,' and so forth.[1]

In later times it seems to have been a constant practice among the Protestant theologians who were combating each other to ridicule each other publicly in comic plays.[2]

An extremely caustic satire in Low German in the form of a comedy and composed with much poetic talent is the 'Gemeine Beicht oder Bekennung der Prädikanten zu Soest' ('General Confession or Creed of the preachers of Soest'). It was written in 1534 under the pseudonym Daniel von Soest, but was not printed till five years later.[3] It has this merit above nearly all the

[1] *Ein heimlich Gesprech*, Bl. B 8^b ; C 2 and 7 ; A 4^b and C 5–6. Cf. Holstein, pp. 221–224, and Holstein in the *Zeitschr. für deutsche Philologie*, pp. 460, 463.

[2] I am in possession of a few short, still unprinted notes of the Hanau Dean Henry Steinhart of the year 1594, in which he says : 'The spirit of vindictiveness is so strong among a great number of the theologians, that some of them get their pupils to write farces in which their adversaries are ridiculed and treated like the filth of the earth, and like devils ; this has happened several times at Wittenberg.' Later on Calixtus the Younger complained of the Wittenberg theologians 'that they had had a disgusting and libellous comedy performed by their pupils, and that Calixtus had been introduced on the stage as a horrible monster, and that the most disgraceful buffoonery had also been carried on, as MSS. still extant bear witness. They also represented in this piece Rhadamanthus, as well as a fiery dragon with horns and claws, on the breast of which the name of Calixtus was written' (Arnold, *Kirchen- und Ketzerhistorie*, ii. 147–148).

[3] New careful reprint in Jostes, pp. 111–230. Gerwin Haverland, guardian of the Grey Cloisters at Soest, who is generally regarded as the author of this piece (cf. Goedeke, *Grundriss*, ii. 336, No. 36), cannot come under consideration as such ; cf. Jostes, p. 57. Jostes (p. 58 ff.) adduces weighty reasons for the assumption that 'Daniel von Soest' was no less a person than the renowned Cologne scholar, and later Cardinal John Gropper. ** On the other hand, Ph. Strauch in the *Anzeiger für deutsches Altertum und deutsche Litteratur*, xv. (1889), p. 229 ff., discussing Jostes's theory about Daniel von Soest, puts

satirical writings of the century, that with regard to the
personalities and events represented it comes very near
to historical truth.[1] Under the leadership of the
escaped monk, John von Campen, a ruined adventurer and impostor, and other disreputable preachers,
a social-religious revolution had been initiated in Soest.
The Catholic Church service was suppressed, systematic
raids were organised against the churches and convents,
the holy vessels were desecrated. A new Church
ordinance, which was to establish the exclusive and
unlimited dominion of the new doctrines, designated
the Pope as a triple-crowned idol, a devil incarnate,
and the devil's faithful vicar ; the convents as syna-
gogues of the devil, the clergy as fatted swine, ignorant
beasts and devil's whores. In the same tone this
document went on to abuse the practices of Catholic
worship.[2] All these things were handled by ' Daniel '
in his ' Gemeine Beicht,' and the pictures sketched
by him are consequently throughout of very gloomy
colouring. If the Protestants regarded the Pope as
the devil incarnate, Luther in the eyes of ' Daniel '

forward ' with all humility the suggestion' that in the search for the
author it might be well to consider Jasper van der Borch, canon at Biele-
feld and rector at Soest.   Jostes also, who no longer adheres to his earlier
hypothesis, seems to think this suggestion worth considering.   See *Allg.
deutsche Biographie*, xxxiv. 539.

[1] See Jostes, pp. 60, 67 ff.   Wherever the protocol books of the Soest
council ' give coincident information the complete truth of Daniel's
statements can be proved ; in no single passage can he be convicted of a
falsehood.'   Many of the incidents, to mention only the earlier life of the
preacher Campen, he might have worked up much more forcibly than he
has done ; he often contents himself with merely indicating details instead
of putting them in : his first readers were quite at home among the incidents
and characters he dealt with.'

[2] Further details are given in Cornelius, *Gesch. des Münsterischen
Aufruhrs*, i. pp. 99–114, and ii. pp. 122–140 ; Jostes, pp. 10–53.

was 'the devil's lackey'; the poet makes the devil come from Wittenberg to Soest in order to champion the preachers, 'his dear children.' The devil instructs them how, under the hypocritical guise of the divine Word, they must preach the people deaf and blind, and insult the sacrament of God.

> And likewise chapels and churches,
> Despise all good works,
> Vilify pope and monks,
> Slander lords and canons,
> Preach : they should be free,
> And teach them all that's evil ;
> That to service dues and rents they are not bound,
> Must no more go to the Pope for confession
> Since they all are priests and popes,
> Be they laymen, women or boys ;
> Shame and sin must you praise up—
> Say you will prove it by Scripture.[1]

These instructions are in harmony with the sermons which John von Campen, 'a chosen rascal among all preachers,' preaches to the people. 'Daniel's' language is coarse, but it never lapses into the grossnesses and vulgarities of by far the greater number of the contemporary satirical writings. The poetic triumph of the piece is the description, unsurpassable in its way, of the wedding of the Soest superintendent : the wit and the sarcasm of the author attain here their highest level.[2] At the end 'Daniel' most urgently admonishes the people of Soest, for whom his work was destined, to turn away from all idolatry :

> O Soest, such noble town of yore,
> Why hast thou so meanly turned thee o'er ?

---

[1] Jostes, pp. 123 ff., 224.
[2] Already noticed by Jostes, who (pp. 73-77) gives an admirable appreciation of the whole piece.

> 'Twas said that seven princes bold
> Could never conquer thee of old.[1]
> Now seven Popes, with nuns to aid,
> Thee altogether low have laid.
> For thy evil deeds, O Soest!
> Thou art despised by all the just.[2]

Polemical feeling against the Lutheran doctrine of justification and the results of the religious revolution is seen in many passages of an allegorical drama, ' Der Sünden Loin ist der Tod ' (' The Wages of Sin is Death '), which the Cologne printer, Jasper von Gennep, arranged in German from a Latin drama ' Homulus,' with use of other original works also, and published repeatedly.[3]

The dissolute ' Homulus ' speaks as follows :

> Can faith alone save us indeed,
> Then fools we are God's wrath to heed.
> I mean according to my will to live,
> And trust that God will all my sins forgive.

In the prologue of an edition of 1548 Jasper says :

> Three kinds of faith are in one home,
> Ah, God, what will of all this come !
> St. Paul long time ago did say
> That when approached the judgment day
> Many Christ's teaching would disown,
> And devilish creeds take for their own.
> Righteousness would be suppressed
> And carnal pleasure lift its crest ;
> The clerical estate is scoffed at,
> He who serves God is mocked and laughed at ;
> Each man on earth seeks only how
> He best may fill his sack, I vow.[4]

---

[1] A reference to the great Soest feud of 1445–1450, in which seven spiritual and temporal princes besieged the town.

[2] Jostes, p. 227.

[3] ** Cf. W. Scheel, *Jasper von Gennep und die Entwickelung der neu-hochdeutschen Schriftsprache in Köln. Ergänzungsheft zur Westdeut-schen Zeitschrift für Geschichte und Kunst* (Treves, 1893), p. 8 ff.

[4] Goedeke, *Everyman*, pp. 46–54.

The most prolific Protestant controversial dramatist was Thomas Kirchmair, styled Naogeorgus, preacher at Sulza in Thuringia.[1]

In 1538 he wrote a Latin drama called ' Pammachius,' which was translated by Justus Menius, superintendent at Eisenach, and published in 1539 under the title ' Vom Bapstum, eine neue sehr schöne Tragödia.' In a lengthy preface Menius impresses on ' all pious Christians ' that it is ' a great sin and shame and misfortune ' that ' we should so lightly and quickly have forgotten the heavy, cruel, hard, and wearisome captivity in which, under the damnable, accursed, and

[1] Kirchmair's plays are all the more deserving of detailed notice as only quite lately they have been praised and admired by distinguished literary critics. Holstein (pp. 198 ff.) says, Naogeorg is ' one of the boldest and strongest controversialists, and the most important "tendency" dramatist of the Reformation period.' ** A similar opinion is expressed in Sybel's *Histor. Zeitschr.* xix. 524–525. In the dramas which he wrote in Latin there is ' an Aristophanic satire which lashes the papacy's many errors.' His play, ' *Pammachius*, is not the Pope but the papacy,' writes Cholevius, i. 277, ' its worth and effect rest on the faithful description of the papacy.' Genée, p. 170, calls *Pammachius* ' an epoch-making play.' Gervinus also, iii. 80, places Kirchmair's dramas among the works which exhibit the spirit of the time and are essentially German and patriotic. *Pammachius* is ' an attack on the Pope entirely in accordance with the spirit of the age, and written in the most honourable spirit.' On the other hand, Erich Schmidt in an article on Kirchmair, in the *Allgem. deutsche Biographie*, xxiii. 245–250, calls him ' a Protestant pamphleteer, especially in his dramas,' a ' fiery Hotspur.' ** In a critique of the new edition of *Pammachius* by J. Bolte and E. Schmidt (*Lat. Litteraturdenkmäler des 15. und 16. Jahrhunderts*, published by M. Herrmann and S. Szamatoloski, Berlin, 1891) in the *Zeitschr. für deutsche Philologie*, xxiv. 423, Holstein repeats his above-quoted opinion, calls Kirchmair, however, a pamphleteer. E. Schmidt and Bolte say (Einl. pp. iv.–v.) that Kirchmair in the *Pammachius* goes beyond everything said by Luther in his pamphlet, *Wider das Papsttum vom Teufel gestiftet* (against popery founded by the devil), and supplies a dramatic commentary to the lampoon, *An den christlichen Adel*, and the grievances and requests therein laid down.'

anti-Christian papacy, we were so long, so gruesomely, and so lamentably plagued and tormented—yea, bled, excoriated, and murdered, both in body and soul ; and it cannot be otherwise than that the damnable devil himself has caused this forgetfulness in us.' [1]   The Pope was a ' rat's king and a devil's head,' his doctrines ' were blasphemous, hellish, devilish abominations,' and could never through all eternity be anything else, ' with which the devil slandered and blasphemed the most high Majesty of God in the most horrible manner.' Therefore ' we ought nevermore to forget him, but on the contrary cherish deadly hatred against him all our lives, and to all eternity, and as strongly and vindictively as we possibly can—but, oh God, who can do this sufficiently ?—revile, curse, and damn him to the very lowest depths of the pit of hell.   The devil's head at Rome was a robber beyond all other robbers.   By his immeasurable villainy with Masses, sacrifices, and so forth, he had robbed and fleeced the whole world, ' he had converted the abbeys and convents into veritable idolatrous temples, brothels, and schools of villainy,' and he had given out that he was ' the true hereditary overlord ' of all imperial, royal, and princely powers, and that he regarded emperors, kings, and princes merely as his servants and lackeys.   In short, the Pope's abominations were of such a kind ' that it was only fitting that the whole human race, yea, all creatures on earth, should in all eternity be in deadly enmity to him as to the damnable devil himself.'

---

[1] Holstein (pp. 206-208) quotes this and other similar utterances in the preface as ' fine specimens of Reformation literature, which like an evangelical sermon proclaim and extol the pure truth that has been brought out of darkness into light.'

' But the worst abomination was that he, the accursed and damned Antichrist, in whom all the fulness of the devilish, hellish wickedness dwells incarnate, exalted himself above God, allowed himself to be worshipped as God, rooted out all true knowledge of God, desecrated the Holy Sacraments in an outrageous and abominable manner, and set up in opposition, and enforced his own idolatry and Satanic abominations.' ' And I am free to confess that long ago I myself should have done what I could to paint the papacy had I not chiefly feared that my brush might be too soft and my colours not strong enough, and that I should not be able to make the diabolical robbers' nest ugly and horrible enough ; for if one is not able to paint one devil with his tricks and wickedness in a sufficiently hideous manner, how much more and greater art is required to paint a whole brood of devils with all their iniquity in one nest as they actually are ! ' Therefore he thanked God that his ' dear master and brother, Thomas Nao-georgus, had, with some others, shown himself equal to the task, and had written this tragedy in which the papacy is so admirably described.' [1]

In the prologue the audience is informed beforehand that the Emperor Julian has accepted Christianity, but that Pope Pammachius has grown weary of the Christian teaching, and, in order to rise to greater glory, has formed the plan with his councillor Porphyrius ' to abjure Christ and to give himself up to the service of Satan.' [2] In his conversations with Porphyrius the

<hr />

[1] *Vom Bapstum*, &c., Preface.

[2] An anonymous translation in Goedeke, *Grundriss*, ii. 334, No. 13, contains the statement : ' Pammachius stands for all popes who have overcome everything by their artfulness, Porphyrius for the Pope's learned parasites, Julianus for the older emperors.'

Pope says that ' Christ had deceived Himself and many
foolish men very grossly with His teaching.' ' This
teaching was contrary to reason and human sense ' :

> Let the foolish and the senseless
> Of the common people follow *Him*,
> With all who court shame and misery ;
> But since Reason I have got,
> I'll follow it to a better lot.

Porphyrius, like the Pope, means to enjoy life, and
not reckon on any reward in heaven ; for it was un-
certain whether the dead rose again or ' were altogether
lost like other animals, horses, cows, and pigs.' They
seek the help of Satan, and Satan appears :

> Great horns he has and bristles fierce,
> A monstrous visage full of ire,
> Round eyes like flaming orbs of fire ;
> A long beak-nose of crooked shape,
> A maul that wondrous wide could gape,
> And all his body black as pitch.

Satan grants the Pope's request, sends for a triple
crown, and receives the Pope's oath :

> I do declare, believe and swear,
> By Prince Satan's head of hair,
> By all his kingdom's noblest might,
> That I my life long, day and night,
> Nought honourable, true, and right,
> Nought holy, godly or innocent,
> Will think, or speak, or do on earth,
> To lessen his dominion's worth.
> But as much as I can and may,
> I will study night and day
> To work unto his enemy,
> Christ and Christianity,
> Without mercy, without pity,
> Injury, disgrace, and spite,
> And root them out, if may be, quite.
> And what in your great presence now
> I have sworn with sacred vow,
> That with actions I will seal,
> And never lessen in my zeal.

Thereupon Satan places the triple crown on the Pope's head, and says :

> Next in the empire thou art to me.
> ' Good luck, good luck ! ' cry all with glee.

Such a scene as this could not fail to make a deep impression on the spectators.

Porphyrius expounds to the Emperor as papal doctrine that by the mere efficacy of the seven Sacraments men obtain forgiveness of sins even if ' they believe nothing ' ; also that the Mass ' compensates for and blots out all sins without faith,' that every saint can help in this work as though he were God, and more of such disgraceful stuff. ' And nothing helps those who want to become sinless and righteous so much as gold ' :

> Where gold is, it quenches hell-fire hot,
> Where gold is, purgatory harmeth not,
> Where gold is, vows may be retracted,
> Where gold is, unlawful ties contracted,
> Where gold is, parents may be murdered . . .

He who steals four horses or kills a man does not commit so great a sin as he who eats meat, eggs, cheese, or butter on the prescribed fast days :

> If anyone by the devil's might
> Is driven, either by day or night,
> To theft, or robbery, or lust,
> The church in haste he visit must,
> Sprinkle himself with holy water for his fault
> Or swallow consecrated salt ;
> These, for sins of every kind,
> Certain remedies he'll find,
> They'll straightway drive the devil thence,
> And are an easy penitence.

In order to figure ' as a new creator like God,' the

Pope institutes cardinals, monks, prebendaries, the worship of saints, and so forth, and decrees :   [ ]

> That from purgatory too
> The dead should rise to view,
> And it may be seen the world throughout
> What mighty wonders come about.

With all these creations Satan is well pleased, and
the Pope then explains to him what are the different
functions of the cardinals, monks, and other servants
of the Church ; for instance :

> Most mighty Prince of earth and hell,
> The duties of all these I'll tell :
> These are the cardinals of thy see
> I've made to serve both thee and me :
> With counsel and deed to be at hand,
> To suck the wealth of every land,
> To guard the empire, raised by me,
> Through all eternity for thee.
> And if a Pope, when I am dead,
> To turn from thee to God be led,
> These cardinals will hold him back,
> Punish him, oppose, attack,
> And if he won't live to serve thy will
> Him with poison they must kill.

Altogether the Pope has arranged everything so beauti-
fully that Satan exclaims :

> Ha, ha, you make me laugh, my son,
> Myself I could no better have done.

'And now,' he said, 'after we have overcome our
enemy the Christ and made all the world subject to
us, we will be of good cheer, and have a right jovial
time.'   He calls to his followers :

> Let's play and dance, and drink amain,
> Let all who beakers can obtain
> Quaff lustily, and refill their cup
> The instant they've drunk it up.

But he who shall so merry make
That his throat with vomiting doth crack,
And then swills again, like swine,
Shall be crowned with leaves of vine.
And if the day too short should prove,
We'll sit on through the night, by Jove! . .
For at my table it's my will
That each should gorge and drink his fill.
Therefore, dear friends, to the feast draw near;
Pope Pammachius shall sit here. . . .

Dromo, Satan's lackey, is sent to invite other guests—cardinals, bishops, deans, besides those of the princes who show themselves subservient to Satan. The monks begin quarrelling for the best place:

DROMO

By the Pope's skin, all merrily goes!
The monks are scrimmaging, with blows,
To see where each shall sit and drink;
They're all quite raging mad, I think.

SATAN

Ha, ha, ha, ha, right quickly go,
And bring some cudgels back, Dromo;
Where Satan holds a festive court
There must be indulgence of this sort.
Strike in with might, none of them spare—
Drink, quarrel, scream, grumble, and swear.

As, however, there is no real enjoyment without women, Satan sends for some harlots:

DROMO

See there, you've harlots in abundance—
Pope's skin, a battle new's commencing!

But Christ comes on the scene, and sends Paul and the Truth to Wittenberg:

Go, Paul, and take the Truth all pure,
Help her and give her convoy sure,
So that the honour of My Name
O'er all the earth may have new fame,
Nor mind though Satan and Pammach
With wrath and rage their bellies crack.

Dromo, who had been despatched by Satan to reconnoitre and see if everything was going on peacefully, comes back and finds all the participators in the devil's feast fast asleep :

> Hoscha !   You're all quite full, that's plain :
> Pope's skin, it's all come up again,
> Tables and benches are all aswim,
> The last trump's blast could scarce wake them.
> Ho, Satan, hear ! you too sunk deep,
> Like all the others, in sound sleep ?

The slumberers awakened receive the news that many enemies have risen up against them.   Paul and the Truth had aroused in Germany a learned doctor, who had denounced them all as criminals, and all their proceedings as downright villainy ; the whole of Germany was tending to apostasy.   Under the presidency of Satan ' a papal council ' is now held in order to discuss measures for demolishing the heretics, and Satan dismisses his associates with the charge to behave all of them in such a manner that it might be said that they were true followers of Satan :

> Quick march ! with fury at them fly,
> Turn all things upside down, awry . . .
> Let eyes, teeth, tongue, and mouth, and hand,
> At every hour, in every land,
> With deadliest poison be well tipped,
> Be with a two-edged sword equipped.
> Not one of those teachers must you spare,
> That none escapes me take good care.
> Strike them dead where'er they're found,
> Like ravening wolf, or raging hound ;
> Whoever of them I meet the first,
> I'll drink myself drunk on his blood accurst.[1]

Another translator of this ' Christian and right merry play, in which the devilish doctrine and nature of the anti-Christian papacy is presented in a wondrous

---

[1] *Vom Bapstum*, C 4 ff.

masterly manner,' John Tyrolf, at Kala-on-the-Saale, executed the work ' for the benefit of the Christian youth of the German nation.' [1]

' The young Christians who knew nothing or very little of the corrupting, scandalous, idolatrous abomina- tions of the papacy ' were to be taught by this work how to protect themselves better against these horrors. ' For without doubt it was chiefly for the sake of tender, innocent youth that this play of Herr Naogeorgo was first written and performed.' [2]   A translation which appeared anonymously, and without mention of the printer's name or locality,[3] has on the title-page a woodcut on which the Pope in the presence of a number of persons is placing his foot on the Emperor's neck, while over the Pope's head floats the devil in an ap- palling shape. The following explanation is given in the preface : ' Pope Alexander III. had driven the Emperor Frederic I. into a gruesome war, and had loaded him with much unjust oppression, for when this excellent Emperor, for the sake of peace and the general welfare, fell at the Pope's feet and begged him for an absolution, the Pope set his foot on the Emperor's neck, and in order to heap still further insult on him gave orders that the following verse from the Psalms should be recited : " Thou shalt tread upon the lion and the adder, the young lion and the adder shalt

[1] Zwickau (1540) ; cf. Goedeke, ii. 334, No. 16.   Tyrolf's *Rhymes* are beneath all art.   The dramatist, Paul Rebhun, however, said in the preface to the translation that the Germans ought also to be pleased with ' such a poem,' because ' among other services ' it was calculated to adorn and enrich the German language (see *Rebhuns Dramen*, p. 176).

[2] Dedication, A 5.

[3] Pammachius, *Ein lustig Tragedi*, &c.   Complete title in Goedeke, p. 334, No. 13.   Concerning the four translations of *Pammachius*, cf. W. Scherer, in the *Zeitschr. für deutsches Altertum*, xxiii. 190 ff.

thou tread under thy feet." [1]   The tragedy had been
written in order 'that the young might be warned
betimes against such tyranny and soul-murdering.' [2]

When Justus Menius sent his translation to a
preacher at Wittenberg on February 8, 1539, they set
to work at Eisenach to have the play performed before
the Saxon Elector John Frederic, who was going to
stop there on his way to Frankfort-on-the-Main to
attend a meeting of the Smalcald League.   It was at a
time when the outbreak of a religious war in Germany
was expected at any moment. [3]

Two years later, when the Smalcalders were planning
their invasion of the duchy of Brunswick-Wolfenbüttel,
and Luther had published his lampoon 'Wider Hans
Worst' against Duke Henry, [4] Kirchmair brought out
another drama, 'Incendia,' which was also forthwith
translated into German, under the title 'Der Mordbrandt, ein neuwe Tragedi, in welcher des Bapsts und
seiner Papisten erschreckliche Anschläge und durauf mit
der That vollstreckte Handel vermerkt und entdeckt
werden' ('The Incendiary, a new tragedy in which
the terrible plots and their accomplishment of the
Pope and his papists are related and laid bare'). [5]   The
Pope Pammachius and Satan appear on the scene, and
the Pope complains to Satan that no one on earth
espouses the cause of the papacy :

> Bring'st thou not rescue, with me here
> All's up, and I wish in my heart
> That thou would'st come, for all my art
> And counsel I see disappear.

---

[1] For this and other Pope-fables of the sort, see our remarks, vol. x.
pp. 11–19.

[2] Pammachius, Preface jjj.   [3] See our remarks, vol. vi. p. 30 ff.

[4] See our remarks, vol. vi. p. 196 ff.   [5] Without locality, 1541.

Satan, however, expresses his dissatisfaction with the Pope. He is no longer, he tells him, worth his triple crown. Pammachius replies:

> I'm just the same as I was of yore,
> No whit better than before,
> And just as dutiful to thee.

On his lamenting that by the death of Duke George of Saxony, the Holophernes of Germany, he has lost his best helper in Germany, Satan says:

> My comrade dear, I know him well,
> Down into the depths of hell
> He's gone, where now his dwelling is.

George, however, Satan informs the audience, had wanted to organise a 'Bundschuh' in hell, and had shown the 'pious monks,' whose acquaintance he made there, how to gnaw their chains so as to get free:

> Already had the prince got in
> The chimney, whom I by the shin
> Did seize, and pull him back with might,
> Then with three chains I bound him tight.

In the presence of Satan the Pope consults with his counsellor Porphyrius, the Archbishop Oncogenes, Albert of Mayence, Duke Pyrgopolynices, Henry of Brunswick, and other trusty advisers as to what should be done in Germany for the eradication of the heretics, but first of all says to Satan:

> Stay outside a while, I pray,
> Till we have sung the sacred lay:
> ' Satan, our God, bad spirit come.'

Satan goes out and the confederates sing:

> Come, hellish spirit, God of ours,
> Fulfil us with thy grace's powers;

With thy counsel bring us success,
Which us and thine own cause may bless ;
And grant us eagerness and zest,
That our bodies may gain peace and rest.
Let Christ's glory be disgraced,
Th' evangel's shining light effaced
By thy powers of darkness, and
As thou hast pushed through every land,
And conquered folks of every tongue,
Let this now to thy praise be sung.

SATAN

Here am I, Pope, what's thy command ?

PAMMACHIUS

Sit thee down here at my right hand.

Duke Henry then proposes that the Protestant lands, Saxony, Thuringia, Meissen, should be visited by hired incendiaries, and that everything should be burnt down :

Field, forest, cattle, village, town,
Guns, gold, land, people, burn all down,
And should some escape alive
Give them not a chance to thrive,
To feed themselves or multiply. . . .
Of soldiers then a little band
With ease may occupy the land,
Lord it over the remains,
Or fully carry out their ruin.
Thereby we may well be singed,
And all heretics here perish.

PAMMACHIUS

Oh blessed, well-beloved son,
Unto thy God whom for the papacy,
The Holy Roman Church, thou hast abjured,
And for us as avenger hast secured,
Let thy heart give thanks, that thus advised
For us and against our foe thou hast devised
Such measures. . . .
I cannot here my wish restrain
To kiss thee, nor can I refrain
My hand, dear son, thy head from pressing—
Then bow thee down to take my blessing. . . .

SATAN

I too herein no zeal will spare.
I will see that everywhere
The incendiaries take every care
To kindle flames, and I will set
The wind astirring through the air
To spread the fire fast and far.

PAMMACHIUS

Yea, that's the very work for thee.
Truly this man delighteth me ;
He seems from heaven to descend
The Church's grievances to mend.

The Pope gives 80,000 florins for the pay of the incendiaries ; the bishops and monks are also to contribute. Henry of Brunswick levies the incendiaries, and the work of destruction begins. Three of the culprits are taken in the act of devastation, are led before Philalethes, the Elector of Saxony, and confess on the rack by whom they were hired ; also

It is the general report
That in some reverend bishops' court,
And with his Holiness's aid,
This resolution dire was made.

At the conclusion of the piece an assembly of princes summoned by the Elector is held, and Probus, chancellor to the Elector of Saxony, proclaims the sentence over Duke Henry.   They are to

. . . let his blood flow, and strike his name
From off the princes' roll of fame,
Then finish him with a sword-hit,
Or with fire, as seems most fit ;
And when his life is overpast,
For his reward he shall be cast
Into hell's devouring flame,
To Cerberus, in the devil's name,
To be gnawed and torn for ever.

PHILALETHES

Say all of you Amen with fervour.[1]

Between 'Pammachius' and 'Der Mordbrandt' falls Kirchmair's drama 'Mercator' (1540), a German translation of which in the following year had already appeared in three editions.[2]

In this 'beautiful and useful tragedy' ' the apostolic and the popish teaching' were to be presented to view, and it was to be shown 'how much each could do in the struggles of conscience, and what sort of an end each was likely to come to.'

A merchant, dangerously ill, sends for a priest, and confesses among other things :

> I was a thief, a profligate, a whore,
> A murderer, an usurer, and more,
> A poisoner, liar, perjurer,
> Of church goods, too, a plunderer ;
> Father and mother I did despise,
> Which made me treacherous likewise ;
> The common goods I made my own,
> My own goods to the winds were thrown. . . .
> My conscience stabs me, I can tell,
> Satan says I shall go to hell ;
> My sins weigh on me heavily,
> As though a mountain lay on me. . . .

---

[1] Holstein (p. 123) says of this piece : ' This tragedy has never been equalled for grandeur of conception.' ' Der Mordbrandt is connected with Luther's lampoon Hans Worst.' The author makes Philalethes, the Elector of Saxony, say of Duke Henry (Bl. D⁸) :

> If he will not as Prince appear,
> Then let him as Hans Worst come here.

** E. Schmidt and Bolte, in their edition of Pammachius, say concerning Kirchmair's Incendia, differing from Holstein, that this sequel to Pammachius does not exhibit the author's talent at its height. ' Pammachius, Porphyrius, and Satan lack the original force and drastic vigour of description. Prince Philalethes of Saxony is a bit of colourless idealism ' (Einleitung, p. 4).

[2] Goedeke, Grundriss, ii. 334, Nos. 19-21. In the poet's Prologue to the readers the conclusion is that ' the papists are all going to hell.'

The priest is ready to absolve him, but says that he must enumerate his good works also. As such the merchant reckons alms, self-castigations, offerings, and listening to sermons.

PRIEST

In order great reward to get
More is needed ; you've not told yet
What to the Church you have presented.

MERCHANT

Altars I've built and ornamented,
Two chalices also I've given
And many lights on the walls suspended.

PRIEST

This will place you high in heaven.

But he must in addition make a pilgrimage, and then he would come all the sooner to God. But the sick man answers that his conscience will not ' allow that,' whereupon the priest exclaims :

Dost listen still to that vile monitor ?
Believe me, I say, by thy body, for
Thy soul is committed unto me ;
I must have gold also from thee.

To give a sum of money, to order the singing of a hundred offices (for the dead) and two hundred Masses, will procure absolution and salvation :

By such things Judas to God came,
Though he had betrayed God's Name ;
Nero also and every knave
Managed thus their souls to save. . . .
To heaven you will certainly mount
When your florins are paid to my account.

Conscience, which still leaves the dying man no peace, is scolded by the priest as a witch or a heretic, who must be burnt.

When the priest speaks of the Sacrament of Holy Unction, the merchant says :

> Had I in a tournament to fight,
> With my mistress gazing at the sight,
> This oil would be a method fit,
> For I could smear my limbs with it.

Now, however, he had to go through a struggle of the soul :

> Not the body, which I heed no jot,
> So keep to yourself your old grease-pot.

During all this and other talk, Satan, who is on the stage, carries on indecent sport, and will not allow himself to be banned by the priest. The priest then moves away, and the sick man calls after him :

> Go hence and break your shinbone, priest,
> Hell's the place for you, drunken beast ! [1]

The sick man is in despair, but Christ sends St. Paul to earth, and the Apostle, with the help of Cosmas, gives the patient an emetic :

> PAUL
>
> Cosmas, bring the basin, quick,
> I'll hold his head while he is sick.

The merchant calls out 'More.'

> PAUL
>
> Vomit merrily away. . . .
> See, at one go he brings up alms,
> Pilgrimages, fasts, prayers, psalms,
> Indulgences by hundreds—who
> Would have thought one dose so much could do ?
>
> MERCHANT
>
> Oh that my throat were wider than . . .

---

[1] The contemptible language which Kirchmair puts into the priest's mouth is, according to Holstein (p. 210), ' the papal law, which makes men pious and takes them to heaven.'

PAUL

Stuff two fingers down it, man.

COSMAS

Let's see, there still sticks here some treasure :
Huge candles that no one can measure,
Bulls, chasubles, and chalice rich,
Whole altars—shoes, two pairs—in which
He meant to take his pilgrimage.

PAUL

I wonder much, indeed, what sort
Of man you can be, if you thought
To enter heaven with such a paunch !

Paul tells the sick man that he has only got to believe in Christ, and he will ' at once be free from sins.'   In a scene of the fifth act Christ Himself appears and says :

Satan had a grand idea
When he raised the popedom here ;
No better work could have been devised
To make My kingdom be despised.
Few now take comfort from my death,
To the Pope they all of them pin their faith,
Who is the devil's loyal friend,
And brings to him souls without end.[1]

In imitation of Kirchmair, John Chryseus of Allendorf, in Hesse, published at Wittenberg in 1545 his play, ' Hofteufel,' being ' the sixth chapter of Daniel arranged as a play, and written in rhyme for the

[1] **E. Schmidt and Bolte in their edition of *Pammachius* (*Einleitung*, p. vi.) criticise the play *Mercator* as follows : ' Scenes of this sort—the priest at the death-bed of the drunken sinner, interrupted by Conscience and rated by the devil, until he is forced to take himself off with his impotent apothecary ; Paul, the teacher of grace (scenes 3, 4); and Cosmas, the heavenly physician, examining the swollen body of the merchant, and, by means of a strong emetic, causing the patient to vomit forth all his " church-works," Masses, indulgences, and so forth, these, forsooth, in the " Aristophanic century " of German literature, are considered master achievements in comedy.'

comfort of the godly and for a warning to the godless ' : [1]

> And it is by the title known
> ' Court-devil,' because in it is shown,
> From Daniel, how the influence
> Of the devil at court was oft immense.

In the dedication of the piece to the Dukes John Frederic and John William of Saxony, the sons of the Elector John Frederic, the author inveighs against ' the wicked, sinister, and raging papists,' through whose ' desperate, bloodthirsty intrigues, financing and secret iniquitous practices ' the devil has brought about that the Elector John Frederic with his allies has been ' as it were thrown before the lions for revenge.' Like Kirchmair's ' Mordbrandt,' this piece is also chiefly directed against Albert of Mayence and Henry of Brunswick, the ' excellent and most willing creatures ' of the Court-devil. The latter, in the guise of a monk, says of them :

> I have in them a first-rate crew,
> In villainy they me outdo,
> And I shall take the greatest care
> Lest they should break away from me—
> My servants they must ever be.
> Beelzebub will triumph much
> To learn that in his kingdom such
> Great, mighty lords I have retained,
> By whom, also, I have gained
> Pammachius's restoration.
> He was well nigh past salvation,
> Too open was his infamy.
> Wherefore I comfort myself verily,

---

[1] Concerning the different editions cf. Goedeke, *Grundriss*, ii. 361, No. 149. The *Hofteufel*, says Holstein, ' belongs to the most important dramas of the Reformation period ; it was the foundation of all the " devil's literature " of the sixteenth century' (cf. Holstein in the *Zeitschr. für deutsche Philologie*, xviii. 437).

That since Beelzebub's given three
Crowns as reward to Pammachius, he
Will bethink him of my zeal also,
And one crown, if not more, on me bestow.[1]

' For the sake of the dear children who know nothing
of the Pope's doings and teaching,' ' Ein frommer
Teutscher ' ('a pious German ') published in 1545 ' a
conference of the most holy father Pope Paul III.,
held with the College of Cardinals, to consider how the
Council of Trent was to be conducted.' In this play
there were introduced ' hymns and collects after the
old popish usage in mockery of the Pope and his crew,
to show that his jugglery was not regarded as any sort
of divine worship.' A woodcut on the title-page represents the Pope and his cardinals in solemn assembly,
with three horrible devils' forms floating over their
heads. The first act begins with an ' office in the
Latin tongue,' with parts set in music, and the office
is the same as in the Roman Ceremonial. The Pope
and the cardinals then betake themselves to the con-
sistorium. The Pope gives the blessing, and the senior
cardinal promises this ' earthly god ' that his Holiness
shall not be withstood even by a hair's-breadth. The
chancellor then explains how, for the last twenty years,
to the injury of all Christendom, strange and pernicious
doctrines have been promulgated by the vagabond and
apostate Luther, whom the devil, if he could, would
soon carry off. Only lately, again, this desperate rogue
and villain had published a monstrous lampoon against
the council convened by the Pope—viz. ' Das Papsttum
vom Teufel gestiftet ' ('The Papacy founded by the

---

[1] Concerning the frequent appearance of the devil on the stage in the
disguise of a monk, see G. Ellinger, in *Zeitschr. für vergl. Litteraturgesch.*
Neue Folge, i. 174 ff.

devil'). The Pope proposes that before opening the council they should consult

> How best the matter to attack,
> And rid ourselves of him, alack, alack !

There then follows a discussion as to whether Luther's lampoon shall be left unanswered, or whether it shall be refuted, or whether they shall keep silence until the council takes place, and then proceed at once. One of the cardinals is of opinion that they should keep silence, or they will strengthen him still further in his villainy :

> Leave him alone in the heretic's mine,
> He is in Germany, the land of swine,
> We in Italy the famed ;
> Nothing from him can be gained.

A second wants to use violence against the heretics and send them into the flames :

> I have nothing more to say
> But kill the villain straight away.

A third, on the other hand, says :

> We priests are not a saintly brood,
> Reform would do us all much good.

The cardinals fall into fierce wrangling, till at last the Pope decrees that four of them shall seek counsel from St. Peter. Before dismissing the ambassadors, however, he wishes ' to bless them like pilgrims.' He goes with them into St. Peter's Church, and ' the ceremony of benediction is devoutly performed with Latin versicles, prayers, and collects, and also musical accompaniment.'

Thus in one and the same piece the Catholic worship was twice over ridiculed on the public stage.

The next act deals with the journey of the ambassadors to St. Peter. At the gate of heaven they meet with Pope Julius II., who with his three successors are waiting in vain for admission, and who complain of the haughty gatekeeper St. Peter. The chancellor knocks at the gate, and as Peter does not open it, he calls out :

> Well, here goes ; I'll knock louder still,
> Maybe he's had a drunken swill,
> And waiting thus outside he keeps
> Us all, the while he soundly sleeps.

After a third knock Peter at last answers :

> Christ will not permit,
> Nor does He think it fit
> That I should answer, or unbar
> To you who all so filthy are.
> Pfui ! the whole great heavenly throng
> Were praising God with holy song
> And music, when you come and howl
> Outside with your behaviour foul,
> And horrid stench and noise obscene
> By which we've interrupted been.

Peter then makes a long speech, in which he deals abundantly in the grossest terms of abuse. All at Rome were 'rogues and villains, thieves, murderers and traitors, conjurers, bell-greasers'—in short, black with every possible vice and crime.

The archangel Gabriel also appears, and delivers the following message :

> Thus saith the Lord of Sabaoth,
> I know you not, you godless lot. . . .
> Your council's only filthy dung,
> Filth is all you've said or sung. . . .

This is what they are to say to their Antichrist, for whom he also gave them a letter.

In the third act the ambassadors lay before the Pope and the cardinals an account of their journey, and hand the letter to the Pope, who reads it, flies into a passion, and calls up the devil. The latter comes, and there is a long talk, which ends as follows :

> Well, hold yourself my faithful knight,
> In due time I'll reward you right ;
> With this I bid you all good-bye,
> And my odour leave in memory.

Whereupon the Pope exclaims :

> Pfui, pfui, oh Sancta Maria !
> O holy Genevieva !
> O all ye saints, pray God for us !
> Pfui, pfui, what stench malodorous !
> Pfui ! Thousand devils, how it stinks !

'After which the cardinals and the Pope make their escape one this way, the other that.' With the singing of Luther's hymn,

> In Thy Word preserve us, Lord,
> Slay Pope and Turk with Thy sharp sword,

this play, ' written for the benefit of the dear children,' comes to an end.[1]

This piece gave the stimulus to the Protestant writer of plays, Joachim Greff, in 1546, to put on to the stage his ' Götzendienst der Bepstler ' (' Idolatry of the Papists ').[2] Greff, a member of the Wittenberg circle, since 1541 a schoolmaster in Dessau, produced a large

---

[1] Extracts from Riederer, *Nachrichten*, ii. 239–248, 353–372. ' I should consider Wittenberg,' says Riederer (p. 240), ' the place where this comedy was printed, even if the resemblance to the writings printed there by George Rhau were not so great as it is. Moreover, it did certainly not come before the public without the knowledge of Luther.' Goedeke (*Grundriss*, ii. 333, No. 12) mentions two editions of the play.

[2] Holstein, p. 144 ; cf. p. 228.

number of Biblical pieces with a polemical tendency
against the papacy.[1] He was much dissatisfied with
the world, as, indeed, the community at Dessau were
much dissatisfied with him. ' I will not conceal from
your Grace,' one of the Dessau preachers wrote concerning him to Prince George of Anhalt, ' that nearly
the whole parish complains of the schoolmaster, that
he lamentably neglects their children whom they have
entrusted to his care to be educated ; and, as I am
told, they are obliged, to their great inconvenience, to
send their children to school out of Dessau.   They are
thinking of petitioning your Grace to provide another
schoolmaster, as this one is so headstrong and obstinate.' [2] Greff, on the other hand, had complained
before this that all rule and order were at an end ;
that art was no more revered, that there was no discipline, no honour, no fear of God ; the children were
all brought up to vice and crime :

> Eating and drinking is all our craft,
> Swearing, abusing, and suchlike ways,
> Rich and poor learn in their earliest days.

---

[1] William Scherer (*Deutsche Studien,* p. 241) criticises him as follows :
' His poetical capacity is slight.   The motives which he selects and works
up are of secondary nature.   The Protestant enthusiasm which animates
him does not inspire him to high flights (in his *Abraham* and in his
Judith his imagination becomes most keenly excited when it is a
question of festive entertainment, of eating and drinking, p. 233).   His
diffusive loquacity often makes him unbearable.   In short in the history
of literature he is rather an encumbrance than a delight.'   With Scherer's
article cf. H. Holstein in the *Archiv für Litteraturgesch.* x. 154–168.
' Even if all critics,' says the author, ' should agree with Scherer, that
Greff is rather an encumbrance in literature than a joy, he is nevertheless
among the number of the most prominent representatives of the drama of
the sixteenth century, and deserves all the more notice as he belongs
to the circle which formed itself around the great men of the German
Reformation.'
[2] Holstein, pp. 144–145.

We teach them thus in their childhood,
And how any conduct good
From such a bringing-up can flow
I would mightily like to know.[1]

The appreciation with which he wrote of the religious plays of the Middle Ages and their aim is very
noteworthy. ' By means of the Passion-plays our forefathers aimed at rousing us to devotion and piety, and
in the play of St. Dorothea they showed us how we
must not allow ourselves, by anything whatever, to
be drawn away from God or from His Word and love,
neither by tribulation nor by persecution; like the holy
Dorothy, who was willing rather to lose her life and
body for the sake of Christ and His Word, than to serve
idolatry and fall away from God. The same lesson
was taught by the play of the " Beheading of John the
Baptist " and many others I could name, as everybody
knows better than I can say.' ' Amid the wholesale
contempt' with which the arts were regarded in his
time, ' there still lay a tiny spark glimmering under the
ashes which with great pain and labour might be preserved and rekindled.' By the performance of good
plays the young might be taught eloquence, courage,
and good manners ; ' above all, plays of this sort, which
are high-minded, chaste, honourable, and Christian,
ought to be performed oftener than they are, and
then much blasphemy, murdering, drunkenness, and
gluttony, and many other evils would be put a stop
to.' [2]   Among the number of such ' high-minded, chaste,
honourable, and Christian plays ' he reckoned Kirchmair's piece, praised by himself, ' Schönes Spiel vom
Papsttum,' [3] and the ' Ratschlag ' of Pope Paul III.,

[1] Holstein, p. 46.   [2] Ibid. pp. 49–50.   [3] Ibid. p. 139.

as well as his own dramas, ' Judith,' in which he wished that the ' papal tyranny ' might be overtaken by the same ruin as had befallen the godless Holofernes through Judith,[1] and the ' Schöne neue Aktion auf das achtzehnte und neunzehnte Kapitel des Evangelisten Lucä.' In this last piece he gave stage instructions that ' the money-changers whom Christ turns out of the temple signify the papacy, and must be represented by courtesans, priests of Anthony, messengers of St. Valentine, monks and nuns, or else the whole clerical pack— Pope, cardinals, bishops, with all the tonsured court followers—might be substituted for the buyers and changers, and in such case one of them must have a holy-water pot, another a censer, a third some other sort of instrument such as appertained to their papacy and idolatrous worship.' [2]

All sorts of Biblical matter was used for polemical attacks. The Hamburg citizen, Henry Knaust, said in the dedication of his 'Tragödi von Verordnung der Stände oder Regiment, und wie Kain Abel, seinen Bruder, göttlicher Ordnung halben, erschlagen und ermord bat ' (' Tragedy of the Institution of Classes or of Government, and how Cain struck and slew Abel his brother by Divine Ordinance '), published at Wittenberg in 1539, that his intention was to present to view the doctrine of God's dispensation as to the two most important classes on earth : Cain was the type of the dissolute and abominable people, who were seen in the papacy, and lately among the peasants and the Anabaptists.[3] In John Baumgart's comedy, ' Das Gericht Salomonis ' (' The

[1] Holstein, p. 104.
[2] Scherer, *Studien*, p. 239 ; Holstein, pp. 143–144 ; cf. p. 228.
[3] Goedeke, *Grundriss*, ii. 392 ; Holstein, pp. 80–81.

Judgment of Solomon'), the devil makes fun of holy
water and consecrated salt, which he compares to 'flail-
pith, midget fat, waggon tar,' and of 'the Pope's benediction and church.' [1]   Duke Henry Julius of Brunswick, in
his 'Tragica Comödia von der Susanna,' could not refrain
from stigmatising the popish 'idolatry' before the great
lords assembled at his court.   The clown of the piece
tells Susannah's father, Helkia, that he has stolen a
'wooden god' out of a church, and that he means to
pray to it, for 'the holy man at Rome, the Pope,' has
'commanded' that people should not only pray to
God, but also to men and women, to the Mother of
God, to St. Paul, and to other saints.   Helkia says we
must worship God alone.   'Do you hold the Pope
higher than God Himself ?   Keep to that which I tell
you, and let the Pope's teaching, which is the devil's
teaching, be hanged.' [2]   In a play written by the
Rostock student, Christopher Brockhagen, 'Von den
klugen und thörichten Jungfrauen' ('The Wise and
Foolish Virgins'), 'the heroine of the piece, the head of
the foolish virgins, Babylonia, is the Roman Church,
the papacy.   Her lover, the most Christian king, sends
her the head of a murdered hostile prince.   Germany is
swimming in blood, France lies stricken, and all these
victims are being sacrificed for Babylonia alone.[3]   The
preacher, Christopher Lasius, actually inveighed in a
Christmas play against 'the Pope's ranting' :

[1] Baumgart, Act v. scene 7.
[2] *Schauspiele des Herzogs Heinrich Julius*, pp. 21–22.   Hans Ackermann, in his *Geistliches Spiel von Tobias* (1539), aimed at showing that
the conjugal estate was ordained by God, in opposition to the teaching
of the papacy which 'to the glory and profit of the devil has hitherto
joined with many liars in extolling the celibate religious life, and exalting
it to heaven' (Ackermann's *Dramen, Einleitung*, p. 2).
[3] Holstein, p. 142.

> The Pope is the Antichrist on earth—
> We say this without any fear,
> And trust we shall not rue it,
> Even were he the devil himself,
> For the true God is living still.[1]

Still more virulent insults against the Catholics were
fired off in the ' Schöne und neue lustige Aktion,' which
Bartholomew Krüger, town clerk and organist at
Trebbin, published in 1580 concerning ' the beginning
and ending of the world, in which the whole history of
our Lord and Saviour Jesus Christ is contained.' [2]

The first three acts deal, in 1900 vigorous verses,
with the fall of the angels and of mankind, the birth,
the teaching, the death, and the resurrection of Christ.
Then follow the last two acts, consisting of nearly
1140 verses, the contents of which are announced in
the prologue with the words : Christ had commanded
His disciples to preach the Word of God, but the Antichrist had perverted this Word through the lies and
deceit of the devil; until Luther, inspired by the Holy
Ghost, brought the pure doctrine back to light again.
The Pope raged against him, but his murdering, burning,
and hanging were of no avail ; God safeguarded His
Word, and the pious Christian gained the everlasting
crown :

> As herein will be shown you well.
> Be still ! I have yet more to tell,
> Here in the briefest way you'll all
> Learn how God's judgments on men fall.

Lucifer sends his disciples forth to mislead the
whole world. Two canons dilate on the subject of the
newly arisen heretic, Martin Luther, whom, however,

---

[1] ** J. Bolte, *Ein Spandauer Weihnachtsspiel* (1549), pp. 112–113.

[2] Goedeke, *Grundriss*, ii. 368 ; reprint by Tittmann, *Schauspiele*, ii.
1–120.

the Pope will certainly put down. The devil, Rapax,
' opens his sack ' and begins to cry out his wares.
Another devil tells him to be quiet, he can ' spare his
rubbish ' :

> With these people you must not do it,
> All their actions only tend
> To hurry them straight into hell,
> They belong already to our band. . . .

Christophorus, a disciple of the new teaching, appears
with the canons, and he expresses his joy at having
found the true Word of God, and makes his two children
sing Luther's hymn :

> In Thy Word preserve us, Lord,
> Slay Pope and Turk with Thy sharp sword.

The canons endeavour to draw him to their side,
the monk Franciscus promises him a remunerative
sexton's post ; but he pushes them off, calls them
rogues and villains and sends them to hell in the devil's
name, and then once more sets his children off singing
the whole of Luther's hymn, with the later addition,
' Overthrow their plottings, Lord,' in order

> To mock and ridicule the Pope,
> Who has made himself as great as God.

The devils also, who on the failure of their ' three
servants ' try their own hands on Christophorus, can
do nothing with him ; the archangels Raphael and
Gabriel place the crown on the latter's head, and with
the choral hymn ' Ein feste Burg ist unser Gott ' the
act closes. In the fifth act Christ appears with His
heavenly hosts on the seat of judgment. The Apostles
Paul and Peter bring charges against the Pope, who,
they complain, with his whole company despises the
Saviour, and deceives the whole world against his better

knowledge, falsifies the Sacraments, forbids marriage, and carries on all sorts of scandal :

> . . . For gold they will forgive men sin
> Which lurketh still the heart within.
> These, Lord Christ, are the complaints
> I bring concerning these Pope's saints.

Christ then pronounces the sentence over the followers of the Pope, the canons and the monk :

> To the devil's realm you appertain ;
> All prayers, entreaties are in vain.
> Be silent ! You're to me unknown ;
> The seeds of error you have sown,
> And much idolatry you've wrought
> On earth, and think thus to have bought
> Salvation, and in Me you've never
> Trusted : now be damned for ever. . . .
> Ho ! devils, carry them all hence,
> They are your spoil and recompense.

' The devils then drag one after another of them off to hell, the victims crying out all the while " Ah ! " and " Woe ! " and howling and weeping.' Christophorus and the elect go into eternal life.[1]

Seven years earlier Philip Agricola of Eisleben had published, ' in honour of the reigning burgomaster of the town of Berlin,' a ' very fine Christian comedy of the Day of Judgment,' in which the Pope did not come off any better. ' As soon as the angel blows the trumpet,' we read in the author's stage instructions, ' all the people in the comedy fall down as if they were dead, and those behind the table expire ; the devils come out of hell with loud cries and take them back

---

[1] Holstein (pp. 78–79) praises this ' fine, humorous new play ' as one of the most distinguished plays of the whole century ; ' it is a thoroughly Protestant play, which must certainly have served for the edification of multitudes.'

with them to hell, and then sit down to table.' Then, after the just ones have been awakened, there follows as the principal scene the condemnation of the Pope to hell.[1]

The centenary of Lutheranism in the year 1617 was used as a special opportunity for inciting the young Protestants against the papacy. Henry Kielmann, co-rector of the gymnasium at Stettin, wrote for the occasion, ' to the glory of God and for the benefit of all the people,' a ' merry comedy,' ' Tetzelocramia,' adapted from John Tetzel's ' Ablasskram.' It was acted by the pupils, and it went through several editions.[2]

In the first act religion complains that her honour is declining in all countries : of her three children her son Gnathaster has become a steward at the papal court ; her daughter Hypocrisis had gone into convents among monks and nuns, and consorted with harlots and rascals ; her daughter Veritas, to whom she had given the Bible, was everywhere mocked and laughed at. Veritas, however, comforts her mother by telling her that a man had appeared to her in the form of an angel, had handed her a shield and a sword, and had admonished her to

[1] Genée, pp. 194–195. ' It is a fantastic and inartistic jumble of angel and devil scenes.' ' Once even the Turkish army appears and is demolished by the Christians with the help of the angel Gabriel,' and so forth. The complete title is in Goedeke, *Grundriss*, ii. 393, No. 329.

[2] The complete title is in Goedeke, *Grundriss*, ii. 395, No. 347. In a Latin prologue to the reader the author says :

> Nec fictis tamen hic notare Papam,
> Sed veris, velut acta sunt, libebat.

G. Ellinger, in the *Zeitschr. für vergleichende Litteraturgesch.* (Koch and Geiger, Neue Folge, i. 176–177), draws attention to the fact that Kielmann, in the places where he makes the Court-devil appear, has copied word for word from the piece of the same name by Chryseus (see above, p. 91).

the diligent reading of Holy Scripture. The mother
urges her daughter to withdraw into the desert, as the
world is the kingdom of the devil :

> See, there's a monk, a creature queer—
> My hair stands up on end with fear ;
> Come, let us go ; come, let us flee,
> Or he will knock us down, you'll see.

A court- or church-devil, in the guise of a monk,
relates how through his son, the Pope, he produces
all sorts of vice and crime :

> If anyone opposes me,
> And will not live as I decree,
> In whoremongering and sodomy,
> In roguery and simony,
> In error and in trickery,
> I visit him with every plague.

At the instigation of the court-devil Tetzel is sent
to Germany ; first of all, however, the spectators are
taken to Rome, where the Pope, carried in a chair,
' with his cardinals, bishops and monks, his pyx and
his holy water,' appears on the scene, and a motet is
played. Tetzel at his own request receives the com-
mission to sell letters of indulgence in Germany, and
the court-devil invites him to join in a spree :

> Tetzel, faithful brother mine,
> Sha'n't we now enjoy some wine :
> Such fortune calls for a good drink,
> And let the courtesans also . . .

To which Tetzel answers :

> Yes, we'll have some merriment,
> Since fortune such good luck has sent.

The Pope then grants permission to a prince, who
has saluted him as ' all holiest Father and God,' on

payment of 2000 crowns, to marry his own sister, and
he breaks out against the bearers who let him fall from
the sedan in the following words :

> You arch-desperate villains, you
> *Potz Wunder, Potz*, what did you do ?
> Are you mad, or drunk, or what ?
> You godless, devilish, dastard lot ! . . .

'Thereupon the children came running up in white
shirts, and began to laugh loudly '; then they danced
and sang the well-known Protestant comic song :

> The Pope has had a deadly hurt,
> Falling from a chair so high, . . .

while on the other hand they glorified Luther, who had
found the right key, and had destroyed the kingdom
of the devil and the Pope.

After all these proceedings Veritas comes forward,
and wonders that

> The earth and rock-cliffs are not riven,
> And all the birds in the high heaven
> Poisoned by such doctrine false
> And devil's venom as comes from
> That son of Satan throned at Rome.
> Such wicked blasphemy doth exceed
> Hell-poison very far indeed ;
> The devil could not outdo it
> Nor equal it with all his wit. . . .
> And now in Germany, they say,
> A fraudulent man is on the way,
> Tetzel, with his bulls and lies,
> The folk to decoy with a money prize.

The author then makes Tetzel read out a Bull of
Leo X, which he (the author) has falsified, in which the
Pope, among other things, invests Tetzel with plenary
power to grant absolution not only from sins that have
been repented of and confessed, but also from un-

repented, unconfessed sins, and also to close the gates
of hell.[1]

They had only got to give money, Tetzel said :

> Yes, dear people, I freely state,
> That nowhere there's a sin so great
> Which I cannot forgive straightway,
> If only money you will pay. . . .
> Though you the worst sin perpetrated
> That anybody ever meditated,
> How monstrous howsoe'er the vice,
> It could be remitted in a trice.
>
> .   .   .   .   .   .
>
> Eternal grace you could ensure
> If one of these briefs you but procure,
> Without penance, pain, or ruth—
> All this I swear is sacred truth.

As a matter of fact Tetzel taught very differently.
God does not ' grant us salvation,' he said, ' for the
works of righteousness which we have performed,
but only through His holy mercy.' ' In the sacred
council at Constance it was resolved anew that whoever
would gain indulgences must both have contrition and
confess according to the ordinance of the Holy Church,
or at any rate resolve so to do.   This is also the purport
of all papal Bulls and letters of indulgence.' ' For those
who gain indulgences are filled with true repentance
and love of God, which do not suffer them to remain
idle and inactive, but stimulate them to serve God
and to do great works for His honour and glory.   For
it is well known that it is Christian, God-fearing and
pious people, and not idle, dissolute people, full of lust,

---

[1] ' A peccatis contritis, confessis et oblitis, ut etiam a non contritis et
non confessis . . . item claudere portas Inferni et aperire januas Paradisi.'
Act iii. scene 4.   ** This work, originally composed as a comedy, was
used by later authors as an historical document ; see *Paulus Joh. Tetzel*
(Mayence, 1899) p. 23, Anm. ii.

who gain indulgences.' And again : 'For all indulgences are granted in the first place for the sake of
God's glory. Therefore, whoever gives alms to gain
an indulgence does it primarily for the sake of God,
as nobody can gain an indulgence who is not filled
with true contrition and love of God, and whoever
does good works out of love to God, refers these works
to God in his lifetime.' [1]

These are the words of Tetzel, whom Kielmann
treats as a 'desperate villain' and an 'apostate scamp.'
When Veritas (in the play) attempts to refute him
with the Bible, Tetzel goes on :

> What say'st thou, *monstrum hominis* ?
> Hold thy jaw or else take this (*striking her a blow*) . . .
> What with your Babel, babble, Bible,
> May the falling sickness smite you !

He leaves Veritas bound as one possessed of the devil
and felled to the ground ; an exorcist is brought on the
scene to drive out the devil.[2] Veritas is then dragged
off to the Inquisition, and Tetzel declares :

> I'll bring her to her senses yet,
> Put her to the sword, or let
> Her burn to ashes at the stake.
> My true acquaintance she shall make,
> And learn to know me for
> A ruthless, fierce inquisitor.

In order to get calmed down he goes to a
'free banquet' in a convent at the invitation of the
exorcist :

[1] Cf. my pamphlet *An meine Kritiker* (new edition, Freiburg, 1891),
p. 73 ff.

[2] Among other incantations, with the following Latin : '. . . adhuc
exorciso te in nomine Patria filia et Spiritua Sancta, sancta Maria.' Act iii.
scene 7.

> Merrily we'll sing and quaff,
> And over all these matters laugh,
> And then to business back again:
> Be calm, my friend, and let God reign.

In one of the following scenes Tetzel, who has sold to a young nobleman and his retinue, for the sum of ten crowns, an indulgence brief which is to remit all their future sins, is then pitched into by the men he has absolved in advance :

YOUNG NOBLEMAN

> Go it, my men, don't spare your blows,
> Pummel his pate, smash up his nose,
> The sin's forgiven, as we've read,
> Though we leave not a hair upon his head.

TETZEL

> Oh ban, hell-fire, murder !
> You rogues, why do you beat me thus ?

The young nobleman's people try to take the money away from him, to give ' the rascal a still better roasting ' and ' pat him on both cheeks,' but their young lord stops them :

> Let be, the tender man might die ;
> We've dressed his hide enough, think I.

In the last act the archangels Michael and Gabriel appear. Veritas is set free, and Beelzebub called up in order to march Tetzel and two of his associates off to a court of justice. Beelzebub tells them that he will spare them if they will fall down and worship him. They fall down at once and pray to the devil.[1] All the same, however, they are carried off to hell. On the other hand Luther and Bugenhagen are solemnly

---

[1] Tetzel prays: ' O Sancte Beelzebub parce mihi misero peccatori.' The two associates pray: ' Esto propitius sanctissime pater Beelzebub. O pater Beelzebub miserere mei.'   Act v. scene 4.

equipped by Michael for their expedition against the Roman Antichrist.[1]

Other religious and polemical plays were written not only against the papacy, but also against religionists who were not Lutheran. To these belongs Nicodemus Frischlin's Latin comedy ' Phasma,' which was acted in 1580 before princes and lords at Tübingen, and was twice translated into German.[2] There is an endless amount of discussion in this piece ; the Lutheran doctrine is defended as the only true and justifiable one, every other is relegated to hell as the work of the devil. Among other incidents in it the audience and readers are treated to a long dialogue in which Luther and Brenz, and Zwingli and Carlstadt are pitted against each other. The first two explain that

> In the Last Supper there are not only both
> Wine and bread, as in a peasant's broth,

---

[1] This play also is warmly praised by Holstein, pp. 240-243. He says, ' It is not only distinguished by skilful and shapely diction, but by correct dramatic structure. The historic incidents of the traffic in indulgences are well represented, and impressive pictures of the religious conditions of the period are supplied. Nor is the piece wanting in humorous features, though these are not present in sufficient number to injure the religious character of the whole.' ' Kielmann's admirable Reformation-play, conceived with so much loving insight,' was used by the pastor Martin Rinckhart as the basis of a *Jubel-Komödie*, written in the same spirit and performed by the pupils of the gymnasium at Eisleben. Genée also (pp. 174, 178-179) considers the polemical plays ' imbued with deep religious earnestness.' ' What a force of conviction lay even in the outbursts of rage which came from the depth of religious sentiment ! ' Besides, ' the yearning for a knowledge of the truth,' ' the heartiest, one may even say the most pious, hatred against the falsifiers of the truth and of the religion of love, was the one idea which was struggling for expression in this exalted movement of the age.' And yet Genée, as he assures his readers in his preface, had ' read the plays himself.'

[2] Goedeke, *Grundriss*, ii. 386, No. 6a and b. Criticism of the play in Strauss, *Frischlin*, pp. 125-129. I make use of the translation by Arnold Glaser, Greifswald, 1603.

but that Christ's Body and Blood are present therein.
This brings on them a storm of invective :

CAROLSTADIUS

Pfui, what vile Thyestean beasts,
On human flesh to make your feasts !

CINGLIUS

Your teeth like knives you use
To tear man's flesh, you cannibals !

CAROLSTADIUS

What blasphemous Centaurs !

CINGLIUS

What savage, barbarous boors !

CAROLSTADIUS

What heretics and idolatrous fools !

CINGLIUS

What blood-suckers and devil's vessels !

Further invectives are strung together. ' The doctrine of the majesty of the man Christ ' is declared by
Carlstadt to be filth

And devil's dirt ; none can receive it ;
Satan himself would be ashamed to believe it.

CINGLIUS

And I do hold it as void and null
As two hairs from a horse's tail I pull.

CAROLSTADIUS

Yea, and about it I say the same
As Beza, my spiritual son,
Who fourth after me has written.
How a sweeter scent proceedeth
From his fine servants' backs
Than from the mouths of those who say
They receive Christ's flesh and blood on earth.[1]

The devil—again here in the guise of a monk—

_____
[1] Act iii. scene 3.

announces that he has carried off Carlstadt and Zwingli, and evinces special delight over the decisions of the Church assembly at Trent. This assembly, in which Pope Pius IV, Cardinal Campegius and Bishop Hosius play a leading part, is interrupted by the arrival of Christ and of the Apostles Peter and Paul.   From the mouths of these new-comers the Pope learns that he is an arch-knave and the Antichrist, and that he belongs to the company of the devil.   The Holy Virgin also comes on the scene, and complains to her Son how ' she has been terribly disgraced by the Pope and his gang.' She has been accused by the papacy of ' committing fornication,' of acting as midwife to a nun, . . . of sleeping with a monk, . . . and the Pope has approved the book containing these slanders.   The Pope pleads guilty, and Christ calls up all the devils to have Pius and his crew cast into hell.

After the Pope, Hosius, and Campegius have cursed the authors of their being, they are carried away by devils.   A like fate befalls Zwingli and Carlstadt, Schwenkfeld, a monk, a nun, and an Anabaptist.   When the devils delay in going Christ urges them on :

> Why tarry ye, devils ! make no pause.
> Tear them away with your sharp claws :
> Off with you to the eternal fire
> Of hell.   The devil is your sire ;
> A place there from the very first
> Has been ready for you.   Go, and be cursed!

Luther and Brenz are to wait for Christ; He will return soon, He tells them, and take them to heaven.

In conclusion choruses are sung alternately by both parties ; Christ with His band sings Luther's hymn :

> Preserve us in Thy Word, O Lord,
> Slay Pope and Turk with Thy sharp sword.

' Satan and his followers,' on the other hand, sing :

> The Roman Church, O Lord, maintain,
> And Luther's mockery restrain,
> Who the Pope Pius, my dear son,
> Would fain hurl down from off his throne.
> Show forth thy might, thou maiden pure,
> Mary, and keep Rome secure ;
> Protect thy Christendom always,
> That she may thee for ever praise.

The devils go on singing in this spirit.

Then follows the lament of a peasant, which is a genuine production of the period ; he complains that in religious matters there are as many different opinions as there are heads, and that it is impossible to know what to believe :

> For this one to the Pope surrenders,
> The next his faith to Luther tenders,
> A third is of Huldrich Zwingli's mind,
> Many to Schwenkfeld's teaching are inclined ;
> Here we've a band of Majorists,
> There a sect of Calvinists,
> Some are Flacians, and some
> Anabaptists have become.
> No one can the number count
> To which these endless sects amount.
> Not even at Lerna Hercules
> So many hydras slew as these—
> These heads which spring up day by day,
> And will each have its own free say.

When one sect is put down, ten new ones rise up instantly in the same place :

> It's all too true, alas ! no joke,
> Dear Corydon, and the poor folk
> Have but a most uncertain way
> To their salvation in this day ;
> For it's plain before our sight
> To what strange and perilous plight
> Hatred, quarrelling, discord, strife,
> Have brought God's precious Word of life.[1]

---

[1] Act i. scene 1.   Strauss (*Frischlin*, p. 125) regards this drama as a

In how high a degree this was the case is shown also by a piece published in 1593 by Zacharias Rivander, superintendent at Bischofswerda, ' Lutherus redivivus, eine neue Komödie von der langen und ergerlichen Disputation bei der Lehre vom Abendmahl' ('A New Comedy of the long and angry Disputation concerning the Doctrine of the Last Supper'). The piece dealt with the controversies which raged round the Last Supper from 1524 to 1592 ; it was based on more than 300 controversial pamphlets which had appeared on the subject, and it left Luther as conqueror.[1] In the following year, at the instigation of his cryptocalvinist opponent, Peter Streuber, superintendent at Sorau, Rivander and his wife were both deprived of life by a poisoned carp.[2]

Of such controversial dramas there were still many more.[3] One of these calls for special notice from the originality of its polemical character. It is known by the very lengthy title 'Der Eisslebische christliche Ritter, a new and fine religious play, in which not only the doctrine, life, and conduct of the last German human wonder, Luther, are set forth, but also those of his, and above all of the Lord Christ's, two principal enemies, the Pope and the Calvinists, as well as other

'strange, formless composition.'   Genée (p. 205) says that ' considered as a comedy it is a model of wearisomeness.'   On the other hand Holstein (p. 62) describes it as ' a great Reformation drama' ; only ' occasionally ' does it show 'fanaticism' (p. 229).   ** Vogt-Koch (*Deutsche Litteraturgesch.* p. 297) calls the piece ' a narrow-minded Lutheran polemical play.'

[1] Holstein, pp. 231–233.   Gottsched, ii. 237–240.   ' A whole cycle of theological controversy is here set forth in the most wretched doggerel rhymes.'

[2] Goedeke, *Grundriss*, ii. 370.

[3] To analyse and dissect all the dramatic productions which the barren, inartistic spirit of hatred brought forth is neither possible nor necessary.

manifold plots and intrigues ; also the end of the world
as revealed in God's Word until the fast approaching
Last Day: both of them in beautiful, poetical and orna-
mental art, and also with historic accurate truth, in
the three brothers Pseudo-Peter, Martin and John, who
are fighting for an inheritance and a Testament, and
all of it depicted and executed by Martin Rinckhart,
deacon at Eisleben in the Neustadt, but acted by the
pupils of the town gymnasium *post ferias caniculares*,
1613.' [1]

In the preface Luther is held up as a second St.
George and ' Knight of God ' against the enemies of
God's kingdom ; ' especially against his own false
brethren, the Pope and the Sacramentarians, by whom
the land of the living, the holy people of God entrusted
to them by the heavenly prince of war and victory on
their souls, has been treacherously administered, and
has become the prey either of the hellish, Babylonian,
seven-headed dragon with his seven Sacraments—the
Antichrist who is honoured in Rome (as was Diocletian,
St. George's worst enemy), or to that generation of
vipers the Zwinglio-Calvinists, the revilers of the
Sacraments, who pour out streams of hellish sulphur-
poison against the majestic person of the Son of God

[1] Reprint by C. Müller (Halle, 1884). Müller (iv.) says : ' This comedy
is much to be commended for its structure, its diction, its enthusiasm for
Luther's character and teaching, and for the childlike naivety and the
purity of spirit which pervade it, as also for the humour which peeps out
here and there.' W. Wackernagel, on the contrary, finds in a passage
quoted by Müller, ' from this hateful poem, that inveterate hatred of sect
against sect, . . . that ossification of soul and deadening of love through
worship of the letter,' by which the sixteenth and seventeenth centuries
were governed. ** Cf. C. Michael, *M. Rinckhart als Dramatiker*. Dissert.
Leipzig, 1894, and K. Reuschel, *Über die ältesten Lutherspiele*, in the
Verhandlungen der 44. Versammlung deutscher Philologen (Leipzig, 1897),
p. 129 ff.

and Mary ; both of these have been slain as one man by the valiant Mansfeldian knight Luther.' . . . .

As the groundwork of his Luther play Rinckhart chose a story which it was well nigh impossible to develop in a dramatic manner, the old tale of the three sons of a king who in quarrelling over their inheritance resolve to shoot at their father's corpse. The king in the play is Christ-Immanuel, His three sons are Pseudo-Peter the Pope, Martin Luther and John Calvin. When Christ dies the sons happen to be absent : Pseudo-Peter in Italy, Martin at Eisleben, and John in Switzerland. In opposition to the express directions of the father's will Pseudo-Peter seizes the crown and sceptre, and tyrannises over the subjects in the most outrageous manner :

> Treats secretly with the devil,
> Buys the shoes of the whore Sarcophil,
> And rules according to his will,
> Yet no one dares to murmur. . . .

Martin remonstrates humbly with him but is repulsed. While they are still quarrelling John returns from Switzerland ; he will neither read nor hear the will, wants to have it all changed, abuses his father and brothers, and makes himself out to have been greatly wronged.[1]

He then proposes that they should shoot at their father's heart. Pseudo-Peter agrees. Martin objects, and is consequently strongly reviled ; his followers, among them Ohm Frühuff and Sixt, who according to the stage directions represent ' all constant Lutheran Christians,' are seized together, and John insists that ' the rascals shall be put to death.'

[1] Prologue, pp. 16–18.

PSEUDO-PETER

Arrange that they be carried away—
Begone, begone, and do what I say !

SIXT

Thou bloodhound !   Do not miss it,
We shall make room for thee in the world
That thou mayest therein eat thy fill :
Our masters must be swillers,
And thou dost swill our blood
As would a cow or a swine.

At the moment when the executioner seizes the
sword, Christ-Immanuel ' comes quite unexpectedly
ex abrupto with a band of angels who blow a trumpet,'
and he says :

You cursed folk,
What are you about ?   Not a blow !

' Then the enemies of Martin all fall down as if
dead and are carted away by Cacangelus, who now
lets himself be seen in the form of a black devil, with
another devil who is dumb.' The prisoners are set
free by angels, and Martin in his shroud is saluted
by Immanuel as his dear child :

IMMANUEL

See, I have made peace for thee, son,
And all thine enemies undone ;
Come thou with Me.   Henceforth thy foes
Shall leave thee undisturbed repose.

KNIGHT MARTIN

Amen, and now the war is ended ;
Well for him whom God has thus defended.[1]

Peace is re-established, but not till after Catholics and
Calvinists have been carried off by the devil.

With his allegorical interpretation of the old story
of the three brothers Rinckhart symbolised nearly the

---

[1] P. 103 ff.

whole history of the religious revolution. In the first
act there appear : Pseudo-Peter (the Pope), Thrasi-
stomus (Cajetan), Polylogus (Tetzel), and Sarcophila,
'the Babylonish whore, with her dragon, the bride of
the Pope as Antichrist,' as is all explained in the stage
instructions.   Pseudo-Peter makes merry over the
death of his father :

> Holla, well done, the father 's dead ;
> In our kitchen we're now head . . .
> What say you, fellows ?   We've orders sent
> From the peasants to get the ' tenth.' [1]

Polylogus is instructed to write an edict to the
effect that the peasants shall bring the tithes themselves, but he first draws the Pope's attention to the
Babylonish whore :

> Lord King, behold your Grace's whore.

> PSEUDO-PETER
> See there !

> AD POLYLOGUM
> Villain, hold thy jaw !

> SARCOPHILA (*seated on the dragon*)
> Will my dear love a drink of honour quaff ?
> You others also ?   Drink ye all enough ;
> Drink, drink, drink as much as you will,
> Full the beaker remains still.

The Pope falls on his knees before her and says :

> Thou goddess great of all the earth,
> Prythee—so it spoil not thy mirth—
> Us honour with thy company,
> I would drink with thee to satiety.

The Pope winks to her and follows her.   Peasants
now come up and lament over the death of the
good king.   ' Somewhat tipsy ' Tetzel joins them

[1] P. 20 ff.

and asks for money. The peasants hesitate, but as
Pseudo-Peter himself appears and threatens them
with the bailiff, they give themselves up to their fate.
In the next scene Pseudo-Peter hears of the arrival of
the Knight Martin, and the question is at once discussed how to make him innocuous by help of a dagger
or an 'Italian soup.' Then Martin himself comes
forward (the marginal note says : 1516) and complains
seriously of his brother :

> My late father, of memory respected,
> Left a will, wherein there were projected
> Measures by which the landfolk's weal
> And liberties might be protected.
> But what now does my brother Peter,
> Pseudo-Peter, rascally creature ?
> The folk like Pharaoh he oppresses,
> And with heavy plagues distresses ;
> Lives a gluttonous life quite bestial,
> And poses like a saint celestial.

The following acts are all in the same style. The
second depicts Luther's conference with Cajetan; the
third, Luther's *début* at Worms and his discussions with
Thomas Münzer, Carlstadt and others ; the fourth, the
beginning of Calvin's preaching and the supposed
league between the papacy and Calvinism for the
extermination of Lutheranism; and the fifth, as has
before been mentioned, the victory of the latter through
the intervention of Christ. But the whole piece is
devoid of artistic arrangement and development. The
poet's fiercest wrath falls always on the Pope, but
Zwingli and Calvin also come in frequently for bad
treatment. In one place there is an allusion to the
Calvinists' rejection of Church music. When the
choir-leader of the Mansfeld miners asks :

> Would my lords like to hear some music ?

the Knight John (Calvin) answers :

> Be off, you fool !   Confound your music,
> And your bald vocatives.   Be off
> With your noise and sow-bleating !

To which is appended the explanation : ' Zwingli's opinion upon Music.' [1]

Another ' fine comedy ' of polemical intent, but of a different kind, and which also depicts the immorality of the period with great coarseness, is Bartholomew Ringwalt's ' Speculum Mundi, Der Welt Spiegel,' which appeared in 1590.[2]   His ' Lautere Wahrheit ' having already gone through at least five editions,[3] the poet set himself to announce the pure truth again in the other ' Comedy,' even though ' the devil with all his associates should burst over it.'

In the first scene the young country squire Hypocratz appears, and complains that he is feeling out of sorts on account of his nocturnal orgies, and wishes that some peasant would ' trample on him with his feet,' which might perhaps ' restore his bones to order.'   His valet Reumaus performs this service for him, and is then bidden by his master to invite again the three young noblemen with whom Hypocratz had caroused the whole night before.   In the meanwhile Hypocratz goes to church and hears a sermon, in which the preacher declares that ' all drunken lords belong body and soul to the devil.'   He waxes furious at this, and threatens to stab the pastor with his lance or to turn him forthwith out of the village.

---

[1] Pp. 98–99.

[2] Frankfort-on-the-Oder.   Goedeke (*Grundriss*, ii. 517, No. 17) mentions three editions of this piece.

[3] Cf. Goedeke, ii. 215, No. 12.

Then follows the description of a drinking-bout of the four young men. A cloth-maker, who brings Hypocratz money in payment for some wool he has bought, is invited to join in the carousal, while Reumaus is told to sing the drinking song: 'Vom Schlemmer aus dem Joachimsthal' ('The Drunkard of the Joachim Valley'). We quote some specimen lines:

> My heart with joy doth spring
>   When I have drink in plenty,
> My best songs I can sing
>   When I am jolly tipsy. . . .
> I can shout finely too,
>   And carry on fool's play,
> Also at evening woo
>   The girls in jovial way. . . .
>   &c. &c. &c.

The cloth-maker, who cannot fulfil all the requirements of a drinking bout, gets a sound thrashing from the young men: he harangues them, calls them hogs, and asks them:

> Since to-day your pastor
> Has blown up all you topers well,
> How can you be so eager
> Again to drink and swill?

Whereupon Hypocratz cries: 'Strike the traitor dead!' draws his sword, and the other three charge with their spears at the cloth-maker, who makes his escape.

The pastor is then fetched up, defends the sermon which he had preached, and receives in reward from the young squire 'a long leave of absence.'

> Mayest thou be rent
> By God's firmament,
> And suffer all torment
> From lightning to gout.

The pastor bids farewell to the parishioners, admonishes them to obedience towards the magistrates, and goes away with his wife and children.

Meanwhile the young noblemen begin another carousal; a hare, which the guests have brought with them, is changed into a cat. . . .

'Look there,' says one of the young men :

> . . . what a grim and horrid sight.
> Its eyes are shining like a light,
> It has all sorts of colours ; see—
> I'm sure it must the devil be.

But Hypocratz will not be disturbed, mocks at the devil, has his glass filled again, dances with his guests on the table, falls under it, and is carried off by three devils who come up, Malus, Pejor, Pessimus.   He

> Bellows like a cow, grunts like a pig,
> And is carried off to the pains of hell.

Pessimus sings :

> Here lies Scharnhans, the precious man,
>   Who died in Beelzebub ;
> To do good deeds was not his plan,
>   In body and soul corrupt . . .
> He set no store by chastity,
>   He brought good folk to ruin.
>
> He was a good-for-nothing sot,
>   Qui contra Deum vixit,
> Sepultus sine lux et crux
>   Et subito morixit.
> Now come, now come, you pious wretch !
> Receive what you have earned :
> Your belly fat we've come to fetch,
>   To be in hell-fire burned.

A relative of the dismissed pastor exhorts the audience to repentance, and tells them the contents of the second part of the comedy.

The first character who appears is a baron, who takes the dismissed pastor into his service. The bishop of the diocese, however, will not tolerate a Lutheran preacher, and consults with a cardinal and the two prebendaries, Porcus and Ruprecht, as to how the newly installed pastor can be got rid of. We poisoned the former preacher, says the cardinal, and we will do away with the new one either by water, rope or fire. But for the help of 'arson, lies, murder and poison,' one of the prebendaries declares, the papacy would long ago have been in ruins, and Luther installed in the Castle of Sant' Angelo. Agents are now despatched to seize the preacher unawares, and then let him starve to death or drown him. Before the agents start the bishop gives them his blessing :

> May the mantle of Burchard protect you,
> Beatrice, Appollonia,
> The indulgence at Bononia,
> And the chair of the Pope,
> Guide you safely in and out
> In the power and might of the Cross.

The plot miscarries, however, and they are obliged to wait till the death of the baron. After he is dead the bishop sets to work, supported by the burgomaster, who offers to make over the little town to him as his fief. After the surrender has been accomplished the bishop gives orders that the baron be taken to the flayer's pit, and the preacher taken prisoner in order to grind him to powder. The agents fell the preacher to the ground and lead him away in chains, while his wife, far advanced in pregnancy, is grossly insulted and faints. The ' heretical beast,' taken before the bishop, begins to dispute about the true doctrine, but is gagged as ' a mad dog ' :

> Seize him this very moment, men,
>   Bind him hand and foot quite tight
> As sheep for slaughtering, and then
>   Fix and fasten him with might
> In a corner on the bench,
>   Until we take him home with us,
> And burn him with fire that will not quench.

A tumult, however, springs up among the burghers, the bishop escapes with his followers, the pastor is set free, and the baron is carried solemnly to burial.

Then the archangel Gabriel appears with a naked sword and tells the audience what a fearful crime the cardinal and the bishops intended to perpetrate : namely,

> In the baron's town whence they
> Had been expelled, the burghers all to slay,
> In one night, with hair and skin
> To root out every one therein.
> For which purpose black and bad
> An army well equipped they had,
> Which in the dead of night should fall
> Upon the town and slaughter all.

By the advice of the devil Malus, the bishop and the cardinal plan a surprise of this sort ; Gabriel, however, strikes the cardinal, who denounces St. Paul as a spermologue, with his sword, throws him on the ground calling him ' a shameless brute,' and says to the devil :

> Take him, Malus, up in the air,
> And drop him in the pool with a splash ;

and when Malus refuses, saying :

> That can I not do, Gabriel,
> For Lucifer likes it not well
> To have his servants by us brought
> When against Michael they have fought . . .
> Take him yourself to punishment,

Gabriel answers :

That's not the task for which I'm sent ;
To take the pious into heaven
Was the sole order to me given ;
To drive the wicked in your cart,
To hell-fire, Malus, is your part . . .
Therefore take him to be burned,
In the place he 's so well earned.
And with this worm high on the church-
Tower let us see you perch,
That everybody, young and old,
Male and female, may behold
The spectacle, a warning to all folk
Who choose the Pope's disgraceful yoke,
Knowing all his blasphemies.

MALUS

Come on, come on into our hole,
Where you shall sweat in body and soul,
And sit you down beside Pope Joan,
The VIIIth of that name on the throne,
Who like a woman bore a child,
And Gabriel, we will let you marry
This same Pope Joan.   Come do not tarry . . .

[They rush off together with a great yell to an appointed place.]

GABRIEL

See, Christians dear, how rightly they
Have served the man who chose to obey
The Pope, and submit to his sway,
Though knowing in his heart full well,
The Pope's deeds were the dung of hell.
Then, Christians dear, this rule resist,
In the right pathway still persist.

.   .   .   .

Keep what God from heaven gave
And never to the devil pray . . .
Just as this man his end has met
So will the others their due get,
And suddenly feel God's great might
A quarter of an hour after midnight.

After this scene a butcher from the country comes
on and communicates to the audience 'true and good
tidings ' :

The cardinal had had a stroke
Of apoplexy, and the folk
Themselves had seen him carried by
The devil right up through the sky.
The bishop they'd found lying dead
In his bed all bloody red,
And no one in the castle can
Discover who has killed the man.
Herr Ruprecht before the bed was lying,
He was heard at cock-crow crying
Horribly, and on his face
His eyes no longer could they trace.
But Porcus still more full of art
In Judas fashion did depart,
And like a sow to roast upstrung,
On a bell-rope himself he hung.
All which before my eyes befell,
And as I live it's truth I tell.

After all the enemies have been destroyed the preacher calls on the burghers to sing a song of praise.

In the next scene the three devils Pessimus, Pejor, and Malus appear again. Pejor tells Pessimus of all ' the grand works ' he has performed or helped on, as for instance, that numbers of Lutherans have been burned, that a wife has strangled her husband, a father has stabbed his son, a daughter has killed her mother, and so forth; whereupon Pessimus exclaims:

By Jove, you've done right well, my boy,
My heart within me laughs for joy.
Come hither, son, and take a fine
Draught from my flask of Rhenish wine.

On the other hand he is highly displeased with Malus, who has not been able to bring about the destruction of the baron's town by the bishop, and the massacre of all the Christians there:

For you're an idle, lazy lout,
You have a greedy, gluttonous mouth,

You have been on the Gart, I guess,
Reading charms on a sorceress,
Old, and bent on crooked business,
Have served her as an incubus.
And while you thus were off your post
Full many a pious lord you've lost,
Who in our ancient game
Might loyally have served our aim.

Malus swears ' by the stool of the Pope' that he has
' to the best of his power shown the good lords all
kind, brotherly treatment'; it was not his fault that
the angel had killed the cardinal :

And commanded me as well
To take the dead cardinal to hell,
In our waggon, in broad daylight,
That every one might see the sight.

PESSIMUS

What ?   Have you carried him away ?
Pitch on you !   It's your turn to-day :
Were you clad in steel from pate to soles,
To-day you shall be hauled over the coals.

He makes Pejor bring him a rod and says :

Now come and lie down here,
Let's see what sort of fat you've got ;
Soon, soon, no prayers will more avail.

' Malus lays himself down on the overturned stool
of Pessimus, Pejor holds his feet, Pessimus stands up
and gives him a sound thrashing.'   After Malus has
promised to amend his ways, the devils proceed to
scatter all sorts of ' devil-seed' about the town, till
Gabriel comes to stop their work :

You slanderers of God, all three,
What may all this villainy be ?
Clear out, there's no room here for you,
Off with you to the Pope's fig-tree ;
And there with plenty of bell-ringing,
Listen to High and Low Mass singing.

Thus you will acquire
Knowledge of purgatory fire,
Useful in your business
Of deceiving the greater and the less.
Be off, you thieves and villains low,
Or I will strike you such a blow
As will smash your skull to dust.
If you won't go, why, then you must.

In conclusion Gabriel admonishes the audience to guard themselves against all false devilish doctrine, and also against the blasphemous and God-forsaken sect of Zwinglianism; the Day of Judgment was at hand, and God's Son would free his brethren from the jaws of the devil.[1]

'I am confident,' says Ringwalt in the dedication of this piece to a councillor and court marshal of a Brandenburg Elector, 'that over these my comedies, whether they be read or acted, there will be more genuine sighs breathed for Christ than hard words of abuse uttered against me, as experience will show.'

Whether a Christian state of mind was likely to be promoted by such plays, we may well be allowed to doubt.

No less full of wild devilry than Ringwalt's plays was a piece by Bartholomew Krüger, town clerk and organist of Trebbin : 'Wie die bäuerischen Richter einen Landsknecht unschuldig hinrichten lassen, und wie es ihnen so schrecklich hernach ergangen' ('How the Peasant Judges let a Landsknecht be unjustly Executed, and how terribly they are Punished for their Sin').[2] One of the judges is struck by lightning, a second

---

[1] Of this 'fine comedy' Holstein (p. 267) says nothing more than that 'Bartholomew Ringwalt in his German comedy *Speculum Mundi* referred to the true preachers, and showed how pleasing they are to honest Christians and how they are delivered out of the hands of their enemies.'

[2] 1580. Newly published by J. Bolte, Leipzig, 1884.

is stabbed at a banquet, a third is hanged. The hangman
Fabian exults over his victim :

'I'll torture him so cruelly that he'll confess to
many more sins than in his lifetime he ever committed,
only to get the hanging over. . . . Hi, Francis, my
faithful henchman, make ready the rack, gag his mouth
as though he were a great farm-horse.'

In an equally joyous mood the servant answers :

> My master, Fabian, look you
> How fortune comes to our rescue ;
> Let's only lustily carouse,
> Luck will be showered on our house.
> The rascals have grown to such a swarm
> We shall have murders enough to perform.[1]

After the execution has taken place on the stage,
two devils appear to fetch the man who has been hanged.

> MORDTEUFEL (*the demon of murder*)
> See how fat the villain is,
> Great cause for joy we have in this,
> He'll yield a ton of grease at least,
> In salt we'll lay the flesh of the beast,
> And to the shoemaker we'll sell the skin
> To make us shoes for walking in.
> Get up and cut the rope and chuck
> The scoundrel down to me ; good luck !

> SATAN
> Why should he hang in the air ?
> I'll launch him fair—
> Catch thou him up, miss him not,
> Lest his bones be broken . . .
> Stay, murdering devil, attention !
> I am already on the gallows' top.

> MORDTEUFEL
> Come down at once, I hold the fellow ;
> Help me carry him to hell.

Another of the peasant judges, the mayor, and a

[1] Bolte, pp. 94, 95, 98.

monk, a personage never omitted in a Protestant play, are carried off alive by the devils.

SATAN

> Mordteufel and my comrades all,
> Throughout hell's region, hear my call ;
> Come here, come here and help me carry,
> I've greased the waggon well, don't tarry.
> A couple of fat roasts I've got,
> We never had so fine a lot ;
> Seize them, brothers, hold them tight,
> And drive them into hell with might.

Satan then directs the singing of a parody of the old Catholic Christmas song, ' In dulci Jubilo ' :

> *In duro Jubilo*, now sing and merry grow ;
> We've got a splendid roast here, *vorate gaudio* ;
> Fortune has befriended us, fat and strong's the mayor
> Whom in his bier we bear.
>
> *In duro Jubilo*, three geese in straw,
> The chickens, eggs and pancakes *vorate gaudio*.
> To fat hell-fire we invite X. Z. F. G. and O.,
> Eat, drink and merry grow ;

and so forth.

First of all (Krüger directs) ' they sing with three voices only, and leave out the bass, but they begin several times over, and stop because it will not go right. They must also put a mask on the mayor, and when they have sung it several times they must fetch the monk to take the fourth part.' The demon of murder says to the monk :

> There, take the bass, emit yells frantic,
> That we may dance a devil's antic.
> Hi, Mayor, you also must make one,
> We have no other kind of fun,
> See'st thou that house, how well it's burning,
> From it there's nevermore returning.

' They set off singing, and when they come to the

three-part time they leap and dance. To the other song they move slowly, one always turning round the other, till at last, with the mayor and the monk, they dance into hell.'

At the end of the play ' the devils come back on the stage with the mayor and the monk, singing, leaping, dancing, and making merry over their splendid booty.' [1]

After this spectacle the audience went home. These, however, were not the first devil's songs and dances which they had witnessed. In the third act Krüger had already introduced songs and dances of the same kind for their edification.

It was not only in religious and polemical dramas, or plays in which polemical episodes were introduced, but in others also that devils played a principal part. ' If, nowadays, religious and moral comedies are to be acceptable to the people,' so a contemporary complains, ' they must be full of devils in horrible shapes ; there must be plenty of shrieking, bellowing, yelling, and abusing, and men and women must be carried off with wild howlings ; in short, there must be as much uproar as possible. This is what the common people chiefly delight in and expect in comedies.' [2]

---

[1] Bolte, p. 98 ff. Bolte (p. x.) is pleased to see ' the Protestant spirit ' of Krüger in the fact that he ' emphasises the unscrupulousness of the monk and the corrupting influence of the theatre,' and ' brings to view the plain innuendoes of *Mordteufel* in the exact manner which has been customary in Lutheran literature, and art.' Holstein (p. 261) accords this play ' an honourable place in the dramatic literature of the sixteenth century,' ' on account of its true observation of life, its popular language, and the skilful manner in which it is put on the stage.'

[2] A Christmas sermon preached at Meissen by M. C. Friedmann. Without locality, 1561, Bl. B.

The Nuremberg Rector, George Mauritius, introduced five devils in his ' Christliche Komödia von dem
jämmerlichen Fall und frölichen Wiederbringung des
menschlichen Geschlechtes ' (' Christian Comedy of the
woeful Fall and joyful Restoration of the Human Race ').[1]

The serpent receives a command from the archangel
Michael to appear in court with Adam and Eve.
Beelzebub binds Adam's hands, Asmodi manages Eve ;
and then, by order of Beelzebub, our first parents are
fastened together like staghounds.   Beelzebub describes
the fate which is in store for them :

> There is a pond in a forest old
> Which, summer and winter, is always cold ;
> Therein they must bathe each day
> Till their hearts in their bodies have melted away.
> A little room I have also
> Where in and out the fire doth go ;
> When I've frozen them up there
> I'll drag them outside by the hair.
> And then I'll roast and drown them too
> With brimstone and with arsenic fumes.[2]

In another ' comedy ' by the same author, ' Von
den Weisen aus dem Morgenlande ' (' The Wise Men from
the East '), Hellebrand, the third devil, boasts of his
power to deceive and take in the people :

> Yes, masterly I am at that,
> Can change at will to a black cat,

---

[1] Leipzig, 1606.   A curious idea in this play is that after the fall of
our first parents God does not know exactly what has happened.   He says :

> To the garden I must needs repair
> And see how things are going there.
> The sky looks dark as at midnight,
> The sun has lost its radiance bright,
> All creatures full of gloom appear,
> Things are not right at all, I fear.
> Where art thou, Adam ?   Come thou forth
> Where art thou ?   Why dost fear my wrath ?
> Are matters not right as before ?

[2] Bl. B 6ᵇ. C 2–3, 7.

To dog, bear, wolf, to cock or crow,
Invisible can also grow,
Sit on a body's tongue or ear
Without his guessing I am there.[1]

In the ' Schöne Tragödie, wie Belial ein Recht mit
Christo anfecht, darum dass er ihm sein höllisch Reich
zerstört habe,' 1570 ('How Belial has a Law-suit with
Christ because he has Destroyed his Kingdom of Hell '),
there are four devils.[2] John Krüginger, deacon at
Marienberg, near Zwickau, in his play, ' Vom reichen
Mann und armen Lazaro ' (1555), introduced, besides
Satan, six other horrible devils, and gave directions that
at the performance ' still more devils might be added.' [3]
Thomas Schmid, of Meissen, stonemason and burgher
at Heidelberg, organised several times over in 1578,
before the Elector Palatine Louis, the ladies of the
court and the knights, the performance of a long play
called ' Tobias,' in which four fools and five devils,
among them a young devil and his Grete, showed off
their accomplishments.[4] In a ' Tragedy of an Unjust
Judge ' (1592) there are actually ten devils.[5] In
Prussia, in the year 1585, an order was issued that
under pain of punishment ' the superfluity of devils
and fools, but, above all, the horrible, abominable, and
alarming masks, and also shameful buffoonery, were to
be left out of comedies.' [6]

[1] *Comödia von den Weisen aus dem Morgenlande* (Leipzig, 1606), Bl. E 7.
[2] Gottsched, ii. 227.
[3] Goedeke, *Grundriss*, ii. 361, No. 147. Gottsched, ii. 214.
[4] Gottsched, ii. 233–234. Goedeke, ii. 462 ; No. 8c.
[5] Goedeke, ii. 521, p. iii. a ; cf. Gottsched, i. 164. Concerning the
Brunswick preacher John Neukirch's *Stephanus* (1592), Gottsched says
(i. 138) that the author in his tragedy has ' exhibited the high council of
all hell.' ** The preacher Christopher Lasius in his ' Christmas Play ' likewise brings in ten devils. J. Bolte, *Ein Spandauer Weihnachtsspiel*, p. 111.
[6] Prölss, p. 198.

It was not, however, for the common people only that 'these things formed the chief attraction of comedies,' for the great lords and ladies also it was necessary that there should be ' plenty of devils, plenty of screaming and bellowing, and carrying people away to hell,' and ' all sorts of noise and uproar.' [1]   This is shown especially by the plays which Duke Henry Julius of Brunswick wrote and had performed before his whole court.   Thus, for instance, in his ' Fleisch-awer' a fraudulent cattle-dealer comes forward : ' (bellows like an ox) Oh, how bad I feel ! oh, how bad I feel ! (Bellows again.)   Oh, what agony I'm suffer-ing ! (Bellows.)   Oh, what shall I do ?   I'm in such agony.   (Tears open his clothes and bellows.) . . . Oh, ye winds, carry me up into the air that I may escape from the wrath of God !   (Bellows terribly several times running, scratches with his hands and feet.)   If none of the elements will help me I must call the devils to my aid.   Oh, ye devils, come, help away my torments ! (The two devils spring forward, seize him by the body, and carry him off.) '   In the tragedy ' Von der Ehe-brecherin ' the deceived husband goes out of his mind, behaves in a wildly insane manner on the stage, is taken away in a ' fool's chest ' ' screaming and roaring horribly.'   The guilty wife hangs a rope, which the devil throws to her, round her throat, and 'the devils leap up and pull the rope, so that she falls on the ground dead, and the other devils come up, also yelling and bellowing, and carry off the dead woman.'   The tragedy ' Von einem Buhler und einer Buhlerin ' had only three devils ; the paramour Pamphilus ' tears his clothes and roars,' gives himself up to the devil, stabs

[1] See above, p. 131.

a watchman, is put to death, and, with the partner of his guilt, who cuts her throat, is carried off by devils. ' Ho, ho, that's right,' cries the devil Satyrus ; ' that pleases me uncommonly. Let the ravens eat the flesh, I have got the souls. But as I have no sack in which I can take the souls away, I must take the carcase with me whole.' He calls up the other devils : ' Holla, Damon ! holla, Lucifer ! come here and help me.' ' The devils carry off the dead bodies, yell and make merry in their own way. They also take the watchman with them, and Satyrus further remarks : Oh, you're also an old sinner, you've been a profligate ! I'll take you also with me, for there should always be three of all good things.' [1] Often the devils' task of carrying off the wicked people was a very difficult one, as, for instance, in the comedy ' Von der Gottvergessenen Doppelspielern,' which Thomas Birck, Lutheran pastor at Untertürkheim, dedicated in 1590 to the Duchess Ursula of Württemberg, and, ' with the sanction of a doctor of Holy Scripture, of numbers of Church officials, and persons connected with the chancellery,' had performed by eighty-two members of his congregation.[2] A female gambler in this piece, who is fetched away by the devil, offers so much resistance that the prince of hell calls up other devils :

> Help, comrades, help ! the wanton bawd
> Makes a stout fight and can't be awed.
> If we had four females as tough
> We'd chase all animals fast enough.[3]

In the comedies of James Ayrer the devils appear now in the form of a dragon, now ' in a plain black

---

[1] *Schauspiele des Herzogs Heinrich Julius*, No. iii. pp. 7, 11.
[2] Title in Goedeke, ii. 387.
[3] Actus tertius, Scena secunda.

garment,' with a crown on their heads and ' Neptune's
trident,' now ' with great spilling of fire.' [1]

'But that all these many devils and devil-stories,
which were passed in review before the gaping people,
and all that was told them about the devils, could be
beneficial to them and fruitful in respectable Christian
conduct and morals, people of insight could well con-
tradict from experience.' [2]

The most repulsive representations of this sort, com-
parable only to the devil-tales and hell-pictures of the
Dutch painters,[3] are to be found in a ' Tragi-Komedia
von einer hochnotwendigen Wallfahrt beides in die
Höll und in den Himmel' ('A Tragi-Comedy of a highly
useful Pilgrimage both in Hell and Heaven'), which
Dr. Klein, of Esslingen, wrote in 1570. In the prologue
Eve appears as the primeval ancestress of the human
race with a gold crown on her head. Whereas the Day
of Judgment, she tells her audience, ' is at the door,'
she has come down from heaven to assist at the tragedy,
and she gives an account

> Of a pilgrimage or journeying
> To the abyss of hell-fire burning,
> And all the horrors seen therein,
> The gruesome punishments of sin.

To the ' Weltmann' (world-man) are recounted the
torments of individual sinners and of different classes.
Those, for instance, who were habitual cursers had

> their tongues torn from their head ;
> This caused me frightful fear and dread,
> For they wailed so woefully,
> Like oxen or cattle raging mad
> Who from the butcher's knife had fled.

---

[1] Ayrer, i. 474, 517, and ii. 1233, 1234, and so on.
[2] In the place quoted above, p. 131, n. 2.   [3] See vol. xi. p. 220 ff.

The proud and haughty ones were 'buffeted with hot brimstone and devil's dung,' the grumblers were dragged hither and thither, and had boiling pitch poured over them. Many thousands were rubbed with rough stone, or else with horrid filth :

These ground and gnashed their teeth,
Which grieved me piteously ;

These, the devil explained, were the peasants whose envy, hatred, and insubordination towards the authorities had always to be purged away in this manner. The most frightful and appalling picture of all is that of Lucifer; he is a dragon with more than 100,000 hands, each of which is one hundred yards long. He is fastened with large chains, and lies

On an iron grating in the midst
Of hell ; beneath, a huge fire roars,
Which monstrous flames and sparks outpours,
For countless devils poke, stir, fan,
And blow it as hard as ever they can. . . .
. . . and how he makes
Souls suffer which his wrath o'ertakes—
Tears them all to shivereens :
Good God, how awful are their screams !
Then with his cruel claws he scratches
The bits up and together patches. . . .
Thus he goes on without a break.
Hear this, dear Christians, and note take.[1]

According to the opinion of the preacher, Thomas Birck, it was desirable that the 'devils' brides,' the witches, should be properly represented on the stage as well as hell and the devils. For this purpose he composed a 'Hexenspiegel' ('Mirror of Witches'), an

---

[1] The first act of the piece in the 2nd, 4th and 5th vols. of Scheible's *Schaltjahr* ; cf. especially ii. 67, 78, 80, 568 ; and further iv. 173, 430–433, and v. 107–108, 289–290.

'extremely fine and well-arranged tragedy,' and had
it printed in 1600 for the benefit of 'all dear pious
Christians.'[1] In order, says the prologue, that the
whole nature and proceedings of witches should 'be
brought accurately to light,'

> everything's conveniently
> Stated in this tragedy,
> Discussed and argued by each side,
> And with many tales supplied.

The piece contains no fewer than four devils and six
witches. Besides these there are a number of 'orators'
who exchange opinions concerning weather-making,
journeying, the courtships of devils, the incantations,
spells, and demoniacal signs of the witches, on devils'
children, cretins, and changelings, on the transformation of witches into animals, and other things; and all
these opinions are given with appeal to the utterances
of distinguished theologians, above all to those of
Luther, who gave detailed information concerning
witches and attributed his illnesses to demoniacal

---

[1] '*Hexenspiegel, ein überaus schöne und wolgegründete Tragedi*, in
which people can see with their eyes what is to be thought of sorcerers and
magicians, how they can scent like dogs, ride in the air, hold nocturnal
meetings, revelries and dances,' etc. (Tübingen, 1600.) On the title-page
it is announced that the book appears 'by gracious permission' of Duke
Frederic of Württemberg. But, 'after nine sheets of 1000 copies had
been printed, the printing was stopped by command of the territorial
prince (Frederic); moreover, the author was sentenced to payment of
thirty florins to the printer, George Gruppenbach' (Holstein, p. 271).
The copy in the royal library at Stuttgart ends at p. 72 with the summary
of the third scene of the second act: four persons 'are talking about the
witches' journey, and on both sides remarkable stories are told. Moreover,
there are talks about apparitions of angels and about each man's guardian
angel. It turns out, however, in the end that, although several men had
ridden in the air, the boasted aerial flights, beginning by the magician's
body passing through a space smaller than itself, are nothing but devilish
hallucinations.'

sorcery.[1] In addition to all these *dramatis personae*
there are twenty-four councillors, three advocates, one
pastor, two executioners, one executioner's servant,
three buffoons, one magician, and other persons ; also
an angel and 'Death.' 'By cutting down many
passages, and performing only the essential parts,' this
tragedy, says the author, ' could easily be acted before
an audience in two or three hours, and the rest might
very profitably be read at home.' Birck depicts,
among other things, the way in which two witches
prepare themselves for their journey, and how two
devils disport themselves with these witches :

> Then soon there appears in view
> The monster Ahalibana, who
> Rides on a camel, and speaks out
> With human language clear and loud ;
> The camel shakes his tuft of hair,
> And turns his head round here and there.

The witch then exhibits a child, which is forthwith
changed into a cat, quite visibly, and springs and runs
about the ' Platz.'

Then follow accounts of several trials. A sorcerer
confesses on the rack ' a number of bad deeds,' but
stubbornly resists penance and contrition. Then the
devil enters the prison in the tower and wrings his neck
like a worm's. None the less, the sentence is then
pronounced that he must be burned to death. A witch
is next ' weighed in the balance.' But the rack draws
no confessions out of her :

> So hardened was she and so wicked ;
> But when they searched her thoroughly well
> They found on her a devil's ticket,
> A compact with the powers of hell.

---

[1] *Hexenspiegel*, pp. 26 ff., 67-68.

> The instant she had lost possession
> Of the bond, she made confession
> Of many witch-deeds terrible,
> And infant-murders horrible.
> Bluntly and plainly too she said
> That with the devil she had made
> A firm compact, which with her blood she sealed,
> And thus to fire of hell herself did yield.

Then when upon inquiry :

> All that under torture she
> Had said was found quite true to be,
> At once went forth the sentence dire
> That with this man at the same stake
> She, this day, be burnt by fire. . . .

A priest urges her to repentance, and she asks for the Sacrament. Then the hangman conducts her to the last meal of those condemned to death, and makes all the arrangements for the execution. Meanwhile two buffoons carry on jests with the hangman's servant :

> And many a mighty theme's discussed,
> That those who hear must laugh till they burst.

At the stake the condemned witch becomes much cast down and frightened ; but the priest administers consolation to her, and by his prayers exorcises the devil, who appears and is obliged to restore the hand-writing ' by which the bond was sealed with blood.' Satan is afraid he is going to get a good thrashing, and, in fact,

> An angel, Uriel by name,
> As messenger from heaven came ;
> ' Begone at once ! ' to the devil he said—
> Swift as an ape the devil fled.

Thereupon the woman was entirely comforted, and went repentant to her death.[1]

---

[1] For the extent to which belief in witches entered into English dramatic literature at the time of Elizabeth and James I., see Wright, *Sorcery*, i. 286, 296 ; quoted by Lecky, i. 82, note 1.

In addition to the great delight which, at the end
of the sixteenth century, the German people took in
devils and devil-scenes on the stage, they had another
and a much more pernicious taste which had been
aroused and fostered by foreign travelling players—
delight in the so-called 'English comedians.' These
English comedians had scarcely any appreciable connexion with the German religious plays, and with the
religious and polemical ones no relation whatever.
They occupied themselves, in the main, almost solely
with those purely mundane materials which had formed
the themes of many of the German poets.

CHAPTER III

SECULAR PLAYS—PICTURES OF THE TIME AND ITS MORALS
—ENGLISH COMEDIANS—DRAMAS OF MURDER AND
IMMORALITY

THE most prolific dramatiser of secular matter was Hans Sachs. Besides turning half the Bible into plays, he composed over a hundred tragedies, comedies, and other plays from ancient mythology, history, medieval sagas, novels, allegories, and humorous matter. In the amazing variety of his materials he reminds one of Lope and Calderon, but in no other respects can he be compared with either of these two. His work betrays everywhere the most limited views : a plain, homely intelligence without a spark of poetic genius. He is not on a much higher level than the artisans in Shakespeare's ' Midsummer Night's Dream.' Like these he assures the audience that they need not be anxious for the safety of the actors, as everything has been so arranged as to prevent any harm happening to them. In a comedy in which Pallas represents virtue, and Venus voluptuousness, the herald and the devil fight together, Epicurus is thrashed by Satan, and Cacus, as administrator of poetic justice, gives him a good horse-whipping, and sings all the while a long moralising song.[1] The ancient gods, heroes and heroines, such as

---

[1] Cf. Devrient, i. 101–106.   Holstein, pp. 70–72.   ** Cf. L. Lier, *Studien zur Gesch. des Nürnberger Fastnachtspiels*, i. (*Leipziger Inauguraldissertation.* Nuremberg, 1889), p. 37 ff.

the Horatii and the Curiatii, Jocasta, Circe, Ulysses, Aeneas, Cyrus, Alexander the Great, Romulus and Remus, become, in the hands of Hans Sachs, plain men and women of Nuremberg guilds. The same may be said about the 'Hornen Seifrit,' 'the patient Griselda,' 'the Queen of France with the false marshal,' 'the banished empress with the two banished sons,' the 'Beautiful Marina.' With what amount of poetic skill he set to work on these pieces is markedly shown by the song which he makes the sirens sing in his 'Ulysses mit den Meerwundern' :

> Ulysses, brave lord of the Greeks,
> Steer in thy bark among our creeks,
> Halt here and listen to our strain,
> From which thy voyage joy will gain.
> Truly no lord did ever sail
> So swiftly past as thou, nor fail
> To stop and listen to our song,
> With which we no one hinder long.
> Of thy great prowess, lord, we've heard,
> And of the loss the Greeks incurred.

And so on.

All pure and simple sentiments of affection, duty, piety, the love of husbands and wives, of parents and children, patience, obedience, trust in God, are treated by Hans Sachs with warmth and feeling, but at the same time almost invariably with insipid platitude. All that is heroic, truly tragic, and soul-stirring, all the great and profound elements in his materials are, as a rule, entirely left out. He delighted especially in dramatising the life of the people on its humorous and comic side, and in his farces and carnival plays he is quite in his element. When he paints the manners of the living present, and creates from the present, he shows keen observation and not seldom genuine humour.   In these also, as in his serious pieces, there is a simple, honest, bourgeois moral.   He lashes the vices and follies of all classes, but he frequently falls into coarseness and boorishness, absurdity and vulgarity.[1]

Hans Sachs was not equalled either in his extra-ordinary fertility or in the excellences of his plays by any one of his imitators.   In rapidity of work he was most nearly approached by James Ayrer, judicial pro-curator at Nuremberg, who died in 1605, whose numerous operas were almost all written each in one day, while his tragedy of 'Lazarus,' of more than 2000 verses, was completed in nine days.[2]   Ayrer moralises as much as Hans Sachs, but the simplicity and honesty of the latter are lacking in the plays of the former.   His carnival plays are almost entirely destitute of popular humour, and they degenerate into vulgar indecency. In all his pieces he had recourse to low methods for gratifying the love of theatrical spectacles ; he dealt in giants, dwarfs, savage men, fire-spitting dragons, sorcery

---

** [1] In his article ' Hans Sachs als Moralist in den Fastnachtsspielen ' (*Zeitschr. f. deutsche Philol.* xxv. 343 ff.), G. Duflon discusses the question how it is consistent with the current opinion of the Meister's moral sound-ness that in most of these plays a dissolute woman deceives her husband with impunity and has her daughter on her side.   ' A satisfactory answer,' says W. Creizenach (*Jahresberichte f. neuere deutsche Litteratur-gesch.* Bd. IV. ii. 4, No. 23), ' the author is unable to give.   It would be well indeed if the author were right in his observation that Hans Sachs, as a rule, for the quieting of his conscience, follows up such pieces with others in which the sinners against the sixth commandment are overtaken by poetic justice ; but out of two cases which he cites in confirmation only one is to the point (*Spiel*, pp. 61–62) ; in the other case (No. 54) between the immoral play and the moral one an intermediary one has been left out.   Moreover, the author is silent as to the fact that in other cases, for instance in Nos. 46 and 56, there is no sign whatever of any such supplementary quieting of the conscience.'

[2] Gervinus, iii. 116.

and fireworks, ' deafening music,' murder, gallows, and fighting scenes.[1]

In numbers, also, of serious and didactic plays, this taste of the period is plainly seen. For instance, in Thomas Birck's comedy of the ' Gottvergessenen Doppelspieler '[2] the gambler Barabbas gets bloody blows from his associates, is robbed of his clothes, and, after he has stolen a coat, is taken prisoner and put to torture. The bailiff Felix says to the gaoler :

> Lysia, go thou quickly out
> To Doeg, to the hangman's house,
> And tell him with thee to come back
> And bring me the screws, the cord and rack.

While the torturing is going on the pipers are to play and the drummers to beat their drums.

' For he will yell without a doubt, though he is treated in all fairness, and no one will like to hear his cries or see his ways and behaviour during the torture.'

While on the rack Barabbas confesses different crimes, and is condemned to be hanged. The judge has the gallows put up, but the executioner understands his business so badly that the criminal falls down, whereupon the bailiff says :

> Oh, you cursed abandoned fellow,
> You've let the thief fall from the gallows !
> Now pelt him with stones and finish him,
> Stone him to death, the villain grim.

---

[1] Cf. Devrient, i. 156–157. Gervinus (iii. 117) says : ' If we want to estimate Hans Sachs's superiority to Ayrer in an unprejudiced manner we must compare the carnival plays of the two men. Many of the shoemaker's, it is true, are nothing but coarse buffoonery, but many others are full of sensible and valuable matter which aims at something more than mere " Punch and Judy " scenes. With Ayrer, however, almost everything turns on coarse jokes about marriage and the best wit deals with nastiness.' ' Ayrer's language in all his plays is devoid of force and originality.' Tieck, i. p. xxi.

[2] See above, p. 135.

> God save us, the devil's in this game,
> And is taking the thief into hell flame.
> Well, well, it is his right reward,
> To such as he belongs the crown . . . .[1]

In Thomas Birck's 'Ehespiegel' ('Mirror of Marriage'), 'a very amusing and instructive comedy about marriage,' there are no such sensational stage tricks, and the play, 250 printed pages long, is therefore intolerably wearisome. George Miller, professor of theology at Jena, praised it as 'a charming and useful poem,' 'a choice piece of work,' &c. The Tübingen professor, Martin Kraus, recommended it personally to the people in verses which fully corresponded to the poetical genius of Birck. The 'Ehespiegel,' he said, should be known by everybody, for all that adorns

> Parents and their children dear,
> Is wisely, merrily, set forth here.

Children must be brought up in 'respectable habits and artistic culture, which form a good conscience and frank character, and prevent their turning into young wood fit only for making sows' troughs; they should earn praise.'

Birck introduced into his comedy, among other things, 'true accounts' of market-women, of the gipsies, of the pleasures of wine, of dancing, of merchants and shopkeepers, of hosts, of givers of banquets, of the 'use of the book of marriage'; he also gave good instructions as to how butchers and vine-dressers should comport themselves, and he inserted also a 'history of how the devil led away two gamblers.' [2]

---

[1] Act ii. scenes 1 and 2.

[2] Tübingen, 1598 ; cf. Goedeke, *Grundriss*, ii. 387. As regards the prolific didactic dramatist Rudolf Bellinckhaus, shoemaker at Osnabrück (b. 1567), Goedeke, ii. 398, No. 631 (in the *German Museum*, 1779, ii.

The cycle of plays which depict school and student life are of great value from the point of view of the history of civilisation.

To the number of these belongs the ' Schulteufel ' ('School Devil') of Martin Hayneccius, ' a Christian, useful, and fine comedy' of the year 1603.[1] The author complains bitterly ' from personal experience ' of the ' devouring cancers and plague sores with which the schools are infected.' ' The world is a stable full of brutes and stinking he-goats ; he who would be the keeper of it is very quickly strangled.' To carry on the office of a teacher, ' to cleanse the Augean stables, or, as Seneca says, the Cloacae, requires a Hercules who will work not only with thought and word, but also with hand, heart, courage, with the whole body and the whole head ; and he will also often suffer in bodily health from the stink and dirt. Those know nothing of all this who simply traffic in abstract ideas. But those do know it who have worked all the days of their life in such Cloacae, who have suffered far more than Tityus, Sisyphus, Tantalus, the Danaides, and others in their poetical purgatories. Therefore a Hercules is needed for the task of schoolmaster. Quite special persons are required, whom God must send and pre-

145–146) defends him against Lichtenberg ; but what Lichtenberg (p. 148) quotes from the *Schöne Komödie*, which he is criticising, is bad enough, and the comedy *Donatus* certainly provokes ridicule. Of the thirty-six religious comedies of this writer Gervinus says (iii. 100) : ' We ourselves know twenty of these, and they are all so bald, clumsy, and crude, so dismal and dreary, so full of mere puppets, that one can easily understand how the entertaining English comedy gained easy entrance.'

[1] ' Heretofore with the title *Almansor von der Kinder Schulspiegel* . . . printed and now improved.' Leipzig, 1603 ; cf. Goedeke, *Grundriss*, iii. 368, No. 195. ** Concerning the new edition of Hayneccius' *Almansor* see *Jahresberichte für deutsche Litteraturgesch.* II. ii. 170.

serve in the work.' But many of them do not stick
to it long. And where one in fifty or a hundred remains all his life, it must be acknowledged that God
has specially preserved him in spite of himself.[1]
Christ Himself, ' in His human nature the patron and
guardian of schools,' appears in this play, and speaks
with horror of the decay of schools and the general
godlessness :

> How many people in the country in these latter
> Days, regard my word as more than monkey-chatter ?
> There's no more earnestness, nowhere, nevermore,
> All are full of wickedness and corruption sore.
> What word ? What word ? Word here and there they say,
> Might, honour, riches I hear praised alway.

St. Paul joins in :

> It grieves me bitterly to see, as I do well,
> What thou aforetime, Lord, didst once or twice foretell,
> How in the last days all desolate would grow,
> This will I now proceed to show.[2]

George Mauritius, Rector at Wittenberg, later schoolmaster at Nuremberg, in a comedy, ' Von dem Schulwesen ' (1606), describes the life of a teacher as veritably
pitiable. In the very first scene he makes the schoolmaster Christianus say :

> Is not mine a wretched lot ?
> So much work and toil I've got,
> Nor day nor night have any rest,
> And only with scant thanks am blessed.
> My like, I think, cannot be found,
> By such tremendous trouble ground,
> So overburdened with hard toil
> Which all my bodily strength doth spoil.

No sooner is a single boy brought into the school
than ' anxieties in a heap ' fall on the schoolmaster :

[1] Preface, Bl. B³ ff.   [2] Act i. scene 1.

> Alas, that on such brats as they
> We should expend our care all day . . .
> For martyrdom indeed I'm born,
> All my powers are outworn.
> With a pack of lads uncivil,
> Lying, thieving, working only evil . . .
> Thus over all the world we see
> Morality is dying out,
> The young are as wicked as can be.

The young are ' so exasperating that it's enough to drive one mad ' :

> The beast the most unmanageable
> Would be tamed with far less trouble
> Than such coarse and clownish creatures,
> Who follow only their own natures.

One of these fellows gives an account of the heroic deeds he performed against other boys :

> I struck him in the face with might,
> Thrashed him till his skin cracked right
> In two, and from his stool he fell . . .
> I drank up all his wine as well,
> And then by the collar took him
> And in a master way I shook him. . . .

The ' school devil ' boasts of his deeds :

> I make the teacher's life so irksome
> That he would rather be a herdsman
> Tending swine or oxen, than
> Be a schoolmaster, poor man ! [1]

The higher arts, said Mauritius in another comedy, were declining, people were ashamed of studying :

---

[1] *Eine schöne Comoedia von dem Schulwesen* (Leipzig, 1606), Bl. A³, B–B², C. The most severe judgment on the youth of that period comes from the lips of the great philologist Joseph Scaliger (d. 1609). ' When anyone has committed some great crime, it is not necessary to send him to prison, let him only have boys given to him to instruct ; that would be the worst punishment that could be inflicted on him ' (Löschke, p. 238).

> The higher arts are also all decaying,
> And men, the fashion of the world obeying,
> No longer study them or prize them,
> But all alike laugh at them and despise them,
> There's nothing more contemptible than art.

'It is so easy to raise a blue vapour and lay on colours enough to drive art beyond the sea.'

> Things cannot thus for ever stay;
> If longer we go on this way
> And the ills do not avert,
> To barbarism we shall revert.[1]

The degenerate condition of student life was most vividly and powerfully depicted by Albert Wichgrew, of Hamburg, in a Latin drama, 'Cornelius relegatus,' which was acted in 1600 by the Rostock students, and in 1605, in response 'to much urgent request,' translated into German by John Sommer, pastor at Osterweddingen. Sommer says in his preface that he had for some time had scruples about undertaking this work, from fear 'that the description of the dissolute life of the students might excite the suspicions of ill-disposed ignorant people.' But other considerations had finally determined him to translate the play, 'especially the breaking-up of school discipline,' owing to which 'the whole world was being overrun by Corneliuses and Hasions,[2] so that now that the Cornelian pestilence has poured in like a flood, all attempts to ward it off are useless, as is complained not only in the towns but also in the academies. For when Mistress Indulgence is introduced among the pupils, they will grow horns, and from calves turn into oxen.'

---

[1] *Comoedia von den Weysen aus dem Morgenlande* (*Comedy of the Wise Men from the East*) (Leipzig, 1606), Bl. A³⁻⁴.

[2] Fools.

Therefore Wichgrew 'did not do wrong in describing this bacchantian Cornelian swine life, although some should take pattern by it, and others should wonder what is going to be the end and outcome of it all.' As the Romans took their children once a year to see a play with mad, tipsy slaves in it, in order to fill them with disgust against drunkenness, so 'this Cornelius,' with his drinking, gambling, and profligacy, and his young Corneliolus, is shown up to public view that all may see him, not in order that young scholars, when they leave private schools and go to the universities, should learn to abuse the privilege and liberty to drink, play, gamble, &c., but that they should be duly warned against indulgence in vices of this sort.' Parents also, culpably negligent and foolish fathers and mothers, come in for their share of reproach. ' Young dandies— I will say nothing now of the old scarecrows and fools who themselves cut out dunces' caps for their children— young dandies, when they marry, and by God's blessing obtain the fruits of marriage, are anxious to educate their offspring in their own image and likeness: the youngsters must wear long French curls, ample miller's hose, and adopt all the new-fangled, utopian, Cornelian manners and ornaments: the fathers admire themselves in their children as old monkeys do in their young. What will be the outcome in the future of such fruit and discipline, posterity, unless God makes an end of this wicked world, will experience with sorrow.' [1]

---

[1] Cornelius relegatus, *eine newe lustige Comoedia* &c. (Magdeburg, 1605 ; cf. Goedeke, *Grundriss*, ii. 372, No. 220ᵇ), preface. Fuller details concerning the play and its contents will be found in the article by E. Schmidt, *Komödien vom Studentenleben aus dem sechzehnten und Siebzehnten*

A woodcut on the title-page gives an illustration of student life. Cornelius is sitting in his room at the table, resting his head in melancholy mood on his hand ; on the floor lie beer-cans, cards, dice, and rapiers ; in a cradle a child is sleeping, and another child is brought in by a servant girl ; the oven is shattered ; on the wall hangs a lute ; at the door the beadle is ' chalking ' a summons ' to the rector.' [1]

' I have heard from many people,' says the father in warning accents to his son Cornelius, about to start for the Wittenberg university, all that goes on in these places,

> How all the vices there abound,
> How the students only fool around,
> Drink copiously, forget their studies,
> Wrestle and make love to ladies.

Cornelius describes the life which he intends leading at the university, and which he does actually lead with his boon companions :

Jahrhundert (Leipzig, 1880), pp. 10–16. The play itself gives as ' argument of the play ' the following :

> Cornelius loathed and hated school,
> Was weary of its rigid rule ;
> He asked his father to permit
> That he to Wittenberg should flit.
> His parents straightway grant the prayer ;
> He flies off to his lady fair
> The news to her to communicate
> That he's going to be a licentiate.
> She gives him kerchiefs, money, ring ;
> He swaggers off, has his full fling :
> In feasts and banquets spends his days,
> Learns nothing, eats, drinks, sings love-lays,
> And when he's deep in debt, the dunce,
> He's fiercely censured, and at once
> Arrested and incarcerated,
> To misery sadly relegated ;
> Then home returns in sorest grief,
> Repents, and turns over a new leaf.

Cf. the ' Kurze Beschreibung des Cornelii von einem Cornelianer gedichtet ' attached to the end of the play.

[1] Cf. E. Schmidt, p. 27.

So soon as I get there and I'm
Enrolled, I'll have a glorious time,
My countrymen I'll all invite,
And spend my money left and right.
I'll riot, gamble, gorge and swill,
I'll follow always my own will,
And should I thus get into debt—
Well, there's good counsel for me yet—
I'll tell a thousand lies, forsooth,
My dad will take them all for truth.
He'll send me money straightaway
That I may riot every day.
But enough of this for the present, I
Must to my young damsel fly.

A carousal scene is introduced with the words :

In the stomach, friends, long time
The dinner-bell has rung its chime,
And our teeth with longing wait
The dainty fare to masticate. . . .
I, too, wait impatiently
The cans and glasses to drain dry.

When once at a scene of this sort one of the students
was overcome by twelve cans of beer, Cornelius was
astonished :

I mind me of the time when you
Full twenty tankards of stout brew
In three short hours have bravely drunk ;
Why then be now in such a funk ?

This student, however, who has been in the war, protests that he is still quite manly :

I still can gamble, eat, carouse,
Smash doors and windows in a house,
Turn gentlemen and ladies out,
With daggers stab, hack, strike about.

An attack on the house of the tavern-keeper Asmus
which Cornelius and two other students perpetrated is
described to the Rector by the officer of the watch :

Herr Rector, there were three, I vow ;
On the market-place they made a great row.
When the watchmen were about to call
Three o'clock, and the people all
Were sleeping their best, they came to the house
Of Asmus and his youthful spouse,
They banged and thumped with angry din,
Insisted he must let them in,
But when they met with no response
They drew their daggers out at once,
And slashed and cut the door in twain
And smashed in every window pane.
The neighbours soon began to gather
Round, to learn what was the matter,
And raised a mighty hue and cry.
I to my watchers winked an eye,
Who with halberd and with spear
Bravely came upon the rear,
One ruffian put to flight, and threw
Down on the ground the other two,
Whom quickly we, as was but just,
Seized and into prison thrust.

Before the university tribunal the prisoners Cornelius
and Grillus deny the whole affair, and abuse Hansius
stoutly in the presence of the Rector :

CORNELIUS

The devil carry thee off with him,
Thy mouth's chock full of lies to the brim.
I'll soon take my vengeance on thee,
With this dagger I'd like to stab thee.

GRILLUS

And I could have no better hope
Than round thy neck to tie a rope,
And throw thee in a stinking pit
And never let thee out of it.

HANSIUS

Hey day, I heed thy threats no whit,
No more than did they issue from
The housemaid who sweeps out my room.
Just try, and see what you will get,
These fists of mine you know not yet.

The Rector tells the insolent youths to be quiet. They are fined thirty florins for the storming of the house, but the amount is finally reduced to fifteen florins, to be paid in fourteen days, and they are let off. Cornelius, however, is soon brought before the magistrates again, and the Rector informs the bench that a 'tradesman has complained that Cornelius, unable to pay what he owed, had beaten and wounded him in the open market, before respectable people who were standing near, and that these last had complained loudly that the Rector let things go too much, was too lenient, and did not punish the lewd rogues and criminals. . . .' The landlord also complains that Cornelius has dishonoured his daughter. A number of creditors demand payment. Cornelius, however, sees nothing out of the way in all this :

> Dear sirs, I really cannot see
> That it rascality can be
> When a young fellow courts a maid,
> Plays, drinks, and riots early and late,
> And borrows money where he can :
> It is the way of every man.

The language in which the dishonoured Lubentia states her case cannot be reproduced.[1]

[1] Act i. scene 3 to Act iv. scene 11. Half a century earlier, in 1549, Christopher Stymmel, of Frankfort-on-the-Oder, in a Latin burlesque, *The Students*, had described the wild, dissolute life at the universities in the same sort of way as Wichgrew. One of the students gives the following account of one of the habitual scenes of rioting and drunkenness : ' We sat on drinking yesterday till one in the morning and were so tipsy that we could scarcely stand ; indeed we fell down on the floor like epileptics. When we were tired of drinking we went out on to the market-place. There we met a large swarm of a students' society who fell upon us with drawn swords. We fought them bravely, till they got the worst of it and finally turned their backs on us, many of them so badly wounded that there was little hope of their living. Soon, aroused by the noise, the night watchers rushed upon us in a troop, bristling with arms. But these also

The Swiss poets Nicholas Manuel and Hans Rudolf
Manuel, amongst others, have given us truly disgraceful
pictures of German national life in general : Nicholas
especially in his carnival farce, ' Von dem Elsslin trag
den Knaben und von Uly Rechenzan mit ihrem ehelichen
Gerichts-handel ' of the year 1530. ' There they lie,
the altars and the idols in the temples,' Zwingli had
preached during the iconoclastic riots in the cathedral
of Bern ; ' the rubbish must be turned out, so that the
untold price you have spent on this fool's work may
at once be made profitable to the living images of
God.' Manuel's ' Elssli ' shows to what a condition of
dirt ' the living images of God ' had sunk in 1530.
The following lines are specially to the point :

> God have pity !   How in the land
> Has vice now gained the upper hand.
> The devil's people and mob they are,
> God teach us how to deal with them ! [1]

When we read the horrible curses and vilifications
which fill this ' charming ' play, the coarse, disgusting
descriptions of low, immoral life, we can scarcely think
it possible that such productions were really performed
before the burghers of Bern. We feel that they were
only fit to be acted by common people, glad to earn a
few groschen, and in the presence of beer-drinkers at
taverns ; and that this particular piece must rather
have been the work of a barber like Hans Folz than of
an artist, councillor, and statesman. In a second

were put to flight. 'Faith, I could have died of laughing to see the men
to whom the safety of the town is entrusted flying so disgracefully.'
(Stymmel's Latin play, *Studentes*, translated by Meyer, *Studentica*, p. 77.)
Stymmel's piece met with such approval that at least thirteen editions of
it can be traced before 1614 ; cf. Goedeke, *Grundriss*, ii. 138, No. 27.

[1] Baechtold, *N. Manuel*, p. 296.

edition it was described as ' amusing to read,' in a third and fourth as ' very entertaining to read and hear.' [1]

Equally repulsive is the piece composed in 1548 by Nicholas Manuel's son, Hans Rudolf, ' Holdsäligs Fast-nachtsspiel, darin der edle Wyn von der trunkenen Rotte beklagt, von Räblüten geschirmt und von Richtern ledig gesprochen wird ' (' Holdsälig's Carnival Farce, in which the noble Wine is Accused by the drunken Pack, but Protected by the Councillors and Absolved by the Judges '). In this play, consisting of 4235 verses, the reigning vice of drunkenness is dealt with and in-veighed against, but by a poet who says concerning himself :

> Of myself indeed I needs must say
> I too grow tipsy night and day,
> Yes, I myself, who this play have done,
> Therefore I can despise no one.

It may therefore be fairly assumed that he writes from personal experience :

> The hound-matins then first strike up
> When we've swallowed the sleeping-cup ;
> Then reason doth no more exist,
> Man is no better than a beast.
> Then we set to hacking, slashing,
> Tubs upsetting, basins smashing,
> The oven must out of the window go,
> Stools and benches after it we throw,
> And then we boil a soup delicious,
> Filled with candle-ends nutritious,
> The wine we measure in tubs and vats
> And eat our viands in felt hats. . . .[2]

---

[1] Baechtold, *N. Manuel*, pp. ccv.–ccvi. ; Goedeke, *Grundriss*, ii. 341, No. 9.

[2] Baechtold, pp. 305–374. The verses quoted are at pp. 354, 359. The publisher has not thought fit to give out the whole of the piece which the author describes as ' charming.' Verses 2584–3139, for instance, are left out with the remark (p. 367) : ' The rest of the wives of the drunken fellows denounce the influence of wine in the most obscene manner ; the

This play also was considered ' quite delightful
to read,' and was acted by young burghers of Zürich.

Another extremely vivid picture of the times is given
by the ' Deutsche Schlemmer,' written in 1584 in
Low German by John Stricerius, preacher at Grobe.
The hero of the piece figures as a universally known
and gay debauchee, whe spends his days and nights
in drinking and profligacy, and as a patron of a church
has acquired ecclesiastical property. God did not
trouble himself about the priests, he said, and whoever
wanted to get rid of them had only to send them away
empty-handed. Let them write and roar that the
church goods brought no blessing to the lords or the
vassals who devoured them, and that they were intended
for the poor and for scholars ; this nonsense didn't go
down any longer, the Pope's ban didn't work any more ;
the only watchword now was : ' Thus will I have it,
thus I command, to us belong the ecclesiastical goods.'
To the good lords who have taken possession of the convents, all is smooth and pleasant ; Christ's bread tastes
very sweet to them, what have they to do with scholars
and the poor ? He had only followed the example
of the lords who, with the approval of their theologians,
court-preachers and superintendents, had taken possession of the convents.   The world was now so demoralised

Landsknecht also calls to witness his whore whom wine has caused to lose
her wreath of roses.   In place of the omitted verses, 3530–3963 and
3996–4157, we read (pp. 370, 371) : ' Sentence is pronounced on the
calumniators of the vine ; they are all to be put on the fools' bench ;
the punishment, the description of which is not fit for insertion, is
carried out and the Britschen song (clown's song) is sung at the same
time.'   Goedeke (*Grundriss*, ii. 348, No. 67) indicates where a complete
copy is to be found.   Genée (pp. 59–60) says it is ' quite inconceivable '
that this play ' should have been able to enthral an audience ' ; but this
was just the sort of piece that the public liked.

that nobody any longer gave anything for church purposes, whether money or corn, hay or straw, even though the churches and parsonages should go to ruin in consequence. He himself would rather drink and gamble away a hundred thalers at a banquet with pleasant people in a jovial mood, than give even one thaler only to a priest. In one scene the proceedings of a dissolute night are described. The drunkard and his cousin tell how they all lay tipsy on the benches, vomiting wine, beer, &c., as though they were knights and heroes on the field of battle. Then begins the description of a fresh drinking-bout : the revellers compete with each other, and whoever cannot drain the beaker at one gulp is treated with contempt. . . . A preacher who comes on the scene, and who will not join them in drinking, but administers serious reproofs to the wild company and threatens them with the ban, is abused and driven away. Finally comes the punishment and the conversion of the drunkard, which are represented in full detail. In the dedication of the piece to the Protestant bishop of Lübeck and Verden, Stricerius says he has had it printed, at the suggestion of godly people, for a Christian exhortation and warning to all ' impenitent and self-satisfied people,' and for the instruction and consolation of suffering mortal men and women. Strange to say, however, he describes this piece, full of such drunken and profligate scenes, as a ' child's poem,' and actually states expressly that it ' has been composed for the pupils.' [1]

The comedies, also, of Nicodemus Frischlin contain in many of their scenes representations of the conditions of that period. In his Latin play ' Rebecca ' (1576),

[1] Goedeke, *Everyman*, pp. 111–131.

repeatedly translated into German, the author gives
an appalling sketch of the rough nobility, usurers,
grabbers and peasant-flayers, and of the inordinate
drinking that went on, especially at the courts. In
his German comedy ' Der Weingärtner,' he makes
the peasants speak their mind about their heavy ill-
luck, and use hard language against the ruling authorities.[1] The comedy ' Frau Wendelgard ' (1597) describes the beggar and swindler life in Upper Suabia,
Alsatia and Northern Switzerland. ' What we have
collected during the day,' says one of the beggars,
' we consume by midnight ' :

> Then come the beggar-wives along,
> With their bodies straight and strong ;
> Then goes round the leathern cup
> Till we've used our money up,
> And when we're drunk, oh, then I ween
> Many wonderworks are seen :
> Then the blind see, then speak the dumb,
> The lame and the cripples straight become ;
> Then in earnest the play begins,
> Then we start the beggars' dance.
> Do you like our beggar-life perchance ? [2]

In the last decades of the sixteenth century the
popular plays which had been acted by all classes,
clergy, nobles, burghers and peasants, schoolmasters
and pupils, began to retreat into the background and
to give place more and more to a kind of professional
theatre the performers of which were for the most part
strolling Englishmen. These plays were almost entirely
of a secular character ; religious matter, in so far as it

---

[1] Strauss, *Leben Frischlins*, pp. 106–112.

[2] Strauss, *Frischlins Deutsche Dichtungen*, pp. 30, 31 ; cf. pp. 44–45,
52–53. John Schlayss in his *Joseph*, Part ii. Act v. scene 3, also depicts
the pleasures of the beggar life. This scene is taken from the Latin
comedy of the same name by Hunnius ; cf. Von Weilen, p. 147.

still had any part in them, was in great measure dragged into coarseness and vulgarity.

Even before the ' English comedians ' had crossed over Denmark and the Netherlands into Germany, Italian, Dutch,. and French actors had already made their way to the German courts and the imperial cities. Italians had appeared at the courts of Vienna and Munich as early as 1568, and even earlier at Nordlingen and Strassburg.[1] They were a special feature at the court of the Bavarian Crown Prince William at Landshut.[2] In the year 1583 the Council of Frankfort gave permission to a French troop of strolling players to ' act a French comedy.' [3]

In 1586, however, they had to reconsider this decision, for the French actors went to such lengths

---

[1] K. Trautmann, in the *Jahrbuch für Münchener Geschichte*, i. 222 ff. : ' In the last decade before 1600 we find in Germany side by side with the Italian comedians rival French and English players—above all the latter. The musical arts were shared by the English in common with the Italians . . . one circumstance, however, decided in favour of the Mimes " who came across the sea," viz. language.   The English players made haste to learn German, and put their comedies on the boards in the German tongue.   The Italians did not follow this example . . . consequently their sphere became more limited to the courts of princes, especially to those of South Germany, which were nearer akin to the Italian language and character, and they left it to the English comedians to gain the favour of the masses of people in the towns ' (pp. 235–236).   ** Cf. Schwering, *Zur Geschichte des niederländischen und spanischen Dramas in Deutschland. Neue Forschungen.* Münster, 1895, a work which was very severely criticised by Farinelli in the *Rivista critica*, 1896, No. 12.   Farinelli also spoke very unfavourably of Schneider's book (*Spaniens Antheil an der Litteratur des* 16. *und* 17. *Jahrhunderts*, Strassburg, 1898) in the *Zeitschr. für vergleich. Litteraturgesch.* xiii. 413 ff. ; cf. Beer in the *Anzeiger für deutsches Altertum*, xxvi. 134–161.

[2] Trautmann, pp. 238 ff.   At the court of Duke Ferdinand II. at Innsbruck Italian comedians are first traced in the year 1589 (p. 232). In Ferdinand's *Schöner Komödie*: Speculum vitæ humanæ (cf. above, p. 11) Italian fools are introduced (p. 297, Note 168).

[3] Pallmann, p. 114, No. 142.   Mentzel, *Gesch. der Schauspielkunst*, p. 17.

in invectives against the papacy, that the council, out
of regard for the Elector of Mayence and other Catholic
prelates, entered into deliberation as to the advisability
of stopping their proceedings.[1] The travelling actors
did not stand in high repute with the council : the
' Italians ' as well as the English companies, which soon
established themselves there, were placed on the same
level as tight-rope dancers and caperers and designated
by the title of ' all sorts of rabble ' ; their performances
were only allowed in order to provide amusement for
the numerous strangers who came to the fairs.[2] Aegidius
Albertinus, secretary to the Duke of Bavaria, makes
his ' Landstörtzer ' associate with these strolling ' new
comedians,' and gives the following account of them :
' They were of all nations, French, English, Dutch,
Italian. Their music and their comedies pleased me
immensely, so much so, indeed, that I addressed myself
to them, and they agreed to take me into their company ;
for I could speak Italian, Spanish, Latin, and broken
German, besides which I could play the lute admirably,
and I represented a Spanish clown with his guitar and
could sing, dance and jump capitally.' These comedians
' were men who could act good pieces, and at the same
time perform absurd farces and tricks of jugglery and
carry on nonsensical talk. They roved from place to
place, and I went with them all through Germany and
the Netherlands.[3] '

---

[1] Mentzel, p. 16.

[2] Cf. Mentzel, pp. 40–41, 49–50, 59–60.

[3] Albertinus, *Landstörtzer*, pp. 284–285.   ** See concerning this adaptation of Mateo Aleman's *Picaro Guzmán de Alfarache*, K. v. Reinhardstöttner, 'Aegidius Albertinus, the father of the German Schelmenromans '
(romance of rogues) in the *Jahrbuch für Münchener Gesch.* iii. 13 and ff.
Cf. also Von Liliencron in the *Allgem. deutsche Biographie*, i. pp. 217–219,

At the courts of the princes English comedians were early appreciated.[1] By the superiority of their dramatic art they drove the performances of the native dilettanti completely into the background.[2] At the Saxon Electoral court at Dresden they performed as early as 1586. Duke Henry Julius of Brunswick and the Landgrave Maurice of Hesse-Cassel were the first German princes who had a permanent theatre, with Englishmen for its chief members; both of them used to compose plays for these actors.[3] Maurice erected in 1605 a theatre in the form of a circus, with a painted roof, which he named the Ottonium, in honour of his son Otto.[4] Besides the Hessian and Brunswickian

concerning the culture and the views of Albertinus ; and for still more comprehensive information, the introduction to *Lucifers Königreich* (Berlin and Stuttgart, 1883, vol. xxvi. of J. Kürschners *Deutsche National-litteratur*), where it is said that the principal works of Albertinus ' with their subject-matter are entirely within the old scheme of the scholastic encyclopedia as it comes down to us from Vincent de Beauvais.' See further Von Reinhardstöttner, *Forschungen*, ii. 87 ff.

[1] For the local dispersion of English comedians in Germany, their repertory and their stage appurtenances, cf. Tittmann, *Schauspiele*, ii. p. xi. ff. and *Englische Komödianten*, p. v. ff.   Goedeke, *Grundriss*, ii. pp. 524–542.   ** It is noteworthy that at Constance English comedians made their appearance as early as 1417 ; see Grauert, *Dante in Deutschland*, in the *Histor. Polit. Bl.* 120, 180 ff. note.   For English actors at Münster, 1601, see Jostes in the *Korrespondenzblatt des Ver. für niederd. Sprach-forsch.* xiii. 37 ; at Rothenburg on the Tauber, see Trautmann in the *Zeitschr. für vergl. Litteraturgeschichte und Renaissancelitteratur*, vii. 60 ff. ; in Austria, see Nagl-Zeidler, p. 732 ff., *Weitere Litteratur bei Greizenach*, ii.

[2] ** Cf. S. Bolte, *Das Danziger Theater im sechzehnten und siebzehnten Jahrhundert* (Hamburg and Leipzig, 1895), p. xvi.

[3] In two letters of instructions to the English comedians Browne and Kingsman, Maurice (about 1598) gave orders that they with their company ' should act all sorts of amusing comedies, tragedies and plays, such as we shall either invent ourselves and give to you ' or such as they themselves should invent and arrange.   The outlines of the letters con-tributed by G. Könnecke in the *Zeitschr. für vergleichende Litteratur-geschichte*, &c., by Koch and Geiger, new series, i. 85–88.

[4] Rommel, *Gesch. von Hessen*, vi. 399 ff.   Cf. Fürstenau, pp. 75–79.

court comedians there sprang up also those of the Electorate of Brandenburg.[1]

All the chief companies of the princely courts also went visiting through the German towns; the Hessian players, for instance, were frequently in Frankfort-on-the-Main.[2]

In a Nuremberg chronicle we read : 'The 20th, 21st, 22nd, and 23rd October, 1612, some Englishmen, court comedians to the Landgrave at Cassel in Hesse, acted in the Hailsprunner Court, by permission of the burgomaster, several fine comedies and tragedies, some of which are unknown in Germany; and they also performed some very charming music; also all sorts of Italian dances with wonderful twistings, hopping, jumping backwards and forwards, turning head over heels, and other eccentric antics which were amusing to see. There was a great concourse of old and young, both male and female, and also of gentlemen of the council and learned doctors. For they had gone round the town first, with two drums and four trumpets, inviting the people to come and see them perform; and each person who came to see these amusing things had to pay half a batze, by which means the comedians made a large sum of money, which they took away with them out of this town.'[3]   In the following year

[1] Fuller details are given in Meissner, 30 ff.   *Archiv für Litteraturgesch.* xiv. 117 ff.

[2] Fuller details in Mentzel, p. 43 ff.   In the year 1605 a company of English players, who had acted for four years at the court of the Landgrave Maurice, performed in Strassburg twenty-four comedies, tragedies and pastorals ; cf. Crüger in the *Archiv für Litteraturgesch.* xv. 116–117. *Über englische Komödianten in Stuttgart seit 1600*, pp. 211–216, contributed by K. Trautmann.

[3] From the original of the Stark Chronicle, contributed by K. Trautmann in the *Archiv für Litteraturgesch.* xiv. 126–127; cf. Siebenkees,

the Brandenburg-English company, under the direction
of John Spencer, acted at Nuremberg ' fine comedies
and tragedies of Philole and Mariane, item of Celide
and Sedea, also of the destruction of the towns of Troy
and Constantinople, of the Turks and other histories,
besides performing elegant dances, delightful music
and other entertainments in the Heilsbrunner Court,
in good German speech, and in costly masquerades
and dresses.' [1] From Nuremberg Spencer went to
Ratisbon and played there while the Diet was going
on ' at different times ' before the Emperor Matthias.
The representation of the ' Taking of Constantinople '
brought him in on the first day 500 florins. ' They were
obliged,' says a chronicle, ' to build for him, at a cost of
135 florins, a great stage and on the stage a theatre, in
which he performed more than ten times with all sorts
of musical instruments, and above the theatre stage
still another stage, thirty feet high on six great pillars,
over which a roof was placed, and under it a four-
cornered aperture, through which their beautiful acting
was visible.[2]

Materialen, iii. 52, 53.   ** And Hampe in the *Mitteil. des Vereins für
Geschichte der Stadt Nürnberg*, xii. (1898), 192 ff., 195 ff.

   [1] Meissner, p. 36.
   [2] Mettenleiter, *Musikgeschichte Regensburgs*, i. 256. ' This " Spund "
was probably a four-cornered opening, in which transparencies or panto-
mimic representations, perhaps also phantasmagoria according to the
fashion of the present day, were seen.' Meissner (p. 54) says : ' In our opinion
the " four-cornered *Spund* " was nothing more than the hole in the floor
through which the devil, spirits, &c. &c., used to leap forth, and which is
so often alluded to by James Ayrer in his stage directions.'   ** Concerning
John Spencer the protocols of the Cologne Council, No. 64, down to the
year 1615, according to a communication of the pastor Unkel to the
deceased author of this work, report as follows :
   February 16.—' When the Burgomaster Hardenrod made known that
the Lord Nuncius Apostolicus had been in person to his Grace's house,
and stated the case of the Master of the English comedians who had

The Emperor Matthias was in crushing pecuniary circumstances. 'Nobody will lend to us,' wrote his minister Melchior Klesl from Ratisbon, ' nobody owes us anything, we ourselves have nothing '; ' the poor unpaid court officials are starving and dying, and scarcely even get enough ox's blood '; the imperial horse-

lately been playing here with eighteen other persons of his company, viz. that he had through the zeal and industry of *Pater Franciscus Capucinus* been so fully instructed in the Catholic religion that there was reason to hope they would all embrace and acknowledge it, it was permitted to the troop to act their plays during the carnival, but with the exception of Sundays and festival days.'

March 11.—' To the English comedians, who have now attached themselves to the Catholic religion, leave has been granted, at the solicitation of the Count of Hohenzollern (*i.e.* the cathedral provost Count Eitel of Hohenzollern) and of the pastor at St. Martin's, to act religious and other edifying plays until the Frankfort fair on working days.'

March 25.—' Whereas a memorandum of the Lord Count of Hohenzollern has been handed in by the pastor of St. Martin's, making request that the English comedians who have become Catholics may be allowed to settle here and act religious pieces about three times a week, it has been decreed that they must send in their request themselves in writing and with their own signature.'

April 1.—' John Spencer, English comedian, has supplicando petitioned and prayed that, whereas he, through God's grace, with his wife and children and his whole company of players and his servants, has been converted to the Catholic religion and has made up his mind to adhere to it, leave may be granted him as a burgher to act instructive and edifying plays on certain days in the week, after Vespers, and on Sundays, and festivals, excepting the high festivals. This has been accorded to him on condition of his qualifying himself properly and remaining faithful to the Catholic religion, and conducting his performances in an orderly and well-regulated manner.'

The *Bruderschaftsbuch* of the *Confraternitas Passionis D.N.J.C.*, Brotherhood of the Cross, founded in 1612 for the maintenance of the converts, mentions among the first converts who were supported by the brotherhood, one Joannes Spencer, M^r. Comoedorum, his two sons, a daughter, and a whole list of English and German names, possibly members of Spencer's troop.

Spencer was converted by the Commissary-General of the Dutch Province of the Capuchin Order, P. Franciscus Nugent, at that time spiritual leader of the brotherhood.

guards and halberdiers, for instance, were obliged ' to go to the slaughter-house and catch the blood of the slaughtered cattle and bring it home to cook, so that the misery of the great is often much worse than that of the common people.' [1] But for the comedians money was easily provided. According to the imperial treasury accounts fourteen Rhenish florins were paid on September 7 to ' a jumper and tight-rope dancer,' on September 14 twenty florins to an English troop, on September 21 fourteen florins to a French comedian, on October 24 Spencer was paid 200 florins. In the following year Italian comedians received, besides free board, nearly 5300 florins from the imperial coffers.[2]

An Italian harlequin was raised to nobility by Matthias.[3]

Great praise was earned by the Englishmen who acted at the ducal court at Graz under the direction of John Green in 1607 and 1608, for the ' very respectable and orderly manner ' in which they performed their pieces. ' They are certainly very excellent comedians,' wrote the Archduchess Maria Magdalena on Ash-Wednesday, 1608, to her brother Ferdinand. Of a comedy, ' Vom reichen Mann und dem Lazarus,' she says : ' I cannot describe to your Grace how beautiful it was ; for there was no suggestion or hint of profligacy in it ; it moved us greatly, so well did they act it.' In the year 1617 the Archduke Charles, then Bishop of Breslau, recommended this English troop to the Cardinal Dietrichstein, Governor of Moravia.[4]

[1] See our remarks, vol. x. pp. 496–498.
[2] *Archiv für Litteraturgesch.* xiv. 129, 442–444. Meissner, pp. 36, 52–53, 56–57.
[3] Meissner, n. 191 to p. 56.
[4] Fuller details in Meissner, pp. 62–63, 74–84, 87 ff.

In general, however, the influence of the 'new comedians' was a very unsalutary one. On the one hand they addressed themselves to the low craving for indecent buffoonery and love 'pranks, on the other to the excitement of fear and terror; they stimulated the ghastly delight in scenes of murder and horrors, and the latent bloodthirstiness which was already far too strong in the demoralised people.[1] Thus, for instance, in the tragedy of ' Titus Andronicus,' which was played by the English company, scenes of the following description are introduced ' for the entertainment and refreshment of the minds ' of the spectators : Titus gets into his power the Empress's sons, who had violated his daughter and cut off her hands and her tongue, so that she might not be able to speak or to write the names of her assaulters. He calls to his people : ' Hallo, soldiers, come quickly here ! Bring me at once a sharp butcher's knife and a slaughter-cloth.   Yes, now I have bethought me of a secret way in which I shall be able to catch all my enemies, and cool my temper nicely on them again.   (Then someone comes up, brings him a sharp knife and a cloth ; he puts the cloth round him as though he was going to slaughter.)   Go quickly also and fetch a tub.   (He goes.)   And you,

---

[1] ** The influence of the English comedians on the character of the stage was far-reaching in its results ; they gave the actual impulse to the development of a professional theatre in Germany, and transplanted to German soil the principle of realistic representation ; in this last respect indeed they went much too far. This is especially brought out by Andreae, who, while paying due tribute to the realistic method of presentation, nevertheless ' polemises ' against the new tendency, because by reason of it ' more store is set by the outward effects, the dresses of the actors, the fools and peasants, the jokes and buffoonery, noise, fighting, scuffling, laughing, &c., than by the usefulness of the plays.' Cf. Creizenach, p. cxvi.

come here with that murderer you've got hold of,
and hold his throat that I may cut it. (The tub is
brought.) And you bring the tub here and hold it
under his throat to catch all the blood. (The eldest
brother is first held over the tub ; he tries to talk, but
they keep his mouth tight shut. Titus cuts his throat
half through. The blood runs into the tub, and when
the blood has all run out they lay him on the ground
dead).' The younger brother is treated in exactly the
same way. Then Titus says : ' Now I have cut both
their throats halfway through ; and what I have killed
I will cook myself ; I will chop the heads up quite fine
and make them into pasties, and I will invite the
Emperor and his mother to come and partake of them.'
This festive meal then takes place, and is followed by
further murders which are also represented on the stage.[1]

After the model of the ' English comedians,' James
Ayrer († 1605) filled his dramas to the brim with
blood and murder.[2] In the tragedy of the Emperor

---

[1] *Englische Komödien*, No. 8. Printed by Tieck, i. 370–407, but
with omission of certain objectionable passages ; compare Act vi. scene 1,
the speeches of *Morian* (Bl. O 7ᵇ) with Tieck, p. 394. The stage effect of
' stabbing oneself ' says Devrient, i. 169, ' had become so worn out
that the more appalling form of suicide by running the head against a
wall had been introduced. We find the following directions : " He falls
into despair, dashes his head up against the wall, so that the blood flows
out from under his hat, which can be done with a bladder." ' In *King
Montalor* the following directions are given in the text : ' Here they begin
to fight, the king's head is hacked ; this can be arranged so that blood
flows from the hat.' ** Cf. also Scherer, *Geschichte der deutschen Litteratur*, p. 312.

[2] ** Cf. Robertson, *Zur Kritik Jacob Ayrers mit besonderer Rücksicht
auf sein Verhältniss zu Hans Sachs und zu den Englischen Komödianten*
(with special reference to his relations to Hans Sachs and to the English
comedians). Dissert. Leipzig, 1892, and also W. Creizenach in the *Jahresberichte für neuere deutsche Litteraturgeschichte*, vol. iv. II. 4, No. 34.
See also Hampe, in the *Mitteil. d. Vereins für Gesch. d. Stadt Nürnberg*, xii.
(1898), 177 ff.

Otto III. and his consort, Otto makes the ears and
nose of Crescentius be cut off ; ' the executioner throws
them away,' and then puts out the eyes of the pope,
who had been elected by Crescentius, ' binds him up
quickly with a bloody cloth and throws him into the
hole ' ; a nobleman, who was living in adultery with
the Empress, is burnt to ashes ; a count, who refuses to
commit adultery with her, is unjustly put to death by
an executioner, who boasts of having already inflicted
the same punishment on a thousand and eight culprits.
As the Countess Euphrosyne ' was carrying her husband's head in a covered dish, the blood spurted out,
and up to a great height.'   The fate of the Empress is
described by the executioner as follows :

> And now I've burnt the Empress quite ;
> With hands and feet she made a fight
> Until the moment that she died.
> By God !   I've driven out her pride.

The devil, who has ' already appeared earlier on the
stage with great spitting of fire and terrible gestures,'
now brings with him ' Pope Gilbertus, who had been
installed at his suggestion,' and who states his wish
that ' when he dies his limbs shall be hacked off his
body.' . . .

Finally the Emperor is poisoned with a pair of
gloves.[1]

In the tragedy of ' Servius Tullius,' Lucius Tar-
quinius cuts his wife's throat on the stage and leaves
her to die in agony ; at the same time Tullia gives her
husband a poisonous drink, and says :

> Therein a sudden death he'll swallow,
> And I escape from all my sorrow ;

---

[1] Ayrer, i. 435 ff.

and turning to the dying man,

> Lucius, henceforth thy brother
> Shall be to me my dearest lover.

The King Servius Tullius is killed by the hangman
and left to lie in the Via Scelerata. Brutus ' agonises '
on the gallows ; the burgomaster Gabinus is stabbed to
death, and other butcheries follow.[1]

Still more terrible things happen in the ' Tragedy of
Theseus, the tenth King of Athens.' First of all there
appears a fire-spitting dragon, which is killed by Jason ;
then come some giants, ' who all pitch into each other,
and Jason also joins in the scuffle, till finally they all die.'
Again and again the devil shows himself in the form
of a dragon, and carries Medea, who is always busy
with sorcery and hobgoblins, away on his back. Then
' enters Minotaurus, a monster, part ox and part man,
carrying in his hands a great club and a child,' and
informs the spectators that he shall devour the child :

> The child I'll eat, I verily swear,
> With lice and nits, with skin and hair,
> And all its intestines beside,
> I'll throw away no single mite. . . .
> Come hither, child ; I'll louse thy head
> Until my mouth overflows with blood.

Five murderers, who come in one after the other, are
demolished by Theseus ; then the latter, with the help
of Ariadne, kills the Minotaur ; Ariadne, dishonoured
and abandoned by Theseus, hangs herself. The wife
of Theseus accuses her stepson Hippolytus, whom
she has vainly tried to seduce, of rape ; he makes his
escape, falls from the carriage and is torn to pieces by
the horses, and Theseus receives the news :

[1] Ayrer, i. 297 ff.

> And your Majesty I would inform
> That his body, all in pieces torn,
> Is scattered right and left about the street.

The stepmother throws herself upon the sword which Hippolytus has left lying. All this, however, does not by a long way exhaust the horrors of this tragedy.[1]

From the ' Schröckliche Tragedi vom Regiment und schändlichen Sterben des türkischen Kaisers Machumetis des Andern,' suffice it to quote the scene in which the Emperor knocks his brother down with a sword, and while the mother, standing by, laments over the deed, is heard to say :

> We are fain to laugh at our Empress mother,
> Who over a handful of blood
> Howls and weeps and makes such a bother.[2]

The horribleness of such tragedies and the coarseness of the sentiments predominant in them could not be overcome or palliated by moralisings at the end.[3] At any rate they do not deserve the praise which was bestowed on Ayrer's works in the preface to the collection published in 1618, that ' more excellent, beautiful, charming and amusing things were not easily seen or heard.' ' Ring-running, fencing, gymnastics,' said the publishers, ' were the pastimes of young people

---

[1] Ayrer, ii. 1207–1303.

[2] Ibid. ii. 737–810.

[3] This is the opinion of K. Schmitt, in his *Jacob Ayrer* (Marburg, 1851), p. 29, note, as opposed to Prutz, *Vorlesungen*, pp. 97–98. That Ayrer himself did not believe that much effect could be produced on the spectators by instructive exhortations is shown by the words which he puts into the mouth of the ' English fool, Jann,' in his *Valentino und Urso*:

> Were I a moral to draw
> From the acting you saw
> You would not listen to me:
> For this is your adage :
> Shorten the sermon, lengthen the sausage.

and of the knightly classes, but in these plays all ages and classes could find entertainment.' [1]

Ayrer's plays were essentially intended for the burgher circles. Duke Henry Julius of Brunswick in all his pieces catered for the wants of higher circles, and this was equally the case with his tragedy of the year 1594, 'Vom ungerathenen Sohn,' which was performed before the assembled court. From an artistic and aesthetic point of view this play is worthless, but from the standpoint of the history of culture and civilisation it is of quite special importance, because it shows plainly how general must have been the decay and corruption of taste if such food could be supplied to the highest classes of society by a prince who in learned attainments excelled many of his social standing. Nothing worse in the way of murder and horror plays was produced in the whole century. The story of the tragedy is as follows. Nero, the younger son of Duke Severus, endeavours to get into his own hands, by 'inhuman and unheard of deeds of slaughter,' the government of the land, which devolves on his elder brother Probus. As, however, his courage is not up to the mark, his counsellors instruct him that 'if he can procure human blood, or the heart of a child, and roast it on coals and eat it, he will be nerved to carry out his enterprise.' Nero adopts the advice, takes his own illegitimate son into a wood, 'puts one knee on the boy's throat, turns up his sleeves, takes a knife, cuts his body open and scoops blood out of it with a glass and places it by his side. Then he takes the heart out and throws the body into a hole; after which he takes up the glass, mixes wine with the blood and drinks it up; he lays the heart on a

[1] Opus theatricum (cf. Goedeke, *Grundriss*, ii. 546, No. 4), preface.

fire of coals, bakes it and eats it. When he has done all this, he goes away, saying : ' Now methinks I am so bold that if the devil were to meet me I should charge at him.' Then he goes ' with an axe in his hand,' to his father, who is asleep in the garden, ' puts the puncheon on his head and knocks it in with the axe,' heedless of his father's cries of anguish. ' Blow follows blow ; and he strikes him on the neck so that he kills him, draws the puncheon out of his head, fills up the hole in the head with earth, and says : What a hard life the old rogue had ! ' Immediately afterwards he strangles the son of his brother, cuts his mother's throat, and goes ' silently away without being seen.' He poisons his sister-in-law, and ' runs a dagger through his brother's body so that he falls down dead.' Then he says : ' I must go now, since all my business has been so success-ful, and order a banquet, and make myself merry and jovial with my guests, for a bad day should be followed by a good evening ; to tell the truth, all this work has somewhat tired me.' Before the banquet begins, how-ever, he ' hastily and in all secrecy ' has the heads of three of his father's councillors cut off, and a chamber-lain ' himself cuts his tongue out of his head and falls on the ground.' The table is then laid. Nero and his three councillors ' laugh, drink, and shout, order the musicians to perform, indulge in exuberant mirth, and call constantly for more food. At last, when their merriment is at its highest, the viands suddenly dis-appear from three of the dishes, and there appear instead the three decapitated heads. At this they all start up from the table terror-stricken, and the heads vanish.' In consequence of this incident two of Nero's councillors ' stab each other to death,' and the physician, who had given the poison to kill Nero's sister-in-law, takes poison himself, 'roars horribly, scratches about him with hands and feet, and finally expires.' Nero 'paces up and down in great terror, and then lies down in the garden to sleep.' But no sooner has he laid himself down ' than his son's ghost appears with a flask hanging round his throat, and in one arm a pot with coals in it, and his breast slit open in front and bleeding ; he is playing on a zither, and walks three times round Nero without speaking a word. Nero wakes up and screams : " Help, oh God ! What is this ? " ' ' The ghost instantly vanishes, and Nero lies down again to sleep. Meanwhile his father's ghost comes, and has the axe in his hand and the puncheon in his head, walks round him playing on a bandore or lute.' . . . Then comes the ghost of his brother's son, with a cord round his throat, and foam on his mouth, and playing the zither ; the ghosts of his mother and sister-in-law also appear. At last ' comes his brother's ghost, with a dagger in his body, and with him are three councillors with heads cut off, and each of them carries his head in a dish ; they walk round him playing on lutes.' Nero quakes and trembles. He goes out into the wood. ' When he comes to the wood he sees the three dead men lying there, and as he comes near the dead men raise them-selves up with eyes turned the wrong way, and wide-open mouths.' Nero's hair stands on end. ' Meanwhile his son appears and says : Vengeance on thee, for having eaten thine own flesh and drunk thine own blood.' The other ghosts all appear again, first singly, and then all together, and call out : ' Vengeance, *Zetermordio*.' ' Nero writhes and cringes, tears open his doublet and bellows frightfully like an ox.' ' He

bellows and screams out, Oh, woe is me, woe is me!'
'Unsheathes his dagger and tries to stab himself; but
he cannot do so, for the dagger breaks in two'; equally
vain are his efforts to hang himself, or to poison himself. When no means avail he again begins 'to writhe
and cringe, to bellow like an ox, to scratch about with
his hands and feet,' and finally he calls up the devils.
'The devils come with great, horrible screamings and
carry him off.'

This 'terrible end,' it says in an epilogue, ought 'to
serve as a warning to the gracious lords, and to everybody of whatever station.'[1]

With such debased, corrupt taste in high circles as
well as in the lower grades of the people it is easily
conceivable that in the new dramatic art, 'side by side
with murder and assassination, the most unblushing
profligacy and indecent buffoonery' should play a
leading part.

In a religious book of instruction of the year 1593,
it is complained that 'most of the comedies no longer
contain godly and useful matter, are no longer Christianly
respectable and sober, but are full of obscene and
immoral things, with all sorts of improper tales, wanton
gestures and maskings, which are most highly pernicious
both for young and old, but especially for the young;
for there is now a swarm of all sorts of foreign people,
for the most part godless Italian and English comedians,
who act such things in many of the towns, and we
may well ask with St. Augustine and other holy
teachers: Is there anything too indecent and disreputable to be represented publicly in plays? The
authorities ought to interfere, and above all to forbid

[1] *Schauspiele des Herzogs Heinrich Julius*, No. 6, pp. 335–400.

the indecent plays of the French comedians and
spectacle-writers under pain of severe punishment.'[1]
'These beautiful writers,' says another contemporary
on this subject, 'introduce into their comedies now a
young fellow who lays bare his burning heart, now a
paramour who triumphantly relates how he has carried
on his illicit loves, now a company of prostitutes,
&c. &c., and then the spectators are shown how all these
people lie, cheat, swear false oaths, scold, steal, mock
at all innocence, justice and honour, carry on lewd
intrigues, dishonour women, and so forth : and all this
is praised, commended to the audience. . . . Dear
reader, what class, what sex, what age or youth do
they not contaminate ?   Are there any women, young
or old, on whose chastity they do not make
attempts ?'[2]

To what extent the 'English comedians'—those in
Frankfort-on-the-Main for instance—laid themselves
out essentially to gratify the lower appetites, is markedly
seen in a description by Marx Mangold in 1597 of the
proceedings at the fair of that place. We are told
that

> On the Main there was such trumpeting and drumming,
> All sorts of people flocking to the show ;
> To see a comedy performed they all were coming,
> A play about Susannah acted like to life
> In honour of each modest maid and wife :
> A play, too, of the Emperor Octavius,
> To whom Knight Galmy was obsequious.

Mangold visited the 'English theatre,' of which he had
heard so much :

[1] Preface to a new edition of Geiler von Kaisersberg's pamphlet :
Wie man sich halten sol bei einem sterbenden Menschen (without locality,
1593), Bl. B 2.

[2] Fickler, *Traktat*, Bl. 35 ff. ; cf. Bl. 75.

> How the fool therein, whose name was Jan,
> At joking was such a capital man :
> Which I endorse with all my heart,
> He is a master of the art ;
> So well, too, he transforms his features,
> That he looks not like any human creatures.
> He wears a never pinching shoe,
> In his trowsers there is room for two,
> And they have such a flap !
> The jumper, too, I fain would praise
> For the height to which he springs,
> And, likewise, for other things ;
> Graceful he is in all his ways,
> In dancing and in all his movements, &c. &c.[1]

In the year 1605 an English troop promised the council that they ' intended to act proper and pleasant comedies and tragedies in the High German tongue ' ; but their ' indecent jokes and foolish get-up ' were so offensive that the following Easter the council would not allow them to perform at all. Later on leave was again granted them to act. At times the rush of the people to these plays was so great that the preachers inveighed publicly against ' their inordinate attendance at the English theatre.' ' The English comedians,' says a poetical ' Discourse on the Frankfort Fair,' ' attract more people than do the preachers.'

> They'd rather stand four hours at the play
> Than one hour in the church, where they
> Quick fall asleep on benches, for
> One hour of church they find a bore.
> And yet they see such worthless stuff
> Acted that they often laugh
> At the fools who parted with their cash to see them.[2]

At Ulm in 1606 and 1609 the English comedians

---

[1] Reprint, by E. Kelchner, in the *Mittheilungen des Vereins für Gesch. und Alterthumskunde Frankfurts*, vi. 355–356, 359–360.   Goedeke, *Grundriss*, ii. pp. 526–527, Nos. 18 and 19.

[2] Mentzel, p. 46 ff. (cf. 26), 58, 59.

obtained leave to act on condition that ' they abstained from godless and immodest things, and all impropriety.' [1] The council at Elbing inhibited the proceedings of an English company in 1605, ' because they had introduced disgraceful things into their comedies.' [2] At the Electoral court at Dresden, in 1617, the ladies of the court expressed the wish that the English ' might not be allowed to play any longer.' [3]

The unutterable indecencies which the actors were pleased to offer for the ' delight and amusement of the spectators,' are soundly satirised in the ' Landstörtzer ' of Aegidius Albertinus.[4]

The ' English comedians,' we read in the preface to the collection of ' English Comedies and Tragedies,' published at Leipzig in 1620, ' have in our days, partly by skilful invention, partly by charm of gestures, and more often still by eloquent language, obtained great praise both from high and low persons.' For this reason, ' For the enjoyment of all lovers of comedy and tragedy these very fine, excellent and choice pieces are now published.' [5] The preface of the second part of this collection which appeared ten years later under the title of ' Liebeskampf,' actually boasted that it might be learnt ' from these tragedies and comedies how people should order their lives as good citizens, maintain themselves respectably and honourably in all virtues, and avoid all evil lusts.' [6] As a matter of

[1] K. Trautmann, in the *Archiv für Litteraturgesch.* xiii. 320–321.
[2] Goedeke, *Grundriss*, ii. p. 530, No. 62. Proelss, p. 153.
[3] Meissner, p. 61.   [4] Albertinus, *Landstörtzer*, pp. 285–289.
[5] *Englische Komödien*, preface, A. 3, and title.
[6] *Liebeskampf* (1630) Bl. A³. A catalogue of the different pieces of the first and second parts in Goedeke, *Grundriss*, ii. 544. Fuller details in Tittmann, *Schauspiele*, ii. p. xvii. ff., and *Schauspiele der englischen Komödianten*, p. vii. ff. ** Bolte, *Die Singspiele* (operas) *der englischen*

fact, ' only the exact opposite ' was likely to be learned
from them.[1] The relations of the sexes were treated

*Komödianten und ihrer Nachfolger in Deutschland, Holland und Skan-
dinavien* (Hamburg, 1893), says of the species of literature which appeared
in Germany in 1596, p. 6 : ' The subject-matter of the operas is for the
most part indecent and vulgar, the humour coarse. In the frequent
presentations of illicit love relations the deceit of the faithless wife and the
cleverness of the lover, who is often a debauched monk, sometimes a
pupil or student, as in the Italian novels and in many German farces, are
generally made to triumph over the simplicity of the cuckold. Other
favourite motives are the quarrelsomeness and love of dominion of women,
the ridiculousness of love-sick pedants and doting old men, the exorcising
of devils and the apparition of ghosts.'

[1] ' The coarseness of these English comedies existed undoubtedly in
the rough originals ' . . . ' but it is probable that those who worked them
up later on heightened the effect from their own love of filth. All in them
that is meant for wit is essentially low and vulgar, full of disgusting obscenities, such as are scarcely to be found in the Nuremberg carnival farces ;
indecent actions on the public stage such as even the Nuremberg play-
writers would not have dared to represent. These professional players
travelled about Germany with their bloody abominations, filthy jests,
and gorgeous rags, gave their services for very trifling pay, and made the
theatre and play-actors altogether contemptible. That they, and they
only, should have met with approval at the courts and in the large towns
is not astonishing in Germany in 1600.' Goedeke, ii. 543. Devrient (i.
pp. 191–192) says : ' It often seems inconceivable—how coarse so ever we
may believe the manners of that period to have been—that women and
girls among the spectators should have been able to tolerate the unbounded
shamelessness and lasciviousness of the scenes which the Pickelhering or
the Hanswurst enacted with his wife or chamber-maid ; the talk and the
actions surpass all credibility.' ' Enough, the whole theatrical life in
Germany ' since the advent of the professional players ' down to the eighteenth century lets us into the secret of a truly brutal condition of taste
and manners.' Cf. also Genée, p. 266. It is striking that W. Wackernagel
(*Drama*, pp. 143–144) should have found it possible to say of the English
comedians : ' It was they who restored the secular drama to honour, who
brought the beloved comic element in tragedy into fitting subordination
and gave it a more artistic character.' In the main it may be said that
at the end of the sixteenth and the beginning of the seventeenth century
the comedians might be classed, as they were later by the young Lassenius,
with ' jugglers and conjurers, mountebanks, tooth-drawers, fortune-
tellers, and such like folk, who serve no other purpose than, by cunning and
dexterity, to draw money out of the purses of the common people.'
Quoted by Wackernagel, *Drama*, p. 143.

as comic matter, and that in the most low, ordinary
language, without any real humour. Actors and spectators found themselves together plunged in the deepest
mire of filth—for instance in the ' Lustiges Pickelhering-
spiel von der schönen Maria und alten Hahnrey,' [1]
or in the ' Kurzweilige, lustige Komödie von Sidonia
und Theagenes,' which were actually the favourite
pieces.[2] This play is in prose, and is adapted from
a play by the Magdeburg jurist Gabriel Rollenhagen,
which appeared in 1609 : ' Amantes amentes. Das ist
ein sehr anmutiges Spiel von der blinden Liebe, oder
wie man's deutsch nennt, von der Löfelei : alles nach Art
und Weise der jetzigen getroffenen Venus-Soldaten, auf
gut sächsisch gereimt ' [3] (*i.e.* ' Lovers are of unsound
mind.' A pleasing play on blind love, in the style of
modern Venus-soldiers—all in good Saxon rhyme).

Still more shameless than this ' pleasant play ' is the
' merry and amusing play : " Hahnenreyerey," in which
seven personages hold up to the men as it were in a
mirror the infidelity of immoral wives.' It abounds
from beginning to end with the very lowest obscenities
of talk taken from gutter language, and mostly put into

---

[1] The ninth piece of the first part of the collection.

[2] The fifth piece in the collection. Proelss (ii. 212–213) says :
' This piece belongs to the coarsest in the collection, and can scarcely be
surpassed in low cynicism and obscenity . . . and yet, down to the following century, it was one of the favourite dramas of the period.'

[3] Gaedertz (pp. 33–35) mentions six editions of this comedy. Its
' skilful composition ' and its ' manifold interest as regards language,
literature and the history of culture are undoubted.' But Gaedertz actually
says at p. 100 : ' It is perhaps to be lamented that our century not only
has no taste for scenes which at that period certainly did not occasion
disgust, but is even revolted by them.' The assumption that numbers
of scenes, as they are here presented (including ' the long, immodest
prayer of Lucretia,' see p. 28), caused no disgust at that time is a severe
condemnation of the age. In the year 1614 the performance of this

the mouth of a monk ' Desiderius,' who plays a principal part in the piece.[1]

On the same level stands a play which, under the name of ' Pamphilus Münnigsfeind,' was dedicated to the ' Pope's highly enlightened Esauites' (Jesuits): ' Nolbruder Curd : *ein umb die Kloster-Nonnen, auch umb der benachbarten Dörfer Bauernweiber wohl verdienter Visitator Venereus.*' The hero is caught in an attempt at adultery and ' puts an end to himself in his priestly raiment ' ; ' very amusing to read.' At the end a hymn is parodied :

> With diligence to God we'll pray
> That many may die in the self-same way.[2]

---

piece met with ' the liveliest acclamation ' at the Court of the Elector John Sigismund of Brandenburg ; so Gaedertz reports, p. 83. In the epilogue of his play Rollenhagen says he hopes that ' it will have a good effect.'

> Since many thereby will be instructed
> As to how love suits are conducted.
> Each one will learn the lesson plain
> That all precautions are in vain
> To escape from love ; each will be taught
> He too must needs by love be caught.
> Love's fire, sweet, all must enjoy,
> Young, old, son, daughter, girl and boy,
> Scholar, burgher, peasant-folk,
> You've seen to-day beneath love's yoke.
> Oh, well for him who so proceeds
> With his love affair that he succeeds !
> But woe to him who what he seeks finds not !
> His is indeed a sore accursed lot.

[1] Without locality, 1618. (Quoted by Hayn, p. 101.) To a great extent in Low German language. Cf. especially what the monk has to say in Act v, scene 4.

[2] Gottsched, i. 175–176. Goedeke, *Grundriss*, ii. 375, No. 234. From the *Nachtbüchlein* of Valentine Schumann (see below, p. 190), to which he refers as his source, Matthew Scharfschmidt, vicar at Zeitz, composed *Ein kurtzweilig Spiel von einem bepstischen Pfaffen im Land zu Franken, wie es demselbigen über der Bulerey mit eines Wintzers Weib so übel ergangen* (' An amusing play about a popish priest in the land of Franconia, and how it went ill with him concerning his love intrigue with a vine-dresser's

'Not least among the causes,' wrote Aegidius Albertinus, 'why the young lapse into immorality and
lasciviousness are the comedies, spectacles and plays,
which are performed at the princely courts, or in the
houses of the great, or in the public buildings devoted
to the purpose.' 'These plays become all the more
objectionable and evil on account of the godlessness and
wickedness of the people who act them.' For they
are generally idle, dissolute, crafty, knavish, shameless
and godless people; yea, what is more, there are found
among them outlaws, anarchists, traitors, gypsies and
vile heretics.' 'Since it is true that immoral talk
corrupts good habits, what must not be the effect of the
horrible, disgraceful things that are presented to view,
seeing that the sense of sight is much sharper than that
of hearing.' 'Whereas also the Holy Ghost forbids us
even to look upon or listen to a dissolute and jumping
or dancing woman, so that we may not fall into her
snares, who shall dare to be so very audacious and
reckless as to go into such manifest danger and into
the midst of such hellish passions against the command of the Holy Ghost? For whereas such female
comedians are generally handsome and seductive, and
destitute of all propriety, they put forth all their arts
like sirens to enchant and bewitch men. . . . Hence
we cannot but greatly wonder that this highly noxious
vermin should be everywhere welcomed by the authorities in the towns, admired and encouraged, and

wife') (Eisleben, 1589); cf. H. Holstein in the *Zeitschr. für deutsche Philologie*, xviii. 435-436.   ** A similar theme is handled in the comedy *Von
zwei jungen Eheleuten*, which was written by the painter Tobias
Stimmer.   *Tob. Stimmer, Comedia*.   With eighteen pen-and-ink drawings
by the same, published for the first time by J. Oeri.   Frauenfeld,
1891.

actually entertained by many princes and lords at
their courts, paid by them and held in honour.' [1]

[1] *Hausspolizei*, Siebenter Theil, pp. 151ᵇ–152. ** The wives and
daughters of the English comedians did not take part in the dramatic
performances ; up to the middle of the seventeenth century the female
parts were always acted by men. Creizenach, p. xv. In Italy, in the
last quarter of the sixteenth century, women had begun to appear on the
stage ; cf. Dejob, p. 216. Pope Sixtus V. in 1588 gave permission to the
wandering players to perform in private houses, and to the company
of ' Desiosi,' the most famous one of Italy, to act in public, but the
performances were to take place in the daytime and the women's parts
to be taken by men. Cf. Von Hübner, *Sixtus V.* (Leipzig, 1871), ii. 142.
Albertinus, who spoke out so strongly about dissolute plays, was by no
means an opponent of the theatre in general ; on the contrary, an eulogist
of ' true Christian dramatic art.' ' If the lives and deeds,' he said, ' of
those persons who have illumined the world by their virtues are presented
to mankind as it were alive in the public drama ' this would tend not
only to the entertainment of the mind, but also to the encouragement of
Christian behaviour. ' Many a godless and erring human being will be
moved by plays of this sort, setting forth either the rewards of the pious
or the terrible punishments of the godless, to repent and lead a godly life.'
Landstörtzer, pp. 284–285.

CHAPTER IV

LIGHT LITERATURE : BOOKS OF JESTS AND LOVE STORIES
—LAMPOONS—WRITINGS HOSTILE TO WOMEN—ON
THE ART OF DRINKING—AMADIS ROMANCES

THE perversion, coarsening and debasement of popular
taste which the stage performances had brought to
light had also become increasingly evident, in the
second half of the century especially, in the domain of
light literature. We can only rejoice, as far as this
branch of literature is concerned, that the popular
books of the fifteenth century still continued to find a
large circle of readers, and that the number of these
books was increased by a few new ones which were
characterised by a healthy tone and an unspoilt instinct
for the feeling of the people.

Among the old books the one that had by far the
widest circulation was ' Till Eulenspiegel,' [1] the most
important production of German popular humour,
unsurpassed in perfection of structure and masterly
style ; the book was frequently translated into foreign
languages.[2] As an imitation of this book there appeared towards the end of the century the so-called
Brandenburg Eulenspiegel, Hans Clavert, whose ' Werck-
liche Historien ' (' True Tales ') were first published in

---

[1] See our remarks, vol. i. pp. 298, 299.
[2] Concerning the numerous editions of this book, cf. Lappenberg,
pp. 147–220. Goedeke, *Grundriss*, i. 344–347 ; cf. also Bobertag, i. 173 ff.

1587 by Bartholomew Krüger, town clerk and organist at Trebbin. This is one of the few really popular books of the period, but, in contradistinction to the earlier Eulenspiegel's propriety in respect of sexual matters, it contains some stories of which it can by no means be said, as Krüger maintained, 'that there is nothing in Hans Clavert but what deserves praise.' [1] A work free from all improprieties, and admirable in its execution, but, viewed from the standpoint of patriotism, a painful monument of German humour, is the ' Buch von den Schildbürgern ' (' Book of Simpletons '), which appeared also at the close of the century, and was announced on the title-page as containing ' Wonderful, extraordinary, unheard of, and hitherto unwritten histories and deeds of the Schildbürger in Misnopotamia.' [2]

This book is compiled in a masterly manner from different ' books of farces '—*i.e.* from collections of little stories strung together, tales, fables, anecdotes, such as, printed in handy, convenient shape, formed an essential part of popular reading.

The first place among collections of this sort, both for form and contents, belongs to the volume ' Schimpf und Ernst,' published by the Barefoot monk John Pauli in 1522. Of this book forty-four editions are known to have been published up to 1618. [3]

[1] Latest edition by Th. Raehse (Halle-a.-S., 1882), p. 5. Cf. *Die Geschichte*, pp. 9–10, 15–16, 33.

[2] Frankfort-on-the-Main, 1597. Goedeke, *Grundriss*, ii. 560. Scherer (*Anfänge*, p. 61) says with truth : ' The classic book of the *Schildbürger* is in its political aspect a melancholy symbol.' ** Cf. *Vierteljahrschrift für Litteraturgesch.* published by Seuffert, vol. i. (Weimar, 1888) p. 471 ff. for the locality and author of the *Schildbürgerbuch*.

[3] A copy of the first impression by H. Österley is in the *Bibl. des Stuttgarter Litterar. Vereins*, vol. lxxxv. Stuttgart, 1866. Pauli's ' good-

To what depth public taste sank later on is seen
by comparison of this book with those books of amusing
stories, which received their first impulse from the
' Rollwagenbüchlein' of Jörg Wickram of Kolmar,
published in 1555. The short stories collected together
by Wickram were intended to relieve the tediousness of
the long journeys in the then customary ' Rollwagen,'
' to enliven the heavy melancholy spirits of the
travellers.' With appeal to utterances of Christ,
Wickram inveighs in his preface against those writers
who introduced into their stories ' scandalous, disgraceful words,' and had little respect for the feelings
of ' modest, respectable wives, or even of young girls.'

humoured way of looking at things maintains the happy mean between
fear of offensive coarseness and temerity,' says Goedeke, *Grundriss*, i. 404.
Gervinus writes (ii. 302–303) : ' What a delicate sense of selection Pauli
had, what admirable naive prose he wrote ! How vivid are his narratives !
They make one feel as if in the very midst of the world he describes, so full
of life and movement ! How wonderfully he localises all that he borrows
from the old, making it all present and living ! ' ' With him the comic
and the serious alternate with wise intention ; the strong repulsion felt by
all sound human understanding against everything that is depraved is the
all-pervading motive which inspired the whole ; humour and wit were the
spice, instruction the substance of the food offered ; they were mixed in
such nice proportions that both satiety and disgust were avoided. On the
other hand all later collections erred in one or other of two directions :
either the didactic purpose and intention robbed them of even harmless
naïveté, or else teaching and serious earnest were left out altogether,
and jesting and nastiness offered for entertainment.' By a confusion of
John Pauli with Paul Pfeddersheim, K. Veith in his work *Über den
Barfüsser Joh. Pauli und das von ihm verfasste Volksbuch Schimpf und
Ernst* (Vienna, 1839), erroneously assumed that Paul was of Jewish origin,
and nearly all later historians of literature, such as Österley, Goedeke
and others, share this error. Cf. Eubel, *Gesch. der oberdeutschen (Strassburger) Minoritenprovinz* (Würzburg, 1886), pp. 64–67. ** In addition
to P. Eubel's proofs that J. Pauli and P. Pfeddersheim were two different
people, cf. *Analecta Franciscana* (Quaracchi, 1887), ii. 534, where P.
Pfeddersheim, in 1504, appears as guardian of the conventual cloister at
Bern. Eubel, *l.c.* p. 66.

But his own book is so brimful of indecent matter [1]
that the Mansfeld Chancellor Lauterbeck, in his
Dialogue on the proper education of the young, expresses himself as follows : ' It fills me with astonishment that such things should be allowed to be printed,
for we pretend to be Christians, and according to St.
Paul's teaching we should use no unchaste language,
still less write it, and have it published in print to
the detriment of the young' ; from the ' Rollwagen '
of Wickram ' the young especially would learn nothing
but scandal and immorality.' [2]   Not less unfit for
youthful readers were ' the fine ancient examples and
histories ' which Wickram wrote ' for the pleasant
instruction and use of the tender young people ' under
the title ' Die sieben Hauptlaster sammt ihren schönen
Früchten und Eigenschaften ' (' The Seven Principal
Vices, with their beautiful Fruits and Qualities '). ' In
idle moments,' he said, ' the young might divert themselves herein.' [3]

A worthy follower of Wickram was James Frey, [4]

---

[1] See the edition of H. Kurz (Leipzig, 1865), pp. 15, 36–44, 78, 135, 139,
165.

[2] Lauterbecken, p. 10.

[3] *Die sieben Hauptlaster* (Goedeke, ii. 464, No. 16), edition of 1556,
preface.   Wickram also wrote a *Schöner und nützlicher Dialogus, in
welchem angezogen wird das mechtig Hauptlaster der Trunkenheit* (' A fine
and useful Dialogue in which appears the strong Vice of Drunkenness '),
Goedeke, ii. 463, No. 13.   He himself ' was greatly addicted to drinking,'
from which his faithful ' friend and brother ' Mathis Ruffer, burgher of
Kaisersberg, tried with small result to keep him back.   Scherer, *Anfänge*,
p. 3.   ** For the life of Wickram see the ' Archivalischen Nachrichten
von Waldner' in the *Zeitschr. für Gesch. des Oberrheins*, N. F. vii. 320 ff.

[4] ** Concerning this writer nothing was known hitherto except what
he himself recounted.   From some Strassburg documents and from the
archives of the courts of justice of Maursmünster, begun in 1553, G.
Könnecke, in the *Zeitschr. f. vergleichende Litteraturgesch. u. Renaissancelitteratur* of M. Koch and L. Geiger, N. F. (1889), ii. 199–205, brings forward

also an Alsatian, author of the 'Gartengesellschaft'
of the year 1556, 'wherein much merry talk, satire, intrigues and other amusing tales, either from history or
fables might be found.' Just as according to its preface
the 'Rollwagenbüchlein' promised to be 'proper and
amusing to read,' so Frey also pretended that he 'would
introduce nothing unsuitable for honourable women
and maidens to read,' for 'to women and maidens all
honour, chastity, and reverence must in every way be
shown.'[1] 'Every delicate-minded young lady,' the
Frankfort printer, Sigmund Feyerabend, assured the
public in a new edition of the 'Rollwagenbüchlein'
and the 'Gartengesellschaft,' 'could read the book
without any offence to her modesty.'[2] On the other
hand Cyriakus Spangenberg reckoned the 'Gartengesellschaft' among the books 'which had come from
the devil to poison the young and to throw contempt
on marriage, and to disgrace the feminine sex,' and he
urgently warned the public against reading such immoral writings.[3] As a matter of fact Frey's collection
contained a large number of extremely objectionable
stories, which were related in anything but a serious
and proper tone.

The 'Gartengesellschaft' was followed in 1557 by
the 'Wegkürzer' of Frey's countryman Martin Mon-

---

proof that James Frey 'was a native of Strassburg, that he bore the nick-
name of *Scharwächter*, was public papal and imperial town clerk at Maursmünster, and had himself recorded as such in 1545, 1549, and from June
24, 1553, to April 29, 1562.' It is probable that his death occurred in 1562,
certain it is that in 1571 he was no longer town clerk. See also, now, the
edition of Frey's *Gartengesellschaft*, prepared by Bolte, which appeared in
1896.

[1] Edition of 1556, preface.
[2] See *Archiv für die Gesch. des Buchhandels*, v. 157.
[3] C. Spangenberg, *Ehespiegel*, pp. 437b–438.

tanus, an equally indecent production, though, according to the verdict of the author, it was 'a beautiful and amusing little book, beyond measure entertaining, and very useful for the young; and written not only for the benefit of young lads, but also for men and women of all sorts.' [1]

Still more morally objectionable than the above-named writers are Valentine Schumann of Leipzig and Michael Lindener from the same neighbourhood,[2] men of dissolute conduct, who in their so-called 'Schwankbücher' deliberately laid themselves out to suit a circle of readers accustomed to all sorts of indecencies. 'The amusing stories' in Schumann's 'Nacht-büchlein' (1559) were meant 'to be read or recited at night after supper, or on the road and in the streets.' In the dedication of the second part of the book he says 'a widow' had reproached him in a letter for having put into the first part of the book 'coarse jests and anecdotes which were not fit for married people to

---

[1] *Wegkürzer*, &c. (Goedeke, ii. 466, No. 4, 1). *Widmung* and *An die Leser*, A 3, 4. Cf. Bobertag, i. 138. 'M. makes most diligent use,' says Goedeke, 'of the out-and-out filthiest expressions, and depicts sexual matters with an amount of detail and with a gusto which make one wonder how he can say of his book that it is calculated to give joy to those who are at the point of death, and that it brings God to the mind.' If the 'anecdotes told by James Frey and Martin Montanus,' says Gervinus (ii. 304), 'are not full of obscenity, scandal and impropriety, that period must have had such strange ideas on the subject that we with our ideas cannot come near them.' ** J. Bolte, also, *Martin Montanus' Schwankbücher* (1557–1566), Stuttgart, 1899 (Stuttg. Litter. Verein), says (p. xii.): 'The first thing that strikes the eye of the critic is the coarseness of his taste and his delight in the most indecent stories. He describes sexual things with a nakedness and an amount of detail such as may be found indeed in carnival plays, but which has hitherto not been met with in German narrative.' Here too, in opposition to Scherer and E. Schmidt, proof is adduced that Montanus was Protestant.

[2] See C. Wendeler in the *Archiv für Litteraturgesch.* vii. 454.

read, for they were too coarse and indecent, just as this
same widow was too modest and refined.' [1] . . . But
even the ' Nachtbüchlein ' is outdone by Lindener's
' Katzipori ' and ' Rastbüchlein.' The author himself
calls his stories ' new pranks, strange freaks, unheard-
of tales, covered obscenities,' and writes for ' good,
pious, select, round and many-coloured " Schaudel-
butzen," called by the Italians " Cazzipori." These
poor fellows in our German language are termed stork's
beaks, duck's feet, goose collars, pig's noses, ass's ears,
goat's horns, wolf's teeth, cat's tails, ox heads, calf's
feet.' The ' Rastbüchlein ' Lindener dedicated ' to the
noble Anthony Baumgärtner, a gentleman adorned
with all virtues,' who will accept this little volume of
tales and anecdotes as the work of a good, pious man.'
In the first pieces of the collection he at once reveals
an intimate acquaintance with the language of brothels,
and he announces his intention ' to arrange and classify
all immodest forms of speech so that the poor devils
who are fond of hearing foolish tales may have plenty
to laugh at.' [2] Whilst, however, in these writings he

[1] ' It is not uninteresting,' says Bobertag concerning Schumann,
' that in the middle of the sixteenth century it was as easy as it is in ours
to make scandal the means of advertising. That our friend occasionally
parades morality, quotes Bible texts in quantities, and brings in the parable
of the bee which takes the good and not the bad out of flowers, is part of
the game, and is a way of gaining favour with the more serious readers,
while for the lovers of " coarse stories " he indicates in the preface to the
second part the pages where these occur.' *Archiv für Litteraturgesch.*
vi. 137. ** Later works on Schumann criticised in the *Jahresberichte für
neuere deutsche Litteraturgesch.* Bd. 3, ii. 3, No. 19 ff. ; Bd. 4, ii. 4, No. 36.
A carefully prepared new edition of Schumann's *Nachtbüchlein,* with a
valuable introductory notice about the author, was published by Bolte
in the *Bibliotek des Stuttgarter Litterar. Vereins,* cxcvii. (Tübingen, 1893).

[2] Both works are newly published by Fr. Lichtenstein in the *Bibl.
des Stuttgarter Litterarischen Vereins,* clxiii. ** ' Frey's *Gartengesellschaft* (1556), Martinus Montanus' *Wegkürzer* (1557), Michael Lindener's

surpassed even himself in dirt and coarseness, he was
all the same ' a pious poet ' ; and indulged profusely
in appeals to Christ, which in his mouth border on
blasphemy.[1]

Out of the ' Rollwagenbüchlein,' the ' Gartengesellschaft,' the ' Wegkürzer,' ' Katzipori,' and other similar
collections, Bernhard Herzog, Fischart's stepfather,
compiled the ' Schiltwacht,' ' for the use and pious
edification of watchmen and other such drowsy and
melancholy beings.' [2]

Insipid, nasty anecdotes and witticisms abounded
also among the ' 627 stories of Claus Narr ' which
Wolfgang Bütner, preacher at Wolferstedt in the
Weimar district, presented to the people in 1572 under
the conviction that ' the pure words and good sayings
of this good man would be preferred to the Eulenspiegel scandals and intolerable vileness.' [3] The book

Rastbüchlein (1558) and *Cazzipori*, and Valentin Schumann's *Nachtbüchlein* (1558–1559), in the opinion of Vogt-Koch (*Deutsche Litteraturgesch.* p. 235), ' are as a ladder leading deeper and deeper down into a mire
of filth.'

[1] Cf. C. Wendeler's *Anführungen* in the *Archiv für Litteraturgesch.* vii.
440 ff. ; ** and A. Hartmann in the *Oberbayrisches Archiv*, xlvi. (1889),
31 ff.

[2] Wendeler, p. 145.   Goedeke, *Grundriss*, v. 472, No. 11.

[3] Cf. Lappenberg, p. 382.   Article on Claus Narr and Wolfgang
Bütner by Schnorr v. Carolsfeld in the *Archiv für Litteraturgesch.* vi. 277–
328.   ' It is interesting,' says Bobertag (i. 194), ' from the point of view of
culture and civilisation, to see the sort of tame, rubbishy jokes that people
enjoyed in those days, and also the indecent—what I might call *abdominal
jests*—which they could tolerate.   And from this point of view it is to be
observed also that the particular circle which Claus amused, and in which,
therefore, the book which immortalised him might be expected to find
readers, was by no means an inferior one either in culture or morals, but
on the contrary it was the circle which had for its centre the court of the
head of Protestant Germany—the Elector of Saxony.' Also ' the compiler of
the Claus-Buch was no obscure scribbler, but a clergyman, active also in
the field of letters.'   ' Our own age has, it is true, anecdote-books of very

had gone through at least ten editions by the year 1617.[1]

'All sorts of improper anecdotes and stories '—such is the complaint of a pulpit orator, Beinhaus, in 1617— 'which are printed in larger numbers every year, and sold by letter-carriers and hawkers in town and country often for a few pennies only, belong nowadays, with innumerable love songs, to the most prized articles, and are read in carriages and ships, at social gatherings and drinking carousals, and boys and girls are even allowed to take them with them to school and to divert themselves with them to the extreme danger of their souls and their salvation.' 'The market is full of Venus booklets of all sorts, and the indecent scribes lay themselves out to attract notice by the shameless titles of their books.'[2]

Like Beinhaus, and even earlier—in 1581—John Fickler, councillor of the Prince of Salzburg, had inveighed against the 'amusing books and tracts, full of good farce and funny pranks.' 'In these,' he says, 'we find very cleverly and skilfully written stories, some of them true, but most of them made up fables, with a semblance of truth, showing in a pleasantly satirical manner the success which numbers of people have had in illicit love intrigues, and describing the way in which men can make themselves attractive to women, and women and maidens to men and youths, and also teaches how in all relations of life people can cheat and lie to one

---

unclean, senseless and objectionable contents, but these are in all respects obscure, and have no recognised place in literature.'

[1] Goedeke, *Grundriss*, ii. 558, No. 3.

[2] Beinhaus, p. 4. Here follows a list of titles not suitable for translation. Readers are referred to vol. vi. of original German, p. 424.

another, citizens to the ruling authorities, parents to children, the wife to the husband, the husband to the wife, the daughter to the mother, the son to the father, the maid to her mistress, the lackey to his lord.' From the reading of such books there followed ' fornication, adultery, disgrace, vice, all which were now in full swing and carried on without any shame.' 'This is the only good that comes out of these beautiful books of diversion, such as the " Cento Novelle," " Gartenge-sellschaft," " Rollwagen," " Cazopori," " Rast- und Nachtbüchlein," and many others, more than we can count up, which are sold here and everywhere in the shops to the ruin of good morals.' . . .

Fickler reckoned as ' foremost among such books Luther's " Table-talk," so full of indecent, stinking tales, lame jokes, and licentious language, such stuff as was also found most improperly intermixed in some of his other secular writings.' [1] Aegidius Albertinus, also, the most important popular bookseller of the Catholic Restoration period in Bavaria,[2] spoke as severely as Fickler against ' the disgraceful, lascivious and unsuit-able books and rhymes.' 'Not only,' he wrote, ' are the bookshops filled with these, but they are exposed openly in the streets and actually offered for sale in private houses, where their packs of cards and their bats (Nachtbüchlein ?) are bought by servants and apprentices, read and glossed over. What do you think such scoundrelly writers, poets, pedants and beggarly grammarians, who thus stir up the passions of the young and make the old cold-blooded fools waste their cash, are worth ? What sort of punishment do you

---

[1] Fickler, *Traktat*, preface, Bl. 2ᵇ–5 ; cf. Bl. 52 ff.
[2] ** Cf. Von Reinhardstöttner, *Forschungen*, ii. 86 ff.

think they deserve ? But justice and law has nothing to say on this matter. When a man poisons his neighbour, everybody curses him and says his head should be cut off, but when anyone spreads the poison of unchastity, with deadly injury to countless souls and bodies, through a whole country, and knows how to smear the poison over cleverly with honey and to offer it openly to the people, that same villain is brought forward everywhere, endowed with great honours, and great privileges are conferred on his books. Yea, verily, and what is still more pitiable, our married men laugh hugely, and consider it a good joke when their wives and daughters have the most wanton jests and obscenities put before their eyes, hear, read, learn them by heart, and can talk glibly about them.' ' With all diligence such books are published, and in order that women and young girls, who care only for pleasure and not for domestic duties, may be able to enliven their idleness and kill time, and that they may learn soft, dulcet words and well-turned phrases, with which to make themselves agreeable.' [1]

' The amorous writers' showed ' especial grudge against the priests.'

> Priests and nuns to rate and scold
> Brings us in honour and gold,

said one of the authors of these ' exceedingly amusing stories, beyond measure edifying for all well-behaved young ladies and budding manly virtue ' :

> The young these stories love
> All other things above.[2]

To ridicule and revile the clergy was considered the chief task of nearly all the books of anecdotes :

---

[1] *Hausspolizei* (1602), Seventh Part, pp. 129–130.   [2] Beinhaus, p. 4[b].

' the accursed, idolatrous papacy was to be reduced to
impotence by their means.' Thus, for instance, Martin
Montanus tacked on to the account of an adulterous
intrigue carried on by a monk in Meissen the following statement : ' All corrupt, devilish, cunning tricks
stick in them,' the monks ; ' under their sheepskins
they are ravening wolves, they devour widows and
orphans, and make long prayers ; and not this only,
but they are on the look-out to dishonour honest citizens, their wives and children, in order to drag them into
the abyss of hell ; see there, this is what their saintly
lives are like.' [1] All sorts of scandalous tales were
taken from earlier writers, especially from Boccaccio
and Poggio, and produced ' as having happened in the
latest times,' in order, says Beinhaus, ' that the young
and others should take all the more delight in
them.' [2]

Two books by the preachers Burchard Waldis and
Erasmus Alber, belonging more or less to the domain of
humorous literature, and which had already appeared
before the ' Rollwagenbüchlein ' of Jörg Wickram,
were couched in very odious polemical style. In the
garb of fable these also in their way were intended for
the amusement and instruction of the young.

In 1548 Waldis published his ' Esopus ' ' made
quite new and put into rhyme, with a hundred new
fables.' In the dedication he assured his readers, just
as Wickram did later in the ' Rollwagen,' that ' he had
published the book for the benefit of the dear young
people, the boys and the young girls,' ' the tender
ears of the dear young folk must not be shocked by
his writing.' At the conclusion of the last ' fable ' he

---

[1] Wegkürzer, p. 98.   [2] Beinhaus, p. 5.

repeated that 'only for the pious edification of the young' he had written this book. Yet his fables, like the 'Rollwagen,' handle a large number of anecdotes and tales in the spirit and the manner of Boccaccio. Waldis exhibits a thoroughly naturalistic representation of marriage. His embitterment against the 'mad papists,' the clergy, above all against the monks and nuns, is abundantly vented in these abusive stories. The nature of his polemics is sufficiently shown by his informing 'the dear young people' that the Pope pretended to be able to release souls from eternal punishment by his absolution, even when 'God did not wish it to be done.'[1] In his calumniation of St. Francis of Assisi and St. Catherine of Siena, Waldis was the precursor of Fischart.[2] The latter, however, did not equal him in the lowness with which he expresses himself in the last fable of the third book. The author's general views of the papacy are summed up as follows :

> So has the scandalous Pope's rabble,
> Like noxious vermin with its poison,
> Overwhelmed us and submerged,
> And with its devil's dung us scourged,
> That we—shame that it should be said—
> Unto their stink and filth have prayed.

In pouring out abuse and vilification of this kind these writers took no heed whatever of their many millions of German compatriots of Catholic persuasion. They counted them as outlaws. The 'dear Protestant young people' for whom Waldis wrote might, with full faith in their instructor's words, rejoice that they were freed from such 'devil's filth'; but could their piety be increased by what Waldis wrote, and the

---

[1] *Esopus*, Book IV. Fable 1.   [2] See our remarks, vol. x. p. 40 ff.

language in which he wrote, ' of a hermit,' ' of a widow lusting after a husband,' and ' of a poor nun ' ? not to speak of many other improper stories.[1]

Erasmus Alber says in his book of forty-nine fables, published as a ' Book of Virtue and Wisdom, for the most part taken from Aesop and put into good rhymes,' [2] in the year 1550 : ' Just as to children who have worms in their bodies we give bitter worm-dust mixed with honey, even so must we catch the poor, rough, stiff-necked people with fables and pictures, for they are sweet as sugar and easy to be retained.' For this reason saintly people and Christ Himself had made use of parables, and even the devil had his fables in the papacy, in Mohammedanism, and in the Talmud, which, however, ' serve no other purpose than to enlarge the empire of the devil, and to draw people away from God and from the truth.' On the other hand, our fables

[1] See especially Book II. Fables 60, 62, 100 ; Book III. Fables 6, 83 ; Book IV. Fables 16, 17, 22, 23, 27, 40, 60, 71, 81, 89, 90, 93. We refer to fables of this kind because in books on literature we not infrequently read of the ' harmless Burchard Waldis.' Even Goedeke (*Burchard Waldis*, p. 17) is of opinion that this writer's fables ' still in the present day kindle lively delight.' ** G. Buchenau in his pamphlet on B. Waldis writes, pp. 24–25 : ' As regards Waldis' fables, Gervinus, Goedeke and Mittler have dealt with them more or less exhaustively ; it is enough here, therefore, to draw attention to the judgment of these men who are unanimous in their praise of his lifelike mode of presentation, often permeated by the finest humour, of his noble patriotic sentiments, and of the rich experience of life which is revealed in these fables. Anyone who has but once turned over the leaves of the *Esopus* will realise how far most writers of fables stand beneath Waldis, who, with the exception of Alberus, has actually only one worthy rival in this line, namely Lessing, who certainly does surpass our genial Waldis and his easy-going narrative in brevity and severity, which he often overdoes.'

[2] Frankfort-on-the-Main, 1550. ** New edition of W. Braune in the Halle collection of reprints of German literary works of the sixteenth and seventeenth centuries (Halle, 1892) ; cf. W. Kawerau, ' Die Fabeln des C. Alberus ' in the *Beil. zur Allgemein. Zeitung* of May 1, 1893, and Schnorr von Carolsfeld, *Alberus*, p. 112 ff.

minister to the service of Him who has given them, and show forth His praise and honour, teach virtue and good morals, and are productive of great benefits.' To such fables belonged, for instance, the account by a frog of the relics at Treves :

> St. Judas' kiss and Malchus' ear
> Are shown us in the higher choir ;
> I saw them all with my own eyes—
> I should have been damned for ever, otherwise.

Another fable depicts the ' great idolatry ' of the Catholics who, like the heathen, ' worship strange gods ' :

> St. Thönges was a god of swine ;
> St. Wendel a cowherd must have been ; . . .
> Vesta was a goddess of fire and flame ;
> St. Agatha was the saving name
> Christians were wont to supplicate
> In danger—all this the prophet false and great,
> The Pope, the Antichrist, has taught.

In a fable ' Vom Papstesel ' (' The pope-ass ') readers were told that by ' the ass's holiness ' adultery was looked upon only as a matter for laughter ; on the other hand :

> Who on a Friday eateth meat
> He overtakes with his lightning fleet ;
> His least command's obeyed by each
> As though 'twere God Almighty's speech.
> The whole world he's deceived, and sold
> Heaven itself for paltry gold,
> Yea, God Himself in heaven he
> Deceived—a proud ass this must be !

The fable ' Von einem Müller und Esel ' (' Of a Miller and an Ass ') gives a description of monks :

> These brothers are at liberty
> To carry out their infamy:
> Lord Belial of hell-fire flame,
> A mighty prince known far to fame,

He doth to them this freedom give
And in return they for him live, . . .
With eating, drinking, gormandising—
Their bodies, as they say, chastising—
And each one every day at table
Must eat much more than he is able.[1] . . .

Descriptions of this sort were to 'show forth the
praise and glory of God' and be of 'great benefit' to
the Protestant people.

Even Hans Wilhelm Kirchhoff's 'Wendunmuth'[2]—
comparatively speaking the best collection of tales and
anecdotes—contains not a few scandalous stories from
clerical life told with polemical bitterness. A veritable
mine of such information is found in a volume published
in 1618 at Frankfort-on-the-Main by Lazarus Sandrub,
'a peculiar lover of poetry,' under the title : 'Historische
und Poetische Kurzweil' ('Historical and Poetical
Entertainment'), 'wherein all sorts of amusing and
clever stories, beautiful and delightful poems, polite
jokes, and anecdotes' are related in rhyme. 'Coarse,
indecent, swinish, shameless and immoral buffooneries,'
says the preface, 'are carefully avoided'; everything in
the book can be read 'without annoyance or disgust.'
However, more than thirty of Sandrub's hundred and
fifty stories are directed against the regular and secular
priests as the quintessence of all immorality. To every
story he attaches a 'reminder,' in which, without any
fear of being wearisome, he repeats himself again and
again, and each time explains that the immoralities he
has been able to recount concerning one individual
apply to the whole class ; for instance : 'The " Geist-

---

[1] Frankfort edition of 1550, Fables 11, 20, 23, 30, 33, 39, 40, 48.

[2] New edition of H. Österley in the *Bibl. des Stuttgarter Litterar.
Vereins*, vols. xcv.–xcix. ** Concerning H. W. Kirchhoff († 1605) see
A. Wyss in the *Centralbl. für Bibliothekswissenschaft*, ix. 57 ff. ; cf. p. 265 ff.

losen "—I mean to say the " Geistlichen " [1]—in the
papacy stain themselves with all sorts of fornication and
profligacy, just as though they were Jews or Turks ':
auricular confession exists for scarcely any other
purpose than ' to entertain the mind with accounts of
whoredom and immorality ' ; ' the clergy of the papacy
were dapper eaters and drinkers.' . . . The Bible ' is
overlaid by the popish teachers with scandalous names
and compared to the fables of Æsop ' ; they indulge
in bestiality and sodomy.   A monk once being attacked
by a wolf, dogs came up and tore the monk to pieces,
as being a more dangerous animal than the wolf.[2]

' The priests,' Beinhaus preached, ' are more hated
in these days in Germany than the Jews, as is abundantly shown by innumerable booklets, lampoons,
rhymes and pictures ; next to them, however, women
are the most detested class, and countless scribblers
make it their business also to disseminate all sorts of
filthy, indecent scandal against the female sex, and
to write against and abuse the married state, in imitation
of the godless writer, Sebastian Franck.   Like him
they say : Nothing good comes from women, they are
all one like the other ; they do not belong to reasoning

---

[1] I have retained these German epithets as it is impossible to reproduce
the play upon words.—TRANSLATOR.

[2] *Delitiae historicae et poeticae.* Frankfort-on-the-Main, 1618.   Nos.
10 and 11 of the reprints of German literary works of the sixteenth
and seventeenth centuries (Halle, 1878), by G. Milchsack ; cf. concerning
the above-mentioned tales of scandal pp. 21, 22, 24–25, 25–26, 29, 30,
32, 34, 35, 36–37, 38, 39, 40, 53, 58, 59, 60, 61, 62, 64, 74, 75, 76, 79, 95,
96, 99, 112, 121.   It is worth while here also to draw attention to this
sort of thing, because Sandrub, like Waldis, is reckoned by many literary
critics as a harmless writer.   ' His writing,' says Kurz (*Gesch. der Litteratur.*
ii. 106), is ' always harmless ; one sees that this poet feels a genial delight
in the witty and humorous incidents which he relates, and does not
concern himself about anything else.'

animals; they are the devil's offspring. And the
youths in the streets sing about them, and have learnt
a lot about them from disgraceful books and anecdotes,
which tell of the wicked things done and said by women,
and how they deceive men, and how everything bad
and profligate proceeds from them.   This sort of
thing is read with delight and gloated over, and these
books and rhymes are the favourite wares; people
often fight for them in the bookshops.   And the sec-
tarian preachers may utter warnings against them and
say what they will, their words are thrown to the
wind; the people say the parson had better hold his
tongue, for he himself has enough to do with his own
wife to keep her respectable and bring her under control,
for the women want to rule everything and are for the
most part bold, hard-headed, unmanageable, immodest
and wanton.' [1]   Long before this a Lutheran preacher
had spoken out in the same way. ' To everybody it is
open as the day that the number of writers that write
against women and censure and abuse them far exceeds
those who have anything to say in their praise, and one
constantly finds such like abusive booklets in ships,
at social gatherings, in drinking-dens, and they are
intended to serve for amusement.   And the scribblers
delight inordinately, to the very great injury of the
young, in raking up all sorts of lewd, immoral tales
and anecdotes against women and young girls, and
publishing them as respectable and useful reading.'
' Not least among the reasons why so many witches
are burnt nowadays is the fact that innumerable writers
say such abominable things about women, and denounce
them all as wicked, venomous, and diabolical in nature;

[1] Beinhaus, p. 5[b], cf. Spangenberg, *Ehespiegel*, pp. 123, 140, 437.

and then forsooth they brag that immeasurably more
women than men are burnt for witchcraft and sorcery,
and that men are much better by nature, and not so
venomous, cunning and crafty.   Whereby the people,
who believe in these writers, are incensed against women,
and when the latter are burnt they say : It serves them
right, for they are hellish and malignant and like
demons.' [1]

> No viler beast on earth is there
> Than a bad woman, I declare,

said Eucharius Eyering in his collection of axioms,

> And a wonder 'tis to see
> That God lets such women be
> With men united, seeing they
> Commit great trespasses each day,
> And always they are worse by far
> Than men, for Satan's brood they are.
> And among all the numbers who
> Are burned for witchcraft, the men are few.
> Nor do we hear that men their wives
> Have poisoned, though the husbands' lives
> Are ofttimes ended by the wives. . . .
> In short, in every evil deed
> Women still bear off the meed.[2]

Every man who did not wish to be a slave in his own
house was recommended ' as a very necessary and exceedingly useful means of discipline ' to thrash his wife.

> He must spare no stripe,
> Be her years however ripe,

---

[1] C. Beermann, *Ein nützlich Osterpredig über die frommen Weiber am
Grabe, für alle Standes-Personen* (' A useful Easter-sermon on the pious
Women at the Grave, for Persons of all Classes ') (1593), A. pp. 3–4.

[2] Eyering, iii. 126–127.   The Magdeburg preacher John Baumgart
said in the prologue to his comedy *Das Gericht Salomonis* (' The Judgment
of Solomon ') :

> With us it is a saying common
> That fraud and cunning dwell in women ;
> The instant that a woman's eye
> Beholds the earth, she coins a lie.

Bl. 133ᵇ.

is the advice of a popular poet.   Eyering emphatically
confirms it :

> Think no ill, the saying goes :
> He who's given his wife no blows
> Has not freed her from the devil.
> What makes the lot of them so evil
> Is that Satan doth in them stick,
> And must be cudgelled out right quick.
> But when a pious woman's found,
> A spinster she—you may be bound !
> As saith an ancient axiom wise :
> ' No quarrelling, no marriage ties.' [1]

Jost Amman, in his ' Kartenspielbuch ' of 1588,
gives a picture of a sound thrashing scene, with the
inscription :

> How justly is this wife o'erlaid
> With cudgel blows, for she essayed
> To get dominion o'er her man
> By force and fraud.   All ye who can
> Not tame your spouses otherwise,
> Keep well this scene before your eyes :
> If once they get the government,
> Servants you'll be unto the end.

On another page, however, he anticipates no good
result from the flogging of wives :

> Hands off, you who with cudgels strong
> Attempt to drive out all that's wrong ;
> If one devil you thrash from your home,
> Ten others into it will come. [2]

The most terrible thrashing scenes between husbands
and wives are those described by Adam Schubart in
his rhymed ' Hausteufel ' of 1565, by which ' he wanted
to frighten somewhat the passionate, self-willed, disobedient, refractory vixens,' but at the same time
did not want to be quite so hard upon them as others
' who had written about the nine skins of women,' or of

---

[1] Eyering, iii. 270 ; cf. p. 435.
[2] Munich reprint, in Hirth (1880), No. 15. 51.

' how a woman had three skins—the skin of a dog, the
skin of a sow, and so forth, item how a woman was one
of the nine reptiles and was possessed with ten devils.'
The woman who is determined to rule is called ' Sieman '
(=she-man) :

> We chased each other in and out—
> In the house, all round about—
> For three hours pretty near,
> Until Sieman quaked with fear.
> I said : This is mere practising,
> In earnest now I shall begin.
> Up I took a sharp halberd,
> Struck Sieman on the head right hard
> And knocked her down upon the floor,
> Then said : ' Wilt thou for evermore
> Obey me ? ' ' Yea, all the devils on thy head,
> Stop, thou lewd blockhead ! ' she said.
> ' If you drive one devil out,
> Ten more will enter, without doubt.'
> Then first was I to wrath inflamed,
> Struck on, while Sieman was so tamed,
> I thought she really dead must be,
> And I from worry set quite free.

But he was mistaken. When he went home drunk
from the tavern he found ' Sieman ' quite revived and
armed with a spear :

> And it was her heart's desire
> To make me instantly expire.
> I in this danger did not quail,
> But seized at once an iron flail, . . .
> Struck Sieman on the head amain,
> And felled her to the ground again :
> She lay stretched out and did not stir—
> With cudgels I belaboured her. . . .
> And now methought she'd had enough.
> I went off to the sexton's house—
> For the grave diggers sorry I was—
> And said : Go to the carrion-pit
> And make a grave for the wicked worm
> That I have murdered in a storm,

and so forth.

'In short,' says the author, 'the whole book is intended to lead wives to obedience when they will not submit.' That Sieman was murdered 'signifies that disobedient wives generally come to grief, as I might show by numbers of examples.' [1]

John Sommer of Zwickau, Protestant preacher at

---

[1] Frankfort edition of 1565. The name 'Sieman' is met with long before Schubart's *Hausteufel*; cf. Scherer, *Deutsche Studien*, p. 224; Spengler, p. 57, note. 'Many men,' wrote J. Stöcker in his *Spiegel christlicher Hauszucht*, p. 115ᵃ, 'are too lenient to their wives, whence it happens that *Master Sieman* is domesticated in almost all houses and bears rule.' In Cyriacus Spangenberg's *Ehespiegel*, p. 51ᵇ, it says : 'The wives will not let themselves be governed, but will always be themselves *Doctor Sieman*.' The name occurs frequently in Eucharius Eyering :

> Those who as subjects first began,
> Are all of them now called Syman,
> Which is not of God, but of Satan.—i. 7.

The men are obliged to carry

> Mantle and child after their wives,
> Obey them in all, for the peace of their lives ;
> Their names too they have altered quite,
> And *Sieman* now they're always hight.—i. 70.

> The wife doth ever her husband fight
> Whether or no she has equal right.
> And Syman in the house will be,
> Herrman with force expelleth she. . . .—ii. 74.

> When a wife two years has had a spouse
> She wants to be the ruler of the house,
> Doctor Syman then she's called, and she
> Quarrels and grumbles endlessly.—ii. 506.

The wives blind the men with fair words to hide the falseness of their hearts

> Till Sieman's gained the lead at home,
> And Herrman's in the fight o'ercome.—iii. 127.

Thomas Murner had already struck the same key when he said :

> There is on earth no heavier woe
> Than when the wives to masters grow.
> Would you bide to the end content,
> Allow no wife the management.

Geuchmatt, 1006 ; cf. 1072.   At the end, 1121, Murner guards himself against the charge of having written against women in general ; he has only censured the bad ones ; good women ought to be justly praised.

Osterweddingen, in his ' Malus Mulier,' published first
in 1609, and reprinted in 1612 and 1614, treats exhaustively, in the very lowest and most obscene language, interlarded with insolent attacks on the lives
and religious practices of the Catholics, ' of the thirst
for dominion of bad wives, of the causes of domestic
dissension, of the management of wives by their husbands, of secret amulets, preservatives and medicines
against the venomous female lust of dominion, and
finally of the superlatively good serviceable qualities
of bad wives,' ' all told in a most comic and amusing
manner, and interspersed with caricatures and anecdotes
and laughable stories.' [1] In a continuation of this
work under the title of ' Imperiosus Mulier—that is,
the wife thirsting for dominion—the old and wearisome
strife and war between the man's trousers and the
woman's petticoats,' Sommer boasts that his ' Malus
Mulier ' had been ' wafted by a favourable wind far and
wide over the land, and had become almost a text-book.' [2]

---

[1] Second part of the *Ethnographia mundi* ; cf. Goedeke, *Grundriss*, ii.
584, No. 9. Sommer sometimes lapses into regular brothel talk; for
instance at pp. 80 ff., 129–131.

[2] Preface to the *Imperiosus mulier*, the third part of the *Ethnogr. mundi*,
which he wrote ' at the suggestion of blithesome people.' The complete
title is in Goedeke, ii. 584, No. 10. All sorts of other writings for and
against women are catalogued by Hayn, pp. 283 (434), 286, 299, 361, 372,
396, 409, 418, 431, 437. ' Some delightful rhymes about the female sex '
(Leaflet of the Year 1587) expressed pleasure that women were particularly angry at the way in which they had been made fun of in the
' Flöhhatz.' This volume, published by John Fischart in 1573 under the
title, *Flöhhatz, Weibertratz, der wunderunrichtige und spotwichtige Rechts-
handel der Flöhe mit den Weibern*, went through many editions (cf. Goedeke,
Grundriss, ii. 492, No. 8). In a revised edition of 1577 the author bragged
that ' this noble booklet ' was ' on a level with the Catechism '; in his
pamphlet, *Aller Praktik Grossmutter*, he urged the reading of this book in
the following words : ' You dear parents, no book more useful for you
has ever been published, not even Albertus Magnus, than the *Flöhhatz,
Weibertratz*. Therein you will find the gem, ' how they caught and

'Because women were so bad' certain coarse-
minded theorisers started the idea that they were
not human beings at all, and put forward 'these un-
Christian absurdities in rhymes and apothegms,' wanted
even 'to hold learned disputations on the subject,' as
though it were a question of 'serious and demonstrable
theories.'[1] Thus, for instance, at Wittenberg in 1595,
fifty-one theses in the Latin tongue were distributed
as a 'new disputation' in proof that women were not
human beings. The Wittenberg theological faculty,
on the other hand, issued a warning to students against
this movement; 'they were to beware,' it said, 'of
burdening their souls with approval and dissemination
of such scandal.' The disputation caused such excitement that Andrew Schoppius, pastor at Wernigerode,
felt it his duty as preacher to come forward, as armed
champion of the female sex, in a comprehensive volume;[2]

scratched the flea: it is your charter of fun and folly.'   M. Scheible,
Kloster, viii. 567–568. Aegidius Albertinus, in his *Hausspolizei*, said that
'people must not give up getting married, although in some parts of
Holy Scripture women have poor praise given them,' and he 'refuted some
of the calumnies which men retail against women.' Part III., 76ᵇ–81.
In his *Kriegsleut Weckuhr*, i. 58ᵇ, he says in praise of women that they
'were somewhat specially endowed by God and nature, and were more
chaste, modest and holy than men.' On the other hand, he says in
Lucifers Königreich, in the section on immodesty : 'Among all the ways
which the devil has devised for gaining the human heart there is none
more dangerous than a woman, for with this instrument he seduced our
first father Adam from the condition of original innocence and brought
him to misery. Almost all men are deceived and led astray by women :
the world is chiefly ruled by women.' Cf. his *Hirnschleifer*, pp. 34–35, 207 ff.
** See also the quotations of V. Reinhardstöttner, *Forschungen*, ii. 109 ff.,
although we cannot say that they are always to the point.

[1] Beinhaus, p. 6.

[2] *Corona dignitatis muliebris* ; it appeared first in 1596, and in a new
edition, 'substantially improved and enlarged,' in 1604. Schoppius
said that he felt all the more bound to stand up against the slanderers
of women, because he knew some more of these 'ruffianly fellows,'

'for how,' he asked, 'could women be bound to lead a human life if they were not really human beings?' From the Bible, from the Church Fathers, and from synods he brought forward twelve reasons to show that women were really human. 'In Holy Scripture,' he said among other things, 'we find that Christ was born of a woman, and was not the son of a man.'[1] 'Whereas women are as much bound by the divine laws of the Ten Commandments as men, it follows indisputably that they must be of the same nature as men, and must therefore be called real human beings.' 'That women are reasonable is clearly shown by the fact that Eve talked reasonably with the serpent, as also did Abigail and other wise women. . . . Does not the proverb say, moreover, "Man's cunning is soon spent, but woman's cunning has no end," and is this not a proof that women are reasonable creatures of God? That they are also mortal it is not necessary to prove, since of all those who have been born during hundreds of years very few are in the world now. In short, since the true description of a human being applies to women as well as to men, women must be regarded as really human.' 'This slanderer further asserts that he has hit the mark well in declaring that women are monsters in nature. But he has not proved this. For monsters and strange abortions are only born seldom, and have not the proper form and nature of the creatures by which they have been generated; as, for instance, when a little child has two heads, four feet, one foot,

'among them certain shallow-brained students, and foolish parsons and mountebanks,' who talked very offensively and scandalously about women. Bl. D 2.

[1] Bl. E 3.

and so forth.   With us, however—thanks be to God !
—women are generally born with the right form and
nature of their species, and therefore it is abominable
blasphemy to vilify their noble sex and call them
monsters of nature, in a way that would make even
reasonable heathens, who know nothing about God,
feel ashamed down to their liver and lungs.' [1]

Schoppius prefixed to the 121 pages of his book
a dedicatory preface of twenty-two pages to three
noble ladies, and was careful to warn his opponent
' not to get among angry and revengeful women, who
would " prick him with needles and tear him with
tongs " to such an extent that he would soon give up
mocking and slandering.' [2]

Balthasar Wendel also thought it necessary to bring
forward proofs that ' women were made in the image
of God just as much as men.' [3]

Another class of books which, according to contem-

[1] Bl. F 4.   G 2. J.   [2] Bl. H 3.

[3] Leipzig and Halle, 1597.   The Silesian physician Valens Acidalius
would not allow that he had written the *Dissertatio nova, in qua mulieres
non esse homines probatur*, &c. ; but he confessed to having had it printed
at Zerbst in 1595.   The pamphlet was reprinted in numbers of places
and translated into many languages.   In refutation of it the Brandenburg superintendent Simon Gedicke wrote a *Defensio sexus muliebris
contra anonymi disputationem*, &c.   Lipsiae, 1595.   Cf. Dahlmann,
Schauplatz, pp. 543–545.   Jöcher, *Allgem. Gelehrten-Lexicon*, ii. 900.
** Th. Odebrecht in the *Märkische Forschungen*, vii. 213–214.   Acidalius
received a judicial rebuke for his share in the pamphlet.   In opposition to
the enemies of women, Cornelius Agrippa of Nettesheim said, in a lecture
on the excellence of the female sex, that ' woman was the actual object
and crown of creation, and that she stood as high above man as man
above the animals, and that the gift of speech which distinguished men
from beasts was possessed by women in a much higher degree than by
men.   In all branches of knowledge and action women had distinguished
themselves, and it was only the injustice and tyranny of men that kept
them limited to their needles and thread, and refused them all public
rights and professions.'   Cf. Sigwart, *Kleine Schriften*, pp. 7–8.

poraries, was no less in request than the buffooneries
and comic stories and fables intended for the amusement and edification of young and old, was represented
by the innumerable tales of ' drinking and carousing,
with which Germany was quite full and so to say con-
gested.'   ' Books of that sort,' Beinhaus complains, ' are
read widely and eagerly, and it makes no difference
whether they are for or against drinking ; for people only
want to hear about drinking because they indulge in it
daily, and if anything fresh is said about drunkards
and the art of drinking they are all agog to hear it, and
they only laugh at those who preach and write against
drunkenness.' [1]

' On the art of drinking,' was the title of a pamphlet
written in Latin by the philologist Vincent Obsopöus,
and translated into German in 1537 by the Colmar
actuary Gregory Wickram.[2]   It begins as follows :

> Who knows not the right art of swilling
> Will learn it here if to read he's willing.
> By art high buildings were erected,
> By art ships o'er the sea projected,
> By art Daedalus flew with wings,
> By art man subjecteth all things ;
> By art, too, drinkers must be ruled,
> Lest they by Bacchus be befooled.

Against a good drinking bout in a man's own house
the author had nothing to say :

> Harmless at home is the drunkenness
> Which outside oft brings great distress.

Away from home it is only permissible to drink with

---

[1] Beinhaus, 5ᵇ.

[2] See Goedeke, *Grundriss*, ii. 460.   ** Concerning the literature of
drinking in Germany during the sixteenth century cf. now also the article
by Hauffen in Suphan-Seuffert's *Vierteljahrschrift für Litteraturgeschichte*,
1889, ii. 489 ff.

pious, God-fearing people; even 'Papists' are not forbidden as boon companions:

> If then thou drinkest with the heathen,
> With them try to keep even.
> Many Papists have I known
> From whom honest pleasure I have drawn,
> Who were better than that sort
> False at heart, just only in word.

On the other hand, they must fly from apostate monks:

> Apostate monks are a wicked lot,
> Avoid them like hell-fire hot,
> Flee from them as from the devil black,
> Chock full of pitch and resin they stick. . . .
> Blacker are they than black horses of the wood,
> Blacker than magpies wearing a hood.

Very vivid is the terrifying description of the dissolute orgies which had become the custom of the world:

> The wine flows over tables and benches,
> The floor, too, it completely drenches;
> On the tables great lakes are seen
> Whereon the empty beakers sail. . . .
> Some will eat things coarse, unclean,
> To make their neighbours nausea feel,
> Some beneath their teeth unkind
> The little singing cage-birds grind;
> Others start a naked dance.[1] . . .

'I herewith frankly declare it to be true,' said Wickram in the dedication of his pamphlet, 'that from experience of society I have found that in these anxious and grievous times so much abuse of drinking has arisen among young and old, that the young will not easily, like their forefathers, grow up in suitable behaviour, wisdom and reasonableness. The older people also, both of high and low degree, who ought to be to the

[1] Bl. A 2ᵇ; B 2. C–F.

fore in government, let themselves be so overcome by
drunkenness that they pay no attention to discipline,
respectability and virtue, in consequence of which the
young are led astray.'

The numerous books written against the habit of
drunkenness were well meant, but they were so detailed
and explicit in their accounts of this ' next to unchastity
greatest German vice ' that they ministered rather to
pleasure than to instruction and warning.'   ' When, for
instance,' so one hears, ' the boon companions, young
and old, men and women, are assembled together, they
say : " Brother, haven't you got any new book about
drinking and carousing from those who complain about
what others do ?   They do a great deal worse themselves, and we will learn from them and imitate them.
Heyday, where's our Grobianus ?   Where was the ' Saufrecht ' and the *Gäuchlieder* printed ?   We will learn
out of these little books how we ought to proceed." '[1]

The ' Grobianus, von groben Sitten und unhöflichen
Gebärden ' (' Of Coarse Morals and Impolite Manners ')
was a little work which was ' written in Latin in 1549
by the very learned Frederic Dedekind, and afterwards
translated into German by Caspar Scheid of Worms,'
Fischart's tutor ; since 1551 or 1552 it had gone through
numerous editions and had had a wide circulation.
The aim of both author and translator had been to
give an appalling picture of their times, and thereby
to influence for good the swarms of profligates who
were wallowing in filth and licentiousness of every
description.[2]

[1] Beinhaus, 5ᵇ.
[2] ** Cf. A. Hauffen, ' Caspar Scheid, der Lehrer Fischarts.   Studien zur
Gesch. der grobianischen Litteratur in Deutschland ' (*Quellen und For-*

'From other nations,' said Scheid in the dedication
of the pamphlet, 'we have received, with regard to
drinking, very fine, subtle, and elegant names, such as
Porco tedesco, *inebriaco*, *Aleman Yurongne* and other
still finer titles—that is, German drunken sows, and
coarse drunken Germans, *Comedones* and *Bibones*.' [1]
'Drunkenness of the very worst and most heinous description has grown to such a pitch that life has come
to be a long drinking bout with us, and he who will not
be a wine-bag, or go to drinking parties, or drink beyond
all measure and reason, and is content with drinking
a little, is soundly abused, rated, if not thrashed.'
Scheid hoped that whereas in his 'Grobian Booklet'
he depicted 'all coarse (*grob*) manners, irregularities,
vices and improprieties,' the world would learn a lesson
from it.   He urged the reader :

> Read this booklet oft and much,
> And always do the opposite. [2]

The indecencies of the Latin original were con-

schungen zur Gesch. der Sprach- und Kulturgesch. der germanischen Völker,
vol. lxvi.).   Strassburg, 1889.   Cf. also Strauch, in the *Anzeiger f. Deutsches
Alterth.* xviii. 359 ff.

[1] In Murner's *Schelmenzunft* ('Guild of Rascals'), No. 48, we read:

> Whatever the German sets about,
> The wine flask first must be brought out.
> For this in Italy we're famed,
> And 'German inebriates' there named.
> And we've become a laughing-stock
> For God and all the world to mock,
> And the whole world says of us, ' Marry,
> Every German a flask must carry,'
> And we compel each other to swill,
> And ourselves with drinking kill.

[2] 'We see at once,' says Gustavus Milchsack, the publisher of the
latest edition of *Grobianus* (Halle-a.-S., 1882), p. viii., 'that its humour is the
humour of despair, which seemed to the author, and to his like-minded
contemporaries, the last resource for keeping themselves above the clogging
slough of universal demoralisation, the last means left for making an
impression on the "Grobianers" weighed down by the curse of ridicule.'

siderably multiplied by Scheid, and yet he declared
that he had only described ' the hundredth part of the
immoral, obscene customs which were prevalent, only
given a specimen, a beginning, a preamble of the greater
iniquities.' [1]

In the ' Zech- und Saufrecht,' so greatly in request
among drinkers, the solemnities and customs of drinking
bouts are described :

> We Germans are born to stand forth
> As drinkers of prominent worth ;
> By day and night our tasks we ply
> Of draining bowls and beakers dry,
> We empty them out on the floor,
> And down our throats the liquor pour.

' But there are many and various ways of drinking.
Some show their skill by taking their glass up with their
mouth ; others bend their heads down to the ground
to pick up the glass ; others again take up two glasses
together and pour the contents down their throats at
the same time ; others do not use their hands at all, but
hold the glass between their two arms. Then there
are other experts who place the glass on the forehead
and let the wine run down along their noses into their
throats. The filthiest among them drink out of the
dirtiest vessels in the kitchen or the bedroom, or out
of dirty shoes.' [2] . . .

' If we look at these *Saufbrüder*—sow-brethren
would be a fitter name—we see that they live up to the
rules of their order. Each brother should stop drinking

---

[1] *Grobianus* (1882), p. 6.

[2] Scheible, *Schaltjahr*, iv. 346 ff., 628, 630. According to the laws of
the Saufrecht (p. 474), they were not allowed to drink to the health of the
Pope, ' for he thirsts for our blood ; blood did I say ?—for our very souls
he thirsts, and if he were to drag them into hell with himself, we should
not even be allowed to ask, " Pope, what are you doing ? " '

first when his eyes are full of water, then when his breath fails him, lastly when his glass is empty. When the contents of his stomach rise to his mouth he should vomit them over the table and on the floor, and spread them all over the place. And if he should bespatter his neighbour he will be all the more thought of by the Order. He should use the table napkin for a hand-kerchief and commit other nuisances—and obscenities —as prescribed in the booklet. Women and girls of the upper classes often witness these scenes.'

Tracts were written with such titles as ' Von acht Tugenden der trunkenen Weiber sammt ihren Eigen-schaften,' [1] ' Von dreien versoffenen Frauen, welche in einer Zech einundzwanzig Mass Wein ausgetrunken haben' (' Of Three Intoxicated Women who at a drink-ing bout drank Twenty-one Measures of Wine '),[2] and it

---

[1] Cf. Weller, *Annalen*, i. 269, No. 402.   Song of the year 1610.

[2] Weller, i. 273, No. 424.   Song of the year 1611 ; cf. also *Facetiae* . . *schöne und kurzweilige Geschwenckh der guten Trinker und Polowitzer Zucht bemeldend*, only lately collected together, short and amusing to sing, 1535.   Weller, *Annalen*, i. 309, No. 89 ; a *Gesang vom Vollsaufen* (Worms, 1561), p. 322, No.161. *Zechbruderspiegel vom Jahre 1612*. Hayn, p. 356. *Die zwölf Eigenschaften der Trunkenen* (' The Twelve Qualities of Drunkards '), by Leonhart Schertlin.   *Die vol Bruderschaft* (' The Drunken Brotherhood ') (Strassburg, 1543), Bl. D.   In this, Bacchus boasts (Bl. B 4) that his kingdom increases daily :

> The clergy do not scorn my pranks,
> Lovely ladies swell my ranks,
> Nobles too both high and low,
> Scholars and learned men also,
> The scribe, the student, and the clod,
> All take me for their Lord and God ;
> All dance round in my merry jig,
> And make my circle wondrous big :
> And all, however high and learned,
> To children and to fools are turned.

From Schertlin's *Künstlich trincken* (Strassburg, 1538) there are longer passages quoted, ' Bacchus zu dem vollen Sileno,' and ' Eigenschaft der viehischen Saufer,' in Wickram, *Sieben Hauptlaster*, pp. 84ᵇ–87.   ** Cf.

was held up as ' a great trophy of drinking power, which
should be a warning to all respectable persons,' that at
a drinking party at Meissen ' two drunken sots of good
social position had imbibed thirty measures of wine
and beer without coming to grief; at the finish they
were still able to sing their drinking songs and dirty
ditties : a thing to be lamented by every Christian
heart.' [1]

From a ' Schöner neuer Kaufbrief zwischen Merten
Drucksferckel und Steffen Quetzs-Quarck, mit allerlei
guten Bossen gespickt,' readers learnt also to recognise
' a fine new mode of salutation between the drinking
brothers.' [2] ' Amusing dialogues about drinking,' which
consisted for the most part of stories of drinking,
fornication, and villainy, with all sorts of mockery of
religion, became more and more licentious almost every
year.[3] The most complete models of such productions

Ph. Strauch in Seuffert's *Vierteljahrschrift für Litteraturgesch.* i. 86 ff.
The ' Beschreibung eines rechten Vollsäufers,' and ' Von mancherlei Art
der Trunkenen ' in Ringwalt, *Die Lauter Wahrheit*, pp. 61–78. Concerning drinking and gluttony and lewd songs, the *Ethnographia mundi*
of Olorinus Variscus (Sommer), Bl. E 2^b ff., E 5^b, E 7. A dreadful
description of gluttonous and drunken women in Aegidius Albertinus,
Lucifers Königreich, pp. 235–238 ; cf. the *Landstörtzer*, by the same author.
James Ayrer makes Pluto, the Prince of Hell, say : ' Out of Germany there
came such a multitude of people

> . . . running, tumbling to hell's brink,
> Who have damned themselves with drink.'

And Mercury puts it more strongly : it is 'A great disgrace to the Germans '
that

> So many of them by wine are killed
> For all their days they've drunk and swilled
> Before they've reached their natural term of life.

Ayrer, i. 517, 520, 568.

[1] *Einblattdruck in Prosa und Reimen*, 1585.
[2] Hayn, p. 397. Of the year 1608.
[3] Beinhaus, pp. 5^b–6.

are to be found in the eighth chapter of Fischart's
' Geschichtsklitterung.' [1]

The favourite light literature of the higher classes
of society consisted of the romances introduced from
abroad, especially from France.   Towards the end of the
fifteenth century the South-west German nobility had
worked zealously by means of translation to domesticate
works of this description in their own land.   The Margrave Rudolf von Hochberg had a translation made of
the wonderful adventures of the sea nymph Melusine ;
Marquard von Stein translated the ' Knight of the
Tower.'   Even noble ladies devoted themselves to this
work.   The Countess Elizabeth of Nassau-Saarbrücken
translated the romances of ' Loher and Maller ' and of
' Hug Schapler ' from Italian into German ; Eleanor of
Scotland, the wife of Duke Sigmund of Austria, translated the romance of ' Pontus and Sidonia.'   These
romances, as well as the pathetic story of Griselda,
the ' Very fine, new story of the exalted love of
the royal prince Florio and his dear Bianceffora,' the
story of ' Tristram and Isold,' and many others of
the same kind, found a rapid sale in the sixteenth
century.   At the Frankfort Lent fair of 1569 there
were sold by the one printer's journeyman, Michael
Harder, 158 copies of ' Melusine,' 147 of ' Pontus and
Sidonia,' 97 of ' Hug Schapler,' 64 of ' Loher and

---

[1] We read there, for instance : ' Duck down, my soul, there's a shower
of rain coming which will allay the fire of hell. . . . I am a brushmaker.
What, have I flayed a dead sow, that nobody brings me nothing ?   I
have a hedgehog in my belly, which must have floated.'   ' Bite the fly ;
bite its eye out ; kiss the ground ; I will be bishop to thee ; I can confirm
thee, I can smear the chrism on thee.'   For other extracts see vol. xi.
p. 376.

Maller,' 56 of 'Tristram and Isold,' and 52 of 'Florio and Bianceffora.' [1]

These books came out in many different editions; of the story of Melusine sixteen can still be identified up to 1601.[2] The stories of the Emperor Octavian and of the 'Schöne Magelone,' translated from the French, also met with immense approval.[3] The German 'Folkbook' of the 'Vier Heymonskinder' ('Four Children of Heymon') did not obtain a wide circulation till after the beginning of the seventeenth century.[4]

The creator of original German romance was Jörg Wickram of Kolmar, who flourished in the middle of the sixteenth century, and was the author of the 'Schöne und doch klägliche Historie von Gabriotto und Reinhard,' the 'Knabenspiegel,' the narrative 'Von guten und bösen Nachbarn,' and the 'Goldfaden, eine schön liebliche und kurzweilige Histori von eines armen Hirten Sohn, welcher aus seinem fleissigen Studieren, Unterdienstbarkeit und ritterlichen Thaten eines Grafen Tochter überkam' ('The Golden Thread: a delightful and amusing tale of a poor shepherd's son, who by his diligence in study, his devotion, and his knightly deeds won the daughter of an earl').[5]

---

[1] *Messmemorial*, vi.–vii. This memorial is not the complete register of the 'bookseller' Michael Harder at the Lenten fair, but only a fragment of a register, in which the entries of ready-money sale of single volumes are missing, and which Michael Harder made after the death of the widow Margaret Gülfferich of what she had bequeathed to her heirs. H. Pallmann, *Archiv für Gesch. des Buchhandels*, ix. 5 ; cf. Pallmann, *Feyerabend*, p. 28.

[2] Goedeke, *Grundriss*, i. 354–355, No. 16.

[3] Catalogue of the different editions in Goedeke, ii. 20–22.

[4] Cf. F. Pfaff in the admirable introduction to his edition of the *Heymonskinder*. Freiburg i. Br. 1887.

[5] Fuller details about these romances are in Bobertag, i. 236 ff. Against Bobertag's opinions cf. E. Schmidt, 'Zu Jörg Wickram' ; in the *Archiv für Litteraturgesch.* viii. 317 to 357. Of the romance, *Von den guten und*

The influence, however, of the German, respectable, bourgeois novel was quickly superseded by the introduction of the French Amadis-romances, the Germanisation of which was first undertaken by Duke Christopher of Württemberg. During his stay in Paris the Duke had conceived a great liking for these stories ; later on he sent ' an emissary to Paris, to learn the French language in order that he might be able to translate books of this sort and have them printed.' [1]   But the death of Duke Christopher cut short his enterprise, and the Frankfort bookseller, Sigmund Feyerabend, then took up the matter, and brought out, in the years 1568–1595, ' The Histories of Amadis of France,' in twenty-four volumes, a veritable giant work in the German book market.   It comprised altogether considerably more than 25,000 pages.[2]   In 1583 Feyerabend published the first thirteen books on 1176 folio sheets of four columns each.   The books which had hitherto appeared separately, he said in the preface, ' had been so eagerly welcomed, bought up and read, that all the copies of these had been sold out very quickly.'   At the request of intelligent persons therefore he had collected these books together in one

bösen Nachbarn, which Bobertag (i. 264) considers Wickram's best work, ' because it is a German family novel,' Scherer says, *Anfänge des Prosaromans*, p. 43 : ' The book made an almost laughable impression on me : Philister life, Philister adventures down through three generations, described with great self-satisfaction, thefts which are discovered, attacks happily warded off, false accusations which are refuted, form the incidents of highest interest ; these things happen for the most part during journeys, and the chief object in travelling is to get home again with sound limbs.' This book found scant welcome among contemporaries ; it went through two editions only, and cannot, therefore, as Bobertag says, have been the popular style of narrative.

[1] Von Keller, p. 461 ; Scherer, *Anfänge*, pp. 67–72.

[2] Goedeke, *Grundriss*, ii. 474–476, where the number of pages in the different books is given.   ** Cf. Steinhaufen, *Die Anfänge des franz. Litteratur- und Kultur-einflusses in Deutschland*, p. 374.

work, and was again offering them to the public ' on
account of their evident usefulness.' [1] Their usefulness,
he said, was recognised by all among the nobility who
loved honour and chivalry, and by all virtuous women
and maidens ; even for young boys and girls the Amadis
books would be profitable and entertaining reading.[2]

Nearly every book of the set was dedicated to some
person of high position ; the twelfth book, which contained 1428 pages, ' filled almost entirely with obscenities,' [3] was actually dedicated to the Freifrau Sibylle
von Fleckenstein, *née* Countess of Hanau.[4]

' The charming, and also true, stories ' comprised
everything ' which was likely to rouse the amorous
passions ' ; gallantry was here represented as knightly
chivalry.[5] It appears in all sorts of ' adventures,' and

[1] Bobertag, i. 349, note 1.
[2] In the preface to the sixth book it says that the publication of these
' charming and at the same time true stories had been undertaken in order
that the young who were becoming more and more inclined to all that
was bad, and who were in danger of becoming subject to carnal desires,
should learn from this little work [it contained only 895 pages ; cf. Goedeke,
ii. 475, No. 6], which at the same time would afford them amusement,
to withstand all those vicious passions and immoral actions which they
were so apt to indulge in ' (Wendeler, pp. 311–312).
[3] So says Bobertag, i. 363.
[4] Goedeke, ii. 476, No. 12.
[5] Bobertag (i. 366 ff.) gives fuller details. ' To the second book there
is an introductory poem which begins as follows :

> When I reflect on gallantry
> And measure it with knight-errantry,
> I find the two are much allied
> Together, and much coincide ;
> For at all times it's ever true
> A lover is a warrior too.

The author then draws in detail a parallel between knight-errantry
and gallantry. ' It appears that this poem is of all prefaces the one
which shows the most insight into the needs of the more distinguished
reading-public, and which explains with most frankness and *naïveté*
how the pages that follow supply these wants.' The knight-errantry

also in 'polite and courtly conversations and letters
which penetrate so sweetly and deliciously into the heart
of the reader.' From this last source Lazarus Zetzner,
bookseller at Strassburg, compiled in 1596 a 'treasury
of choice and elegant orations, epistles, dialogues,
discourses, exhortations and so forth,' which went
through several editions.[1]

Zetzner was of opinion that 'those who had translated the highly esteemed "Amadis" from French into
German had done no less—indeed quite as much, if
not more—for the German language than the author
of the book had done for the French. They had 'so
greatly embellished their language and developed it
that it could not easily be further improved, and also
enriched it with such well-turned, delightful, graceful
phrases that Germany could now boast of its language
as much as the French could of theirs.' Even that
'essentially feeble quantity, the female sex, had begun
to store their minds with the charming elegancies and the
elegant charms of the German "Amadis" with peculiar

depicted in the *Amadis* is 'a hollow, dead form without any living principle
or real aim,' as contrasted with 'the older poems and romances from the
Breton and Frank sagas,' in which knightly chivalry appears sketched in
bold and true outlines, and exalted, by a living principle of religion or
of politics, to universal, historic significance' (pp. 372–373). Some of the
Amadis books, 'like the first and the fourth, are actually protestantised,
though indeed only superficially and clumsily, so that a comic effect is
produced when the heroes, before starting on their enterprises, instead of
the Mass listen to a rapid sermon' (p. 348 ; cf. Von Keller, pp. 453 ff., 464 ;
F. Wolf in the *Wiener Jahrbücher der Litteratur*, lix. 44 ff.). The manner
in which works of medieval literature were intentionally remodelled
and falsified in a Protestant spirit in the sixteenth century is discussed
in detail by Simon Schäfer [*Zur deutschen Litteratur des sechzehnten
Jahrhunderts* ('Inaugural Dissertation,' Bonn, 1874)], in connection with
the edition of Hugo von Trimberg's *Renner*, which appeared at Frankfort
in 1549.

[1] See Goedeke, *Grundriss*, ii. 479, No. 26.

delight and profit.' [1] Martin Opitz in his 'Aristarchus' cites the German translation of the 'Amadis' as an incontrovertible proof of the splendour and beauty of his mother-tongue.[2] This was the age *par excellence* in which, in Germany, 'almost everything foreign was set up as a model,' and those Germans who retained a true patriotic spirit complained bitterly that 'the foreign craze was increasing more and more to the veritable ruin of the people.' [3] This 'foreign craze' was already showing itself very conspicuously in the language.

In the fifteenth century it had been found possible to express the most profound and abstract ideas clearly and appropriately in German, without the help of any foreign forms and phrases; but in the course of the sixteenth century there sprang up an unmanageable medley of speech, and foreign words were heaped on in such abundance that in 1571 it became necessary to have a dictionary of foreign words, which was published under the title 'Deutscher Diktionarius, *i.e.* an interpreter of difficult, unknown German, Greek, Latin,

[1] Preface of July 7, 1596. ** How high-born ladies in their letters imitated the style of *Amadis* is seen from the correspondence between two Countesses of Wertheim at the close of the sixteenth century ; cf. A. Kaufmann in the *Archiv des histor. Vereins für Unterfranken*, Bd. xix. Heft 2. pp. 54–56.

[2] Which remark 'is as characteristic as possible of the tendency of that epoch as well as of the true child of his epoch Opitz,' says E. Höppner in the *Zeitschr. für deutsche Philologie*, viii. 468. In the original edition of the *Aristarchus* of 1617, as Höppner has established, Caspar Dornau, rector of the Schönach Gymnasium at Beuthen, has put Fischart's *Bienenkorb* instead of *Amadis*.

[3] Beinhaus, 6ᵃ. ** Cf. the valuable treatise of Steinhausen, 'Die Anfänge des französischen Litteratur- und Kultureinflusses in Deutschland,' in Koch's *Zeitschrift f. vergleichende Litteraturgesch.* vii. (1894), 349 ff. Concerning the Spanish influences cf. the two works of Schneider and Farinelli cited at p. 400 Anm.

Hebrew, Italian, French, and other words, which have
been incorporated by degrees into the German language.'[1] Fischart, who was very fond of ridiculing this
kind of language,[2] is by no means himself free from it.[3]

George Rollenhagen complained in his didactic
poem, ' Der Froschmeuseler ' :

> The Roman, and likewise the Greek,
> Can both artistically speak
> Their mother-tongue—their pride it is
> That they are able to do this.
> But Germans most of all prefer
> The diction of the foreigner ;
> In foreign tongues they speak and write,
> Their mother's tongue neglected quite.[4]

But he himself in his writings brought in all sorts
of Latin, Greek, and even Hebrew phrases, in order
to show off his learning.[5] The jurists also used by
preference quantities of unintelligible foreign words, as
though in the very language itself every trace of native

---

[1] By Simon Rote. Cf. Wackernagel, *Gesch. der deutschen Litteratur*,
p. 388, note 25, p. 390, note 36.

[2] Cf. Dederding, p. 10. His ridicule of it is wittiest in the speech
which he makes Janotus of Bragmado deliver in his *Geschichtklitterung*,
ch. 22. In this one stumbles up against half-Latin, half-German words
and sentences, and hears of the ' substantifickliche Qualitet der elemen-
tarischen Complexion, welche in der Terrestritet und Irrdigkeit ihrer
quidditavischen Natur intronificirt ist,' and such words as ' extranesirt,'
' narrirt,' ' parlirt,' ' arguirt,' ' commendirt,' and so forth.

[3] For instance, in the dedication to his *Podagramisch Trostbüchlein*
and in the address to its readers, in the space of a few pages he intro-
duces expressions such as ' tesaurisiren, Discipulus, tractiren, Antidotum,
Preparativ, Ethici, Tractat, Medicament, Arrestirung, offeriren, Repu-
tation, unnodisirt, simple Conversion,' and more of the kind. Scheible,
Das Kloster, x. 643 ff.

[4] Dedication of March 21, 1595. ' Our own language disgusts us,' wrote
the Hessian superintendent, Henry Leuchter, in 1613, ' and we must needs
jabber French, Italian, and so forth. In our clothes we do not even
know ourselves. O God, the pity of it ! ' Leuchter, p. 33.

[5] Cf. what Goedeke says in his *Froschmeuseler*, vol. i. p. xxxv.

German law was to be obliterated by the Roman law.[1]
Even in love songs the mixture of languages made itself
apparent.[2]

The deeper ground of the evil lay in the shattering
of German national force and in the permeation of the
entire nation of Germans with foreign elements.   From
all directions foreign influences poured into the intellectual life of Germany : Rabelais and his coarse satires,
the English blood-tragedies, the Italian pastorals, the
Spanish romances of rogues ; above all the ' Amadis '
with its whole sequel of debased knight-errantry.

' Among the light and frivolous tales and tracts which
have been translated from Italian, Spanish and French,'
said John Fickler in 1581, ' the " Amadis de Gaul "
deserves special notice on account of its wide circulation.'
All the world knows ' how popular this book has become
with men and women both of high and low classes,
but most especially with a goodly number of great
ladies who all the same pose as being very evangelical ' ;
by these ' this worldly and amorous book is handled
far more than their prayer-books and studied much
more diligently than the Gospel of Christ.'   At the
Frankfort assembly of Deputies in 1577, he said, he
had heard from the mouth of a distinguished printer
' that this time the " Amadis de Gaul " had brought
him in more money than Luther's " Postilles," ' which
nevertheless was one of the books most in demand
among nobles, burghers and peasants, ' they could
scarcely indeed get enough copies of it printed.' [3]   The

---

[1] Wackernagel, *Gesch. der Litteratur*, p. 390.

[2] See our remarks, vol. xi. pp. 307, 308.

[3] Fickler, *Traktat*, Vorrede, Bl. 2ᵇ-5.   Cf. Bl. 52 ff.   On the spread
of immoral books in France, Bl. 25 ff.   Cf. Bl. 58 ff., *Complaint on
the Italian Scribblers and their Immoral Poems.*

Protestant school rector, Sigmund Ebenius, reported with grief that the young pupils ' actually amused themselves during divine service in church with reading the frivolous stories of the " Amadis " and other such indecencies.' [1]

Many earnest-minded men drew attention to the demoralising influence of the ' Amadis ' romance.   One named it a poisoned work, highly injurious to the young ; another called it accursed ; a third said it was a devilish book.   The Protestant theologian, John Valentine Andreä, was of opinion that ' it was best to burn such highly objectionable books and altogether obliterate the memory of them, in order that innocent hearts might not be led astray by them.' [2]   Fischart went so far as to declare that whoever could read these romances without blushing must be as proof against moral poison in his own immovable virtue as Mithridates was against physical hurt.[3]   The invectives which Andrew Henry Buchholtz, professor of Theology at Brunswick, hurled at ' the scandalous "Amadis " book ' reveal at the same time the reasons why it was so popular.   The book, he said, ' has also many lovers among women, none of whom are improved by reading it, but on the contrary stimu-

---

[1] Evenius, p. 83.   ' To have learnt from the *Amadis* how to practise gallantry was considered a sign of distinguished breeding.'   Even in 1601 Theobald Höcks (cf. Wolkan, *Gesch. d. deutschen Litteratur in Böhmen bis zum Ausgang des sechzehnten Jahrhunderts.* Prag, 1894) speaks in his *Schönes Blumenfeld* of the ' gallantry ' and the ' pursuit,' which is now called *Galanisiren*.   M. v. Waldberg, *Die Galante Lyrik* (Strassburg, 1885), pp. 4, 5.   The gallant poets who compared their mistresses with everything imaginable had a precursor in the new-Latin poet, Matthew Zuber, and his *Amores et Suspiria*, which appeared at Wittenberg in 1599 ; cf. Von Waldberg, p. 88, note 3.

[2] Quoted in Scherer, *Anfänge*, p. 66.

[3] *Vorbereitung in den Amadis*, in Kurz, iii. 29–32.   Cf. Bobertag, i. 360–362, 363.

lated to unseemly boldness, by having painted before their eyes incidents which even the most shameless persons would shrink from dragging before the light of the sun.' 'The wantonnesses of behaviour are spun far too coarsely, and the unseemly goings on between young lovers of the higher classes are so offensive that modest-minded people cannot read them without disgust.' 'I will not speak . . . of the part idiotic, part godless cases of enchantment of which there are such frequent accounts, and which are as much wanting in good taste as in credibility, although this devilish art claims not only to be good and permissible, but even Christian and godly, such as Christian emperors, kings and knights have practised without scruples of conscience, thereby, through special providence of God, escaping many a misfortune and being strengthened to fulfil much good. I need not say how easily thoughtless, lascivious women might hereby be incited to give themselves up to witchcraft.' [1]

[1] Bobertag, ii. 115–116.

CHAPTER V

LITERATURE OF WONDERS AND HORRORS

THE 'Amadis' romances owed their wide popularity not only to the taste of the period for 'conventional gallantries,' for sensual, coarse love adventures and fantastic, monstrous pictures from knightly life, but also, and chiefly, to the prevalent delight in all sorts of wonders, horrors and magic apparitions.

The predilection for tales of marvels which had come down to the sixteenth century from earlier times had by degrees degenerated into such a craze for prodigies and wonders that the ability to distinguish the possible and thinkable from the unthinkable, as well among the high and cultured classes as among the lower ones, had almost entirely disappeared. Since the foundations of religion had become tottering, since hatred and discord had ripened everywhere, and even in public life there was no longer any firm basis to go upon, there had grown up a world of illusion and deceit in which every imaginable fable and fiction passed muster as truth, and those who 'could offer the most extraordinary and unheard-of goods for sale' were believed in the most.[1]

Whilst the 'wonders' related in the legends of saints or in Catholic books of sermons, as also those

---

[1] *Von der Werlte Eitelkeit*, Bl. 4.

which according to Catholic report were found frequently at pilgrims' shrines, were covered with scorn and derision,[1] the credulity of the people was fed with the most absurd tales of so-called supernatural character ; and these were not confined only to the region of things childish and preposterous, but were connected also with matters of a thoroughly degraded nature, and mocked and desecrated things holy and divine ; besides which they were supplied with the most extraordinary explanations.

Down to the middle of the century narratives of this sort had only been the exception in the book-market ; [2] afterwards, however, they increased and multiplied, and, in connection with all sorts of tales of horrors, crimes and magic, they poured like ' a new sin-flood ' over the land, so that, to quote the words of a contemporary, ' it might well be thought that in those days in Germany the majority of writers and poets were intent only on stimulating lust, and exciting fear, horror and superstition.[3]

[1] That all sorts of books were distributed among the Catholics which contained ' spurious marvels ' and ' fabulous stories about sacred things,' is sufficiently proved by a decree of the papal nuncio, Felicianus Ninguarda, who, during his residence in Bavaria, issued on May 1, 1582, a special enactment that all such books must be removed. H. Reusch, *Index der verbotenen Bücher*, i. 478 (' Index of Forbidden Books ').

[2] Von Liliencron (*Mitteilungen*, p. 138) has lately drawn attention to this fact.

[3] ** A. Musculus (*Vom Mesech und Kedar, vom Gog und Magog*, and so forth—Frankfort-on-the-Oder) remarks (Bl. A 3ᵃ) : ' Of late years so many marvellous portents have happened, have been written about, printed and painted, that there was never anything like it before from the beginning of the world, and if all the miracles, wonders and portents out of all old writers and historians were collected together and counted up, I am certain that whatever the number of these, they would not be so many or so alarming as those which have happened and been reported within about the last forty years.'

By the theologians and preachers of the new religion the circulation and confirmation of all sorts of tales of wonders which they heard of was considered an exceptionally good method for proving the truth of the new evangel, and at the same time for stimulating to penitence and improvement the demoralised people sunk in licentious and bestial living.[1] Moreover they did not fail to draw attention to the fact that it was only since the advent of the new teaching that the number of these wonders had become so enormous. An expounder of the Revelation of St. John spoke in the year 1589 of a ' sea of wonders, which had happened and been seen during the last fifty or sixty years by the

[1] ** 'During the last few years,' says the Hildesheim chronicler, John Oldecop, for the year 1561, ' the rabbis and sophists of the Lutheran sect have published a number of books and trashy compilations, full of strange figures and pictures, and they have depicted wonderful visions of storm winds, thunder and lightning, fiery clouds, here three, there five suns, here a little child, and many other wonders. And when the Catholics and pious Christians, whom the Lutherans call papists, publish such pictures and glosses, they are denounced and cursed from the pulpits by the Lutheran preachers. But to these Lutherans all things are allowed ; they are free to say and invent just whatever suits their mouths. Now it might well be asked : What are our Lutheran heads and preachers aiming at with these pictures and ungodly glosses ? Answer : They see and observe that the Lutheran brethren and other rough fellows are growing more and more wicked from day to day. The nobles lie in ambush in the streets, the merchants heap up gains with great cunning and deceit, the government officials, under pretext of the new doctrines, tyrannise over the poor peasants and burghers with taxing, flaying and fleecing. To such an extent have vice and scandal, violence and injustice gained the upper hand, that sermons are no longer of any avail to make tyrants and oppressors become more pious. These fables and tales were printed in this manner, read out to the misguided crowds and the poor blind Lutherans, and explained with special glosses, in order that the people might by this means be brought back to righteousness and obedience. I, however, have my doubts about them, seeing that the portents are so falsely explained by their own authors, who do not abide by the punishment, but dissemble and flatter the Lutherans in the glosses.' *Chronicle of John Oldecop* (published by K. Euling), pp. 474–475.

glorious light of the dear, true evangel.' Enumerating
the various objects briefly, he went on : ' Sea-marvels
more wonderful than any former books of history had
ever described : fish with popes' heads, monks' hoods
and Jesuit hats ; new-born infants with two, three and
more heads ; women who had given birth to little pigs
or donkeys ; children who had come into the world
with gold teeth, or wearing trousers or neck ruffles, and
who had spoken and predicted wonders the instant they
were born ; fiery signs, bloody rain, blood-red comets ;
Christ in the sky encompassed with blood ; angels who
had been heard preaching in the clouds ; as, indeed,'
he said in conclusion, ' the reports of these true and
wonderful events are all over the land, and all the people
are acquainted with them.' [1]

'If any,' wrote another preacher, ' wish to speak of
the great wonders which are happening almost every
day, and foretelling the judgment of God, it is fitting
that they should first make mention of the prodigies
and abortions which are born into the world, and
of which credible reports are circulated everywhere
in print.   Is it not indeed a wonder well adapted
to warn and terrify the people that, by way of
example, a woman in the Voigtland, in this very
sixty-second year, should have given birth all at
the same time to seven children, who had together
thirty-two hands, nine heads and only eleven feet,
and one of which had a moustache, while another wore
a Jesuit hat ? Portents and prodigies of this sort, well
authenticated, have happened in endless number, and
their truth cannot be disputed.' [2]

[1] See our remarks, vol. x. pp. 48, 49.
[2] *Von grewlichen Misgeburten*, &c., Bl. B.   As early as the end of the

After the second half of the century the number of
'new, alarming, but quite true, tidings' increased with
almost every year ; these, most of them in rhyme,
gave notice of all sorts of abortions which had come
as signs of divine chastisement, and they were abundantly supplied with illustrations in order 'to impress
them still more deeply on the human mind.' Thus,
for instance, the Hamburg preacher, Joachim Magde-
burgius, ' made an exact picture of a calf born in 1556
with six feet, two heads, and two tails.' A preacher of
Werringschleben described in 1563 ' a frightful birth
and visible portent which had taken place in his village ';
new editions appeared from his report in Augsburg,
Erfurt and Strassburg. A Zurich newspaper announced
' a terrible abortive birth of a pig in Hesse,' a Tübingen
paper ' a birth prodigy never before heard of in the
village of Franckenau.' [1] In the year 1565 there
appeared an official report stating that, on the property
of the lord of Bernstein, a child had been born without
a head and without bones ; on the left shoulder it had a
mouth, on the right one an ear, and so forth ; it had been
delivered over to the flames by the hand of an executioner as a devil's abortion, but it had been necessary
to cut it up into quite small pieces, and to use a great
deal of wood and powder before it could be burnt.' [2]
Equally remarkable was an announcement in 1576 of
' a gruesome child, born in November 1575, at Arnheim

fifteenth century abortions had already been the subject of special literary
attention. The humanist, James Locher, published in 1499 a *Carmen
heroicum de partu monstrifero in oppido Rhain* . . . cf. Hain, *Repertorium*,
2ᵃ, No. 10, p. 162. ' Ein Lied vom Jahre 1517 auf eine Misgeburt in
Strassburg,' in the *Archiv für Litteraturgesch.* ii. 136–137.

[1] Weller, *Annalen*, i. Abt. 2, Nos. 142, 181, 189, 238, 240.
[2] Wolfius, *Lectiones*, ii. 825.

in Guelderland.' This child, covered all over with rough hair, immediately after its birth ran under a bed ; it had two horns on its head, two feet like a peacock's and its hands were like bird's claws ; 'numbers of people saw this monstrosity both alive and dead.'[1] With all such frightful portents 'announcing the day of the Lord,' it must have seemed scarcely worthy of notice that once, as David Meder said in a sermon, in the county of Hohenlohe a whole case full of threads and little bits of linen rag were taken out of a child's eyes.[2]

Horror was caused especially by 'all sorts of monstrous forms and abortions of animals born of women or human beings born of animals ' ; these were not indeed ' quite frequent everywhere,' but nevertheless occurred ' constantly in those terrible times.' A woman of Augsburg, ' of this there is not the slightest doubt,' gave birth at the same time to a human head, without any other limbs, wrapped up in a skin, a snake with two feet, and a pig with body and limbs complete.[3] What John Fischart told as a well-established fact of a Jewess at Binzwangen, who in 1574 'had brought into the world two little live pigs,'[4] happened also in the following year in a Bohemian village.[5] The Hessian superintendent, George Nigrinus, was able to report a few years later that a child had been born at Erfurt with monkey's claws, a horse's nose, and a tall hat.[6]

---

[1] *Fliegendes Blatt* in Scheible, *Schaltjahr*, iii. 627–630.

[2] Meder, p. 77. The Landgrave William of Hesse showed Count Philip of Hohenlohe ' a whole glass full of flies and gnats which had come out of the eyes of a boy of noble birth at his court ' (Rüdiger, p. 310).

[3] Scheible, *Schaltjahr*, ii. 460.   [4] See vol. xi. pp. 374, 375.

[5] *Eine Wundergeburt in Böhmen*, 116 rhymes. Without locality, 1576.

[6] See our remarks, vol. x. p. 28.

At Prague, in 1591, the daughter of a cook gave
birth to a beautiful boy and at the same time to five
monsters, one of which was a dog and another like a
monkey.[1]   A terrible report of the year 1595 was to
the effect that a woman at Liegnitz had had three
children at one birth, one of them with three heads
which began to speak and to prophesy wonders directly
after its birth.   At Nebra in Thuringia, on one occasion,
flames burst out of a woman during childbirth; the
fire danced round the room and made a great stench
of powder and brimstone, 'many honourable matrons
being present at the time, and also some of the nobility,
who saw and bore witness to the event.'[2]   At Bacharach
in 1595 the wife of a drunkard gave birth to a monster
the upper part of which was human, the lower part a
snake, with a tail three yards long.   As the father was
coming home from the ale-house, the creature shot at
him like a falcon, wound round him and killed him with
poisonous stabs.[3]   The year before, according to an
Erfurt 'veritable new tidings,' a woman at Blanken-
burg in Saxony brought a devil's child into the world :

> On its body it had a head
> Which none could look at without dread ;
> Upon its head two horns there grew—
> Ye men and women, this is true ;
> Its eyes to look upon were dire,
> Fierce and flaming like red fire ;
> From its mouth, too, fire blazed . . .
> Five men, who thereupon had gazed,
> Died in the same hour of fright,
> Terror-stricken by the sight.

---

[1] Chmel, *Handschriften*, i. 402.   Concerning *Schauermären* (shudder-
fables), accounts of which were sent to the Archduke Ferdinand II. of
Tyrol from Vienna and Prague, cf. Hirn, ii. 512.

[2] Scheible, *Schaltjahr*, ii. 91–92.

[3] Wolfius, *Lectiones*, ii. 1027.

Scarcely was it born when this devil's child fell upon its
blasphemous father,

> Through the window dragged him out—
> This was seen by old and young—
> And in a moment his neck wrung.[1]

In order that both present and after times 'might,
by such manifold and dreadful spectacles, be more
deeply moved to the fear of God and the shunning of
sin,' Doctor Schenck of Grafenberg published, in 1610,
reports of nearly ninety 'monstrous births from unreasoning animals.' Once 'a cow gave birth to two
human beings, a male and a female'; another time
there was 'an unheard-of birth of a calf which, to
the unbounded astonishment of everyone, was like a
clerical person'; further, there was 'an abortive birth
of a pig, which in many points resembled a priest';
this last wonder 'occurred at Hall in Saxony on the
high and sacred festival of our Lord and Redeemer.'
Schenck's 'Wunderbuch' closed with the picture of
an 'extraordinarily unnatural' egg, 'in which was found
a man's head with young snakes for hair'; 'on the chin
also, instead of a beard, there were three snakes of the
same kind.' [2]

'It was the duty,' said the preacher Balthasar
Rietesel, 'of every pregnant woman to search out her
heart and acknowledge her sins, for she could not tell
what fruit she might bring into the world,' and whether,
'in special punishment of all the prevalent vices,
monstrosities such as are described and copied in the
little book "Elucidarius," which is in everybody's

---

[1] Printed at Erfurt by George Bawman, 1594.
[2] Schenck, Preface and pp. 121–162. Cf. our remarks above, p. 229 ;
for the rest Schenck was a physician of merit ; cf. Sprengel, iii. 165.

hands, showing what happens in distant lands, might not also be brought into the world in Germany.' [1]

This 'booklet' 'Elucidarius, concerning all sorts of creations of God,' enjoyed, at any rate, the widest circulation.[2] It supplied the people from the writings of different cosmographers with accounts of the following nature : 'There are numbers of Ethiopians, Moors, or Indians who have no heads, but eyes and mouths on their breasts.' 'There are people in the Indian land who bark instead of talking ; they are of both sexes, male and female, but they all conceive and bear children, the men as well as the women. Their right breast is male, and the left one female.' 'In the land of Sicily there are people who have ears so enormous that they cover the whole body.' 'In Ethiopia some people have horns, long noses, and geese's feet ; some have four eyes ; there are also people there with horses' hoofs, also people who have one broad foot, and they often shade themselves from the sun with the breadth of their foot. In Eripa there are handsome people with crane's necks and bills ; some of them live in water, and are half-human and half-horses ' ; and many more such 'marvellous apparitions,' all which were brought vividly before the reader's eye by illustrations. To entice customers three of these human prodigies were painted on the title-page.[3]

In order 'suitably to convince the people that these marvels and monstrosities were really signs of God's

---

[1] *Busspredig für alle Stände* (Ursel, 1617), Bl. C.

[2] Cf. *Messmemorial*, p. vii., and Pallmann, p. 156.

[3] *Elucidarius*, Bl. C 2 to C 4. In Sebastian Münster's *Cosmography* (Basle edition of 1545) there are also numerous pictures of abortions, ghosts, and abnormally formed human beings and animals, pp. 71, 230, 354, 421, 507, 615, 729, 749, 752, 763 ff

wrath' they were plentifully explained and illustrated, 'with good Christian intent.'

Luther and Melanchthon, as early as 1523, had published a compilation entitled 'Deutung zweier greu- lichen Figuren' ('The Meaning of two horrible Por- tents'), which was supplied with illustrations and went through several editions.   One of these was 'a dreadful animal' which the Tiber had thrown up at Rome, and the other a 'monk-calf,' the abortion of a cow, which appeared at Freiberg-in-Meissen.   The people were to look upon them as 'signs from God.'   In the animal prodigy at Rome, said Melanchthon, 'God Himself' had counterfeited the abomination of the papacy, in order that people should be on their guard 'against the accursed Antichrist and his followers.'   Still more emphatically Luther declared that 'the whole world must tremble and shudder at this monster because the high, divine Majesty itself had begotten and created it, in order to show forth what was in His mind.   Was not everybody frightened if a ghost or a devil ap- peared, or a mysterious noise is heard in a corner?   And this was mere child's play compared to this mon- strosity, through which God Himself appeared openly and showed Himself in such awful guise.'   The horrible animal at Rome, 'the pope-ass,' signified the downfall of the papacy, the 'monk-calf' the downfall of monks; for it was sufficiently 'declared by this calf that God was the enemy of monasticism.'   The Papists must learn to see 'in the calf and the cow, as in a mirror before their eyes, who they are in the sight of God, and what is thought of them in heaven.'[1]   Dr. Simon

[1] Luther's collected works, xxix. pp. 2–16. Cf. our fuller state- ments, vol. iii. pp. 339–342, and ** K. Lange, *Der Papstesel. Ein*

Pauli of Rostock, in 1578, wrote no fewer than ten explanations of the 'terrible unnatural birth' of a child in Mecklenburg. Among other things it pointed to the imminent invasion of Mecklenburg by the Papists, Turks and Russians, who would then 'deal with us as mercilessly as Antiochus and the other heathen kings dealt with the Jews.' The fact that the unnatural child 'with a long, tall, Turkish and Russian hat, was born of a tailor's wife,' plainly showed how abominable in the sight of God the Lord were the new-fashioned clothes then made by the tailors.[1]

With constant appeal to Luther, and with the most frightful slander and abuse of the papacy and the Papists, whom he denounced as 'more wicked than devils,' the preacher Christopher Irenaeus published in 1584 a book of nearly seven hundred pages on the 'occurrence, origin, and signification of strange and wonderful abortions.' Even without bearing any special marks of the devil in his body, man, said this preacher, in and of himself after the Fall, and before his regeneration in Christ, was 'the most hideous monster and image of the devil.' The special monsters, which to the horror of the whole world had been born in countless numbers, were not, as was asserted, works of the devil or of nature and chance, but God Himself had fashioned

Beitrag zur Kultur- und Kunstgeschichte des Reformationsalters (Göttingen, 1891).

[1] S. Pauli, Bildnuss und Gestalt, &c. (Rostock, 1578). Cf. especially the explanations of abortive births in Fincelius, Wunderzeichen, pt. iii. (Jena, 1562), Bl. K 2 ; L 5 ff. ; N ff. That in the times of Calvin, Beza, Zwingli, many children were born with dogs' heads, was 'a sign of the times in which everything was barked out after the manner of dogs.' Wolfius, ii. 954.

** Cf. also Mart. Weinrichius, De ortu monstrorum Commentarius (Leipzig, 1595).

them as a punishment to mankind.[1] He referred to
the many monsters which, especially since the middle
of the century, had already been made known to the
people by printed matter and by illustrations, and he
introduced a number more to the knowledge of ' distressed ' Christendom, the following among others :
In 1580 at Hildesheim a mare gave birth to two little
boys, ' who were in every way and in all their members
shaped exactly like other boys.' At the same time
' two hideous monsters were born of a woman at Havel-
berg-in-the-Mark on December 12. One of them was
beyond measure dreadful, deformed, and disgusting,
none other than a disguised or masked monk and
Jesuit.'[2] In a little town near Göttingen a woman
gave birth to a wolf. A wife in the Netherlands bore
' a little boy with seven heads, each of which had only
one eye ; they had seven arms and two feet like the
feet of a wild animal or beast. The foremost and
principal head had, as it were, two pig's ears.'[3] A
woman at Bünigheim in the Habergau gave birth to
no fewer than fifty-three children, ' nearly always four
at a time,' and once ' in twelve weeks she had seven
children.' Even worse was the case of ' a woman in
the Cleverland, who in 1555 gave birth all at once to
365 little children. Half of them were boys and half
girls, and they were carried to church and all baptised.'
' They are said to have been so tiny that they were
scarcely bigger than a little finger, but they were all
of perfect human form, and all born alive.'[4] All these
prodigies Irenaeus could quite easily explain ' with great
clearness from the revelation of God's Spirit.' For

---

[1] Irenaeus, Preface of sixty pages, F 4ᵇ. V 4ᵇ. c–eᵃ.
[2] Bl. T 3ᵇ—T 4.   [3] Bl. R. S 4. o 2ᵇ.   [4] Bl. O 3. L ll.

instance, the meaning of 'those strange monsters and abortions which had such extraordinary mouths and more than one tongue, and which were born so quickly one after another, has, alas! been shown by after events and experience' in the double-tonguedness of Melanchthon, of the Wittenbergers, and of other theologians. 'The children with two, three, and even more heads' were, among other meanings, to be regarded as a foreshadowing of the pretended formula of concord of James Andreä and his followers :

> There's no abortion to us sent
> But comes from God as punishment
> For mankind's wickedness, nor can
> We find a monster worse than man,
> For, since the fall of Adam, he
> Has been corrupt as he can be.[1]

No less terrifying than the innumerable cases of abortion were 'the equally countless wonderful apparitions in inanimate nature and in the sky which were undoubtedly attested,' and which 'were issued in print every year for a warning to all true-hearted Christians,' who, the preacher Rietesel hoped, 'would buy all these accounts and take them well to heart.'[2]

As early as 1556 the physician Job Fincelius had published a whole collection of these 'fearful portents and stories,' which, 'since 1517, when God's Word had begun to be preached in Germany, had been seen in heaven and on earth and in other creatures.' 'Whereas the gravest offences,' he said in his dedication of his work to the Duchess Maria of Pomerania-Stettin, 'such as contempt of God's Word and persistence in gross sins and shame, were in full swing among us, and are

---

[1] Bl. Ee 2–4. Gg. 2 to JJJ 2b, LLL 2b.   [2] See above, p. 236, n. 1.

increasing and multiplying from day to day,' God's wrath can no longer be withheld. 'The supernatural signs and wonders were penitential preachers and heralds of this wrath, and must therefore be driven into the people's minds by written descriptions.' [1]

'If all histories are read through it will be found that never at any time did so many signs and wonders happen as in the present day, when one scarcely leaves room for another. No sooner has one gone by than another comes, so that without doubt God has something great in His mind, and that great distress will befall the Christian Churches, and terrible changes will take place among worldly rulers, with war and bloodshed.' No value must be attached to the objection that 'in the present age people are already quite enough terrified without these portents,' and that 'they cannot be made more anxious and frightened with any amount of threatenings ; for the godless must learn to fear and tremble, and earnest Christians also must acknowledge their sins with awe before God's everlasting judgment. All this that he had made known to the public he had not put together lightly and without forethought, but he had collected it from the experience of pious, trustworthy persons, who in part had been themselves witnesses of these wonders.' [2] For instance, in Hesse, in the year 1530, a child screamed so loud in its mother's womb that the whole household heard it. At Pilsen in Bohemia, in 1542, a child was born that resembled a crucifix. In many places in

---

[1] Fincelius, A 2-3.   ** Janssen quotes from the edition of 1557. The first edition printed in 1556 appeared at Nuremberg, and is now in the Hof- und Staatsbibliothek at Munich.

[2] Bl. B 4 ; C 3-5.

Germany cockchafers appeared with monks' hoods—grey, yellow, and black. In Silesia there fell hail as big as a fist, ' in which there were clearly seen the objectionable clothes worn by Landsknechts and other fantastic sort of garments.' Stones with Turkish hats were also seen to fall. Near Erfurt, in 1555, a wolf tore about, hugging and squeezing the women in the field, and it had an unusually large mouth. ' All these things have been seen and related by trustworthy people.'   Among a hundred other such-like ' dreadful portents and demoniacal apparitions ' Fincelius told as serious truth that in 1554, in a village near Cammin, a filly had been born with the ears of a staghound and a mouth like two pot-ladles. ' When it neighed everybody thought it was a full-grown horse. If any of the nobles went up to it, it assumed a strange and ferocious attitude, and pranced up at them with loud howling.' Burghers and peasants, on the other hand, it allowed to approach quite quietly.[1] Fincelius ended with the words : ' After I had collected these wonders of God, not without great trouble and industry, into a book, I was afraid that either unfriendly people or unscrupulous disdainers might set about to falsify the work, either by deducting from or adding to it. I therefore make my petition to all and sundry that they will allow my book to remain unaltered and unimproved. If anybody wishes to serve the common welfare, let him make a book for himself.' [2]

Fincelius added to his work a second and even a third part, and he could with justice boast that ' his books met with the most cordial approval and esteem.'

[1] Bl. E 2b, J 3. J 8. N 8. Q 5b. R 3–6. T 3b–4. V 7 ; cf. Irenaeus, P 2.
[2] Bl. X 3.

Michael Harder, at the Frankfurt fair of 1569, alone
sold 171 copies of the three parts together,[1] and the
firm of Sigmund Feyerabend, in the Lent and autumn
fairs of the following year, sold 233 copies.[2]

An imitator of Fincelius appeared in 1557 in the
preacher John Herold of Basle, who published in a
folio volume a German translation, with supplementary
additions, of a Latin work of the preacher Conrad
Lykosthenes (Wolffart) on 'God's inscrutable wonder-
works in strange creatures, and abortions, and apparitions in the heavens, on the earth, and in the waters.'
His book was intended 'for study and Christian medi-
tation by the elect, and for the wicked for punishment of their unbelief.' Although his readers, he says
in the preface, 'may find in this work many things
which are beyond human understanding and belief,
such as oxen, snakes, and dogs that talk, trees and
mountains changing place, grapes growing on elder
trees, corn on oaks, women turning into men, the sea
in flames, and new islands starting out of it, and many
other things which are hard for the inexperienced to
believe,' they must nevertheless accept them in humility
of mind. For all these wonders he had taken out of
the books of trustworthy people, and some of them
he had also seen with his own eyes, and 'heard tell of
by people who were truthful.' 'Human reason, dear
reader, must not dive too deep into God's works, of
this I would have you admonished, for these same
works are wonderful, great and incomprehensible, as
the man of God, Job, bears witness, and as the prophet David everywhere exclaims, and also exhorts all

[1] *Messmemorial*, p. vii.   [2] Pallmann, p. 160.

R 2

believers to do the same.'.[1]   The author mentioned all
the different writings from which he had taken these
wonders, and named seventeen learned men who had
helped him in his work: Conrad Gessner, Henry
Bullinger, Huldrich Merian, John Grell, John Oporinus,
Rudolf Lavater, and others.[2]   A child born in 1543,
with fiery eyes, mouth and nose like an ox, dogs' heads
at its elbows, and a yard-long tail with a scorpion
hook, is said to have spoken the following words:
'Awake! your Lord and God is at hand!' whereupon
'throughout all Europe there was great mortality.'
'In Hungary, in the year 1549, snakes, vipers, and
toads grew in people's insides.   Among these there
was one much greater than the others, which said in
a clear voice: It's of no use, however hard you set
yourselves against punishment from God.'   'In Meissen,
in 1550, a man was walking across the churchyard,
when a grave burst open, and a loud voice was heard
from it: " Woe, woe, the town! "   The good man was
so terrified that he fell down in a swoon.   It is said
also that a fish was caught in the sea of Denmark which
resembled a monk.'[3]

The number of 'Wonder-books' was very great.
Adam Ursinus published a 'Beschreibung der Wunderzeichen von 1568, 1569, und 1570'; [4] Caspar Goldwurm
a 'Wahrhaftige Beschreibung vieler Wunderwerke'; [5]
Abraham Saur a 'Diarium historicum' or a 'Chronika,

[1] Herold, a 5. b 3ᵇ. c 4.   See our remarks, vol. xi. pp. 227–229.   ** A
German and a Latin edition of the work of Herold, both of them printed
in 1557, and preserved in the Hof- und Staatsbibliothek at Munich.

[2] Bl. b 5.   [3] Herold, pp. 497–546.

[4] Erfurt, 1570.

[5] Frankfort-on-the-Main, 1579.   ** The first edition appeared in
Frankfort, 1557, the second in the same place in 1567 ; both are in the
Hof- und Staatsbibliothek at Munich.

in which on each day some special stories, remarkable and true, alarming wonders which have happened, are described ' ; [1] Ambrosius Taurer a ' Bericht von mancherlei erschrecklichen Wunderzeichen.' [2]

Great excitement was caused in the year 1549 by what was considered ' a very extraordinary vision,' related by Doctor Nicholas Medler, superintendent at Brunswick, as having been seen in the sky by four young Brunswick burghers in the week of Pentecost. Among other things they saw a fiery wolf, an eagle with two heads, the whole exact image of the captive Elector of Saxony, Christ on the Cross between two malefactors, and besides all this a great and terrible person with a tremendous sword in his hand. ' With the two who saw the vision most plainly,' the superintendent declared, ' I myself have spoken, and they agree perfectly together.' A messenger from Leipzig ' had also seen Christ on the Cross, but not in Christ's own form, for he had a grey beard ' ; he had also seen two angels and

[1] Frankfort-on-the-Main, 1582. ** Second edition in the same place, 1594. A *Catalogus prodigiorum, miraculorum,* &c. had already appeared at Nuremberg in 1563. On the Catholic side Abraham Nagel published at Flochberg (Ingolstadt, 1583) a true description of an ' unerhörtes Wunderwerk.' Valentine Leucht published an *Historische Beschreibung vieler Wunderwerke, welche bei dem heiligen Kreuz geschehen* (Würzburg, 1591) ; another work on the *Wunderwerke welche bei dem heiligen Altarssacrament geschehen* (first edition, Würzburg, 1598 ; second edition, Würzburg and Mayence, 1606) ; and further a German *Viridarium miraculorum* (Mayence, 1611). ** To this series belongs also Tilm. Bredenbach's *Collationum Sacrorum libri VIII.* Coloniae, 1584, 1591, 1592, 1599, 1609, an uncritical collection of marvellous tales.

[2] Hall, 1591. In the same year there appeared at Tübingen a Latin pamphlet, which had already been printed in 1571, entitled *Disputatio de miraculis,* by James Heerbrand. ** Among Protestant writings belonging to this set there still remain to be mentioned : (1) Wolfg. Bütner, *Epitome Historiarum.* Selected Christian tales and histories . . . Short epitome (Leipzig, 1576). (2) Andrew Angelus, *Wider Natur und Wunderbuch* (Frankfort-on-the-Main, 1597).

a man with a sword, who was about to cut off the head
of one of the figures kneeling before him.   All this was
a tremendous warning, which God was sending forth in
connection with the present day abundant revelation of
His sacred Word.   In the preface to this narrative the
author inveighed fiercely against the Papists, who ' were
possessed with the devil,' and were ' consciously sinning
against the Holy Ghost.' [1]

A particularly deep impression must have been
produced by ' nature-wonders ' of the following description.   In a village in Mecklenburg ' there grew in a
wonderful manner a hand and a face out of the pillar
of the pulpit in the church.' [2]   At Zweibrücken, in
1597, ' a stone in the town was heard to call out, and
after this in five days nine hundred people died
suddenly.' [3]   Some time before this the moon had
spoken out distinctly.   ' On March 23, 1582, between
eight and nine before midnight,' so the astronomer
Lambert Floridus Plieninger reported, ' trustworthy
people at Morthingen in Lorraine had seen the moon
come down close to the earth in the form of a veiled
woman, and heard it cry out distinctly : " Woe, woe ! "
six or seven times one after another, after which it
returned to its accustomed place and orbit.'   By this
exclamation of woe the moon meant to warn the Protestants against the acceptance of the new Gregorian
Calendar, just as before ' when the Roman were-wolf
and Antichrist Gregory was publishing his wicked
Calendar work, to the ruin of the poor evangelical
Christians, the moon had come down to earth in a

---

[1] *A Wonderful Vision, seen in the Sky near Brunswick*, &c., 1549.
[2] Lisch, *Jahrbücher des Vereins für Mecklenb. Geschichte*, xxii. 263.
[3] Weller, *Zeitungen*, No. 848.

village in the Voigtland and with an angry, almost ferocious aspect, had said several times quite plainly : " Woe, woe, blood, blood, Pope and Jesuits ! " '

If the ' powers of heaven were thus moving and speaking,' ' heed must also be taken of the many bloody tokens which were credibly reported in hundreds of newspapers in all the German lands.' In the Saxon village of Ichtershausen, Plieninger related, in July 1582, ' the fish-stream Piscina had been changed into pure blood, and had remained in this state for six days.' In 1597, according to a trustworthy newspaper, ' blood and brimstone had rained down in and outside the town of Stralsund at different times, and fire from heaven had fallen on the Church of St. Mary in the same place ' ; at the same time ' God allowed blood to rain on the town of Schilbrick in Silesia.' [1] In a ' Donner- und Wunder- predigt ' (' Thunder and Wonder Sermon ') which lasted several hours, Hartmann Braun, pastor at Grünberg in Hesse, in 1603, told his congregation from the pulpit what horrible things had happened in different places : on the Rhine, in the Allgäu and in Bavaria there had been hailstones as big as hen's eggs, in which sulphur and pitch had been found ; in Saxony and Meissen fire-balls had fallen from heaven ; at a place in Silesia the hailstones had been as large as hens' and geese's eggs, and some of them had the appearance of ruffles, such as are worn at the present day, with a stamped, open-work pattern.[2]

---

[1] Weller, *Zeitungen*, Nos. 840, 843, 845, 848, 849 ; Weller, *Annalen*, i. Abt. 2, No. 318.   ** In 1552 blood and flesh rained down at Hofstadt in Franconia, so says Goldwurm, *Wunderzeichen*, 1567, Bl. 83ᵇ. Concerning the ' Kalenderwunder ' see our remarks, vol. x. pp. 35–39.

[2] Braun, *Drei christl. Predigten*, pp. 177–189.   The sermon consists of full eighty pages of print.

Of a more cheerful nature was the tale of the Göttingen burgomaster, Tilmann Friese, who ' had heard from certain experienced people ' that pennies had fallen from heaven ; he did not doubt the story, for God had worked many other miracles ' in the air with stone-blood and corn-rain.' [1]   At Klagenfurt in Carinthia and round about Villach, wrote Herold, ' on March 23, 1550, corn had rained down for two hours long and the country people had picked it up and eaten it : I, John Herold, myself saw this corn.' [2]   Corn had also rained down in Brandenburg, Thuringia, Silesia, in Austria and Bavaria ; in other places milk ; once a great black loaf, and another time bits of meat.[3] In the year 1579, in Norway, a shower of monks had fallen, according to the report of James Krüger, preacher in Hamburg.[4]

All unusual phenomena of nature were regarded as portents of misfortune. ' When new portents in manifold shapes,' wrote Theophrastus Paracelsus, ' fall from heaven to earth, it behoves us to consider what is the cause, for such things do not happen except they are intended as presages ; and they do not occur in the ordinary course of nature, but are introduced by the ordinance of God as tokens and presages ; for God is the Master and Maker, the disposer and shaper of such presages.' [5]

The Darmstadt superintendent, Henry Leuchter, in a pamphlet of 1613, made out that even high winds and rainbows were not to be explained by simple natural

---

[1] *Müntz-Spiegel*, pp. 45–46.   [2] Herold, p. 523.

[3] Weller, *Zeitungen*, Nos. 359, 516.   Fincelius, i. Bl. Q 5ᵇ ; cf. R 3 and 5. See the remarks in Kornmann, pp. 96–97.

[4] ** Weller, *Zeitungen*, No. 537.

[5] Schindler, p. 214, note.

causes, but must be regarded as signs of divine chastisement.   For did not history show what heavy ills, for
instance, had followed after the great winds of 1606,
namely famine, plague, illnesses among leading people
and deaths of great potentates ?   The divine judgments
which followed the appearance of rainbows were war,
tumult and sedition in the land, and unfortunate
alliances.   When in 1525 a nocturnal rainbow had
been seen, the death of Duke Frederic of Saxony and
the terrible revolt of the peasants had immediately
followed : 'many thousands took flight in consequence.'
Now, too, melancholy events would again take place ;
for in the past year, among other portents of nature,
'there had been high winds, and here and there rainbows had been seen.'   But in the midst of all these
'sinister occurrences' men and women were as uncon-
cerned as wild beasts about the great signs from God
and the Day of Judgment so close at hand.[1]

The portents which caused the greatest alarm were
miraculous stars and comets.   'Of the new miraculous
star which appeared on September 26, 1604, and remained visible till the year 1606,' Paul Nagelius
prophesied that 'there would scarcely be a house or
a corner where there would not be terrible misfortunes
to bewail and lament.'   In particular this star signified 'persecution among the clergy and their expulsion
from Germany'; the Jesuits especially 'would not
escape the chastisement and rod of the Almighty';
general scarcity and famine, pestilence, great conflagra-
tions and unheard-of deeds of murder would follow.
Albinus Mollerus said, 'The meanings of this new star
are much greater, much more terrible, more sad and

[1] Leuchter, pp. 10, 14, 32–35, 37 ff., 43, 46.

more injurious than is a comet, because it has surpassed all the other planets on high, and the like of this has never happened before since the world began.' Among other things it presaged ' change in religion and great and unheard-of misfortune for the Calvinists; and, besides the Turkish war, a dreadful war of princes with dire tumult, murder and conflagration.' David Fabricius Frisius explained the star as foretelling ' the cruel maladies of the Roman eagle.' ' The subjects of the Roman empire would be invaded by the surrounding and neighbouring peoples, and ruthlessly robbed and plundered ; many long for foreign domination,' but the eagle will not perish; the holy light of the evangel will suddenly begin and shine in many dark places, and a ' great light of the Church ' will arise. Should there be any attempt to resist this light there would in all like-lihood be a violent reformation, by which the Church's estate would be lamentably dismembered and the ec-clesiastical states transformed into secular dominions. John Krabbe at Wolfenbüttel saw in the star a pre-diction that a new prophet ' would work great signs and wonders, and draw many people to himself.' This meaning ' is powerfully confirmed by the great conjunc-tion of the previous year.' [1]

The mathematician and house-physician of the Count Palatine of Veldenz, Helisäus Röslin, was of a different opinion about the meaning of this portent ; not this star, he said, which smiled on them in such a friendly way, but the comets were the presagers of divine punishments. ' Nothing remarkable ever hap-pens in the world,' he wrote in 1609, ' without God

[1] *Kurtzer und gründl. Bericht von erschreckl. grausamen Zeiten*, &c. (Halle, 1612), Bl. B 3ᵇ–C 4.

first warning mankind by special signs in heaven and
on earth, in the upper and the lower world ' ; ' does not
every-day experience teach that whenever God has some
special design for human beings, either removal by
death, or else some great disaster, he gives them warning beforehand in many ways ? ' All the more did this
apply to the great signs, the comets ; for these were
' the actual critical signs of the world and of rulers, who
after their occurrence were instantly stricken with
diseases.' ' With reference to the comets which had
appeared since 1600 ' Röslin compiled an ' Historischer,
politischer, und astronomischer Diskurs von heutiger
Zeit Beschaffenheit, Wesen und Stand der Christenheit,
und wie es inskünftig derselben ergehen werde.' ' I am
by no means one of those,' he emphatically assures the
Margrave, George Frederic of Baden-Hochberg, in the
dedicatory pages of the work, ' of whom there are such
swarms nowadays, who fill the world with wordy, useless chatter and astrological humbug, and with lying
books ; from such iniquitous arts God has wonderfully preserved me.' [1]

Towards the end of the fourteenth century Henry
Langenstein, professor of Theology and Mathematics

---

[1] It was not inauspicious but auspicious events that the stars betokened,
hence the Basle doctor, who considered the miraculous star of 1572 the
presager of all the disturbance and bloodshed which had followed in
France and the Netherlands, was a bad philosopher or Magus. It was
different with the comets, which ' with their long tails like rods, signified,
in natural magic, judgments and plagues, war and bloodshed.' There
was, moreover, another difference between stars and comets, namely that
the first referred to ' universal events,' while the latter referred more to
' private events occurring here and there in the world.' Besides which
the results of the comets did not happen immediately, but sometimes
not for seven years. ' So also from this present comet I opine that the
influence will not be fully felt for seven years, when there will be great
disturbance.' Röslin, Bl. b³, E 1, F 1ᵇ–F 2, H, K, N.

in Vienna († 1397), one of the strongest opponents of
astrology and chiromancy, had publicly combated the
superstition that there was any portentous significance
in comets.[1] After the middle of the fifteenth century
John Müller, called Regiomontanus, after his home
Königsberg in Lower Franconia, an equally zealous
opponent of astrology, had determined the distance,
size, and orbits of the comets, thus bringing them into
the region of scientific observation ;[2] in the sixteenth
century, however, scholars, with few exceptions, fell
back into the old superstitions about comets.[3]

The Protestant preachers and theologians also set
themselves up especially as interpreters of these extraordinary celestial apparitions.[4] They were first and
foremost, wrote one of themselves, in duty bound
' to explain to the people by preaching and writing
the terrible meanings, histories and examples of the
comets, and thereby to infuse wholesome awe and
dread of the divine judgments.'[5] To this end the
theologian James Heerbrand published, in 1577, a
' sermon about the dreadful sign and wonder in heaven,

---

[1] Cf. Wolf, *Astronomie*, p. 85.

[2] See our remarks, vol. i. pp. 139 ff. Wolf, pp. 181, 388.

[3] Peter Apian, professor of Mathematics at Ingolstadt († 1552), and
John Richter or Praetorius, professor at Altorf († 1616), were the only
ones who opposed these superstitious ideas ; cf. Wolf, pp. 102, 265, 407–
408. Among the Catholics Peter Binsfeld, bishop-auxiliary of Treves,
in his *Tractatus de confessionibus maleficorum* &c. (Treves, 1591), pp.
418–425, was the chief advocate for the supernatural significance of
comets (' . . . ex speciali Dei dispositione apparet ').

[4] ** Comets, according to Luther, portended only evil. Luther's
works, Erl. edition, pp. 62, 319. John Richter, or Praetorius, was a
perfect slave to the superstitions about comets ; cf. *Narratio oder Historische
Erzelung dern Cometen, so vor diser Zeit sind gesehen worden*, &c., &c.,
written by Joh. Praetorius (Nuremberg, 1578). (It is here shown in
detail that comets portend disaster.)

[5] *Von den grewlichen Misgeburten*, &c. Bl. C 2.

the new comet or peacock tail.' [1]   The preacher
Christopher Irenaeus wrote in the following year a
'Prognosticon aus Gottes Wort, a necessary reminder
and Christian penitential sermon in these last evil days
. . . about the comets which have been seen by Martini from 1577 to the beginning of 1578, together with
accounts of many other comets and terrible signs,
and what always followed after them.' [2]   At the same
time the superintendent Andrew Celichius wrote a
'Theologische Erinnerung von dem newen Cometen.' [3]
L. Hamel composed in German rhyme a 'Theologischer
Bericht von dem erschrecklichen Kometen und seinen
Effekten.' [4]   The Elector Augustus of Saxony, 'by
reason of this doleful and dreadful sign of God's wrath,'
caused a Church prayer to be formulated by Selnekker
and James Andreä, and sent into all the parishes.[5]
In the year 1580 Adelar Praetorius, preacher at Erfurt, dedicated to 'the whole of Christendom' a
'Selige Erinnerung von dem erschrecklichen fewrenden
Kometstern am Himmel,' 'seen and observed in the
evening, through October and November of this current
year 1580, by Christian eyes and hearts.' [6]   Zacharias

---

[1] Tübingen, 1577.   Out of this sermon the Leonberg schoolmaster
Kreidweiss, in 1578, composed *A True Warning to Repentance*, &c.   On
account of the general wickedness, Germany, he said, was ripe for destruction ; pious people were looked upon as fools :

> Herewith I give an illustration
> Of my simple speculation,
> How this comet means, in my opinion,
> Mahomet's teaching, might and dominion ;
> How the Turk's rule it signifies,
> And the papal power typifies . . .
> Is like him in his tyranny,
> And causes great idolatry . .

[2] Without locality, 1578.   [3] Magdeburg, 1578.
[4] Frankfort-on-the-Main, 1578.
[5] Weber, *Anna von Sachsen*, p. 363.   [6] Erfurt, 1580.

Rivander, preacher at Luckenwalde, went more deeply
still into the meaning of this comet, which he said
foreboded war and the speedy advent of the Day of
Judgment; he gave an exact description of its shape,
size and colour, and at the same time drew attention
to many other wonderful signs which had occurred at
Berlin, in the lordship of Mansfeld and elsewhere. A
prodigy in Mansfeld, he said, 'was painted on a large
sheet of parchment, and carried about for sale with an
accompanying printed memorandum.' From the dedicatory pages of his pamphlet, addressed to the Magdeburg Captain Otto von Amsdorf, we learn that 'many
people' were of opinion that it was not the business of
the preachers but of the mathematicians to interpret
the comets. But for such people, Rivander said, he
cared not; they might 'make sour faces and assume
terrible airs, and, as their father the devil had taught
them, abuse him, the preacher, to their hearts' content;
he, however, was resolved to put out to the best interest
the pound entrusted him by his Lord.'[1]

In a great many publications the comet of 1618 was
regarded as the loudest actual 'trumpet' announcing
the advent of Christ.[2] Mövius Völschow, among others,
formerly professor of mathematics and librarian at the
university of Greifswald, and afterwards pastor and
praepositus at Bergen in the principality of Rügen,

---

[1] *Von dem newen Cometstern des vergangen Jars*, &c. (Wittenberg, 1581).
Wendelin von Helbach published 'carefully written and explained in
rhyme,' an *Eigentliche und wahrhaftige Beschreibung dreier erschrecklichen
Commeten, deren Deutungen* (Frankfort-on-the-Main, 1580); cf. Weller,
Annalen, i. 247, No. 252. Concerning the interpretations of the comet
of the year 1607 cf. *Kurtzer und gründlicher Bericht,* &c., Bl. C¹–H².

[2] ** Cf. for instance the pamphlet, *Cometa, oder ein Predigt von Cometen
gehalten in der Pfaukirche zu Darmstadt von Henrico Leuchtero, Pfarrer und
Superintendent daselbst* (Darmstadt, 1619).

searched very minutely into ' the message and creden-
tials ' of this celestial wonder.   ' It would,' he thought,
' greatly grieve the dear Lord God if we did not all of
us inquire into the meaning of this His work.'   ' The
trumpet sounds very clearly, the lion roars; who shall
refuse to hear ? '   In addition to His Word and the
prophetical threatenings which God ' causes daily to be
reiterated by His ministers,' He sends ' other signs also
with all sorts of unusual and alarming apparitions,
strange visions, flashes of fire, and rainbows, which are
seen in the air at unwonted times at night.   This has
God done, and these things are terrible to behold, and
we are greatly concerned and troubled about them.'
' If we follow God's Word we shall not err.   For
Jeremias says expressly in chap. xviii. 11 that the
Lord is framing evils which he enumerates, and David
also warns us that God prepares great misfortunes.' [1]
Also ' quantities of old and new heresies of the Arians
and Photinians, Schwenkfeldians and Anabaptists,
Jesuits, and such-like devilish doctrines,' played a part
in the comet-sermon, which must have taken several
hours to deliver, for the printed copy contained fully
ten sheets.[2]

[1] All this was proved by the Christian preacher from the comet, from
its ' *mala indole, ominosa facie, qualitate materiae, infaustis aspectibus.*
Saturnus ran forward a mile *in domo mortis*, turned *retrogradus* back,
Mars *in domo religionis* first gives its hand to the comet, still closer follows
on foot the clerical *vertumnus Mercurius in cuspide prima* in the Scorpion,
the Sun is involved in the Sagittarius, Jupiter is exactly under the earth ;
above, in the Cor Leonis there stands in diametrical opposition,' &c.
Then follow proofs for the significance of the comet.   They are drawn ' 1. *ex
Gnomone*, from the tail pointing at us like a finger ; 2. *Horizontis nostri
descriptione* : how as a *communis visitator* he walks about the borders of
Germany ; 3. *Materiae abundantia* ; 4. *Quotidiana imminentia* ; 5. *ex causae
concurrentia.*'

[2] *Auszug bei Biederstedt*, pp. 45–54.

Another form of alarming portents, which grew more numerous almost every year, was the countless 'forecasts and prognostications' by which 'far-famed mathematicians and physicists' announced to the people extraordinary and terrifying prophecies.[1] 'Fear and terror have already for many years past been the daily bread of all the people, and rightly so,' it says in a 'Prognostikon' of 1585, 'because with every year things grow worse in the German land, and all kinds of vice and scandal increase and multiply among high and low. And in this present Prognostikon, you can plainly see, you true-hearted Christian readers, how many divine punishments will come on all lands in

---

[1] See, for instance, the *Practica und Prognosticacionen von Carion und Salomon*, printed by Cammerlander at Strassburg in 1545, and predicting events down to the year 1560. At the same time there appeared from the same printing-house another similar work, *Grosse Practica*, down to 1581, with 'great, important, obscure, terrible, and never before heard-of doings and prophesyings which all classes should give good heed to.' Cf. Roskoff, ii. 322 ff. In 1574 Paul Grebner published a *Sericum mundi filum seu vaticinium, quo nuntiatur subita et plus quam miraculosa orbis terrarum mutatio, h.e. Antichristi Pontificis occidentalis et Mahometi orientalis horribilis interitus*, &c. He presented it to the Elector Augustus of Saxony, and predicted first to him, then to the Elector Christian I., and finally to the Elector Christian II., the imperial dignity ; cf. Adelung, iv. 65 ff. ** Concerning the Brandenburg court astronomer, John Cario, who had studied at Wittenberg, cf. Möhsen, p. 429, Sprengel, iii. 413. See also G. Th. Strobel, *Miscellanea litterarischen Inhalts, Sammlung* 6 (Nuremberg, 1782), p. 141 ff. Thirteen of such Forecasts are known as belonging to the one year 1587. *Märkische Forschungen*, vii. 194. In the Cologne town collections a copper engraving is preserved which represents street criers of the sixteenth century. Among these is a vendor of Forecasts, who is holding a tablet with the inscription 'An. 1598. Amen.' The verse underneath, which no doubt the crier shouted about the streets, runs as follows :

All these Forecasts, and tidings, both
Are true and genuine by my troth.

(Cf. *Organ für christl. Kunst* [Köln, 1866], p. 259.) Norrenberg, *Kölnisches Litteraturleben im ersten Viertel des sechzehnten Jahrhunderts*, pp. 29–30.

the next ten years in the shape of scarcity, famine, pestilence, war and bloodshed, for you know well

> That all lands are in dire woe,
> As though to ruin they would go.[1]

The year 1588 was indicated as specially disastrous by numbers of astrologers, soothsayers and weather-prophets, among others George Ursinus of Plauen, 'a lover of the science of mathematics' : 'Everything will be sad ; all elements will mourn, all men on earth, and the birds in the air. Item, everything that lives on earth will be sad and distressed through great misfortune and future evil. Nobody must doubt this, for it is certain that a great change will come over the whole world !'[2]

At Basle there appeared in 1587 a ' New Tidings and terrible prophesying or soothsaying about Germany, Poland, the Netherlands, Brabant and France, which would begin to be fulfilled in the eighty-eighth year, together with an account of the signs which would presage the Day of Judgment.'[3] At the same time it was announced, in an ' unheard-of horrible and terrifying newspaper ' of Augsburg, that in Bohemia several hundred people had had such a vision, ' that they could

---

[1] *Practica und Prognosticacion bis auf das Jahr 1605.* Without locality, 1585.

[2] Köhler, *Lebensbeschreibungen,* i. 258–260. ** The Hildesheim chronicler John Oldecop reports in 1561 : ' Many years ago the preachers and star-gazers wrote and predicted of this year, 'Anno sexagesimo sibi caveat omnis homo,' and did their best to frighten their misguided people and thus drive them to repentance, as I have often before mentioned, that in Magdeburg and Strassburg they printed heaps of lies, examples and visions, spooks and poems concerning the one little child, in order that the Lutherans might be induced to repent, otherwise God would withdraw his Word from them.' John Oldecop's *Chronik,* published by K. Euling, p. 469.

[3] Weller, *Zeitungen,* No. 656.

only think that the Day of Judgment had already come,' but God had heard and answered their fervent prayers for aversion of the evil.[1]

Since Luther had so often announced the speedy coming of the Last Day, the belief in the imminence of this event had grown tolerably general among the Protestant preachers and men of learning. ' What Luther, the new Elias and Paul, has prophesied cannot possibly fail to happen,' wrote a preacher in 1562, ' and they are sceptical, godless, papists, epicures, sodomites and fanatics, who presume to doubt the prophecy. Has not everything become so dreadful and brutish with blasphemy of God, cursing, swearing, profligacy and adultery, usury, oppression of the poor, and all other vices, that we may well expect to hear the last trumpet calling us all to judgment ? What else can all the countless portents and visions, never before heard of, signify but that Christ is coming immediately to judge and to punish ? '[2] Philip Agricola (1577), Maurice Seydel (1582), John Holtheuser (1584) sang in songs and didactic poems of the speedy advent of the Day of Judgment.[3] The Hessian superintendent, George Nigrinus, informed the people in 1582 that an angel had already appeared in the sky with a drawn sword in its hand ; he himself had seen ' fiery beams, long spears and muskets in the heavens ; what else could these fiery signs betoken but the Day of Judgment, which would come with fire ? '[4] Michael Mästlin, professor of Mathematics at Heidelberg, was so convinced

---

[1] Weller, *Zeitungen*, No. 659.
[2] *Von grewlichen Missgeburten*, Bl. C 2.
[3] Weller, *Annalen*, i. 252, No. 281 ; 334, No. 214 ; 340, No. 254.
[4] See our remarks, vol. x. pp. 28, 29.

that the end of the world was close at hand that he said reproachfully of Pope Gregory XIII. that 'whereas the latter had made no mention whatever of this imminent event in his Calendar, no other conclusion could be formed than that he and all his followers did not at all believe in the Day of Judgment, and consequently did not believe in Christ or in the end of the world, and indeed troubled themselves less on these matters than the Epicurean scoffers, spoken of by the apostle Peter, whose throne the Pope pretends to have inherited.'[1] The Saxon preacher, Caspar Füger, taught the peasants that the Pope feared Christ's coming too soon and had therefore made the new calendar 'in order that Christ might be puzzled and not know when would be the time for Him to set up His tribunal, and that the Pope might thus have less cause for fear, and longer time to pursue unpunished his rascality, blasphemy, and iniquity. May God punish this villain!'[2]

On the Catholic side George Wizel had already expressed himself very strongly, in the years 1536 and

---

[1] See our remarks, vol. x. p. 40 ff.

[2] See our remarks, vol. x. pp. 42–44. 'Whereas Germans nowadays will only read what is put into rhyme, and everything else is too difficult for them which is not written in rhyme, we are obliged to print all the accounts of divine chastisements and portents of judgments, and of the speedy coming of the Last Day, in rhyme if we want to alarm the people and make them examine their own hearts.' For this purpose, for instance, Melchior Ambach, preacher at Frankfort-on-the-Main, published a volume of 'Old and new prophecies about these last evil times, quite serviceable to read, put into rhymes,' with the title *Vom Ende der Welt und Zukunft des Endechrists*. (Without date. Frankfort-on-the-Main.) In 1614 there appeared (without locality) a *Bettglocke wegen dess Römischen, dess Mahometischen und des Bepstlichen Reiches Endschafft, daraus jüngster Tag stündlich zu vermuten, die Christen aufmunternd, gegossen durch Albertum Hitfeld, Magdeburgensem* ('A passing bell of the Roman, the Mahommedan and the Popish Kingdoms, giving hourly warning of the Last Day, and encouraging Christians ; cast by Albert Hitfeld of Magdeburg').

1548, against the belief in the near end of the world and the interpretation given by the new religionists of natural phenomena as signs and portents. 'In order to frighten the world and bring it round to his new doctrines,' he wrote, 'Luther had invented the story of the end of the world being at hand and of there being signs that the Antichrist had come.' 'He has written about the signs of Christ's advent being near at hand, and he goes on reiterating this opinion of his, which has already been refuted, and driving it forcibly into his hearers. Preposterous stubbornness of the man to defend this crazy nonsense! We are bidden, forsooth, to see "signs and portents" in the overflowing of the Tiber in Italy, in the fall of Ghent in Flanders, and rough winds and storms at sea must be taken to signify the speedy coming of Christ. And these follies are not only read by numbers of people, but accepted with credulous veneration as the oracular utterances of a celestial hierarch. Not one of these people, however, reads and ponders the oracles of the Gospels by Matthew and Luke, but all of them pin their faith to the mere assumptions of these trumpery books.' 'If there is fierce lightning in Silesia, is this a portent? The north wind carries off roofs, does this mean that the Lord of heaven is hurrying down to judgment? Some one has seen fiery coals, the earth has heaved, thunder has roared, lightning has flashed, a very thick cloud has overshadowed a town, but do such things happen seldom in the world? At Breslau a tower has fallen down—lo and behold, what a wonder! In Silesia a woman has given birth to a child at the wrong time. This is indeed astounding to hear, but how shall such an event as this belong to the signs of the Lord's second

coming ?   O you precious interpreters !   The new evangelists ought to produce new signs and wonders ; as,
however, they are quite incapable of doing this, they
ram down our throats thunder-claps, winds, meteors,
tumble-down buildings and premature births as signs
and wonders.   These they proclaim with marvellous
pomp of rhetorical language, and cry wonder on
wonder, so that the people, utterly befooled, thank
their stars that it has been permitted them to live in
the time of these wonders of God, and so that they
may be able to stop the mouths of the Papists when
they ask for wonders.' [1]

Because the numerous prophecies of the end of the
world were not fulfilled, it came to pass, as many of the
preachers experienced, that ' a large mass of the people '
ceased to believe in the Last Judgment.   ' If we threaten
Epicureans with the Day of Judgment,' wrote the
Tübingen professor, George Sigwart, in 1599, ' they
answer, "It has been preached about for a long time,
when is it going to come ?   We are beginning to think
there is nothing in it ; meanwhile, all we want is enough
to eat and drink, or money enough to spend." ' [2]

So, again, in a leaflet of the year 1581, we read :
' Many people make fun of the Day of Judgment, and
of all those who preach about it, and say : " We have
heard so much and so often about this Day of Judg-

---

[1] Quoted by Döllinger, *Reformation*, i. 118–119.   ** The Jesuit, G.
Scherer, ridicules the Lutheran announcement of the Day of Judgment in
the *Bericht, ob der Papst zu Rom der Antichrist sey. In etliche Predigen
kürzlich verfasset durch G. Scherer* (Ingolstadt, 1585), p. 62 ff.   So, too, does
Cochlaeus, *In quatuor Andreae Osiandri Coniecturas de Fine Mundi Velitatio*
(Ingolstadii, 1545), and Bellarmin, *Conciones habitae Lovanii ante annos
circiter quadraginta, nunc consensu auctoris publicatae* (Coloniae, 1615)
p. 18.

[2] Sigwart, 123[a] and 123[b].

ment, and yet nothing has come of it ; what has become
of the Day of the Lord ? " ' [1] A leaflet of the year
1594 directed attention to those persons who, ' in order
to appear clever in the eyes of the world, declared the
Day of Judgment to be an old woman's fable.' [2]

In order, therefore, ' at least to preserve the common
people as much as possible from the raging, godless,
epicurean unbelief around them, and to fill them with
wholesome fear and alarm,' fresh wonders betokening
the impending judgment of God were perpetually
announced, and ' to this purpose,' said one preacher,
' the portents from the dead and from the world of
spirits were beyond measure useful.'

' Is it not,' he asked, ' an appalling portent that in
the Mark of Brandenburg, in a village not far from Berlin,
there were seen, in this year 1563, two dead persons,
who had been buried a long time before, but were seen
alive by some twenty people, and also heard to speak
prophetically of the judgment God would send as
punishments to mankind ? ' [3] At Honschotten, in
Flanders, ' three horrible corpses ' came to life and
exhorted the people to repentance ; ' the body of one
of them looked just as if he was standing in the fire and
burning ; another gnashed his teeth and cried out in
a dreadful voice : Woe, woe to the godless ! ' then they
disappeared and the graves closed again ; but the
burgomaster and the council made haste to record this
' great, unheard-of wonder ' in writing, and to send it
round the neighbouring towns and villages.[4] In another
place thirty people who had lately died were heard

[1] Scheible, *Schaltjahr*, iv. 646.   [2] *Ibid.* iv. 133.
[3] K. Althaus, *Predig von kommenden Gerichten* (1563), Bl. C.
[4] Scheible, *Schaltjahr*, iii. 501–504.

' singing and playing on instruments.'   In a Bamberg
newspaper this ' song of the dead was set to the tune
of the last "Stündlin Niklas Hermanns," and in addition
it was announced how in the same place a bear, a lion,
a cuirassier, and a clerical person had been seen in
dreadful forms.' [1]   ' A musician who had been in his
grave seven years appeared in ghastly form at the
wedding of his son, and to the terror of all present said
that all secular music was from the devil, and that
he himself was on that account condemned to burn in
hell.' [2]

Angels preaching repentance came into vogue at
an early date.   The preacher Wendelin von Helbach
published at Dresden, in 1564, ' veritable new information of how three angels from heaven had by command
of the Lord Christ warned the town of Carsaw in
Hungaria to repent of its sins.' [3]

At Eisleben there appeared in rhyme, to be sung to
the tune of ' Wilhelmus von Nassau,' an equally ' true
account of two angels who had been seen for three days
and nights together in front of the town of Oppenum
on the Rhine, near a wayside statue, and who had
exhorted to repentance, and had prophesied what
was to happen from the year 1594 to the year 1600.' [4]
Even before this an angel had appeared to a girl at
Prague, another to a woman in a village near Nachod,
and a Nuremberg ' trustworthy paper' reported what
the angel had said to her, and how he had told
her what terrible things would soon happen in the

[1] Weller, *Zeitungen*, Nos. 600, 606.
[2] *Eine newe unerhörte schreckliche Zeitung*, &c.   Without locality.
1587.
[3] Weller, *Zeitungen*, Nos. 600, 606.
[4] Weller, *Annalen*, ii. 411, No. 1162.

world, and charged her to make them known to all
people.' [1]

Near Cologne, on June 24, ' a little child was found
in snow-white clothes, and it prophesied wonderful
things ' ; a second account placed the event on July 29,
and added that ' the child had been found with a rod
and a bloody sword ' ; a third account gave Laibach
as the scene of the discovery, and 1593 as the year.[2]
The earliest of these angelic appearances was seen by
Paul Runge, a burgher of Schönau, who declares a
little boy appeared to him in a wood and informed him
of God's fierce wrath and vengeance ; ' and as I was
parting from the child,' he says, ' it went up into the
heavens like a spider.' [3]

' As if for special consolation in these last distressful

[1] Weller, *Zeitungen*, Nos. 323, 749.   [2] *Ibid.* Nos. 510, 770.
[3] *Wahrhaftig Geschicht eines Kindes*, &c. ; cf. Weller, *Zeitungen*, No. 221.
Weller (*Annalen*, ii. 414, No. 1183) mentions a Strassburg paper with
an account of an apparition of the archangel Gabriel on April 23, 1602.
** ' James Frolich, a printer at Strassburg, published this year (1557) a
book, and wrote that Paul Runge, burgher and resident at Schönau,
found a little child sitting on the trunk of a tree in a forest. The child
earnestly enjoined him to tell all the preachers that they must exhort the
people to repentance, and admonish them to abstain from usury and not
to sell corn at such a high price ; also that they must abolish the terrible
curses and grievous oaths. Otherwise God would visit the world with
fire, water, hunger, feuds and famine, and the Day of Judgment would
speedily come. And there would soon be a great pestilence, so that
scarcely a fourth of mankind would survive. Many dreadful things
were in James Frolich's book ; and I gather from it, as I have already
written before, that the Lutheran preachers see, hear, and know that by
their gospel, with its freedom, they have led astray their flocks, and that
now they are powerless to tame the roughness, licentiousness and wickedness of the young lads, above all of the nobles, and bring them back
into the path of salvation. For among the people there is no longer
any fear, any obedience, any love or loyalty. And therefore they use
examples of this sort, and try hard by this show of horrors to make them
once more pious and obedient.' *Chronicle* of John Oldecop, published by
K. Euling, p. 428. See also above, p. 257, n. 2.

times, in which so many devils showed themselves in bodily form, God also sometimes allowed friendly, instead of chastising, angels to appear, and, indeed, I myself knew an old man whom an angel carried five miles through the air to the bedside of his sick son.' Thus wrote a preacher in 1593.[1] Two preachers re-counted in the year 1581 that ' on Easter Day, at Alber-hogen-on-the-Main, two angels had carried a young fellow up to heaven, where he had seen the heavenly Jerusalem with wonderfully beautiful towers, and had been charged by the angels to make known this vision to everybody, but first of all to the pastor of the village ' ; it was only so sad that the world treated all such signs and wonders with contempt, notwithstanding that they stared them in the face, and that in spite of the signs they grew every day blinder and more obdurate.[2]   To despise such wonders and portents, they said, was all the more pitiable and lamentable, because God, at the very first, when the dear evangel appeared, had sent His angels down from heaven to spread it everywhere.[3] Thus, for instance, the superintendent James Weber, in his ' Historische Predigten,' stated as an authen-ticated fact that ' angel-messengers had distributed Luther's first writings, in four weeks, throughout the whole of Christendom, and that angels had appeared to the promulgators of the new gospel, the Elector John Frederic of Saxony and King Christian of Denmark.' [4]

The people were also supplied with ' suitable in-struction ' concerning new prophets. In 1586 there was published ' for the admonition of all Christians a

---

[1] *Wahrhafftige newe Zeitung von der Erscheinung eines Engels,* &c. Without locality. 1593.   [2] Scheible, *Schaltjahr,* iv. 646.
[3] The *Zeitung* quoted at note 1.   [4] Weber, pp. 98, 115–116.

true and actual description of the person and form, as
well as all the predictions and preachings, of the new
prophet who had appeared in the Mark before the town
of Stettin, and foretold terrible things which were to
happen all over the world during five consecutive
years.'[1]   Prophets also arose in Switzerland, in Ulm,
Nuremberg, and other places.   Respecting the prophet
Noa Kalb of Ulm, a baker, who uttered divine revelations in 1606, and threw the people into consternation
by the announcement of the Day of Judgment, many
councils and synods were held.   This prophet pretended
that he was the same Noa of whom Luther, in his exposition of the twelfth chapter of Daniel, says that God
would awaken him immediately before the Day of Judge-
ment.   John Bartholomäi, preacher at the cathedral
of Ulm, and Wolfgang Holland, preacher of Grimmel-
fingen, regarded the prophecies of Kalb as divine; but
Kalb ended on the scaffold, as it turned out that he was
a drunken sot and a most profligate character.[2]   A
still greater prophet, Philip Ziegler, concerning whom
'truthful tidings' were also published, carried on his
avocation at Nuremberg.   He called himself 'Origines
Philippus, by the grace of God King elect and crowned
of Jerusalem, Shiloh, Joseph and David, the brother of
the captain of the Rose-cross and invincible sceptre of
the King in Zion.'[3]

A very sinister end overtook the prophets Esaias
Stifel, tradesman at Langensalza, and the chemist of
the same place, Ezekiel Meth, who had constructed for

---

[1] Weller, *Zeitungen*, No. 637.   ** Concerning this same prophet a
Zeitung appeared as early as 1585; see Weller, *l.c.* No. 623.

[2] Weyermann, *Nachrichten*, pp. 370–371.

[3] Soden, *Kriegs- und Sittengeschichte*, i. 561.

themselves a new system of religion out of the writings
of Theophrastus Paracelsus, and with the help of their
followers had attempted to spread it in Thuringia and
the surrounding country. They rejected baptism, and
the Lord's Supper, and the resurrection of the dead ;
for ' they lived here already in the most perfect enjoyment of what Christ had called the joys of eternal
life.' Stifel declared that he himself was ' Christ not
only according to strength, but also according to his
nature ' ; Meth posed ' as the great prince of God,
Michael,' also ' as the living Word of God,' and ' as
God's new first-born son of holiness.' Their doctrines
gained a wide footing among the people, until, at last,
the Elector John George of Saxony, in 1614, issued a
severe penal edict against them, which was then circulated in print as a ' Neue Zeitung ' for a warning ' to
all and every in these perilous times, when all sorts
of errors and false prophets were gaining the upper
hand, and leading many Christians astray.' [1]

Besides the endless reports concerning prophets,
' those about the Antichrist also gave people plenty
to think about.' While the latter, according to the
Protestants, had already been bodily present at Rome
for several centuries, it was announced elsewhere that
' he had been born at Babilonia, on the borders of
Labea, in 1574 ' ; another account placed the birth in
1578, and finally ' he was born in this current year
1592, in a town called Consa.' [2]

To what extent superstition of all sorts had taken
hold of people is seen plainly from the ' House-book,'
written down by Joachim von Wedel-Wedel for his

[1] Fuller details concerning these prophets and their fate are in Köhler,
Lebensbeschreibungen, ii. 144–173.   [2] Weller, *Zeitungen*, Nos. 498, 747.

family, one of the most delightful and instructive of Pomeranian chronicles. Wedel († 1609) was landrat (sub-prefect) to the Prince of Pomerania, a cultivated, conscientious, capable, and experienced man. In the preface of his book he assures his descendants : ' This with truth I can indeed say, that I have never delibe- rately, either from liking or misliking, mentioned any- one with flattery or with spite, but have, as far as I could, respected the plain, unvarnished truth.' Side by side with the most important information Wedel recorded, almost in every year, all sorts of wonderful events by which God interposed in the world, in order to warn His people and prepare them for great things. Thus, for instance : ' When the Elector Maurice of Saxony died, blood and fire, as Joachim Camerarius relates, poured in showers out of a giant form in the sky ; in Thuringia a woman gave birth to a toad. In the year 1555, at Freiberg-in-Meissen, in broad daylight, the Lord Christ was seen sitting on a rainbow ; in the duchy of Cleves 364 children were brought into the world by a woman at one birth.[1] On September 5, 1556, at Küstrin a quantity of flames and burning pillars appeared in the heavens, and a voice from out them was heard saying : Woe, woe to Christen- dom ! In 1559, during the oat-harvest, in a field near Berlin, in broad daylight, twenty-seven spectres of masculine form—amongst them twelve without heads—were seen mowing vigorously with scythes. The Elector called on the theologians for an opinion

---

[1] This story of the Countess Margaret of Holland ranked as a ' historia valde memorabilis ' ; cf. Stieve, *Über die ältesten halbjährigen Zeitungen oder Messrelationen, Abhandlung der histor. Klasse der bayerischen Akademie der Wissenschaften*, xvi. 211 ; also p. 205, note 119. See above, p. 239, the statement of Irenaeus.

on the matter, and they decided that the spectres
foreboded pestilence to come.   In 1562 figures of
Christ, with blood flowing down, hosts of warriors
and bloody crosses were seen in the sky.   In 1568, on
August 16 and 26, and also on September 14, Caspar
Forchheim and three other noblemen saw the figure
of Christ first hanging on the cross, and then, surrounded
with numbers of angels, sitting on the seat of justice
and holding a tribunal; also close by the flames of hell
and a number of devils.   On January 10, 1570, fire
fell from heaven and consumed a number of people.
On January 1, 1574, in Poland, an angel was seen with
two contending armies, and the angel had a rod, a
sword, and a trumpet in its hands, and it cried out
twice with a loud voice : Woe, woe !   The noise and
shouting of the army and the roars of the great muskets
so terrified a number of people that they seemed as if
struck down by death, and a quantity of blood flowed
down on the earth.'   The book also contains a great
many other wonders.   'In Hesse a child was born with
a Turkish moustache.   In Salzwedel cabbages grew
with women's ruffles ; a child also was born with a
Turkish face, who warned the people to repent, and then
immediately after died.   In Silesia a boy had a tooth
of pure Hungarian gold ; it is said that he grew up to be
an arch-villain.' [1]   ' Now although these supernatural

---

[1] Concerning this golden tooth James Horstius, professor of Medicine
at Helmstädt, wrote a pamphlet in 1595, *De aureo dente maxillari pueri
Silesii* (Leipzig, 1595).   He says that he himself saw this tooth which had
grown in the mouth of the seven-year-old boy Christopher Müller.   This
wonder signified that the Emperor Rudolf II. (to whom the pamphlet was
dedicated) would gain a great victory over the Turks and live to see his
empire considerably enlarged.   Concerning the history of the golden
tooth, see also Sprengel, iii. 403–406.   There were accounts also of children
who were born with golden teeth ; see above.

things,' says Wedel, ' may seem somewhat incredible,
they are, nevertheless, confirmed by other even more
incomprehensible things which Almighty God causes in
the elements, metals, stones, and so forth, contrary
to nature.' The only report that seemed incredible to
him was that of ' two angels in Moravia who preached
for three whole days in the presence of a number of
people ' ; this he found it hard to believe, as there was
at that time no dearth of faithful teachers among the
people : the devil, he supposed, must have disguised
himself in the form of angels.[1]

In addition to all the countless tales of marvels,

[1] Wedel, pp. 168, 171, 175, 187, 197, 204, 207, 216, 224, 238, 240, 269,
278, 301, 315, 318, 346. ** ' In the summer of this year,' so the Hildesheim
chronicler Oldecop says in 1556, ' a book was printed at Magdeburg on
the outside of which a crucifix was stamped ; in this book it was related
that the form of Christ Jesus had been seen in the clouds hanging on a
cross, and that afterwards He had come down from the Cross and seated
Himself on a stool, holding a sword in His hand.   The book says further
that many patriarchs fell on their knees before the judge, and called on
Him with outstretched arms.   Also a number of angels stood by holding
trumpets, and looking as if they would very soon blow the trumpets.
There was also seen standing by a host of devils who were driving a number
of black horsemen to hell.   The book further relates that several of the
devils seized people by the hair, put them behind them on their horses and
rode with them to hell.   The vision is seen to have occurred not far from
Plauen and Elslerberg on the day of the Visitation of Mary, and the writer
mentions four noblemen as witnesses, namely the Honourable Caspar von
Forchheim, Albin von Rab zu Schoditz, Christopher Dhes zu Adorf,
and Friedrich von Doberneck ; von Forchheim's household, and the wife
of a peasant, says the book, saw it all quite plainly.   And I, John
Oldecop, Deacon, have read the whole of this book, which was published
under the seal of the town of Magdeburg.   As, however, the name of the
author is not given in the book, I imagine that some Lutheran preacher,
knowing that he has misled many thousands of people with the
Lutheran doctrine and the Lutheran freedom, and now cannot bring
them back to obedience, piety, discipline and honour with all his cries of
" Repent, repent ! " has put forward this terrible vision which may
perhaps, God willing, make the Lutherans better.'   *Chronik des Johann
Oldecop*, published by K. Euling, pp. 403, 404.

made up chiefly of horror and woe, there was another
species of popular literature which had the widest
circulation—viz. stories of the most gruesome crimes,
martyrdoms, and executions. These also were intended
to serve the purpose of warnings, but at the same time
to gratify the craving of the masses for sensational
excitement. Narratives of this sort, whether in prose
or rhyme, could not exercise an ennobling influence;
on the contrary they could only fill the readers' imaginations with pictures of murder, immorality, and cruelty,
and accustom them to look upon crime as an everyday
matter.

'When I was still young,' said the preacher Leonard Breitkopf in 1591, 'forty or fifty years ago, there
was not so much known about all the horrible deeds
of murder, such as nowadays are described every year
in all sorts of papers. They are Christians in name,
but in reality devils in human form, who by their own
confessions have committed such deeds of murder, and
thereby brought on themselves the just punishment
of being pinched with burning tongs, or put on the
wheel, or burned and quartered, or having their eyes
put out and their noses, hands, and ears chopped off,
by the Christian authorities'; all this was written for
the 'instruction, warning, and entertainment of the
people.'[1] Thus, for instance, in 1570 the people were
entertained with accounts of two murderers who had
brutally killed 124 people. A song printed in 1577
at Tübingen told of 'Peter Niersch and his company

[1] *Charfreitagspredigt* (without locality, 1591), Bl. B. Breitkopf recommended 'earnest Christian reading' of such papers as these which 'were
written in clear style, or in charming songs,' and 'often supplied with
illustrations.'

who had committed 440 murders.' At the same time,
at Augsburg, were sung the deeds of six incendiaries
who had 'been guilty of much murder and arson.'
Caspar Herber von Cochem on the Mosel described, in
1581, the execution of a murderer 'who from his youth
up had committed or caused 964 murders': this seems
almost incredible, 'but the register has been found, in
which the murderer himself entered the records from
day to day.'[1]

In 1583 there appeared in Wesel 'Ein neu kläglich
Lied' of the great evil of the sorcerers, which they have
committed in Westphalia at Aschenbrügk and other
places during this present year 1583, and of how 180 of
them were miserably burnt, to be sung to the tune of
'Kommt her zu mir spricht Gottes Sohn.'[2]   Five
years later it was announced in another 'Truthful
new paper' that in 1588, on one day, in the one town
of Osnabrück, 133 sorcerers had been burnt;[3] and,
again, three years later, there came from Erfurt, together
with 'another wonderful and amusing new song,' a
report, written in verse, of how 'on February 9, 1591,
133 sorcerers had been burnt in one day.'[4]   Grim and

[1] See concerning these and other criminals, who were written and sung
about, Weller, *Zeitungen*, Nos. 360, 361, 416, 442, 481, 482, 513, 517,
524, 543 (also Scheible, *Schaltjahr*, v. 12–16), 546, 548, 570, 587, 590,
592, 593, 621, 705, 707, 815, 844, 845, 853, 870. Further Weller, *Annalen*,
i. 203 ff. Nos. 18, 37, 42, 50, 130, 141, 184, 198, 207, 208, 212, 213,
214, 215, 222, 237, 242, 271, 288, 289, 292, 299, 302, 315, 317, 388, 415,
422, and ii. 434 ff. Nos. 582, 583, 590, 595, 600, 606, 610, 615, 616, 619,
626, 630, 634, 636, 644, 657, 661, 672. Prutz, *Journalismus*, p. 167.

[2] Weller, *Annalen*, ii. 438, No. 609 ; cf. the *Strassburger Zeitung* of
the year 1583, according to which on October 15, 19, 24, and 28, 1582,
134 sorcerers were burnt to death 'for their inhuman deeds and horrible
confessions.' Weller, *Zeitungen*, No. 572. See our remarks above, vol. xi.
p. 388.

[3] Weller, *Zeitungen*, No. 633, and *Annalen*, i. 256, No. 308.

[4] Weller, *Annalen*, ii. 439, No. 618.

ghastly songs were also written about people who could change themselves into wolves, and in this form commit frightful crimes. We quote two verses of a song about a peasant who was executed in Bedburg, near Cologne, on October 31, 1589 :

> Frightful it is to hear, and bad :
> A magic girdle the man had,
> So soon as he had bound the same
> Around him, he a wolf became.

> He murdered thirteen children small,
> And his own son therewithal ;
> Their skulls he split and eat up too,
> And also three old people slew . . .

whereupon follows a description of all the tortures which the unhappy man had to suffer.[1]

In order to keep up a constant supply of fresh news, and to ' cool the natural instinct for cruelty,' the most frightful crimes were invented, and so little fear was there of investigation that they even printed in Augsburg ' horrors said to have happened at Munich, but of which nobody there had heard a word.' Thus, for instance, the Augsburg preacher Bartholomew Rülich published in 1604 a ' Jesuiterische newe Zeitung,' containing the information that the Jesuits in Munich had murdered young women in their church, and that as a punishment for the crime the town council had sentenced five fathers to be pinched with red-hot tongs and to have strips of flesh cut out of their bodies. In a document signed with the Munich town seal the council replied that the whole report was a deliberate lie.[2] Another news-writer, with whom, ' as with so many, writing and

---

[1] From the *Zeitung* : ' Der Post Bot bin ich genannt ' (1590), B 3 ; cf. our remarks, vol. xi. p. 388 f.

[2] See our remarks on these and other crimes attributed to the Jesuits, vol. x. p. 299 ff.

lying were one and the same thing,' in a ' Truthful and
New Gazette ' of 1614, accused the Jesuit Bellarmin of
the most unnatural crimes, and also of murder and of
mixing poisons ; he (Bellarmin) ' died in abject despair '
—Bellarmin died in 1621—' and even at the present day
he appears in the air, in broad daylight, on a fiery hell-
flaming horse with wings, and is heard in his palace
uttering ghastly shrieks and lamentations, and he
frightens many people so much that they die in a few
hours.'   The Basle bookseller Ludwig König, by whom
this ' Famos-Zeitung ' was said to have been printed,
issued a public declaration to the effect that he had no
printing press ; all the same a new edition of this
' truthful historical report ' announced on its title-
page : ' Printed first at Basle by Ludwig König.' [1]
The historian Sebastian Franck had complained before
this that all manner of fabricated stories were sold as
truth.   ' Whereas, nowadays,' he wrote, ' it is, alas !
permitted to everyone to lie, and the world shuts its
eyes and nobody takes any notice, or asks how or
wherewith money has been got of the public, or what is
said, written, or printed, it has at last come to this, that
when the writers have no more money they invent some
wonderful tale and sell it as a true story.   Thereby not
only is the world misled and the common people filled
with gaping wonder, but the public is cheated out of its
money, and lies are brought into the land and paid for
in cash as if they were truths.   The consequence is
that historians can no longer be sure what they may
hand on as truth, for among all the books floating
about there is no warrant for their trustworthiness.' [2]

---

[1] See our remarks, vol. x. p. 317 ff.
[2] Franck, *Chronica*, Teil ii. 270[b]—271[a].

As regards the reports of and songs about crimes ('Verbrecher-Zeitungen und Liedern'), it was 'for the most part murders of fathers and mothers, brothers and sisters and children, which in view of the wholesome terror and dread of the people must not be kept secret.' [1] 'How do you feel,' asked the preacher Leonard Breitkopf of his congregation on Good Friday, 1591, 'when you hear of such inhuman deeds—for instance, that a woman at Bretteburg, some years ago, murdered her husband in the night, and cut his left arm and his left side down to the hip, and salted the rest of his body to be devoured later! What do you think about the appalling news that an innkeeper in Austria, in 1582, as he himself confessed, put 185 people to death! When they were dead, he chopped them up in little bits, had them cooked and gave them to his guests to eat. For this he underwent the just punishment of having a limb cut off his body every day until the eighth day, when he was torn with red-hot tongs and impaled alive, till the devil incarnate carried him away in the sight of all present. That was verily a righteous punishment which everyone will gladly hear and read of'; 'it is also useful for the young, in order that they may be warned and preserved from such horrible deeds of murder.' [2]

[1] In the newspapers and songs, quoted above at p. 272, note 1, crimes of this sort are told in multitudes.

[2] See above, p. 271, note 1. In order that the young might receive wholesome warning parents ought, it was said, 'whenever executions took place, to take their children to see them with their own eyes.' But what sort of an impression must these sights have made on children? Felix Platten of Basle gives an account of an execution which he witnessed in his youth : 'A murderer was taken to the gallows, where there was a great crowd of people, so that I was filled with wonder. He was fastened alive to the wheel, and his limbs were crushed. The last blow was given him on the breast and it made his tongue start out ; they tied him on to the wheel and raised him up.' Shortly before this a criminal who had

When at Frankenstein in Silesia, in the years 1606–1607, seventeen people—amongst them two boys—were executed with hideous torture, for having distributed poison, and for other crimes, the preacher of the

assaulted an old woman of seventy 'was scorched alive with red-hot pincers . . . by the executioner, Meister Niklause, who had come from Berne on purpose. There was a mighty lot of smoke as I myself saw. One of his breasts—a pretty good-sized one, for he was very fat—was torn out of his body. After this he was led back to the gallows. He was terribly weak and the blood was streaming out all over his hands, and he kept on falling down. In this condition he was beheaded, and afterwards thrown into a grave with a stake thrust through his body, as I saw with my own eyes, for my father took me to see the sight.' Boos, pp. 152, 153. School children were indeed officially summoned by the magistrates to be present at these gruesome executions. In a 'Dreadful newspaper account of two fiendish boys, who, though not more than fourteen and fifteen years old, had already committed several thefts and murders, and, worst of all, had poisoned their father and their uncle, whom they had found lying drunk,' we read,

> Now hear ye, Christians all,
> What horrors did befall
> At Alberhogen-on-the-Main. . . .
> To see the punishment
> Young boys and maidens went,
> And 'twas the magistrates who did
> To the sight the young folk bid.

The two boys were first stripped naked and whipped in such a manner all over their bodies that 'blood streamed from every part.' Next the executioner applied red-hot irons to the wounds, whereupon 'the boys screamed and howled so murderously that words cannot describe it'; after this 'both the boys' two hands were hacked off,' and so forth. 'And all this torture down to the final execution lasted full twenty minutes; boys and girls, besides many other people, old and young, were present in order to be witnesses of God's righteous punishment and to be warned by it.' 'And several Psalms from God's Word were sung at the same time.' The preacher strove in vain to bring the bloodthirsty boys to confession, for by the devil's instigation they stubbornly denied everything, and would not acknowledge that they had committed the murders, notwithstanding that there was a great deal of evidence forthcoming, and that several persons witnessed against the boys.' 'They came of a devilish race, for their mother and sister had been burnt as witches and devil's whores several years earlier, and by them they had without doubt been instructed in all sorts of secret magician's arts and in poison-mixing.' Without locality. Printed by Karl Allwin Schultze, 1603.

place, Samuel Heinnitz, gave a full description of these 'poisonous deeds of the infernal hunter.' He delivered six sermons, which he afterwards published in print, about these criminals and their righteous punishment. 'Many pious and reasonable people,' he said, 'when they saw how the malefactors were tortured with red-hot tongs, and how at last four were mutilated and four were burnt, said without any pity: "It is but fair that they, by whom others had been burnt, should be burnt in their turn." ' [1]

'Nothing but dread and alarm,' Leonard Breitkopf went on in his Good Friday sermon of 1591, 'devils and spectres, sorcerers, witches, prodigies, earthquakes, fiery signs in the heavens, three-headed visions in the clouds, and numberless other signs of God's wrath. And yet in spite of them all vice of all sorts remains in full swing, horrible murdering and poisoning increases every year in all lands. At the same time superstition-mongers, spiritists, and all that class of people carry on their work more and more audaciously and dishonour and revile the divine Word of revelation. Doctors of magic write books and pamphlets both for the learned and for the common people; others go about as gold-makers, deceiving high and low; others spread the strangest superstitions, pretending that they are able with their own minds to rule other minds and to control the stars, and to put people to death without external means. And these secret, devilish arts are multitudinous, and the whole world is deceived with them, so that it is verily high time that the Day of Judgment came.' [2]

---

[1] Heinnitz, pp. 1–70 ; *Predigten*, pp. 1–208 (cf. p. 61).
[2] See above, p. 271, note 1.

CHAPTER VI

LITERATURE OF OCCULT ARTS, MAGIC, AND DEVIL-LITERATURE [1]

To the secret arts which, 'in many books and in all sorts of tracts for the common people,' were made known abroad and perplexed all heads, belonged in the first rank the 'magic-medicine' which was bound up with astrology, alchemy, and the Kabbala.

Philip Aureolus Theophrastus Bombastus Paracelsus Eremita, of Hohenheim in Suabia, had come forward as a great reformer of medicine, and had gained the highest esteem and a great crowd of followers. He was called the 'Luther of the healing art.' As Luther had burnt the ecclesiastical canons in public, so Paracelsus, in 1526, at the opening of his lectures as professor of Medicine at the Basle University, burnt the

---

[1] The literature dealt with in this present section, as well as the earlier descriptions of 'Wonder-newspapers,' will forcibly remind readers of the accounts in Lucian's *Lover of Lies*. In the sixteenth century, as in the time of Lucian, high and low, statesmen and scholars, believed in all sorts of supernatural arts, and tales of magic and ghosts ; and the words of Lucian might well have been spoken to all the innumerable recounters of such things : ' If you have so little respect for yourselves, you ought at any rate to spare these young people, and also make it a matter of conscience not to fill their heads with all these preposterous and dreadful fables, which, when once they have taken possession of their imaginations, will disquiet them for the rest of their lives, cause them to tremble at every rustling leaf, and make them a prey to all manner of superstition and fear of ghosts.' Cf. Wieland's translation of Lucian (Leipzig, 1788), i. 193–194.

works of Galen and Avicenna, which he combated most energetically. He was the first professor who delivered his lectures in the German language. For therapeutics and chemistry many of his discoveries were important. 'Follow me,' he wrote, 'you of Paris, you of Montpellier, you of Suabia, you of Meissen, you of Cologne, you of Vienna, and so forth; it's for you to follow me, not I you—mine is the monarchy'; for he gained his learning not from books but from the pure source of nature : his shoe-latchets knew more than all the ancients, his beard had more experience than all the colleges put together.' He loaded his opponents with the most exquisite vilifications. After he had fled from Basle, where he had made himself many enemies, he perambulated the greater part of Europe now as magic-doctor, now as theologian, now as sorcerer, now as alchemist; Africa and Asia, according to his own account, were also visited by him. In Spain he took up his abode with a master of the black art who, by his magic clock, called up all sorts of wicked spirits around him; in Constantinople, so he said, he had acquired the philosophers' stone from a Greek abbot.[1]

He pretended to possess the art of prolonging human life to 600 years, but died himself in poverty and misery in 1541, barely forty-seven years old. Besides the

[1] Bullinger describes him as a dirty, dissolute man, and his servant Oporinus said of him : ' He was seldom sober ; he took delight in drinking with the peasants, and in making them drink till they were all tipsy. For two whole years he never undressed himself ; when he came home drunk late at night he would throw himself down on his bed, with the great sword which he had got from an executioner by his side, and then jump up again and brandish it about so wildly in the air and at the walls and ceiling' that more than once his Famulus trembled for his head. Sigwart, *Kleine Schriften*, p. 35. ** Haeser in his *Gesch. der Medizin*, ii. (3rd edition) 79, attempts to disprove the charge of drunkenness ; the learned man, however, goes a good deal too far in his defence of Paracelsus.

works which he really wrote, mostly in German, many others were circulated in his name. The disciples of his healing method and his cabalistic philosophy, the so-called Paracelsists, most of them Germans, magnified him as the hero of the century.[1]

Paracelsus taught among other things that 'in all the four elements God has created living creatures : in the water, nymphs, water-nixies, melosynes and sirens; on the earth, gnomes, sylphs, mountain sprites and pigmies ; in the fire, vulcans, salamanders and so forth. As all things are emanations from God, so all bodies are invested with a certain celestial essence which determines their form, figure and colour. The stars are peopled with spirits of a higher kind which govern the destinies of men. Human diseases are most efficaciously healed by magic.' 'If you wish to know what magic is,' he said to the professors of the college, 'seek out the matter in the Book of Revelation. Since you cannot prove and establish your philosophy from the Bible and from Revelation, your tricks and pranks must come to an end. The Bible is the true expositor and key. John not less than Moses, Elias, Enoch, David, Solomon, Daniel, Jeremiah, and the other prophets were all magicians, cabalists, and soothsayers.' With sympathetic salves and talismans wounds could be healed without contact ; the talismans were the pots in which the heavenly influences were preserved. The 'magisterium of the magnet' was a

[1] ' Numbers of wonder-working doctors and German tract-writers' merely traded on ' the fame of Paracelsus.' In the year 1594 there appeared (without indication of locality) a pamphlet 'against the power-grasping, presumptuous, vain-glorious, apostate, quack doctors and disreputable alchemistic vagrants who call themselves Paracelsists,' entitled a *Klage Theophrasti Paracelsi über seine eigenen Discipel und leichtfertige Ertzte, aus seinen Büchern auf das kürzeste zusammengezogen.*

specific to draw all diseases out of the human body.
' The body proceeds from the elements, the spirit from
the stars.' ' In sleep the astral body goes back to its
fathers ; it holds converse with the star. After death
also it goes back again to the star world, just as the
earthly body returns to the universal lap of earth.'

The power and influence of the spirit was unlimited.
Thanks to his power of imagination and will and his
connection with spirits of nature man could see through
nature as through a glass, and discern the inner qualities
of bodies and all the secrecies of his fellow-men. ' It is
possible,' he declared, ' that my spirit without the
help of the body, and by the indwelling word alone, and
without a sword, could stab or wound another person.
It is also possible for me to bring the spirit of my adversary into a figure (statuette), and then bend or mutilate
it at my pleasure. You must know that the influence
of the will is a great point in medicine. By will we
can by cursing produce diseases in men and cattle, the
imagination alone conveying the influence, and not
either strength of character or unbleached wax or any
other such thing. The powerful imagination of another
person directed against me may suffice to kill me.' [1]

[1] Sprengel, iii. 430–493 ; Adelung, vii. 189–364 ; Ennemoser, pp. 878,
888–902 ; cf. Lessing, *Paracelsus, sein Leben und sein Wirken* (Berlin, 1839),
Marx, *Zur Würdigung des Theophrastus von Hohenheim* (Göttingen, 1842) ;
Lindner, *Theophrastus als Bekämpfer des Papsttums* (Leipzig, 1845) ;
F. Mook, *Theophrastus Paracelsus, Eine Kritische Studie* (Würzburg,
1876) ; Sigwart, *Kleine Schriften*, i. 25–48. Cornelius Agrippa of Nettesheim also, in his work *De occulta philosophia*, in which he gave a summary
of all secret arts, advanced the theory that ' It is the fact that all influences are in their origin spiritual, which gives their might to imagination,
will, and strong faith ; one man grows horns on his head if he thinks
vividly of a stag-fight, another through the force of his will is able to kill
a camel ; the most wonderful results can be produced by the glance of the
eye, and the pulse of the lover will reveal the name of his beloved.' Sigwart, *Kleine Schriften*, pp. 9–11; cf. Sprengel, iii. 22 ff.; Ægidius Gutmann at

As a 'learned pupil of the wondrous Paracelsus,' from whom ' he had learnt all arts, George Am und von Wald at Dürnhof, near the imperial city of Dünkelspiel, licentiate of law, doctor of philosophy and both medicines,' came into possession of a 'universal medicine, named Panacea Am Waldina,' by which ' he threw nearly the whole of Germany into wonder and amazement.'[1] Every medicine, he said, which removes all impediments and afflictions of the spirit, the life, heals also all diseases. The panacea Am Waldina takes away all impediments and afflictions of the spirit, the life, and therefore it heals all diseases.' When he was called on by the renowned Andrew Libavius, 'doctor of medicines, physicist, poet and gymnasiarch, at Rotenburg,' to reveal the recipe for his secret method ' as a pious German,' he unhesitatingly refused to do so. ' It is best to keep silence,' he said, ' for the high gifts of God must not be revealed to the unworthy and the unthankful.' Libavius himself, he said, would never succeed in the preparation of the

Augsburg wrote : it only depended on faith to be able to practise all sorts of secret arts, and also to fly through the air ; cf. Gmelin, *Gesch. der Chemie*, i. 286 ; Kopp, *Alchemie*, i. 212, note 3.　**Concerning Paracelsus and Cornelius Agrippa of Nettesheim cf. also Haeser, *Gesch. der Medizin*, ii. (3rd ed.) 71 ff. ; cf. Schubert and Südhoff, *Paracelsusforschungen* (Frankfort, 1887–1889) ; Jul. Hartmann, ' Theophrastus von Hohenheim, sein religiöses Standpunkt und seine Stelle zur Reformation,' in the *Blättern für württemb. Kirchengesch.* Jahrg. ix. (Stuttgart, 1894) p. 1 ff.　See also our remarks vol. vii. (German *) 357 ff., and *Jahresberichte für neure deutsche Litteraturgeschichte*, vols. iv. and v.

[1] In a *Kurtzer und zum andermal gemehrter Bericht*, &c. (Ursel, 1594) (the title of this ' short report ' is over thirty lines long), Am Wald, in no less than some 150 pages, published every imaginable testimony in Latin and German, in prose and rhyme, which had been given to him by doctors, pastors, superintendents, advocates, schoolmasters, counts and lords concerning the wonderful effects of his panacea.

* Vol. VII. is not yet translated into English.

panacea, and that for seven reasons. 'First of all he despised the Word of God, for he would not believe that
this preparation was contained in the Bible, although
Luther in his "Colloquia" says that the Bible is head
and empress of all arts. Secondly he will not acknowledge that God is so powerful and merciful as to have
ordained a universal medicine, but he attributes it to
the devil. Thirdly, as he himself acknowledges, he
does not understand the doctrine of Hermes, Hamuel,
Albumazar, Theophrastus Paracelsus, and the other
true philosophers and doctors of medicine, who have
written about the philosophers' stone, and he does
not scruple to talk abusively about them.' 'The
saintly man Luther says in his "Colloquia," that the
true art of alchemy is the veritable philosophy of
the wise, and that it commends itself thoroughly
to him, not only for its great usefulness in smelting,
separating, purifying and preparing metals, but also
on account of its allegorical and secret meanings which
are extremely beautiful, especially those which refer to
the resurrection of the dead at the Day of Judgment.'
Am Wald let fly at his opponent so mercilessly in
lampoons, libels and devilish slanders, that Libavius
in a refutation 'counted up a hundred and eighty
or more gross lies' which Am Wald had circulated
concerning himself, and on his part urged on all 'honour-
loving' readers that they ought 'to spit upon this
slanderer and cry " Pfui! you devil!" ' [1]

---

[1] *Vortrab Dr. Georgen am Wald auf die im Truck ausgefertigte Spott- und
Schmähkarten Andree Libavi*, &c. (Hanau, 1595), pp. 11, 15, 29 ff., 51 ff., 69;
A. *Libavius, Panacea Ambaldina victa et prostrata* (that is to say, renewed,
unaltered, counter-report, &c.), (Frankfort, 1606) preface, 'Instruktion,'
p. 14 ff. In one of his writings Libavius pointed out that the famous
panacea was nothing more than ordinary cinnabar (Sprengel, iii. 516).

'It's just the same thing over again,' said a 'lover of suffering humanity' in 1608, 'the doctors of medicine are doing just like the controversial theologians and preachers, they carry the Word of God and Holy Writ in their mouths and pretend to be instructed out of them, but they abuse each other like street urchins. At the same time they lead all the world into uncertainty, error, waste of money and misery.'[1]

But Am Wald did not enjoy a monopoly in his trade. Like him the Suabian Ægidius Gutmann had a universal medicine for the prevention and healing of all diseases, and one which had in addition the power of producing gold. The preacher John Gramann also, widely known as a Paracelsian enthusiast, was the possessor of an elixir of life.

Still more renowned through their writings than even the Paracelsian-cabalistic magic doctors were the house physicians of the Prince of Anhalt, Julius Sperber and Oswald Croll, the second of whom was also in the service of the Emperor Rudolf II. 'Man,' so Croll declared, 'is in organic connexion with the firmament, from which he derives all his knowledge: the astral influences fashion him into a true sage, for his mind emanates from the stars, his soul, however, from the mouth of God.' All the different parts of the body correspond with certain elements, planets, forces, and numbers; the actual genius of a human being, the inner, astral ego, the imagination, is the 'Gabalis,' which like a magnet draws all visible objects to itself, and with the help of which we are able to produce all that we see with our eyes. The most powerful among

---

[1] *Von der natürlichen Kunst zur Kurierung von Krankheiten und vielen Gebrechen* (1608), preface.

all magic agencies is ' the word ' : through this agency,
above all through the alphabetical characters and talismans prepared at stated times, all diseases can be
healed. All remedies work by virtue of the magnetic
force which they derive from the stars ; these, however,
manifest themselves chiefly in balsam, which is in close
connexion with the life-balsam in man, through which
it removes all ills. By means of magic physicians
must search through nature for this balsam, and they
will find the secret for prolonging life. No less enthu-
siastic was Henry Kunrath of Leipzig, who practised
medicine at Hamburg, and published later on, at
Dresden, an ' Amphitheatre of eternal wisdom,' and
managed to establish for himself the fame of having
discovered the stone of wisdom, the highest elixir of
life.[1]

From foreign lands also there were brought into
Germany, ' for the benefit of all sick people in the
whole country,' the works of every imaginable ' wonder-
doctor and merchant of secrets,' among others those
of the Bolognese Leonardo Fioravanti, a dissolute,

---

[1] Sprengel, iii. 528–530, 533–534. Concerning a publication, *Arznei-
Kunst- und Wunderbuch*, published in 1592, at Leipzig, by the Paracelsist
Michael Bapst von Rochlitz, preacher at Mohorn in the Meissen circle,
Sprengel says (iii. 514) : ' In the whole range of our medical literature there
is perhaps no other book which contains such an enormous quantity of
most wonderful fables, most preposterous remedies, and absurd twaddle.'
Besides this book the same preacher-doctor published at the same time,
at Leipzig, a *Giftjagendes Kunst- und Hausbuch*, and four years later at
Eisleben a *Wunderbarliches Leib- und Wundarzneibuch*. See also our
remarks, vol. vii. (German) p. 363 ff. [The English translation of vol. vii. is
not yet out.] There were also many *Harnpropheten*, doctors who pretended to know and to cure disease by inspecting the patient's urine.
They were in great request ; at the princely courts it was the doctor's duty
to enter every morning the prince's bedchamber to make inspection.
Sprengel, iii. 314–315, 315–318, where doctors are named who opposed this
practice.

wandering adventurer. A publication by this person, ' Physika, das ist Experienz und Naturkundigung,' was translated into German in 1604, under the auspices of the Frankfort bookseller, John Berner, ' on account of its unspeakable excellence and superiority, and its many secrets,' and because ' in the removal of diseases almost all the most famous physicians had erred grossly and only made darkness darker.' ' This work far excelled all medical treatises of our time because, as may be seen in it, it disclosed so many secrets, so many beautiful wonders of nature concerning which other men were either silent or ignorant'; for instance, ' secret, never before heard of experiments, in surgery and medicine,' all sorts of alchemistic mysteries, &c., &c. Another work by the same ' dealer in secrets,' entitled ' Krone der Arznei,' contained no less a number of beautiful secrets of medicine and surgery and of the alchemy of man and of minerals. Each and all among the people ought ' to have a special longing for such wonderful treasures.' [1] As Fioravanti with his magic balsam, so Thomas Bovius pretended to cure all imaginable diseases with his liquid gold.[2]

There were other tracts on medical secrets and wonders which were specially devoted to showing that all human diseases came from the stars. ' A true physician,' says one of these writings, ' is only he who is master of the high art of astrology and knows all about the stars, from which the great Paracelsus learnt that all planets have in men their image and reflection and their offspring, and that each human being has

[1] Both works printed at Frankfort, 1604. Fioravanti, said Crato von Crafftheim, the house physician of Maximilian II., was a *nebulo pessimus* (Sprengel, iii. 440, note 16).

[2] Sprengel, iii. 536.

in him or herself the sun and moon, Saturn, Mars, Venus and all the other signs. The various kinds of diseases correspond to the various stars, their origin and nature—the one is of Mars, the other of Luna, the other of Sagittarius and so forth, and the nature of ill-nesses can be discovered in no other way. Who, then, that has not studied all this can cure illness ? Rejoice, O German people, that, with the dawning of the dear evangel, and with improved knowledge and science, all this has become known and established ! ' [1] ' Patricius ab alto Saxo ' published in 1613, at Frankfort-on-the-Main, a volume entitled ' Wegweiser, die Krankheiten zu heilen durch astronomische Konkordanz.' ' When a doctor is going to give medicine to a patient,' he said, ' he must first of all acquaint himself with the position of the planets at that moment.' For to each planet particular herbs and plants are subject, and ' the friendships and enmities of planets, which love and hate each other,' must not be left out of account in treating the sick.[2] The pestilences which raged so frequently were attributed to Saturn, the child-devourer, who acted in the capacity of ' God's schoolmaster and executioner.' [3]

The belief, set in general circulation both by learned books and by little tracts for the people, that most diseases originated in magic, had an extremely corrupt-ing effect. ' Be it known unto you,' says a compilation of this sort, ' that out of seven kinds of maladies which in these last unhappy days have attacked mankind, such as lamenesses, blindnesses, caries, curvatures, cramps,

[1] *Etliche chymische und verborgene Mittel* &c., Bl. B 2.
[2] *Methodus*, &c. Now first published for the general use and profit of mankind (Frankfort-on-the-Main, 1613).
[3] See Sprengel, iii. 255.

leprosy and others, at least four or five proceed from
sorcery and other arts, and therefore cannot be cured
with apothecary's drugs, but require anti-magic means ;
indeed the wise and highly famed doctors of medicine
say themselves that their ordinary practice in no way
suffices to heal the innumerable diseases caused by
magic.' 'The best teacher in such matters,' they said,
was Paracelsus. 'From this man's highly famous books,
dear reader,' said the author of the 'Volksschrift,' 'I
promise to bring you, by the next Lent fair, certain little
tracts which will instruct you in these most important
things and in the diseases which by God's judgment are
produced through magic.' [1] Paracelsus taught, among
other things, that 'some sorcerers can make an image in
the form of a man whom they have in their minds and
thoughts, and strike a nail into the sole of his foot. In
this way the real man is undoubtedly struck, and carries
the nail undoubtedly in his foot. Thence it follows
that the man must limp and can never stand properly
on his foot as long as the nail remains sticking in the
image. But when the nail is taken out of the image
the man also is relieved. So, too, it often happens that
boils, scars, and blue marks may suddenly appear on a
man's body, and it may become sore all over, just as
if he had been beaten with sticks ; and even if there
is a simple natural cause, he will explain it in no other
way than that he has been unknowingly struck by
a sorcerer through an image. Further it also happens
frequently that a person becomes blind in one or both
eyes, or deaf in one or both ears, or speechless, palsied,
limping, or even is struck dead : all this in the judgment of God happens through these arch-sorcerers.'

[1] *Etliche chymische und verborgene Mittel*, &c. Bl. A 3, and preface.

And whenever such ' magic seizures ' occur, the doctors must not regard these ' supernatural ailments and illnesses ' as natural, and attempt to heal them with materia medica, for then they would become a laughing-stock and a disgrace. ' To be a perfect doctor ' one should, on the contrary, know that such complaints can only be relieved by the same methods which produced them—that is ' through faith and through the imagination.' ' And the right procedure is at once to make an image which shall be a facsimile of the hand or foot, or whatever limb it may be, that is suffering pain, or a whole figure in wax, and anoint or bind up this image, and not the man himself who is afflicted with boils, scars, blue spots, &c., and these affections will all disappear from the man. If, however, the man is so strongly bewitched that he is afraid he is going to lose an eye, or his hearing, to become dumb, lame, palsied, then an entire image of the man must be made in wax, and the imagination must be fixed strongly on this image, and it must even be burnt in the fire according to proper regulations.' They must not, he said, trouble themselves about the sophists of the colleges who made fun of such cures. ' Physicians do not learn and discover everything that they ought to know in the universities ; they have often to go to old wives, gypsies, masters of the black art, vagrants, old peasant-folk, and learn from them. For these people have more knowledge of such things than all the colleges and universities.' [1]

---

[1] Schindler, pp. 126–130, 350–352. Johannes Hiller instructed the Elector Augustus of Saxony in a special kind of magic, ' which taught how to make or paint images in the name of some particular person, on which images, by the force of imagination, everything could be

As a disciple of Paracelsus, Bartholomew Carrichter of Reckingen, house physician to the Emperor Maximilian II., compiled a 'Practica aus den fürnehmsten Secretis,' and a book entitled 'Von gründlicher Heilung der zauberischen Schäden.' [1]

brought to pass which otherwise would have happened to the said person.' This art can be turned both to good and bad uses. 'A sorcerer abuses the art when he uses it to injure an enemy whom by this means he can strike with sickness, blindness, lameness, or even kill at once. He constructs an image, as described, in the name and likeness of the man whom he wishes to injure, and all that he does to this image, by striking it, sticking nails into this or that limb, &c., takes effect in the corresponding limbs and parts of the body represented by the image.' The right and legitimate use of this art, on the other hand, consists in this, that by its means 'all bewitched people, whom no natural means in the world is able to help, can be relieved' (Von Weber, *Anna von Sachsen*, pp. 283–291).

[1] Sprengel, iii. 511–512. A passage from this book quoted by Sprengel shows the degree of intelligibility with which books of this sort were written : ' The disease of magic hemorrhoids belongs at the beginning to the third degree of the *Heustor resolutus*. But the instant it becomes insensible, it is classed under the *uviatoria Arsoluta inflaculecta Capoi Cori*, made up by the beginning and the end of the third and fourth degrees,' &c. The Strassburg doctor Melchior Sebisch, in 1580, summed up the reasons why medicine 'in these our days has fallen into disrepute, abuse and confusion.' Many people, he said, ' boast of their great knowledge, imagine that they can cure all diseases, keep their pretended art beyond measure secret, and are all the time less learned in it than a cow is in the Psalter.' ' They excogitate in a most wonderful manner, how this or that herb must be gathered with special ceremonies, under this or that planet : this one on a Friday, that one on a Sunday ; this root must be disenchanted with silver, the other must be dug out with gold or copper ; one must be gathered from above one's head, another from under one's feet, and in this way, by all this juggling, they cause distrust in the remedies of experienced doctors. There is so much of all this fantasticalness that it is impossible for me to describe it all.' ' As if, however, these charlatans were not enough, the devil and his associates must also have their part in it all ; and we see the blasphemous God-forsaken Jews, the witches, the exorcists, the makers of wax figures, enchanters, and all the rest of the noxious vermin that proceeds from the devil, joining in the sport. The people flock after them. They are looked upon as gods. They give them as much money as they like to ask for ; enchanters read in the urine not only the diseases but also the name, status, fortune and other circum-

No less fatal was the confusion of heads and brains produced by the ' science' of alchemy, which was brought into connexion with ' magic medicine' and ' planet spirits,' and which had numerous practitioners and disciples both in town and country.[1] On this subject

stances of their clients. Under the same category comes the practice of attributing every disease to this or that old wife by whom the patient is said to have been bewitched. Also those who cure every ill of man or beast with blessings, crossings, written formulas and such like fooleries.' 'Finally there are the vagrants, the peddlers who sell vermifuges and theriac, who trudge about with their knapsacks and are for the most part hangmen, players and such like disreputable people ; they deceive the world publicly and palpably : they cry out a salve or a medicine for all ills. They recommend their human fat for everything' (Birlinger's *Alemannia*, vi. 185–187).

[1] The enormous number of books on alchemy which the German book-market produced almost every year, especially after the beginning of the seventeenth century, shows what a widespread interest this occult art had for the public. In Frankfort alone there appeared the following works in the first two decades of the century : 1600, *Paradisus aureolus Hermeticus*, by Benedictus Figulus ; 1603, the compilation, *Thesaurus Chemicus*, with a collection of the chemical writings of Arnaldus Villanovanus ; 1604, a German translation of the most important of the just-mentioned writings on alchemy ; 1604, Gerhard Dorn's *Sammlung Philosophiae chemicae quatuor vetustissima scripta* ; 1608, Hildebrand von Hildebrandseck's *Auriferae artis, i.e. der Goldkunst . . . uhrälteste Autores und Anfänger* ; in the same year *Hortulus olympicus aureolus*, i.e. a heavenly, golden, hermetical pleasure-garden, planted by old and new Philosophers, &c., by Benedictus Figulus ; 1610, Michael Potier's *Compendium philosophicum*, &c. ; 1611, *De lapide philosophico tractatus* ; 1613, an *Alchymie-Spiegel* (or a brief summary of the practice of the whole chemical art, &c.) ; in the same year a second *Alchymie-Spiegel* ; in the following (1614) again a *Speculum alchimiae* and *Opuscula quaedam chimica* ; 1615, a German translation of Michael Maier's *Lusus serius* ; 1617, Michael Potier's *Philosophiae pura, qua . . . vera totius mysterii revelatio filiis sapientiae offertur, quod typis nunquam visum, quamdiu stetit mundus* ; in the same year Michael Maier's *Jocus severus, hoc est, tribunale aequum, quo noctua reginae avium, phoenice arbitro, agnoscitur* ; 1618, Michael Maier's *Tripus aureus*, &c. ; and the same author's *Themis aurea, hoc est, de legibus Fraternitatis roseae crucis tractatus* ; further, in 1618, Chr. Nigrinus, *Sphynx rosacea* (i.e. the discovery of the Brotherhood of the laudable order of the Rosicrucians and a probable opinion on their creed) ; and simultaneously a *Fratrum Roseae Crucis Buccina jubilei ultimi*. At Oberursel near Frank-

also there must have been special 'newspapers' for the people, to judge from the complaint of the preacher Leonard Breitkopf: 'Eager is the demand for papers which announce that gold and silver can be made out of baser metals; and all the tailors, shoemakers, servants and maids who hear and read about these things, give all the coins they can spare to the numbers of perambulating and fraudulent artists who pretend they can make gold, when they come into their towns and villages, hoping to have it turned into gold; and they are miserably deceived. 'Therefore, my friends,' the preacher warned his hearers, 'throw the wise booklet which you have got into the fire, and save the pennies with which you would buy more such rubbish, and beware of everyone who tries to take you in with this pretended art.' The magistrates, if they were concerned about the duties of their office, should have an eye on these mischievous scamps, who are a veritable plague with their fraudulent writings and inventions, and the practice of their false art.[1]

'Inexperienced doctors,' wrote John Porta, 'ruined apothecaries, greasy barbers, good-for-nothing, lazy gold- and copper-smiths, shameless charlatans, tooth-drawers, mountebanks, dissolute jugglers and conjurors, quacks, treasure-seekers, beerhouse fiddlers and vagrants boast of their power to make gold, and read books on alchemy instead of the Bible.'[2] In a pamphlet

fort there was published in 1602 a three-volumed *Theatrum chimicum*. See Kopp, *Alchemie*, ii. 330–389. ** In the British Museum there is a splendid illuminated work, *Splendor Solis*, treating of alchemy, written in German, and illustrated by German artists with the most exquisite miniatures and marginal arabesques.

[1] See above, p. 271, note 1.

[2] Schindler, p. 203.

published in 1518, 'Die phantastische Alchemie,' Virgilius of Salzburg said :

> From alchemy occult
> Eight evil things result :
> Smoke, ashes, multitudes of lies,
> Labour hard and heavy sighs,
> Dishonour, poverty and need :
> Would'st thou escape such things ?   Be wise,
> Of alchemy beware indeed.[1]

For a warning to the people Rollenhagen, in his 'Froschmäuseler,' showed up the whole fraudulent procedure of the alchemists, and exposed them to scathing ridicule by making one of the alchemists say concerning the secret of his art, the 'philosophers' stone,' that it is

> The supersoul of metals all,
> And every metal that doth fall
> Below the nature of pure ore,
> It sweeps out like an angel broom.
> That no impurity or sore
> In our bodies may remain
> Of this powder take one grain,
> And the sick man will be well again,
> As Theophrast with his azote
> The people cures just like a God.
> *Aurum potabile* rescues
> When all the doctors hope refuse ;
> Yea, the life of longest span,
> E'en a hundred years old man,
> Grows young and sound and strong again,
> Renews his heart, his bones, his brain ;
> The spirit, above all, grows whole
> Wherein inhabiteth our soul.[2]

Occasionally also intelligence reached the people of the fate of the gold-makers who perambulated round the German princes' courts. Thus, for instance, in 1597, there appeared a 'strange and unheard-of new

---

[1] See Kopp, *Alchemie*, i. 227–228 note.
[2] *Froschmäuseler*, Part i. c. 15.

report of the manner in which George Hanober (Honauer) of Olmütz, so-called alchemist and gold-maker, was executed at Stuttgart.' He was hanged on the gallows ' in a coat gilded all over.'

> Of iron was the gallows made,
> And all with gilding overlaid ;
> On it were spent great sums untold,
> It shone and sparkled with bright gold.
> A hundred and eighty men on horse,
> And of the folk a large concourse,
> Came to see the culprit die.
> Take warning, all of you, thereby.

' This gallows weighed twenty-five hundredweight and cost 3000 Oberland florins, and on it was hanged on April 2, 1597, the above-mentioned Jörg who, among other charges brought against him, had robbed the Duke of two tons of gold.' [1]

Duke Maximilian of Bavaria issued a public order to the effect that ' alchemy, or the art of making gold and silver out of any material that was not gold and silver, was wholly and entirely forbidden, because it was seldom practised without sorcery and superstition, and such like devil's work. Any who disobeyed this command were either to be fined a certain sum of money or, if they could not pay this, be punished with imprisonment, banishment, or in some other just manner.' [2]

---

[1] Scheible, *Schaltjahr*, i. 45–50 ; cf. ii. 389–391. Concerning the proceedings of the alchemists at the court of the Emperor Rudolf II and at the courts of the German princes, see our remarks, vol. viii. p. 185 ff. (German). [The English of vol. viii. is not yet out.]

[2] J. Müller's *Zeitschrift für deutsche Kultergesch.* 1873, p. 102. The Augsburg doctor, Daniel Keller, in order to make money, offered to sell his secret for 400,000 florins. As he found no purchasers he made (in 1570) a contract with Marx Fugger securing him one fourth of the proceeds. All hopes and all expenses, however, were in vain (Von Stetten, i. 226).

The number of books on alchemy and on 'secret wonder-working medicines' was extraordinarily large.[1] The Venetian alchemist Laurence Ventura boasted that he had written 250 books on this art which he had made over to the Palatine's library, besides fifty others which he had kept for himself.[2] 'All these innumerable books,' however, 'were deliberately veiled in the greatest obscurity.' Theobald von Hohenland, in 1610, gave twelve reasons for this obscurity, the first of which was, that it might not be revealed and that no one might know, that the art was true and in all respects certain'; and a second, 'that the philosophers might not be called to account or held responsible for all the evil that wicked people might do if they became initiated into this art.' ' The philosophers to whom this " magisterium " was revealed have sworn together,' said one of the adepts, ' by the most terrible curses and malediction of God, that they will never describe this high godly work to any single human being in plain language, so that it may not fall into the hands of wicked, godless people.'[3]

The 'Aureum Vellus,' or 'Gulden Schatz und Kunstkammer,' which appeared in 1598 was prized as a most important and invaluable book for the use and instruction of people in general. This treasury of art was said to contain the ' most highly distinguished, most excellent, most select, most beautiful and most authentic' writings of the old Oriental kings and sages, translated

[1] See above, p. 291, note 1.
[2] Von Hohenland, p. 155. The Frenchman, Dionysius Zacharias, in 1539, made acquaintance in Paris with a hundred alchemists (Schmieder, p. 272). Concerning John Fischart as a publisher of alchemical writings see Wendeler's article in the *Archiv für Litteraturgeschichte*, vi. 487–509.
[3] Von Hohenland, p. 48 ff.

into German by the philosopher Solomon Trissmosin, the preceptor 'of the great philosopher and doctor Theophrastus Paracelsus,' and now collected together and published by one of the lovers of this art. Trissmosin tells how he 'snapped up the whole treasure of the Egyptians' and learnt to know the decoctions of the greatest heathen kings. 'And it is a matter of wonder that the eternal God should have revealed such things to the heathens; they, however, kept them very secret.' 'Now the red lion is the greatest treasure in this world; so that the children of man to whom he is granted may work great miracles and obtain health and wealth.'

This lion is an unspeakably tincturial being. 'In the book "Suforethon" is found the lengthening of life of a man in this world, and men can prolong their lives many hundred years, were it not against the will of God; . . . for example, the all-powerful heathen King Xopholat preserved his life to the age of 300 with the accompanying Arcanum.' . . . 'All apothecaries must humble themselves before this "Suforethon" with their syrups which only produce putridity and uncleanness in the blood.' The medicinal alchemical 'arcanum' begins with instructions to 'get sulphur from the mines where gold grows.'[1] For the next autumn fair the author promised treatises and receipts about the 'green lion,' 'philosophical dialogues about the yellow and red man,' and so forth.[2] Not less 'clear and useful for everybody to study' was the 'Neue gebenedeite philosophische Rosengart,' in which it was shown by the most wise King Solomon, by Solomon Trissmosin and

[1] *Aureum Vellus* (Rohrschach, 1598), A 1–4.
[2] Bl. 2ᵇ—4ᵃ.

by other sages, how the blessed golden bough and treasury of tinctures is to be reached and broken off from the everlasting Oriental tree of the Hesperides by divine grace.[1] Very extraordinary also is the pamphlet which appeared in 1616 by Stephen Michelbacher, 'Cabala, Spiegel der Kunst und Natur in Alchymia.' 'God appeared to me with great grace,' says the author in his preface, 'and to me, all unworthy, revealed His great secrets'; it was consequently his duty to make these known through a mirror, as well for the physical health of mankind as for the salvation of their souls.[2]

One of the most renowned practisers of, and writers about, alchemy and occult magic medicine, was Leonard Thurneissen zum Thurn, born at Basle in 1530, and house physician to the Elector John George of Brandenburg since 1571. In Berlin, where the so-called Grey Cloister was made over to him for a laboratory for his occult arts, he set up a private printing-press, and employed writers, setters, proof-correctors, typefounders, mould-cutters, copper-engravers, and bookbinders—sometimes over two hundred workers at the many publications issued by him. He lived in very grand style, dressed in velvet and silk, drove in a carriage with a four-in-hand, accompanied by boys of the nobility, counted among his guests the most distinguished members of the court. For he made an abundant harvest of gold out of his magic medical practice, his annual calendars and prophesyings, his horoscopes, and the talismans which he sold for the

---

[1] *Rosarium novum et olympicum et benedictum*, 2nd part by Benedictus Figulus (Basle, 1608).

[2] Cabala . . . in honour of all toiling lovers of the art, with the help of God presented as clearly as in a mirror. Augsburg, 1616.

warding off of threatened evils. Half an ounce of
magic cinnamon oil cost twelve thalers; the same
quantity of Tinctura Antimonii sixteen thalers.

In one of his numerous works, ' Quinta Essentia,'
Thurneissen, through the length of twelve books,[1] expounded ' the wonderful subtlety, power, and effect of
the two most excellent arts of medicine and alchemy,
which were both most highly beneficial to mankind,
and he also showed how closely the two are allied and
bound up in relationship, and that neither is of any
use without the other, or has any power to affect
human bodies.' The tenth book dealt with the ' Zwölf
Hauptstücken der Alchimy,' the eleventh of the ' Seel
Solis und Lunä und Zubereitung zu dem Lapidi Philosophorum ' (' The Soul of Sun and Moon, a preparation
of the philosophers' stone '); the twelfth of the ' Ordnung
der philosophischen Heimlichkeit ' (' Discipline of the
philosophers' arcanum '—or search). In his epilogue
concerning the twelve preceding books he said that his
work ' was compiled and written truthfully, but at the
same time obscurely, as before announced, in order
that each and every one might not fall upon it, like
the unreasoning brutes of the stalls.' [2]

In an earlier work, ' Archidoxa,' he had already
' summed up all the hidden mysteries of alchemy and
seven liberal arts, and expounded them in rhyme in
eight volumes.' [3] This work taught the secrets of
' 108 beautiful art processes '—for instance : ' To trans-

---

[1] New edition, Leipzig, 1574.

[2] Pp. 175 ff., 202. ' Medicine,' he says at p. 204, ' is in a deplorable,
contemptible condition.' Theophrastus Paracelsus comes in for great
praise, p. 34.

[3] *Archidoxa* (Berlin, 1575). The complete title is in Goedeke, *Grundriss*, ii. 571.

mute lead into silver and tin ' ; ' to change lead into oil ' ; ' to make gold out of lead ' ; ' to change iron into copper ' ; ' to change iron into gold ' ; ' to change gold into oil,' and so forth.   In 1575, simultaneously with the second edition of this work, he published what he called ' a sufficient, plentiful, and exhaustive explana- tion ' of this same work, ' in which will be found, with- out especial trouble, many profound explanations and revelations of a number of vexed questions concerning gods, angels, devils, human beings, animals, characters, seals, enchantments, ghosts,' in particular also ' revela- tions from the heavens, stars, planets, zodiacal signs, items about the elements, the comets and their forces, faculties, influences, procedure, modes and qualities, together with the astrolabe and its use, by means of which nativities are determined, fortune and misfor- tune, death and life, war, famine, and other things forecast, according to astronomical method and mathe- matical calculation.'   This work, he prides himself, ' has been compiled and written for the benefit of the common Fatherland,' and, moreover, ' in elegant and flowing German rhyme,' after the pattern of Mercurius, ' who is said to have written and published thirty thousand books in verse.' [1]

[1] He had, indeed, a very large number of renowned precursors in the investigation of things earthly and heavenly.   Thus ' Adam, Aristotle and Paracelsus have been of high repute in the understanding of natural things ' ; Seth, Ptolemy and Stöfler were three grand lights in astronomy.' ' We know what Enoch, Abraham, and Luther, not to mention Plato, have done in the discovery of things divine, celestial and spiritual.'   ' What splendid fame have not Mercurius, Trismegistus, Cicero, and of late John Sturmius, earned in the art of eloquent speaking ! '   ' Are we not still in our own days living for the most part under the laws, policy and organisation, religious and secular, of Socrates and Moses, coupled with the admirable statutes and civil regulations of the Emperor Trajan ? ' Preface, Bl. 2 and 3.   ** The Electoral Prince of Brandenburg, Joachim

Another man who gave himself out as 'highly renowned in the knowledge of occult art' was John Faulhaber, 'arithmetic master and modist' at Ulm. Among other writings he published at Nuremberg, in 1613, an 'Andeutung einer unerhörten neuen Wunderkunst, which the Spirit of God has seen fit, down to these last days, to keep sealed and hidden in certain prophetic and Biblical occult figures.' This pamphlet, which was dedicated to Duke John Frederic of Württemberg, was twelve pages long, and contained 'irrefutable demonstrations, such as had never before been seen in any tongue or speech.'[1]   In the same year Faulhaber dedicated to the Emperor Matthias, who had summoned him to his court on account of his 'newly discovered mathematical and philosophical arts,' another no less wonderful pamphlet of thirteen pages, which appeared under the title : 'Heavenly Secret Magic, or new cabalistic art and marvellous reckoning of Gog and Magog, from which the wise men, the initiated, and the learned, who are sufficiently experienced in this art, can secretly observe and carefully calculate the nature of the great enemy of Christ, Gog and Magog.' By means of the Ulm notary Helias Steudlin, Faulhaber

Frederic, requested von Thurneissen, in 1575, 'to inform him confidentially in what places the events assigned in his calendar to each day, such as murders, incendiaries, tumult, decease of high personages, and so forth, would happen.'   When the Prince's wife, the Margravine Katharina, heard secretly of this request, she also begged the calendar prophet to send her an almanac 'in which it was quite clearly and truly explained how each event was to be understood, such as he had sent her husband, and to keep back nothing from her' (Moehsen, *Beiträge*, p. 121).   In the royal library in Berlin, says Moehsen, there is a calendar of 1580, interleaved with paper, on which Thurneissen is supposed to have written and explained such prophecies for the Margravine Katharina, apparently before the events happened.

[1] Nuremberg, 1613.

got certificates of authenticity for several testimonies that he had given 'concerning the incredible mathematical magic art which was hidden in the prophet Ezekiel,' and 'concerning the newly discovered wonderful art of war against the hereditary enemy, which had been sealed up in the Revelation of St. John.' Unfortunately 'the remaining testimonies of future events and other secret matters, which were still hidden in the Holy Scriptures, were, for certain reasons, not introduced here this time.' [1]

Other 'friends of the German people' were less abstinent in their communications of future events. 'Nowadays,' wrote the Zurich mathematician Conrad Holtzhalbius, in 1618, 'the world has become so highly favoured and so wonderful since the advent of the holy evangel that the mathematicians, physicists, philosophers, and other learned men of the reformed and pure religion have had more prophetic arts revealed to them and more power given them of seeing into the future than ever before in many thousand years, and it behoves all intelligent Christians who wish to be certain of the future, and of all that is impending through divine judgment, to buy and to study diligently all the many booklets and newspapers which are printed on these subjects every year in greater and greater numbers. Almost everything in the world has now become a wonder, and one of the greatest wonders undoubtedly is the certain prediction of the future. Therefore buy and read.' [2]

At this period, more than ever before, the science

[1] *Himmlische geheime Magia*, B B 2—C.
[2] *Zweiter Sendbrieff über die wunderkünste Johann Faulhabers*, &c., 1618, preface.

of astrology was considered one of the first and best means for penetrating into the future. It was believed in almost everywhere even by the most famous men.[1] Princes and towns held their own, often highly paid, astrologers. 'This astrology,' wrote John Kepler, 'is indeed an idiotic little daughter; but, goodness me, where would her mother, that most reasonable dame, astronomy stop if it were not for this foolish daughter of hers? The world is still more foolish, so foolish, in fact, that for its good the wise mother has to be introduced to it by her daughter's foolish prophecies and lies. Then the mathematicians' salaries are so slender that the mother would starve did not the daughter earn some money.'[2] Kepler himself was obliged to publish calendars, in which the nature of the weather during the coming year was predicted according to astrological rules, and forecasts concerning political events were also given. He also told to distinguished people the fortunes of their future lives, and gained such high renown that the Emperor Rudolf II. appointed him his court astrologer.[3] David Fabricius, also, of East Friesland, a distinguished astronomer, who earned lasting fame by his discovery of the spots on

[1] * Concerning astrology in Italy during the epoch of the Renaissance, see Pastr, *Geschichte der Päpste*, iii. 3-, 112 ff. In Italy, unlike Germany, this craze was slowly disappearing.

[2] Wolf, *Astronomie*, pp. 82–83.

[3] Wolf, pp. 284-286. 'He compared his own destiny, in strict conformity to astrological rules, with the positions of the planets, and as it were dissected himself by the rules of his art and appraised his character accordingly; nevertheless in spite of it all the thought of the untenableness of this phantom knowledge is always obtruding itself, and we find frequently both in the public and private writings of Kepler such remarks as this: "Verily, with all my knowledge of astrology, I have not attained to so much certainty as to be able confidently to predict one single special event."'

the sun, was a friend of astrology.[1] The astrological follies gained entrance to the homes of burghers and peasants chiefly through the calendars and planet-books, which belonged to the most widespread class of popular literature, and which furnished, from the position of the stars, all manner of superstitious rules and recipes for house and home, health and life.[2]

---

[1] See Wolf, p. 317. Among the antagonists of astrological follies and predictions of the future was the Franciscan John Nas, who made fun of them all in his *Philognesius Practica Practicorum*; i.e. ' a sure and certain forecast of many future years, in which all sorts of happiness and sorrow is foretold from strange aspects, and briefly and amusingly described ' (Ingolstadt, 1571 ; cf. Schöpf, p. 34). Next to him John Fischart came forward against the astrologers and prognosticators. ' They turn the beautiful stars into hangmen, murderers and mischief-workers.' ' All that we do out of inborn wickedness is put down to the stars.' ' They fasten on to the stars all the sanctity of religion, the secrecy of the conscience, the God-power of miracles. They say whoever prays to God while the moon is in the dragon's tail will obtain his petition. Do they not even worship the moon and the stars and the blue firmament ? ' Hippolytus Guarinoni also spoke out strongly against ' the lying soothsayers, the readers of horoscopes, the chiromancists and charmers of wounds and diseases.' ' Trample on the thing with your paws, for no power of sky or constellation can affect either the length or the shortness of your life, because no star is as noble, as strong, as free as you are, nor has any power even to move itself ; how much less then can it move the reasonable soul of man. Why, even the pagan sages, by the light of nature only, discovered the impotence of the heavens, and freely acknowledged that they were incapable of moving themselves, but needed to be continually turned round by angels and spirits. Understand then what any child should understand, that the heavens are governed by the angels, and not the angels, spirits, or souls by the heavens.' See A. Pichler, in the feuilleton of the *Wiener Presse* of March 11, 1884.

[2] See fuller details in Schindler, pp. 84, 210, 235. The production of calendars was an extremely profitable business for the booksellers ; cf. Kirchhoff, *Beiträge*, ii. 14–16. Thomas Erast complains on this score that, at the court of the Count of Henneberg, he did not dare open a single vein or give a purging draught without consulting the calendar (Sprengel, iii. 411). At the Easter and autumn fairs of 1568, Sigmund Feyerabend sold nearly 400 planet-books, and over 520 guide-books for farmers. See the Register in Pallmann, pp. 156–160. ** For calendars and guide-books (*Practica*) in Austria, see Nagl-Zeidler, p. 557 ff.

In the Austrian dominions the preachers used the
' Praktiken ' in order to incense the people against the
Catholic Church, and also against the ruling house.
John Rasch, organist of the Schotten cloister at Vienna,
came forward as opponent of such practices. He declared it to be an abuse of Holy Scripture ' to invest
astrological practice with Bible authority.' He complained bitterly of ' the lying booklets which were
bought up in such quantities in Austria, Moravia, and
Bohemia, and which caused so much terror and despair
among the people.' In verse and prose Rasch made
merry over the astrologers and soothsayers and their
' star-gazing foolery.' In special satires, such as the
' Ketzer Katz,' he lashes the ' sham prophets ' and
astrological preachers and preaching astrology. His
chief opponents were the preacher Mark Volmar
and the Danzig physician William Misocacus, who
had prophesied the downfall of the House of Habs-
burg.[1]

Dreams were another important means for reading
the future, and these were explained in all sorts of
' dream-booklets,' among which one, published in 1551
by Walter Ryff, deserves special notice. It was entitled ' Wahrhaftige, unbetrügliche Unterweisung über
Träume, Erscheinungen und nächtliche Gesichte,'[2] by
which future events are made known to men. For
instance, if anyone dreams that he has golden teeth
' this is a very good omen for orators, but for other

---

[1] The above-mentioned according to Nagl-Zeidler, p. 561 ff.

[2] *Warhafftige, gewisse und unbetrügliche Unterweisung, wie alle Tröum,
Erscheinungen und nächtlichen Gesicht . . . natürlich und recht erklärt und
ausgelegt werden sollen, als dann solches von den alten Philosophis und
Weissagern der Heiden . . . warhafftig und gewiss erfunden ist*, &c. Strassburg, 1551.

people it signifies fire in their houses, or to some people it means illness.' 'To dream that one has horns like an ox or some other strong and dangerous animal means a violent, unnatural death—generally that the person who had the dream will be beheaded.' 'I have learnt from frequent experience that it is very fortunate to dream of eating human flesh, provided it be the flesh of a stranger and an unknown person, but to dream of eating a friend or acquaintance means that the latter will shortly die. But to eat the flesh of one's own son is the very worst and most unhappy omen, for it means a very speedy death.' 'Dreams about creatures of hell, devils, plagues, and tortures of hell are bad and unlucky, and even alarming for good and pious people, for they mean calamity, tribulation, grief, suffering, and sadness. It should, however, be remarked that if anyone dreams of devils and hell-creatures the dream should be explained with reference to the shape, manner, behaviour, and dress of the apparition.' 'To dream of eating and devouring books is a good omen for schoolmasters, orators, and all who seek to earn a living out of books ; but for other people it means a sudden and unexpected death.' 'To dream of hanging or strangling oneself signifies great anxiety, calamity, and danger.' 'To dream of taking something from a dead person or robbing him of his clothes portends death to the person who has dreamt the dream.' And so forth.[1]

Besides the dream-books there were also quantities of books on herbs and animals, from which the people might learn 'many wonderful secret arts for the prediction of the future, and also for guidance in daily

[1] Pp. 23, 30, 61, 135, 138, 140, 143, and so forth.

life and business, and even in love and in sorrow.'[1]
One of the most widely disseminated of these books
went by the title of 'Albertus Magnus,' or 'A new
Albertus Magnus about women and the births of children, about the virtues of certain valuable herbs, about
the power of precious stones, about the species and
nature of certain animals.' . . . This volume tells us,
for instance, that if anyone has had anything stolen
from him, and he lays the herb chokeweed under his
head at night, he will see who has committed the
theft, and all his appearance and qualities. If one
places the heart and the right foot of a screech-owl on
a person asleep he will tell all that he has done, and
will answer everything that is asked him. If one eats
the heart of a weasel whilst it is still alive, it makes him
foresee future events. The right eye of a wolf, tied
up in the right-hand sleeve, preserves from all injury.
And so forth.[2]

The advertisements and the written ' explanations '
of the ' magic mirrors indispensable for finding out
hidden things ' which were sold publicly were positively
dangerous.[3] These mirrors were made of gold, silver,
copper, and other metals, and they were used respec-
tively for different purposes. ' In the first kind,' says
Paracelsus, ' may be seen the counterfeit presentments
of people, such as thieves, enemies, and other persons ;

---

[1] *Etliche chymische und verborgene Mittel,* &c., B2.

[2] *Albertus Magnus,* &c., and *Ein newer Albertus Magnus.* . . . By Q.
Apollinares (Frankfort-on-the-Oder, without date), Bl. 11 ff., 23–31 ;
cf. *Messmemorial,* pp. vi. and ix.   At the Lent fair of 1569 Michael Harder
sold 135 copies of *Albertus Magnus* ; the firm of Sigmund Feyerabend at
the Lent and autumn fairs of 1568 more than 200 copies ; cf. Pallmann,
p. 156.   It became one of the popular books which were printed afresh
every year : ' Printed in this year.'

[3] *Etliche chymische und verborgene Mittel,* &c., preface.

also military armour, battle ordnance, sieges—everything, in fact, that men are doing, are going to do, and have done.   In the second one sees written down all past speeches, words, intrigues, where and of whom the talk was, together with all that has been discussed and concluded in councils ; but in these no future events can be learnt.   In the third one sees all that has ever been written in letters and books all over the earth.   Thus then hidden treasures are discovered ; thus, then, all that is covered is laid bare and brought to sight ; thus is shown the spot where anything has lain concealed, and all that has been stolen is brought to light again.' [1]

Itinerant students went about towns and villages selling booklets, leaflets, broadsheets, and parchments, with magic recipes and signs against the devil, against sorcery, witchcraft, drowning, and fire.[2] Talismans and the charms against musket-balls for soldiers going

[1] Schindler, p. 253.

[2] ' Itinerant students ' had long been known as a plague of the land, and in the middle of the century they became more and more numerous under the added names of gold-boilers, exorcists, and sorcerers.   About the year 1544, so Crusius relates (*Annal. Suev.* pp. iii. xi. 653–654), there appeared in Germany a lot of godless, dissolute fellows, loutish, demoralised students, who gave out that they had been in the Venusberg, had seen all sorts of wonders there, knew all about the past, the present, and the future, could get back things that had been lost, and protect people against witchcraft and sorcery.   They muttered strange unintelligible words through their teeth, and carried people away with astonishment, especially women, and cheated them out of their money.   They assured the credulous folk that by the words they uttered they could save people from being stabbed with a sword, or bewitched with magic, fruit from being destroyed by hail and animals from dying all through the year. They pretended further to have power over the raging hosts in whose ranks were all unbaptised children and all who had fallen in battle.   The belief in the Venusberg, where these strolling students pretended to have seen all the wonders they recounted, was tolerably widespread among the people.   The most splendid festivities and revellings were said to be held

to battle were in special demand.[1] Spirit seals, or the
signs of the planets in their sevenfold conjunction were
reckoned infallible against enchantments. Paracelsus
wrote concerning them : ' These spirit seals must be
made when the moon is on the increase, on a Wednesday,
and in the twelfth hour ; they must be made with
genuine red cinnabar on virgin parchment, and worn
round the neck on a black ribbon—*nota bene*, on a
bare breast. These seven new seals, made when the
moon is growing, in the twelfth hour, are, verily,
efficacious in all dangers and troubles for frightening
away and disabling spirits.' [2]

As another ' extremely powerful means for driving
off wicked spirits and sorcerers, for ensuring happiness
and health, and also for seeing into the future,' the
people were recommended to buy mandrakes (elves),
which invariably, unless God had some special plan of

there, huntings, jousts, dances and banquets. Cf. Dolch, *Geschichte
des deutschen Studententums* (Leipzig, 1858), p. 110 ff. Hans Sachs in his
carnival play, *Der fahrend Schüler mit dem Teufelsbanner*, makes the
students say of themselves :

> The duty is on us imposed
> Ever through the land to wander,
> From one high school to another,
> And the black art we must learn,
> And other kindred arts in turn.
> If any's robbed another man
> We can restore the goods ; we can
> Hang a charm around the neck
> To cure sore eyes and sharp toothache ;
> We have also a magic spell
> For making bullet wounds quite well ;
> We can dig up treasures and soothsay,
> And ride on a ram at night away.

[1] When the chief burggrave of Dohna, in 1587, led 15,000 auxiliaries
to the help of the French Huguenots and suffered a heavy defeat, there
were found on the bodies of nearly all the prisoners and the dead talismans and magic charms, which were supposed to make the wearers proof
against bullets and victorious ; cf. Moehsen, *Beiträge*, p. 134.

[2] Schindler, p. 126 ff.

chastisement in His mind against anyone, were found efficacious.' [1] Mandrakes, so it was believed, grew out of the tears of agony which fell to the ground under the gallows from the thieves who were hanged, and the executioners drew great gain out of elves.[2]

Complaints were frequent among contemporaries

---

[1] *Etliche chymische und verborgene Mittel*, &c., pp. 5–6.

[2] How strong was the belief in these elves is shown by the letter of a Leipzig burgher in 1575 to his brother in Riga (Scheible, *Kloster*, vi. 180): ' Brotherly love, and loyalty and everything else that is good to you, dear brother. I have received your letter, and in part understood well how you, dear brother, have suffered calamity in your house or farm ; that your oxen, pigs, cows, horses, and sheep have all died, that your wine and beer have turned sour in your cellar, that your food is altogether failing, and that you and your good wife are consequently in great distress, which makes my heart ache sorely on your account. I have therefore taken a great deal of trouble on your behalf, and I have been to the people who have understanding about these matters, have taken counsel with them for your sake, and have also asked them from what cause all this evil has come upon you. Their answer to me is that all this misfortune has not come to you from God, but from wicked people, and that you cannot be helped unless you procure a mandrake or elf, and that if you had one of these in your house or farm, things would soon be very different with you. I therefore further, for your sake, went to the people who supply these things—our executioner, for instance—and I paid him sixty-four thalers and a tip to his attendant, for this one which I now send you as a present out of love and loyalty. And you must attend to the directions which I write in this letter. When you receive the mandrake at your house leave it alone for three days before you look at it. After the three days lift it up and bathe it in warm water. With the water in which it has been dipped you must sprinkle your cattle and the thresholds in your house which you and yours cross over, and you will then find that your affairs will all come right again, if you will only make use of this mandrake. You must bathe it in water every four years, and every time that you do so you must put it back again into its silken coat and lay it with your best clothes, and then do nothing more to it. The water in which you bathe it is also specially good for a woman who is in travail and cannot bring forth her child. Let her take a spoonful of it and she will then be delivered of her child with joy and thankfulness. And whenever you have to go to law or to seek counsel, stick the mandrake under your right arm and you will gain the cause whether it be just or not. I herewith commend you to God. Dated Leipzig, Sunday before Lent, 1575. Hanss N.'

concerning the quantities of 'misleading books and pamphlets on magic,' which were either distributed secretly or sold openly. 'Books with fictitious names,' wrote Anton Praetorius, 'are carried about secretly, and are held in high worth on account of their age and of the honoured men who wrote them ; for it is made out that Adam, Abel, Enoch, Abraham, Solomon, Raziol whom they call Adam's angel, and the angel Raphael who taught Tobias to drive out spirits, and the angel Uriel who taught mighty and hidden secrets to Esdras, have written them.' Besides the books of wonders and magic, written in Latin and sold publicly, there are 'other well-known books of the same kind in the German language which I dare not mention for fear of over-curious, prying people.' To these also belong 'the sibyl-books, dream-books, planet-books, and others of the kind, especially those which pretend to teach how a man's character and temper, fortune and ill-fortune, present and future, may be learnt from the colour of his hair and eyes, the shape of his nose, his voice and speech, the lines of his hands, his gait, the size of his limbs.' [1]

The Italian doctor and philosopher Hieronymus Cardanus († 1576) passed for an 'extraordinarily wise master in many occult arts.' 'From Cardanus,' says a booklet on medicine and marvels of the year 1584, 'everything secret and hidden can be learnt quite infallibly, for his father before him, as he himself says, was instructed in these matters by a familiar spirit, and he, the son, was in such remarkable communion with the spirits that, whenever he wished, he could see

[1] Praetorius, pp. 166-167 ; cf. Gödelmann, pp. 91-92, 455 ; Fornerus, *Panoplia*, pp. 87-88.

into the future. Hence it is easy to understand why
it was that what he wrote was held in such high esteem.'
' Thus, for instance, if you want to know what can be
read in hands, you should not go to the gypsies, but to
Cardanus, who can inform you in this matter better
than anyone else.' [1] Cardanus had, in fact, reduced
chiromancy to a complete system. The separate
fingers, he said, were all under the dominion of the
stars and planets. The thumb was ruled by Mars, the
index by Jupiter, the middle finger by Saturn, and so
forth. From the different fingers the capacities and
qualities, as also the destinies, of human beings could
be foretold. From the middle finger, for instance, one
could learn what capacity a man had for the magic
arts and for varied labour, what liability to poverty,
distress, and sorrow, quartan fever, and captivity.
From the ring finger, on the other hand, friendship,
distinction, and power were foretold. In the triangle
in the middle of the hand ruled by Mercury one read
the signs of erudition, cleverness, and thieving.[2]

There were also books of instruction as to how fate
could be foretold from crystals, from earth, ashes,
coals, fire, and figures in the smoke, from springs and
waves, and, above all, from air, clouds, fog, wind, and
storm ; ' for the spirits,' Paracelsus had said, ' which
dwell in the elements know everything that can possibly
happen in nature—that is to say, how men will come
to an end, everything that goes on in town and country,
and among all people, item, all good fortune and all
bad fortune.' [3]   ' The class of men who practised all

---

[1] Without locality, 4[b].

[2] Sprengel, iii. pp. 401–402 ; where also several other books of instruction on chiromancy are quoted.

[3] Schindler, p. 213 ff.

sorts of secret, juggling, and magic arts, and of those
who sold pamphlets and letters on these subjects was
extremely large.' They carried on their business as
star-gazers, as readers of the motion of the planets,
interpreters of dreams, interpreters of signs from the
flight of birds, from the sitting or screaming of birds,
as soothsayers, wise people, discoverers of stolen property ; moreover, as ' wondermen, ringslippers, mist-
makers (=humbugs), illusionists, mandrake-hawkers,
quacks, howlers, spider-eaters, conjurers, benison-
dealers, hare-catchers, bullet-stoppers, sure-shots, stab-
proofs, sword-dancers, love-compellers, mice-drivers or
rat-leaders, spear and sword doctors.' [1] An itinerant
magician and crystal-seer who was taken up in Lemgo
was found possessed of a quantity of printed matter,
' letters, tables, and so forth, an exorcising book,
numbers of charts, collects both German and Latin,
circles, characters, crosses, several large letters' giving
fuller instructions as to how the magic charms were to
be used, the crystals read, an eye struck out from a
person, and so forth.[2] In a ' short, truthful narration
of extraordinary secrets which he had learnt and practised for many years, not in the service of the devil,
but by especial and unfathomable grace of God,' an
adventurer, in 1573, boasted among other things of
possessing the art of selling wind and weather.[3] The
Meissen superintendent Gregory Strigenicius, however,
warned the people in his sermons to beware of such
arts. ' With the wind-sellers,' he said, ' it's all sorcery
and devilry.' [4]

---

[1] Enumerated in Praetorius, p. 33 ; cf. Scultetus, p. 6.

[2] There is an account of this incident in J. Hocker's ' Der Teufel selbs
in the *Theatrum Diabol.* i. 95b–96.

[3] Printed at Erfurt, p. 2.   [4] *Predigten über Jonas*, p. 90b.

'As a thousandfold artful knave,' wrote John of
Münster at Vortlage in 1591, 'the devil works in manifold ways either through oracular soothsaying, pre-
monitions, dreams, divination by the earth, water, fire,
air, and oil, by the soot which is swept out of chimney-
flues, by rings, crystals, mirrors, by the song of birds,
by the entrails of sacrificial victims, and even, as some
say, by the bodies of people who have been hanged.'
'Whosoever reflects seriously on this terrible power of
the devil, will not say with the world of to-day that
the devil is not so black as he is painted, but, on the
contrary, will gladly acknowledge with me that the
devil, the prince of darkness, is far blacker and more
terrible than anybody ever could paint him.' [1] 'As
true as it is,' said a preacher emphatically, 'that God
in heaven lives and reigns, so true is it also, as the
true evangelical theologians teach, that we here in the
world are now in the kingdom of the devil. And
things have never before been so terrible as they are
now, when the devil has so gained the upper hand that
he has got men almost entirely into his power, and
works through them whatsoever he pleases. And even
should a hundred zealous and godly theologians and
writers paint the devil with his thousand wiles and
arts as black and horrible as they possibly can, and as
they are bound before God to do at all times, they
could still never paint him as black and terrible as he
really is.' [2]

---

[1] Münster, *Ein christlicher Unterricht von Gespensten* (Hanau edition
of 1591), pp. 87–88.

[2] 'A Sermon on the Day of Judgment which is standing at the door,'
by M. Henry Riess (1605), p. 3. The utterances concerning the power of
the devil are almost the same as J. Hocker's in his 'Der Teufel selbs,'
in the *Theatrum Diabol.* i. 33.

The devil had also played an important part in the literature of the Middle Ages, especially in the biographies and legends of the saints, in which his wiles and intrigues are as numerous and various as the modes of his outward appearance. Thus, for instance, in the narratives of Caesarius of Heisterbach he appears now in all sorts of animal forms, as a horse, a dog, a cat, or a monkey, now in human form, as a giant or as a finely dressed gentleman or as a seductive woman; sometimes, too, he appeared as an angel, and sometimes in the shape of some person still living.[1] Reports often ascribed to him flaming eyes, fiery hair, and fire-spitting jaws. But however multitudinous his forms of disguise, however indescribable his lies and frauds, his assaults and his rage, he was invariably conquered and humbled by the saints and the pious people, and he served only to prove and purify them, to strengthen their faith in God, their Christian confidence and Christian love. If the belief was universal and undisputed that the devil exercised his influence over human beings incessantly and from all directions, in order to separate them from God and draw them to himself, there was an equally universal conviction that he had no power over any person against that person's free will; that every human being, by help of the means of grace and the benedictions of the Church, was in a position to overcome the wicked enemy and put him to flight. For this reason the demoniacal apparitions did not call forth any overwhelming terror;[2] they by no means dominated the life of that period. If the prince of

[1] Cf. Kaufmann, *Caesarius*, p.139; see also the same author's wonderful and memorable stories from the works of Caesarius, in the *Annalen des hist. Vereins für den Niederrhein*, Heft 47.

[2] Lecky, i. 28–30.

darkness was presented to the people on the stage, he did not appear as a clever and victorious devil, but as a stupid and hoodwinked one.

But after the end of the fifteenth century belief in the power of the devil acquired an immensity of scope and an intensity before unknown. The study of cabalistic and talmudic literature enormously encouraged the representation of all sorts of demoniacal and magic arts; the study also of classic antiquity revived in countless minds the faith in all those works of demons and their associates on which in pre-Christian times doubt had scarcely ever been cast; Greek and Roman mythology filled even learned heads with all manner of new phantoms from the kingdom of the devil.[1]

Formerly protection and comfort had been found in the universal Church. Soon, however, it came to be said the old Church itself was an 'appanage of the devil.' And when the doctrines of the Church came to be attacked, and even the fundamental principles of Christianity largely called in question, the minds of the people became more and more a prey to Satanic influences. Fear and anguish before the all-conquering might of the devil became greater and greater as life grew more and more disquieted and dismal, amid the uninterrupted strife of religious partisanship. The old fear of God was converted into fear of the devil, and the doctrine of the wholesale corruption of human nature and of the non-freedom of the human will was least of all calculated to stem this faith in Satan.

---

[1] Concerning the belief of the Italian humanists in demons and spectres see Burckhardt, *Die Cultur der Renaissance in Italien*, pp. 410–426. (** Edition of L. Geiger, Leipzig, 1899, ii. 251 ff.).

This condition of things produced a literature of its own, comprehensive and many-sided, and which can only be called literature of the devil. In so far as it appeared in the German language, it was almost exclusively of Protestant origin, and in its main features it corresponded with what Luther had taught about the kingdom of the devil.

Luther, in his entire scheme of thought, attributed to the devil a power and influence far exceeding anything that had ever before been conceded to his Satanic majesty. His faith in the power of the devil and in the arts by which he seduced souls was all the more unshakable because of the personal experiences of demoniacal apparitions, which he believed in firmly, and which he recounted as all-sufficient proofs of the devil's unremitting activity. 'The devil,' he said, in his 'Hauspostille,' 'sometimes, as I myself have seen, disguises himself as a sow, as a burning wisp of straw, and so on.' He told his friend Myconius that at the Wartburg the devil had twice come to him in the form of a dog with intent to kill him; that in his garden he had seen the devil in the shape of a black wild hog; at Coburg in the shape of a star.[1] From the pulpit he spoke more at length of his conversations with the devil, and dwelt repeatedly on his relations with the night side of the spirit world. He also learnt from his friends and fellow-combatants all sorts of stories about the devil which 'had veritably happened.' At Sessen the devil 'carried three servants bodily away'; in the Mark he turned 'the head of an innkeeper round and carried off a Landsknecht into the air. At Mühlberg a piper, who had been drinking wine and horse-dung,

[1] Myconius, *Hist. Reform.* p. 42 ; Mathesius, *Historien Lutheri*, p. 184.

was treated in the same manner ; at Eisenach, also, a
piper was carried away by the devil, although Justus
Menius and other preachers ' watched by him day and
night, and guarded the doors and windows to prevent
his being taken off ' ; the first piper was found the next
day dead and black as coal in a stream, the other was
found dead in a hazel-tree. Things went better with
a young journeyman in Thuringia, who got the better
of the devil, when the latter tried to carry him off.
' These are indeed,' said Luther, ' no vain and profit-
less stories invented merely to frighten people ; they
are truly terrible, and by no means child's play, as the
clever heads declare.'

' The devils that are overcome and humiliated
turn into hobgoblins and wild Laplanders, for they
are spoiled devils. It's my belief also that monkeys
are only devils.' ' Snakes and monkeys are more
than any other animals in subjection to the devil,
who travels about in them, holds them in possession,
and makes use of them to deceive and to injure people.'
' In many lands there are still places where devils
dwell. In Prussia there are a quantity of wicked
spirits, and also in Pilappen (Lapland) there are numbers of devils and sorcerers. In Switzerland, not far
from Lucerne, on a high mountain, there is a lake
called Pilate's Pond, in which the devil carries on a
grim and dreadful existence. In my Fatherland, on a
high mountain, called the Poltersberg, there is a pond,
and if a stone is thrown into it a great storm arises,
and the whole neighbourhood is thrown into excitement
and alarm. It is the abode of devils who are imprisoned
there.' The following is among the remarkable stories
of devils which Luther recounted. Once the devil

appeared to a doctor ' in the form of a hairy he-goat with long horns, and he was also seen on the wall. The doctor perceived that it was the devil, and, screwing up his courage, he seized the goat by the horns, tore him away from the wall, banged him on the table, kept the horns in his hands, and the body disappeared. Another man who witnessed this proceeding thought to himself : " So, so, has the doctor done this ?   I'll do the same, for I've been christened as well as he." When the devil encountered him also in the shape of a he-goat, he thought to perform the same miracle and daringly seized the creature by the horns. But the devil twisted his neck round and strangled him.' [1]

In all writings which antagonised him Luther saw the inspiration of the devil ; his opponents, the Elector Joachim I. of Brandenburg and Duke George of Saxony he declared to be personally possessed by the devil ; of his former friend and later adversary, Carlstadt, he asserted that he had been strangled at Basle by the devil.

The most terrible proof which the devil had given of his power was, according to Luther, the fact that he had succeeded, after a short space, in spoiling the whole Church which Christ had founded, in deforming the Sacraments instituted by the God-man, and in setting up the abomination of a false and idolatrous worship, and establishing dominion for his ceremonies in the south and in the east.   The devil, Luther declared, had changed the Church into a den of murderers, and for long centuries had freely ruled the whole vast kingdom of Christendom in the place of the Christ whom he had dethroned. The bishops were, in the

[1] In *Förstemann*, iii. 27–30, 34, 36, 38, 48, 49–50, 52, 57–58, 62, 65.

eyes of Luther, ' servants of the devil,' the monks
' creatures of the devil ' ; purgatory and celibacy a work
and a phantom of the devil. Even the saints with
their ascetic practices were under the guidance and
the influence of the devil, and while in their blindness
they imagined that they were serving God, they were
really servants of Satan. In the ' Smalkald Articles '
it was taught that the ' wicked spirits accomplished
much villainy, that they appeared as human souls,
and asked for Masses, vigils, pilgrimages and other
alms, with unspeakable lies and rascality.' The holy
Mass was especially reviled by Luther as an invention
of Satan, and as that heathen abomination which the
prophet Daniel predicted under the name of Mausim.

In his ' Short Form ' of the Catechism of the year
1520, Luther still adhered to Catholic ground in the
statement that it was a sin against the first commandment to attribute ' one's misfortunes or adversity to
the devil or to wicked men.' [1] Later on, however, he
taught that just as the devil played a part in the life
of the Church, so he did also in life in general. In his
larger Catechism of 1529 he said in plain language that
the devil stirred up ' hatred, murder, sedition and war,
likewise storms and hail in order to spoil the corn and
the cattle and to poison the air ; that he was incessantly
plotting against the lives of Christians and wreaked his
vengeance on them by injuring them in every possible
way. Hence the numbers whose necks he broke, or
whom he drove out of their minds, or drowned in
water, or brought into many other dreadful straits.'

[1] Cf. Löschke, pp. 36–37. ' How to reconcile with this definite statement of Luther the fact that he constantly attributed his sorrows and
calamities to the devil is a puzzle to me ; neither do I remember having
read an utterance of the sort in his later writings ' (p. 37, note 1).

Thus in the catechetical instruction given to them, boys and girls were taught to consider themselves as constantly under the influence of Satan, not only as regards their souls, but also in their bodily lives: every unusual disease, all morbid spiritual suffering, every violent natural phenomenon must be looked on as a special contrivance of the arch-enemy of mankind ; the whole of existence was as it were enveloped in an impenetrable web of demoniacal influences.

What the most ancient councils had condemned as Manichaeism now asserted itself afresh in the life of the nation.

' No illness,' said Luther, ' comes from God, who is good and only does good to everybody ; but it comes from the devil, who causes all evil and interferes everywhere in life, and sends pestilence, fevers, and so on.' In another place he said emphatically, ' The devil is such a clever fellow that he can cause death by the leaf of a tree. He has more pots and vessels full of poison for killing people than all the apothecaries all over the world.' And again : ' The devil injures and kills people by ways of his own ; he poisons the air.' ' There are quantities of devils in the woods, the lakes, the waste places, and in damp marshy districts ; they dwell also in black thick clouds, and these make storms, hail, thunder and lightning, and poison the air and the pasture land.' ' At the time of a pestilence the devil blows into a house ; whatever he hits he takes away.' ' Much deafness, lameness, blindness, &c., is also caused by the wickedness of the devil. Consequently, it must not be doubted that pestilence, fever, and other heavy plagues and diseases are the works of the devil, because it is from him also that

bad weather, flies, and famine come, and by him that
the corn and fruits in the fields are destroyed.' 'It
is also my opinion that it is the devil who makes people
crazy and mad, and robs them of their reason. And
the reason why the doctors ascribe so many kinds
of illness to natural causes, and sometimes try to alle-
viate them with medicine, is that they do not know
how strong and powerful the devil is.' Once when he
was told how one man had been choked in eating a bit
of bread, and another had fallen from a house and
been killed, he said : ' All this has been done by the
devil, who is so close behind us ; but the world will
not believe that it all comes from the devil ; they think
it happens by accident.' [1]

Luther regarded as specially devilish tricks the
goitres with which people were plagued, and the
changelings, ' which Satan substituted for the right
children.' He will drag maids under water, make
them pregnant, and keep them with him till they are
delivered ; then he substitutes their children for legitimate children, whom he carries off. In Dessau, Luther
saw a child ' which,' according to his story, ' was
twelve years old, had its eyes and all its senses complete,
so that people thought it was a *bona-fide* child. But
it did nothing but eat, and as much, indeed, as four
peasants or corn-thrashers. If anyone touched it, it

---

[1] Förstemann, iii. 2, 14, 15, 16, 33–34, 63, 94. Cf. iv. 244–246, 253.
' The illness I am suffering from, vertigo and other things, is not natural.'
Squire Satan is venting his wrath upon me through sorcery (vol. iii.
pp. 41, 97). The doctors, he says, ' non considerant Sathanam impulsorem
naturalis causae in morbo, qui causas et morbos illico et facile mutat '
(Lauterbach, p. 109). ** See also Cordatus, *Tagebuch* (published by
Wrampelmeyer), No. 659 : Omnia mala et morbi sunt opera Sathanae.
No. 1051 (The devils in the air make the storms).

screamed. When things went wrong in the house and disaster occurred it laughed and was merry, but when all went well it cried. I said to the Prince of Anhalt : " If I were prince or lord there I would throw this child into the water, into the Mulde, which flows near Dessau, and I should not be afraid of being charged with homicide." But the Elector of Saxony, who was at Dessau, and the Princes at Anhalt, would not listen to me.' When he was asked later on why he had given the advice to drown the child, he answered, he was firmly convinced that changelings of this sort were nothing more than bits of flesh without any souls, ' for the devil could easily make such things ; he himself dwelt in these change-lings as their soul.' A tale about changelings, which he heard from the Elector John Frederic of Saxony, provoked him to exclaim : ' It is verily an abominable and dreadful thing that Satan can thus plague people, and that he can beget children.' [1]

Associated with all these opinions, and raising the power of the devil to tremendous height, was Luther's doctrine of the ' slavish will,' and the dualistic conflict between the good and the bad principle in man : ' The human will,' he said, ' is midway between God and Satan, and lets itself be led and driven like a horse or any other animal. If God takes possession of this will, it moves where and as He wills. If the devil takes possession of it, it moves and acts as the devil wills. And the human will is not free, neither has it any power to choose by which of the two it will be

---

[1] Förstemann, iii. 56, 69–71. Further references on this subject occur in Döllinger's *Luther und das Zauberwesen*, ii. 413 ff., and in the article, ' Über das Verhältniss und die Stellung des Glaubens an den Teufel zum Luthertum ' in the *Histor.-Pol. Blätter*, xii. 39–48. ** See, now, also Cordatus, *Tagebuch* (published by Wrampelmeyer), No. 660.

governed and guided, but the two strong powers fight and struggle to get possession of it.' [1]

In consequence of the great repute which Luther enjoyed as a theologian, his opinions and assertions concerning the devil and his influence on earth became authoritative in the new Church which was named after him. These opinions and statements formed the basis of a multitude of publications—almost all of them the work of preachers—which ranged all the vices of society under the name of Satan, and enriched popular reading with a vast storehouse of so-called 'devil-literature.' Thus, for instance, Andrew Musculus contributed a devil of breeches, a devil of oaths, a devil of marriage ; Matthew Friedrich, a devil of drunkenness ; Cyriacus Spangenberg, a devil of the chase ; Albert von Blanckenberg, a devil of avarice and usury ; Joachim Westphal, a devil of idleness and a devil of pride ; Louis Milichius, a devil of magic and a devil of finance ; Florian Daule, a devil of dancing ; Andrew Hoppenrod, a devil of whoredom ; Jodocus Hocker a pamphlet under the title ' Der Teufel selbst ' (' The Devil himself '). Many more writings of this kind appeared. A collection of twenty was published at Frankfort-on-the-Main in 1569, in a folio volume entitled a ' Theatrum Diabolorum,' and from these we learn that ' we in this world do not have to fight with emperors, kings, princes and lords, or other potentates, but with the devil himself.' Six years later another edition of this work appeared with four additional devils in it,[2]

---

[1] See our remarks, vol. iv. pp. 102–104.

[2] Fuller information on this kind of devil-literature is given in Goedeke, *Grundriss*, ii. 479–483. ' The Protestant teaching about the devil,' said

and in 1587 a third edition, containing ten new devils,
'devils of dress and ruffles, of envy and flattery, of
parsonage and benefice clippers, of speculation and
lying, of tribunals and procurators, of beggars, of
Sacraments, &c., which had never before been seen
in print.' The last named, the Sacrament devil, was
described by the preacher John Schütz 'with his
thirty-seven assistants.' This work, dealing in its third
edition with thirty-four devils, covered in its two parts
over 1360 pages of large folio with double columns,
but, by the wish of its publisher, Sigmund Feyerabend,
it was to be a sort of Vademecum for all the world as
'a true warning against all the cunning and murderous
wiles of the devil.' It would be 'useful not only for
laymen and ordinary Christians, but also for many
of the learned men, such as pastors, chaplains and
other high officials of the Church, and I may add also
for those who are learned in law and medicine.' For
it shows abundantly 'how the devil not only lays
snares for the souls of men, but also for their bodies
and their possessions, and how he misuses the latter not
only in violation of secular law and natural order, but
also in opposition to God's Word; yea, verily, against
all sense, wisdom and reason, in proof of which numerous examples are taken from ancient history and
from everyday experience.' The different devils, we are

the author, 'favoured the demoniacal personification of vices and objectionable customs, which were banned by the name of the devil. Theological
zeal created a species of recreation-literature, which is instructive as
regards the history of morals, and much of which is written in vivacious
style.' ** See, now, the important work of Osborn, *Die Teufelslitteratur
des sechzehnten Jahrhunderts* (*Acta Germanica*, iii. 3), Berlin, 1893, and
also Kawerau in *Gött. Gel. Anz.* 1893, p. 165 ff., and Pastor in the *Histor.
Jahrbuch*, xv. 884 ff. Osborn also published a new edition of the *Court
Devil* of Musculus (Halle, 1894).

told, ' are, as far as possible, ranged in the order of the Ten Commandments of God,' and thus the work, with its numerous lessons and admonitions, forms 'no slight part of our Christian catechism.' 'And it is inter-larded and adorned with a variety of entertaining stories, apothegms, maxims, rhymes and parables, so that it may prove agreeable and amusing also to people of the world who find the Holy Scriptures and Church teachers wearisome.' [1]

And the world did truly respond. The new kind of literature appealed with wonderful force to the popular fear of the devil and curiosity about the devil which prevailed at that period. Feyerabend alone, at the Lent and autumn fairs of 1568, sold about 1220 of the many devil-books which had appeared earlier in single volumes.[2] At the Lent fair of 1569 Michael Harder sold 452 copies of such books, most of which went off to Leipzig and Magdeburg.[3]

The Catholic controversialist, John Nas, was a zeal-ous opponent of this new kind of popular literature. 'Within the last years,' he wrote in 1588, 'a great quantity of devilish books have been published, books written in the devil's name, printed in the devil's name, bought and read in the devil's name, and cried up as great works of art; and the writers of these books are not the least among the renowned ministers of the Word.' He quoted whole lists of devil-books that had been published, and then went on : ' The pious Christians of old would not allow their children even to mention

---

[1] Preface to the enlarged edition of 1587, printed at Frankfort-on-the-Main by Peter Schmid. The preface to the second part, also signed by Sigmund Feyerabend, is dated February 8, 1588. This third edition is not mentioned in Goedeke.

[2] Cf. the register in Pallmann, pp. 156–160.   [3] *Messmemorial*, p. ix.

the wicked fiend with his horrible devilish names,
and as for cursing him nobody was allowed to do so;
as the wise man says : " If a wicked man curses the
devil, he curses his own soul." The world nowadays
preaches and writes books in the name of the devil,
and it is considered quite the right thing to do. And
why ? Because their grandsire and patriarch Luther
began the game. . . . The son follows the father. As
the preachers receive, so do they give out.' The
Catholics must not follow in this path. ' I myself was
present more than twenty years ago when this devil
yelping first began, and there were several learned
Catholics gathered together, and they were talking
and laughing about the black angel. Then one of
them, a highly learned man, of blessed memory, said :
" I, too, will bring forth a devil." This was taken
for a joke at first and laughed at, but when it was
discovered that the man was in real earnest, some
of them said : " Eh, mein Herr, devils must not be
hatched by us Catholics ; we will not grudge them to
the sects, like and like belong together.' [1] Duke

[1] Nas, *Angelus Paraeneticus* (1588), pp. 2–9. In another of his writings
Nas remarks that in the Protestant books a devil is met with on every
page, while of angels there is scarcely ever any talk ; cf. Schöpf, p. 64,
note 3. Gervinus (iii. 17–18) traces the whole of this devil-literature
back to the precedent of Luther. ** So, too, does Osborn in the work
cited above. ' Luther,' it says here, ' was the pioneer, the model, the
instructor of all the compilers of devil-books. He seemed to them blame-
less, almost sinless. The fanatical antagonists of the Catholic world of
saints did not even scruple to canonise their dead oracle as Sanctus
Lutherus ; he was extolled as a prophet, and compared most unsuitably
to the myth-shrouded Old Testament figure of Elias. This conception was
not new then, and it lasted on into the eighteenth century. To the pastors
of the *Theatrum Diabolorum* Luther was infallible. They called his
style moderate, and his polemics mild. His writings were ranked with the
Bible ; like the texts of the Sacred Book, their contents were their own
proof ; to carp doubtingly over their accuracy or their credibility was in

Albert V. of Bavaria had already in 1566 inhibited ' all the new publications which were named after the devil, such as breeches devil, gambling devil, and so forth.' ' For,' says he in his enactment, ' although they all have the appearance of being written only for the sake of good discipline, they can nevertheless not be tolerated on account of the objectionable examples which they bring forward, and they are composed in such a way that they serve chiefly to further the kingdom of him whose name they bear. And it is not necessary that Christian people should be deterred from vice by books about the devil, for the good and wholesome scriptures in the Catholic Christian Church are quite sufficient for this purpose.' [1]

With a view to filling up a gap which still remained in the devil-literature, the Mecklenburg superintendent, Andrew Celichius, published in 1595 a pamphlet giving a detailed account of demoniacal possession, ' Des Satans letzten Zornsturm.' ' Although others,' he said, ' had not only painted one devil after another separately, but had also depicted the whole region of hell, besides the whole Theatrum Diabolorum, I do not think that anybody has attempted the particular task which I have now undertaken, and for the instruction and comfort of possessed persons written anything systematic and fundamental on the subject.' [2] And yet a book on the subject is urgently wanted. ' Far and near in all directions the number of people possessed by devils is so large that it is a wonder and a pity : maybe

itself sinful. Whoever had any fault to find with them was without further ado branded as being possessed by the devil, and sent about his business in the rudest manner ' (Osborn, pp. 170, 171).

[1] *Archiv für Gesch. des deutschen Buchhandels*, i. 180.

[2] Celichius, *Notwendige Erinnerung*, Bl. B 3ᵇ.

they are the true vermin which is about to ruin our Egypt and the whole decaying world.' 'Some thirty possessed persons had spread terror and consternation in Mecklenburg.' 'Weak and timid women and girls had been no little terrified by such strange spectacles ; but many of them entirely forgot all Christian faith and love, for they either sought counsel of the devils in these persons in an idolatrous and un-Christian way, or else fled piteously away from the grievously afflicted patients, denying them all hope of salvation.' [1] 'Here in this very neighbourhood there are at least three preachers deranged in their minds, and, as it appears, possessed with devils in their bodies.' 'Nowadays, also, it is quite common everywhere for young people to be afflicted with epilepsy, so that they fall down on the ground in church or in the street, and Christ Himself classed such patients among those possessed with devils. And this is the reward and wages of all those children who will not submit any longer to the disciplinary rod . . . and who behave like the wicked children at Bethel, so that at last they are torn to pieces and devoured by hellish bears.' [2] From his own knowledge Celichius brought forward evidence that these were just punishments of God. 'I have known in the course of my life a woman who was the wife of a blacksmith who favoured the Interim, and she used to be suddenly and wonderfully possessed, and a number of devils would talk out of her at the same time ; this wife had to atone for her money-grubbing husband.' 'A well-known jurist, whose name I gladly, and for good reasons, keep secret, had amassed for himself more than a ton of gold, and was still

[1] Celichius, Bl. A 3, B 2.   [2] Bl. D 2, G 3ᵇ.

unsatisfied ; he scarcely ever came to hear preaching or to absolution and Communion, and at last he was reduced to crouching like a dog under tables and benches ; by what sort of a spirit he was influenced those may know who associated with him.' There was a certain ' soup-eater ' (monk) who favoured none more than the members of the Calvinistic faction, until at last Satan became his abbot and plagued him both at home and abroad, raising all manner of spectres around him, and muddling his empty head and con- science to such an extent that he became a death- jumper, *i.e.* attempted suicide by jumping from win- dows, &c. Of those transgressors who took possession of Church property ' some were carried away, body and soul, by the devil, some were lamed in hands and feet, and some became raging lunatics.' [1]

Seeing that the world in general was full of sin, crime and disgrace, there was no need to wonder at the large number of possessed persons ; nor to be astonished that it was chiefly women, old and young, who were afflicted in this way. For ' it is the habit of Belial to address himself first and chiefly to Eve and her daughters, for it was through Eve that he first brought in sin and death. And, moreover, women are weak vessels, and they are generally full of melancholy and sadness. St. Paul, too, writes from experience that they are wild and forward. . . . Besides which they are by nature proud and voluptuous, and the *Diis eritis similes* sticks always in their throats ' ; their love of finery and their stinking pride opens doors and windows to the hellish Leviathan, and because he is king over all proud people, he sometimes

---

[1] Celichius, Bl. G 1ᵇ, H 1-2, H 3.

punishes such stuck-up dolls by twisting their necks round while they are in front of their looking-glasses, or shows them in some other way that they are no longer like anything human.' 'Besides this, women are attracted to sorcery much earlier and more often than men.'[1]   The Duchess Anna of Mecklenburg, to whom Celichius dedicated his pamphlet, cannot have been specially edified by these remarks on women.

Among the causes of all sorts enumerated by Celichius 'why our Lord God sent this gruesome plague of possession by devils,' he says, 'it is to be carefully noted that by such terrible signs he generally meant to announce great changes in the Church and the State, as old and new examples prove.'[2]

At the time when Celichius composed his work for the consolation of distressed Christians, all sorts of 'terrible and wonderful news' concerning the arts which the devil practised in possessed persons had already been published broadcast over the land. As early as 1538 a 'Wonder Gazette' had appeared 'of a money-devil, a strange, incredible, yet true story, which had happened at Frankfort-on-the-Oder.' The preacher Andrew Eber and the judges and sheriffs of the town gave authentic evidence in this paper of the way in which the devil had possessed a servant-girl, who had before been weak in intellect. 'Whenever this girl touched anybody on the coat, biretta, jerkin, hand, sleeve, head or beard, or put her hand on a table or bench, on wood, stone, earth and so on, she always took up money, which she would put in her mouth and bite, so that you could hear her teeth crunching it and see the coins shining in her mouth.'

[1] Bl. D 3–4.   [2] Bl. F 2–3.

'In like manner at night, when she was lying in bed beside her attendant, if she touched the feather-bed, the bedposts, or what not, she took up money and filled her mouth with it, so that it made a gruesome rattling, and she seemed as if she must be choked.' 'Sometimes, too, when she grabbed up handfuls of money in this way, she distributed it among honest men and women, and it was all sorts of current coin, such as Mark groschen, pfennigs, Stettin, Meissen, Polish and Bohemian coins, Prussian groschen, and among these also some bad red coins. And when she was questioned, she answered in strange and wonderful speech.' In corroboration of the truth of this story the preacher affixed his seal to the document, and the town judge, with the knowledge of the sheriffs, added his seal.[1] In four different editions there appeared in 1562 a 'Neue Zeitung' of a man, Hans Vater by name, 'whose hands the devil had tied behind his back with cord, women's veils, and maiden's tresses and braids of hair, and then mercilessly tormented. On April 24 the said man came here to Nuremberg and was veritably seen by some hundred persons.'[2] Three years later, another 'gruesomely terrible and extraordinary story' was reported from Nuremberg, 'which really and truly happened in this present year 1559, at Platten, two miles from the Joachimsthal; there was a smith there

<hr />

[1] In Scheible, *Schaltjahr*, iv. 616–620. ** Weller, *Zeitungen*, No. 118. Concerning the Frankfort story, see also Angelus, *Wunderbuch* (Frankfort-on-the-Main, 1597), pp. 203–208. And in the same place, 400 ff., a letter from Luther to Andrew Eber about the case, dated August 5, 1536.

[2] Weller, *Zeitungen*, No. 252. ** Hans Vater von Mellungen was unmasked in Nuremberg in 1562 ; see Waldau, *Neue Beiträge z. Gesch. der Stadt Nürnberg*, ii. (Nuremberg, 1791) 273 ff.

who had a daughter, who was seized and possessed by
the devil, who uttered through her the most wonderful
and strange things to the priest who came daily to talk
with the girl.' [1]   A terrible report which went out in the
following year from Erfurt, of a shepherd in Thuringia
who had been attacked by the wicked devil, was printed
six times over in Nuremberg, Augsburg, Hof and other
places.[2] Exorcists, who perambulated the country in
large numbers, boasted in printed billets of how much
they had already accomplished against the devil, and
invited ' all distressed and devil-possessed Christian
men and women to come and let themselves be healed,
for they were the true and powerful exorcists of the
wicked enemy and his assistants among all the devils
of the earth and the air.' [3]   At Lemgo, in 1533, a
preacher made a great deal of money by the driving
out of devils, which he pursued as a trade.[4]   At these
ceremonies of exorcism, wrote the Lemgo preacher,
Jodocus Hocker, in 1564, ' one sees and hears nothing
else but empty pushing, thumping, screaming and
calling : " Begone, begone, you shall and must come
out ! " These exorcists cared only for vainglory and
worldly goods, as is well known to the whole world, and
as many people have experienced to their cost.   And
I, too, have seen in several places how the poor, foolish
people, both high and low, take money to these charlatans in handfuls and do not seem able sufficiently to
honour them.   And it is piteous that the world should
be so ready to give with full hand to the devil, when
they will give nothing to the living God.' ' It's all in

[1] Weller, *Zeitungen*, No. 233 ; three editions.
[2] *Ibid.* No. 236.
[3] Sermon against the exorcists, by L. B. Kornmann (Erfurt, 1561), p. 3.
[4] Clemen, *Einführung der Reformation zu Lemgo* (Lemgo, 1846), p. 28.

vain that our so-called evangelical exorcists varnish the
matter over with the pretence that they use no un-
Christian means, but only the Word of God, Christian
songs of praise, and holy prayer, and by this cant and
rant they persuade the common people that their
performances are of great value and pleasing to God.
This is no exculpation, for a godless Papist might
defend his idolatrous Mass in the same way, and say
it was nothing but sacred words that he made use of.' [1]
' In Meissen,' so a preacher complained in 1563, ' I have
seen in a village where there were no fewer than seventeen persons of both sexes possessed with devils, three
drunken exorcists, who, notwithstanding that they
were in ill odour with everybody on account of their
dissolute lives, carry on their trade with the foolish
people, and earn a great deal of money, besides presents :
it's a case of driving out the devil by the devil, and old
and young indeed believe more in the devil than in
God and His holy evangel.' [2]

A remarkable case of exorcism took place in 1565,
when ' a devil was driven out of a noble lady, Kunigunde
von Pilgram,' by the Lutheran pastor at Schremberg.
When the devil was exorcised, so the report goes, ' he
screamed in such a way that the people could not
remain in the church ; and he threw the head of the
possessed lady backwards and forwards a whole yard
from her body, as though it did not belong to the body.
He was then seen visibly in her face and body in the
form in which it has been the custom to paint him.
Then he cursed and blasphemed God, and said at
last : " You talk a great deal about your almighty

---

[1] *Bannteufel*, pp. 8, 12, 19, 34 (in *Theatrum Diabol.* i. 136 ff.).
[2] *Von Höllenzwängen*, pp. 5–8.

God ; where is His power now ? how well you're able to drive me out ! I am stronger than He is," and so on with blasphemies innumerable.' [1]

The people were also entertained with accounts of frequent cases of ' horrible possessions,' in which Catholic and Protestant exorcists had entered into competition for the expulsion of the devil. Thus at Ingolstadt, in 1584, ' a terrible and perfectly true story' was printed of the wife of a burgher at Spalt on whom ' a young Lutheran preacher had vainly tried his powers of exorcism, the devil only playing a monkey-game with him,' while a Catholic exorcist had succeeded in driving out the evil spirit. ' Certain persons who were standing by declare and affirm that they saw a black bird in the shape of an ousel fly out of the woman's mouth. We ourselves do not give this as truth, because none of us saw it, and we will not vouch for more than, if called upon, we could confirm with our priestly honour and highest oath and a good conscience.' [2]

On the other hand, the Lutheran preacher at Dohna, Nicholas Blum, in an ' Historische Erzählung' of the year 1606, showed up the powerlessness of Catholic and Calvinistic exorcism. The case he cites was that of a noble Bohemian student ; the devil had ' whirled him round in the air, tormented him cruelly, afflicted him with deafness and dumbness, and torn his tongue out of his throat. This devil had the special characteristic of being ' now popish, now Calvinistic, and of

[1] Weber, *Aus vier Jahrhunderten*, New Series, ii. 304–312. In 1566 George Silberschlag, Protestant pastor at the Kaufmannskirche at Erfurt, drove the devil out of the wife of a baker. Jaraczewski, *Zur Gesch. der Hexenprozesse in Erfurt und Umgegend*, p. 27.

[2] The report printed at Freytag, ii. 361–374.

disputing now on the popish side, now on the Calvinist side, but Lutheran he would never be; he had never done anything but dispute against Lutheranism.' To a Lutheran preacher who tried to exorcise him he said: ' Bah, if I come out I'll go straight into you!' The Lutheran, however, met him valiantly and said: " Devil, I am God's creature and property; in me thou hast no part; go to the Pope at Rome, he is a fine creature of yours.' The devil screamed back at him: ' Verily is the Pope a fine creature of mine, but I have still another fine creature, Gottlieb at Prague is also my fine creature.' The question was then asked whether there was anyone at Prague called Gottlieb, and the answer was that this was the name of the chief Jesuit there. ' A Calvinist priest absolved the pos- sessed person and administered the Communion to him, but the evil only became worse: the devil raged and stormed more than before.' On being asked whether he would like the devil to be exorcised by a Jesuit or by a Capuchin, the student answered: ' I will not have one devil to exorcise another.' On the other hand he begged to be taken to Meissen, ' to a land, that is, in which the true Church has its abode.' He was taken to Pirna, and here occurred the exorcism and expulsion of the devil, which Blum, who was present at it, describes in full. For six whole days the dispute lasted with the devil, who spoke of election by grace in the spirit of the reformed faith; finally, however, ' he came out in the shape of a fiery barley-corn and in smoke.' When ' the liberated youth went home again to Prague and entered a Capuchin church, a monk ran up to him and touched him, whereupon an image came down on the monk's head and struck him so hard that he fell on the ground

and died at once.   Perhaps the exorcised devil wanted
to kill the student, but he failed in his aim and killed
a monk.'   Blum heard of this ' wonderful work ' from
the student himself.[1]

On the subject of the expulsion of a devil at Vienna
the Jesuit George Scherer, in 1583, published a sermon
entitled ' Christliche Erinnerung,' in which he told
' on the evil spirits' own unwilling confession, extracted
from them ' by how many thousands of devils a young
woman named Anna Schlutterbäurin has been possessed.
The Bishop of Vienna ' did not intrude himself into
this business, but his services were solicited by the
imperial court, and he was informed how the Jesuits,
far from wishing to be present, had actually refused to
attend.   Every time that the act of exorcism was performed on the possessed damsel there were always
men and women present, and in the last days, indeed,
the exorcism was witnessed by illustrious lords, both
from the imperial and royal courts and from other
princely courts also, item from the town council, also
by doctors and magistrates of the university, and
captains, nobles and burghers.'   If the common people
should ask, ' how it could have been possible for so
many thousand devils to dwell in one person,' they
must be answered : ' how many evil spirits were there
in possessed people of whom it is said in the Gospels
(Matthew viii., Mark v., and Luke viii.) that after they
had come out they went into two thousand swine and
were drowned in the sea.'   Were there not, moreover,
a legion of them by their own statement in answer

[1] *Historische Erzählung*, p. 1 ff.   On pp. 4–6 Blum enters into details
of which the gist may be given in Latin : ' Sedebat diabolus non in corde
quod est templum SS. Trinitatis, sed, salva venia, in genitalibus.   Juvenis
mingens eadem patiebatur quae mulier parturiens etc.'

to Christ's question ? If so many of them could be
in one person then, why not now also ? ' Scholars
and men of understanding know that devils have
neither flesh nor limbs, but are spirits, and therefore
need no place or space as do our bodies. A hundred
thousand legions of spirits could all be collected together
on the point of a needle.' Scherer's admonition was as
follows : ' The Christian should not be over-confident or
careless as if no enemy were at hand, but also by no
means cast down. " Watch and pray." Above all take
the shield of faith, wherewith you shall be able to quench
all the fiery darts of the wicked one. And take the helmet
of salvation, and the sword of the Spirit, which is the
Word of God.   In short, work and quit yourself valiantly
like a good soldier of Jesus Christ.' [1]

Tremendous excitement was caused in the empire
by the ' truthful reports ' of the demoniacal occurrences
in the Mark of Brandenburg.   In the year 1593, so said
report, there was ' a terrible panic in the Neumark, in
the little town of Friedeberg, for it was said that the
devil had taken bodily possession of more than sixty
people, young and old, male and female, and that at
different times he had tortured them frightfully, and
that there had been a great deal of trouble with these
afflicted people in the churches and elsewhere ; even
the pastor of the place had been himself seized in the

---

[1] Scherer's Works, Munich edition, ii. 179–196.   In 1589 there appeared
in Würzburg, published by J. Schnabel and S. Marius, a ' veritable and
dreadful story of a young smith's apprentice, Hans Schmidt, of Heydings-
feldt, who was violently possessed by a whole legion of devils, and saved
by means of the Catholic Church.'   Concerning a strange case of exorcism undertaken on the imbecile Duke John William of Cleves, by two
Ambrosian Fathers, see the account in the *Zeitschrift des Bergischen
Geschichtsvereins*, ii. 201–211.

same manner while he was preaching.'[1] The con-
sistory ordered public prayers to be offered up in all
the churches of the Mark for the liberation of these
people from the power of the devil. The evil, however,
was not removed by this means, but it spread more
and more. The number of possessed persons in
Friedeberg rose gradually to 150.[2] 'Whilst the evil
was still going on in the Mark, it happened also at
Spandau, in November and December 1594, that over
forty persons, most of them young boys and girls,
became possessed. If often took five or six strong
men to hold down one individual thus possessed.' The
council had iron rings fixed in the walls and the victims
fastened to them. In Berlin also 'the devil carried
on his work.' Here, as at Spandau, 'before Christmas
1594, gold and silver coins were found, and anyone
who picked them up was at once invaded by the
devil, which caused tremendous agitation in the Mark of
Brandenburg as well as in the adjacent districts, and
great alarm among the people.'[3] Praetorius, superintendent at Frankfort-on-the-Oder, in an ' Erschröckliche und wahrhaftige Geschichte,' written in 1595,
gave a more detailed account of how the wicked spirit
in Friedeberg, Spandau, Berlin and Küstrin ' possessed
people and tormented and plagued them daily.'[4]

It was also observed that 'since the advent of the
dear and holy evangel as preached by Luther the devil
had tormented Christians more than before with visions,

[1] Cramer, iv. 53.
[2] Moehsen, *Gesch. der Wissenschaften*, ii. 500.
[3] Cramer, iv. 53–54. ** Cf. Jac. Coler, *Bericht von den vorhin unerhörten Wunderwercken, so sich neulicher Zeit in der Mark Brandenburg
zugetragen und noch täglich geschehen*, &c.
[4] Moehsen, p. 501.

spectres and ghosts of all sorts, as though he was raising
all the storms of his wrath because he knew that the
Day of Judgment was at hand, and that his own kingdom
on earth was drawing to an end.' Under the papacy
there had been numbers of hobgoblins; now, on the
contrary, the superintendent Andrew Celichius complained, ' we have instead of these the grimmest of all
grim plaguers of men from the abyss of hell, and they fill
every nook and cranny with their horrors and abominations.' [1] In a ' Christlicher Unterricht von Gespensten '
the indefatigable controversialist, John of Münster, asked
at Vortlage in 1591 : ' Who does not daily see and hear
all manner of ghosts, screaming and howling, tumbling
down, rustling and rattling, shutting down coffins,
making graves and so forth ? Item, who does not see
every day numbers of faces in the air, on the earth and
floating over the water, in the spot where somebody is to
be drowned or meet with some other disaster ? Item,
who is there who cannot tell of lights, great and small,
which appear at night and also frequently by day ;
the great ones, as the common people know from daily
experience, portending the death of old people, the
small ones the death of young people ? ' Münster gave
more detailed information on the subject, showing
how it could be known ' whether the ghosts were good
and from God, or wicked and from the devil '; also ' of
what substance the ghosts were made,' and ' how
Satan knew how to use nature so as to produce ghosts
therefrom,' and ' what sort of a body he assumed.'
For instance, ' to make a flaming ghost the devil used
the sun in the daytime and the moon at night ; to make
a vaporous apparition, or others that appear in human

---

[1] *Notwendige Erinnerung*, Bl. D.

form, he used the earth and other natural objects in his own masterly way.' If these tales seem incredible to any persons, ' let them look at the conjurers, and see how dexterously they eat bread and instantly spit out flour, or how after having drunk wine they can tap it out of their foreheads,' and so on. ' If such things are possible to conjurers who are only men, how far more possible and credible is the skill of the devil who takes the materials for ghosts in a wonderful manner from nature ?   Secondly, he assumes a body of a kind which will enable him to make his apparitions more visible and terrifying, and whereas he is a more powerful and skilful spirit, no one can deny that he takes on either dead or living bodies to deceive mankind.' [1]

Especially in times of plague ' the devil,' says preacher Samuel Heinnitz in 1609, ' does fearful things to the corpses in their graves, preferably to those of women ; strange noises are heard as of sows devouring their food, and after such noises the plague increases and carries off people wholesale.'

Ludwig Lavater, preacher at Zurich, in an article on ghosts, ' Von Gespensten,' written in 1570, had warned his readers against too great credulity.   ' Most

---

[1] John von Münster, *Ein Christlicher Unterricht von Gespensten*, &c. (Hanau edition), pp. 18–19, 76 ff., 91–95.   He wrote this book because ' certain distinguished and pious people who were troubled and visited by fiery ghosts' had asked him for his opinion about them, and also ' how to encounter and oppose these ghosts, and to ward off their terrible effects and influence with God and a good conscience' : Preface, a². P. 41, it says : ' We read that in 1569 a Jesuit, at Augsburg, dressed himself up as the devil to frighten a maid-servant.'   To which is added the remark : ' In my opinion the Jesuits do not need to dress up in the devil's clothes, since they openly practise and defend the teaching of the devil of which Paul speaks.'

of the things,' he wrote, ' which are commonly taken for
ghosts are nothing of the kind.'   But ' none the less,'
he added, ' ghosts and other similar apparitions are
very often seen and heard.'   ' The very learned Philip
Melanchthon says in his book, " De Anima," that he
himself had seen monsters or ghosts, and that he knew
many trustworthy people who declared positively that
they had not only seen ghosts, but had had long talks
with them.'   ' Numbers of God-fearing, pious, honourable, truthful men and women affirm that they have
both seen and heard ghosts, sometimes at night and
sometimes in broad daylight.   And that sometimes
also they have seen people riding or walking, with
a fiery appearance, who they knew well had either been
dead a long time or had lately died.'   ' Frequently
ghosts have been heard shuffling along at night, coughing,
moaning and sighing piteously.   And when asked who
they were and what ailed them they have answered
that they were this or that soul.'   ' The miners declare
that in some of the mines there are spirits or ghosts to
be seen dressed exactly like the miners, and running
hither and thither and seeming to be working just like
other miners.'   ' On the other hand one often finds
wicked and dangerous mine-sprites who often baulk
the miners from going into the shafts and pits, and
play all sorts of other wicked tricks.'   George Agricola,
a renowned and distinguished mineowner, who has
written excellent books about mines, says that at
Annenberg, in a mine called the Rosenkranz, an evil
spirit of this sort killed twelve miners, and ' although
the mine was rich in metal they were obliged to leave
off working it.' [1]

---

[1] L. Lavater, *De spectris, lemuribus,* &c. (Tigur. 1570), in the German

The Leipzig bookseller, Henning Gross, in 1597, dedicated to Duke Henry Julius of Brunswick a ' work extremely useful to all Christendom ' on ghosts, spirit-apparitions, and all sorts of other demoniacal sorceries.[1] In an ' Historischer Tempel der Natur ' Henry Korn-mann of Kirchhayn in Hesse, in 1611, ' related so much about ghosts and devils that it must have caused everybody horror and shuddering.' In correspondence with Paracelsus he made out that there were ' four different kinds of beings—water-sprites, mountain-sprites, fire-sprites, and wind- or air-sprites—which were to be regarded as human beings, though they did not proceed from Adam, but from another creature, different from us men and from all animals.' ' A marriage contracted with such spirit-men could not be dissolved so long as life continued, even if the nymph or water-maid had run away.' ' And on this subject,' wrote the Lutheran theologian Arnold Mengering, ' Kornmann

translation in the *Theatrum de veneficis*, pp. 116 ff., 138–140. Cf. Roskoff, ii. 428–431.   ** Concerning apparitions and ghosts, Oldecop gives the following notes—p. 380 : ' 1555, on January 7, near Gerden, in Hanover, there was an apparition ; a number of soldiers, who fought first in the air and then on the earth.' Pp. 452–453 : ' 1559, Tuesday before St. Vitus' Day, in the village of Berl, to the right of Lechlenberg, a battle between cavalry soldiers, four snow-white on one side, and four coloured ones on the other side.' Pp. 473–474 : ' 1561, on the day of the Holy Innocents, a fiery cloud at Dorygen, afterwards seen over Wittenberg ; on Thursday after Invocavit a terrible apparition between Eisleben and Mansfeld at sunset, a crucifix and two large rods, which were striking two great stone pillars, and underneath a picture of the sunset.' Pp. 529–530 : ' At the beginning of the year 1563 there were seen in many places terrible fiery clouds in the heavens and unusual storm winds.' An account of ' many gruesome and devilish spectres and ghosts,' which were seen in 1601 in a castle of the Bamberg Bishop, near Cranach, and which especially molested ' those who were not attached to the Catholic religion ' (Von Hormayr, *Taschenbuch*, new series, xv. 292–293).

[1] Gross, *Magica*, preface.

is so obstinate and determined, that those who differ
from him and regard all his rubbish about nymphs and
Venus-company as devil's work, are not, in his opinion,
sound theologians.' [1] In a work published at Frankfort-on-the-Main in 1589 it was related that one of the
spirits of the air had said : ' I am neither a good nor a
bad angel, but I am one of the seven planet-spirits, who
govern intermediary nature, and to whom it is commanded to rule over the four different divisions of the
universe, namely the firmamental, the animal, the
vegetable and the mineral parts.   There are seven of
us, and through our skill we bring all the astral virtues
and influences of the upper circle to bear on the three
inferior divisions by ascensions and descensions.   For
the planets cannot come down corporeally.' [2] ' How
rich, indeed, are our present times in wonderful explanations of nature and of supernatural and demoniacal
apparitions ! '   Such in 1562 was the boast of a ' truthful
and wonderful account—the outcome of the newly
arisen and highly enlightening science—of several
heavens, and also of subterranean, chymic beings, water-
sprites and nixies, air-sprites, fire-sprites, dragon children, ghosts, and also of devilish changelings, which
indeed always have existed but till now have been
more concealed, and are nowadays to be found in almost
every country district, wood, lake, town or village.'
In the preface the author says : ' Oh, the wonderful
judgments and decrees of God, which are so clearly
manifested !   But the pity is that so many Christians
pay no heed to these judgments and will not recognise

---

[1] Kornmann, pp. 49–50, 78, 113, 171–174 ; cf. Waldschmidt, p. 446 ff.
[2] Alchimia, D 5 ; cf. Waldschmidt, pp. 459–460.

the devil, who does not confine himself to hell, but prowls about, appears and governs in the air, in water, woods and wildernesses.' [1]

In full agreement with the prevalent belief in ghosts and devils, Aegidius Albertinus, court secretary to the Duke of Bavaria, told the most extraordinary stories in a work destined for the people (1616). 'Besides the devils in hell and in the upper airs,' he wrote, 'there were others in the under airs, and these take on different forms and bodies from the thick airs, and appear visibly to men, vex, trouble and tempt them, and also produce thunder and lightning. The third class are called earthly devils, and they dwell partly in the forests, where they lie in wait for the hunters and mislead people wandering at night, partly in open fields, partly in caverns, hollows and pits, and sometimes also among men in dark and sombre places. These creatures are partly wicked, partly not so; the latter only frighten people by all sorts of apparitions. Some of them also predict future events. Others move people to melancholy, insanity and despair, and cause them to jump into fountains or lakes and drown themselves, or to jump out of windows, or to stab, shoot or hang themselves. They also make people believe that they, the devils, dwell in glasses, crystals, mirrors, from where, if conjured or commanded, they will converse with them, and assist them in word and in deed. The fourth kind are called water-sprites; they live in damp, watery places, near to ponds, streams and lakes. These devils are very spiteful, restless, false and deceitful; they stir up the waves, make ships go down and destroy much human life. Sometimes also

[1] Without locality. Preface, Bl. b.

they assume bodily shapes, generally that of a woman, for which reason they are called water-nymphs. But those who live in the dry places appear in the visible form of men. They also take the shapes of different animals according to their respective characters. The fifth kind are earth-sprites, and live under the earth in caves and holes of mountains. These devils prey upon the men who dig out springs and metals, and who search for the treasures hidden in the earth. They cause great disturbance in the earth, wind and flames of fire ; they destroy and shatter the foundations of the earth. At night-time they pour out in shoals from the mountains, perform frightful demoniacal dances in the field, and when their leader gives a sign, they disappear instantly and return to their accustomed abode. Sometimes a sound of bells is heard among them, and sometimes they give themselves out as spirits of the dead. They have no other object than to cause fear, terror and wonder to human beings. It sometimes happens, also, that they entice people into the holes of mountains and show them wonderful things, as though they were the friends of mankind and that these caves were the abode of the blessed. Some of these devils are the guardians and preservers of the treasures which are hidden away by misers. In order that such treasures should never fall into the hands of men and women, they steal them themselves, and carry them from place to place to take care of them. The sixth kind are called Lucifugi, or fliers from the light, for they hate and fly from the light, and take on bodily shape only at night. For this reason they roam about only in the dark, they elude discovery, are wicked and turbulent, and cause death to numbers of people at night-time either by violence, or by blowing upon them, or by touching them.' [1]

With the accounts of the dwelling-places and the thousandfold arts and practices of the devil on earth, ' possession, molestations of all sorts, ghosts, apparitions and all the other innumerable demoniacal plottings,' there were also combined other ' no less terrible, but truthful, stories of the magic arts which the devil practised on earth through his necromancers, and also of leagues and mantle-journeys with the devil, exorcism of devils and so forth.' [2]

Quantities of such accounts, given in perfect faith, are actually found in a publication by a man of remarkable mental calibre, who took his stand intelligently and emphatically against the horrible and insensate persecution of witches which was the fashion at that time. This was a book published at Heidelberg, in 1585, under the name ' Augustin Lercheimer von Steinfelden,' and entitled ' Christlich Bedenken und Erinnerung von Zauberei.' It was reprinted at Heidelberg in 1587, at Basle in 1593, at Spires in 1597, and again in 1622 at Frankfort-on-the-Main. [3]

---

[1] *Lucifers Königreich*, pp. 5–6 ; cf. the way in which the abbot Trithemius replied to the questions asked him by the Emperor Maxmilian I. respecting the devil ; German translation of his treatise in the *Theatrum de veneficis*, pp. 361–363. In the *Elucidarius*, one of the most widely circulated popular books, it says : ' All the way from the earth to the moon there are wicked spirits called Cacodaemones ; their business is to torment human beings up to the Day of Judgment ; they take from the air the bodies in which they appear ' (preface and Bl. B 4). In the preface the book was recommended in the following words : ' Doctrines which are treated obscurely in other books are here admirably explained ; things which have to be hunted for laboriously through the Scriptures are here well summed up in few words.'

[2] In the *Wahrhaftiger und wunderbarlicher Bericht* quoted above, p. 343 ff. Preface, Bl. c.

[3] The Basle edition of 1593 is the one which we make use of. ** See

The Calvinistically minded author, without doubt the Heidelberg Professor Hermann Wilcken, styled Wite-kind,[1] has not the slightest doubt that ' everywhere the whole universe, inward and outward, water and air, is full of devils, of wicked, invisible spirits ' ; this, he says, ' is especially known and vouched for by the mariners and miners, to whom they appear in manifold shapes and for no good object.' ' Among the men of learning there are some who have a familiar spirit which predicts to them what they want to know, shows them in what place to find this or that, tells them what is written in books which lie concealed and unknown to anyone, yea, in books which once existed but have since mouldered away, been torn up or burnt, but the contents of which the devil still knows well.' To the devil's race belong also ' fencers, wrestlers, warriors, whom the devil is bound to stand by for a time, whom he protects from being scourged, stabbed, shot, like that soldier who fled from the battle into the town of B., shaking the bullets out of his sleeves like pottles of peas ; not one of them had been able to wound him.' Further, ' those also belong to this class whom the devils employ indoors to serve them, and out of doors send about in the shape of little mannikins, which in Saxony and the Baltic are called Drolls, as they are well known and not rare, especially in Sweden and Norway. They attend to the horses, feed, wash and comb them, clean out the stables, sweep the houses, carry water and

our remarks in vol. viii. p. 562 ff. [German original. The English trans-lation of this volume is not yet out].

[1] Cf. A. F. Vilmar in the *Zeitschr. des Bergischen Geschichtsvereins*, v. 228–230, and the reprint of the Spires edition of 1597, by Karl Binz (Strassburg, 1888), where there is fuller and careful information on the person and the writings of Witekind.

wood into the kitchens, drive the carriages, guide the ships, and then end with murder, fire or some such disaster in houses, upset carriages outside, so that legs and necks are broken, and sink the ships.' [1]

Witekind was also able to tell all sorts of things about devilish arts from his own experience. ' A very mischievous, dare-devil youth, whom for his father's sake I will not mention by name, also carried on this devil's play, and rode on the magic cloak with his boon companions. When the span of life which the devil had fixed for him had elapsed, he travelled from place to place, visiting his friends and relations, and seeking in their company to forget his fear and anxiety. When he was at table with some of them, his head was suddenly turned round hind part before, and he was as one dead. They thought he had only looked round behind him, but it was the invisible devil who had done it.' ' When in my youth I was a student at Frankfort-on-the-Oder, in the lifetime of Doctor Jodocus Willichius, it was reported to him that in the month of August, in Mecklenburg, there was brought to the noble family of Malzan from their neighbourhood by their subjects a great hound with a white collar. At once the staghounds fell upon it and began biting it. But when they could not succeed in hurting the creature the stable-men came running up with pitchforks and spears, and cudgelled and stabbed him unmercifully. Then suddenly it turned into a man, then into an old woman who begged that they would have pity on her and spare her. It was then seized and imprisoned. This proceeding incited Doctor Willichius, a professional medical man, to dispute openly in the college the legitimacy

[1] *Christlich Bedenken,* pp. 3, 7, 45–46, 52.

of such transformations of men into animals. He proved and established, with the consensus of all the scholars who were present, that it was only an optical illusion which in these stories, just told, worked on the animals as well as on the human beings. The devil had advised and helped the woman to appear as a dog until at last she was put into prison; then he had had enough of her and abandoned her.'[1] 'Sometimes the devil gets hold of dead bodies from the gallows, from a battlefield, or from elsewhere. He carries these corpses about, makes them move and act, and uses them just as if they were alive, as long as it pleases him. To prove this I will relate what I have heard from the pious and very learned Philip Melanchthon, and from hundreds of other scholars. In Italy, at Bologna, there was a female lute-player who after her death walked about, talked, ate, drank, played on the lute just as she had done when she was alive, until one day at a banquet a sorcerer noticed her and said to the guests, " That woman is dead." The company only laughed at him, whereupon he seized her under the arm, drew out a little bag containing a magic charm which another sorcerer had tied under her arm, and straightway she fell on the ground, and was a lifeless corpse.' Not far from Rotenburg on the Tauber three devils appeared once in a tavern disguised as a noble-man with two servants, who, on being exorcised by the host in the name of Jesus, ' instantaneously fled away, left a horrid, unbearable stench behind them, and also three corpses which had hung on the gallows, lying in the room.' 'I have myself heard of a sorcerer that, in

---

[1] Pp. 16, 54–55 ; cf. pp. 61–63. ' The dreadful story of a nobleman who could cut off heads and put them on again.'

company with others, he travelled more than one hundred miles from N. in Saxony to Paris, and went uninvited to a wedding, riding on a magic cloak. But they soon, however, took themselves off when they heard a murmur going round the saloon : " What sort of guests are those, and whence do they come ? " This same sorcerer had in reality got red eyes ; perhaps it was the journey that made them so.' [1] The stories current among the people about the necromancer and exorciser, Doctor Faust, who had also carried on his practice at Wittenberg, found full acceptance with Witekind. Thus he writes : ' Faust and his company came once in Lent, after they had had their supper at night, from Meissen in Bavaria to Salzburg, more than sixty miles, for a night-cap drink to the bishop's cellar, where they drank wine. And when the cellarer came in by chance and addressed them as thieves, they went off at once and took him with them as far as a wood. There Faust set him up on a tall fir tree and left him sitting, while he flew on further with his associates.' Another of his communications runs as follows : ' At K. in Pomerania one of the workmen who boil salt there had an old wife, a sorceress, with whom he was not at all happy. He gave out that he wanted to visit his friends in Hesse where he was born. The wife feared he would not come back again, and would not let him go. All the same, however, he set off on his journey. After he had been gone a few days, there came up behind him a black he-goat, which slipped between his legs, lifted him up, and carried him back home again through fields and forests, over water and land, in a few hours. The wife welcomed him with taunting words : " And so

[1] *Christlich Bedenken*, pp. 130, 147, 149.

you're back again, are you ?   And so they've taught
you to stay at home, have they ? "   She dressed him
in a fresh suit of clothes, and gave him food to eat, so
that he came back to himself.'   The conclusion says :
' In short, it is undoubted and undeniable that the
spirits, although they have no bodies of their own,
yet carry bodies and corporeal things from one place to
another.' [1]   ' Whenever and wherever the imperial Diet
was in session the devil was sold openly and without
concealment in rings and crystals, from out of which
he would answer whatever he was asked.' [2]

' To enter into relations with the devil, to have him
close at hand in rings and crystals, to conjure him, to
enter into alliance with him and to carry on hundreds
of magic arts with him,' says a pamphlet of 1563, ' is
more in vogue nowadays both among high and low,
learned and unlearned, than ever before, and newspapers
full of these things are published, which seem indeed
quite incredible, but which are none the less true and
deserve to be believed.   Who is there who can point to
a single country where these devilish necromancers do
not settle, attract crowds of people, perform magic
journeys, and conjure heaven and earth, the dead and
the living, with their magic and demoniacal sorceries ? '
In every class of society ' these practitioners are found
in large numbers ; but most especially among huntsmen
does the black art prevail.' [3]   ' Among the huntsmen,'

---

[1] *Christlich Bedenken*, pp. 131–132.

[2] *Ibid.* p. 88.

[3] *Von Höllenzwängen und Teufelsbeschwörungen*, pp. 3–4.   ' And if
you are not a sorcerer yourself, then, when anything does not fall out
according to your wish and pleasure, fly straight to the devil and say : " he
shall and must help me, in the devil's name I will accomplish the work " ;
and you will be able to make your boast that the devil has helped you.'

said the Meissen superintendent Gregory Strigenicus, in the year 1602, ' there are a great many who are able with magic arts to gather together in one place all the hares and stags in a whole forest. There are also people who by the help of these arts can bring all the birds round them from more than five miles distance. Necromancers have often been known to collect all the snakes of a whole hunting district into one hole; item, to entice the rats and mice all together out of a town ; but they have not always had full success.' [1]

James Ayrer makes a necromancer boast of his magic skill :

> I can dig up treasure that's hid,
> I can make people love as I bid.
> On a goat, too, I can ride for miles,
> O'er sticks and stones, o'er bushes and stiles.
> There's never a lock I can't undo,
> Nor wall so thick I can't get through.
> I can make donkeys, children, cats,
> Can poke out eyes and cut off ears,
> With one finger I can iron pierce,
> On a man's head grow a stag-horn fierce.
> And if no trust in me you lack,
> I can chop off your head and put it back.
> I can also fire quench,
> Cause thunder to peal and rain to drench ;
> Right well, also, I can soothsay,
> A house on my hand I can carry away,
> Can eat a whole cart-load of hay,
> And spit out fire any day.[2] . . .

Thurn von Thurneissen counted up no fewer than twenty-four different kinds of magic arts which were

In a record we read : ' Once when at Hof a bell had been twice cast and still went wrong, the bell-founder cast it a third time in the devil's name, and it then came perfectly right.' Spiess, *Archivische Nebenarbeiten*, i. 63 note.

[1] *Diluvium*, p. 599.
[2] Ayrer, iv. 2401–2402.

practised in his day, among them 'a new and very
excellent art,' which

> Ostendiomantia we call,
> By means of which we exhibit all—
> Battles, cities, people, land,
> Ancient patriarchs, prophets, and
> Emperors of olden time,
> The same in habits, dress and clime,
> As of yore they did appear,
> Now to-day presented here :
> But secretly the sight is shown,
> It's meant for the great folks alone.

By means of another kind it was possible to keep
the soul of a friend with one :

> If anybody, when a friend who's dear
> Of this world leave takes,
> Holds back the spirit that escapes,
> And mutters something in his ear,
> Then, so 'tis said, the spirit will,
> Be ready service to fulfil
> One, two, or three years for his friend,
> Until the spell shall end.

Another 'newly discovered' art, called Animali-
magia, 'more wicked than all the others,' exorcised
wild beasts 'in the name of God with holy words so
that they became quiet and tame, conquered by the
devil who spoke through them.' [1]

'That exorcisers of devils, spirit-rappers, and traders
in many other magic arts and sorceries are so palpably
multiplying and deceiving and ensnaring the whole
world, is, without doubt,' said a preacher in 1605, ' a
sure sign of the speedy advent of the Last Day and the
Day of Judgment. In some towns, as we learn from
newspapers of all sorts, there are men who can make
tables jump up in the air, and who can rap up the
spirits of the dead and get them to reveal hidden things

---

[1] Εὐποραδήλωσις, Bl. b 47–49.

and future events.'[1] 'There is no doubt whatever,'
says a pamphlet of 1563, 'that by means of witchcraft spirits can be rapped up and made to appeal,
for there are many people who have been present at
such performances, and who have testified on their
word and honour to what they saw and heard. But
it is not the spirits of good and pious men who can be
thus called up and who will reveal hidden things, but
wicked people who have found no rest after their
death, and are obliged to roam about incessantly.'[2]
' The souls of those who have died in their sins,' wrote
Cornelius Agrippa of Nettesheim, ' are, like the demons,
still wrapped in darkness and fog, by means of which
they become manifest, and can be called up by the
sorcerers.'[3] As regards table-turning Samuel Brenz
of Osterberg, near Memmingen, a Jew who had been
converted to Christianity, made a charge against his
former co-religionists that ' By means of sorcery[4]
they can make a table go up and down in a merry
dance, and they whisper the devil's name to each
other, and then the table, even should it weigh many
hundredweights, will jump up in the air.' The Jew,
Solomon Zebi of Offenhausen, did not in his defensive
pamphlet, ' Jüdischer Theriak,' published at Hanover
in 1515, dispute the fact of the table's jumping up, but
he maintained that it was not done by devil's work or
sorcery, but by the practical Cabala with invocation
of holy names.[5]

---

[1] 'A Sermon on the near approach of the Last Day,' by M. Heinrich
Riess (1605), p. 5.   [2] *Von Höllenzwängen*, p. 7.
  [3] Cf. Sprengel, iii. 400–401.   [4] *Kischuph.*
  [5] Cf. Schneider, *Geisterglaube*, pp. 59–60. According to this, Perty's
statement (p. 389) that table-turning and table-rapping are of North
American origin, is incorrect.

In several cabalistic and talmudic books it was stated that 'the service of the demons reaches the highest grade when the human being surrenders his soul with full consent to a formal league with Satan, carries on personal intercourse with him and his associates, and at stated times joins with them in dances, feasts, and other excesses. Many sorcerers take on the forms of animals and do injury to men, or traverse great spaces in very short time. They also make frequent use of outward means, especially of salves from certain herbs and oils.' [1] 'When the sorcerers want to fly away into space,' said Sigmund Friedrich of Lindau in 1592, ' the goat and the mantle are not the only means always used for the purpose; they also make use of a salve and a special kind of fat-oil, which we might mention by name if we were allowed. With the same moisture and oils which their lord and master the devil has learnt to apply they smear and anoint themselves until they are in the right condition for flying off to another place.' [2]

There were ' special booklets and leaflets ' in which, as a contemporary complained, instructions were given ' as to how one might take magic rides with the devil and practise other demoniacal and ghostly arts, and how one could invoke him so that he would do just what one wanted. The devils, so this book represented to the people, manufactured money and property at stated times, and the devils themselves undoubtedly had a hand in making the book.' [3]

[1] Cf. Görres, 4ᵇ, 50–55.
[2] *Von wunderlicher Verzückung*, Bl. A 4 ; cf. A 3.
[3] *Von Höllenzwängen*, pp. 3–4. An instructive pamphlet on the nature of magic is *Des Teuffels Nebelkappen* ; i.e. a short summary of the whole business of sorcery, by Paul Frisius. Without locality, 1583.

To this collection of books belonged the work entitled 'Höllenzwang' ('Hell Subjugated'), published in 1575 under the name of the great magician and astrologer, Doctor Faust, by whom ' the devil and the spirits were compelled and exorcised to bring to pass what he wanted and to do what he required.' Thus, for instance, ' With the Word of Jesus Christ I command you, Seloth, to appear to me this instant in human shape, without any noise or tumult, without any horrible form, yea, without injury to our body and soul. I conjure thee, Seloth, to bring hither silver and gold, to the value of seventeen hundredweights of Oriental gold, and moreover in such state and condition that it may be recognised and accepted by everybody in all countries.' If the invocation did not succeed it meant that it had not been made rightly ; for there was a special art in this matter which Doctor Faustus described as follows : ' Anyone who is a lover of gold, silver and precious stones will be able to obtain as much of these as he will find marked in this book ; but he must condense from my discursive volume the force and the words of the exorcism in such wise as to be able to read them out or say them by heart in three times three hours, and he must bless the round circles with the silver tripod, with the names, words and letters of the bystanders,' and all this ' according to their rank.' [1]

' Those sorcerers,' says Thomas Sigfridus, Bl. A 4, ' are the most pleasing to Satan who sacrifice children to him ; of such was a count, who was also a sorcerer, who strangled eight young children and presented them to the devils, who then told him he must further tear his own son out of the mother's womb and offer it up to them.'

[1] In Adelung, vii. 365–408. At the court of the Emperor Rudolf II., at Prague, there lived from 1584 to 1589 the famous English magician Dr. John Dee, who with his Famulus, the apothecary Kelley, was able by means of a crystal ball to call up all manner of spirits. Dee kept full

Doctor Faust is the actual representative of all the necromantic and magic developments of the century. Just as all sorts of writings on ' occult arts ' appeared under the name of Theophrastus Paracelsus, so under the name of Doctor Faust, who lived contemporaneously with Paracelsus, there were collected all conceivable reports on the practice of such arts, credited both by high and low, learned and unlearned. As early as 1539 the Worms physician Philip Begardi had compared the fame of Faust with that of Paracelsus. A later writer coupled the name of Faust with the no less renowned ' arch-magician ' Cornelius Agrippa of Nettesheim.

' Of late years,' says Begardi, ' a remarkable man has been travelling through nearly every province, principality and kingdom, has himself made his name known to everybody, and has boasted highly of his great skill not only in medicine, but also in chiromancy, necromancy, physiognomy, crystal gazing, and other kindred arts, has also described himself as a renowned and experienced man, and has also not denied that he is, and is called Faustus ; and has further signed himself Philosophus Philosophorum.' [1]

diaries concerning these apparitions, one of which was printed in 1659. Cf. Meissner, *Untersuchungen über Shakespeares Sturm* (Dessau, 1872), pp. 42–46, and Meissner, *Die englischen Komödianten*, p. 26.

[1] These and other earlier and later testimonies of contemporaries concerning Faust are recorded in Goedeke, *Grundriss*, ii. 562 ff. ** There is also the more extensive literature on the subject ; cf. further *Jahresberichte für neuere deutsche Litteraturgesch.* Bd. 4, ii. 3, No. 25 ff. and Bd. 7, ii. 3, No. 21 ff. F. Kluge (' Vom geschichtlichen Faust,' in the *Allgemeine Zeitung*, 1896, Beil. No. 9) comes to the following conclusion : ' Concerning the end and the last biographical events of the historical Faust, we know nothing certain, nor have we any information from any authentic source concerning the year of his birth and the course of his development.'

The oldest popular book on Faust appeared in 1587 at Frankfort-on-the-Main.   It was a specimen of the strong Lutheran tendency which the publisher John Spiess manifested in his whole work as bookseller.[1] There is no trace whatever of Catholic belief in this book; on the contrary, the Catholic worship and the Catholic clergy are ridiculed and slandered in it after the manner of the Protestant polemics of the day.   Mephistopheles appears in the form of a monk.   In the course of his travels Faust finds at Cologne 'the devil in the Church of St. Ursula with the 11,000 virgins.'   At Rome, where he stands three days and nights in the papal palace, invisible all the time, he learnt, so he says 'all the godless ways of the Pope and his rabble.'   'These pigs at Rome,' he says, ' are fatted and all ready to roast and cook.'   After his immoral conduct, told in the most immoral manner, in the harem at Constantinople, the author of this book makes him ' mount up in the air in the vestments and ornaments of a pope so that everybody could see him.'[2]

[1] See Fr. Zarncke, 'Joh. Spiess, der Herausgeber des Faust-Buches und sein Verlag,' in the *Beil. zur Allgemeinen Zeitung* (1883), No. 246.

[2] 'Faust became the favourite hero of those tales of magic which the German people can never hear enough of or relate too often ; the religious interests of the period are, moreover, bound up with these stories, and this gives them their particular stamp ; Faust is the accursed and deplorable man who has apostatised from Lutherdom, subscribed to the devil, sold himself hopelessly to hell, and whose character and destiny are made to serve as a warning example to all good Christians.'   Wittenberg figures in the popular books, ' as the second home of this anti-Lutheran Magus ; although he is not allowed to have learnt magic at Wittenberg, but only in such places as were strangers or enemies to Lutheran doctrine : according to one popular book he studied his occult arts at Cracow, according to another at Ingolstadt.' ' How narrowly Lutheran and anti-popish ' the author of the first people's book of 1587 was, 'and how anxious he was to exhibit his state of mind in the history of Faust, is nowhere so glaringly seen as in the passages describing the sojourn of the two world-travellers

'Whereas now for a great many years,' says the editor in the preface of the book, 'there has been a widespread legend in Germany concerning Dr. John Faust, the far-famed magician and necromancer, the hero of all sorts of adventures, and whereas at all social gatherings there is much inquiry concerning the history of the said Faust,' he had published this book the

in Rome and in Constantinople.' 'Islam and the papacy, moreover, appeared so like each other in the eyes of our narrator, that the rôle of the Prophet and that of the pope were easily fused in one, and could be played by one and the same person—either the godless Magus, or the devil himself—with the best effect. In the palace at Constantinople Mephistopheles appeared before the Sultan as Mohammed in papal attire, and after Faust had spent six days and nights in the harem, playing the part of the Prophet for the multiplication of the faithful, he took his departure in pontifical robes. And on both occasions the pope was highly gratified by the honour which had befallen him.' K. Fischer, pp. 99–100, 114–115. Oscar Schade remarks : Were there in the book ' any Catholic additions, Mary and the dear saints would not have let the poor sinner perish.' ' As in all the earlier sagas of leagues with the devil, Mary would have taken pity on him and undertaken to intercede for him with her Son ' (*Weimarer Jahrb.* v. 242). ** Cf. now also E. Schmidt, ' Faust und Luther,' in the *Sitzungsberichte der kgl. preuss. Akademie der Wissenschaften* (1896), i. (Berlin, 1896), p. 567 ff., where the relation of the *Faustbuch* to the theological teaching of Luther is thoroughly exposed. According to Milchsack (*Historia D. Johannis Fausti des Zauberers*. Wolfenbüttel, 1897 ; cf. Kampers in the *Histor. Jahrbuch*, 1897, p. 713) the *Faustbuch* strikes into the middle of the battles between the strict Lutherans and the Philipists ; for it attacks one of the chief points in these discussions, namely, the synergism of Melanchthon, *i.e.* the assertion made by him from practical considerations of the necessity for co-operation of the individual in the work of conversion and redemption ; we have, therefore, to deal not only with a popular saga, but also with a problem-tale produced by the spirit of strictest Lutherdom. 'The proofs in justification of this view,' so G. Ellinger concludes his *Referat* (*Allgem. Zeitung*, 1897, Beil. No. 216), 'are so far only in the smallest degree to the fore, and we must wait for the second volume of Milchsack's book before we can pronounce a final judgment. In the volume already out, Milchsack confines himself, with a view to establishing the tendency of the *Faustbuch*, to a very careful exposition of the book, which throws much clear light on the structure of the work, as well as on certain points hitherto little noticed ; but even here the correspondence of the book with the most fundamental doctrines of Lutheran theology stands out markedly.'

matter of which had been communicated to him by a
friend at Spires, ' for a warning to all Christians ' as
' a terrible example of devilish deceit and murder of
body and soul.' [1]

[1] Catalogue of the numerous editions in Goedeke, *Grundriss*, ii. 564–568.
K. Engel, *Zusammenstellung der Faust-Schriften vom sechzehnten Jahrhundert bis Mitte 1884* (Oldenburg, 1885) ; and also, by the same author,
' Nachricht über drei höchst seltene Faustbücher ' (of 1589, 1597, and
Wagnerbuch of 1596), in the *Zeitschr. für vergleichende Litteraturgesch.*
i. 329–333. The *Faustbuch* of 1589 contains six new stories which are
not included in the oldest editions of 1587, among others, chapter 55 :
' Ein Mönch will Dokt. Faustum bekehren.' ** Fr. Zarncke, *Die Biblio-
graphie des Faustbuchs* in the report on the transactions of the Gesellsch.
der Wiss. at Leipzig, 1888, p. 181 ff.—*The oldest Faustbuch . . . with
an Introduction by W. Scherer* (Berlin, 1884).   In the sixteenth century
traditions concerning Faust, Scherer distinguishes three classes : an
Upper Rhenish, a Wittenberg and an Erfurt tradition.   Schwengberg,
Das Spiess. Faustbuch und seine Quellen (Berlin, 1885) ; G. Ellinger, in
the *Zeitschr. für deutsche Philologie* (1887), xix. 244–246. Further, by
the same author, ' Zu den Quellen des Faustbuches von 1587,' in the
Zeitschr. für vergleichende Litteraturgeschichte, New Series, i. 156–181,
and in the *Vierteljahrschr. für Litteratur*, ii. 314 ff.   In Michael Lindener's
Katzipori there are three Faust stories, two of which, in a not advan-
tageously altered form, have been incorporated in the Faust book.   ' We
have in these stories the more original form in which they were known
to the people a generation before the compilation of the *Faustbuch*, and
even earlier.   The hero of these stories is called in Lindener not Faust
but Schrannhanss ' (Bobertag in the *Archiv für Litteraturgesch.* vi. 142).
Further articles on the sources of the oldest *Faustbuch* of Szamalotski and
Hartmann are in the *Vierteljahrschr. für Litteraturgesch.* i. 161 ff. (the
natural science dialogues about hell and paradise, and about celestial
phenomena are borrowed from the medieval *Elucidarius*), further from
Fränkel and Bauer, *ibid.* iv. 361 ff. (quotations from Agricola, Franck,
Brant), and finally the remarks of Milchsack already referred to in the
preceding note (p. 359).   Of special importance is the correspondence
here pointed out by Milchsack between the *Faustbuch* and the *Zauber-
teufel* of Ludwig Milichius (1563).   Ellinger (*Allgem. Zeitung*, 1897,
Beil. No. 216) considers the agreement of the *Faustbuch* with the *Zauber-
teufel* in certain parts as undoubted ; on the other hand it appears
to him likely that in many of the places where Milchsack thinks to detect
the influence of the above-mentioned book, the correspondence is only
accidental, and not the result of any opinions of Milichius (*Aufzeichnung*).
Concerning the MS. copy of the oldest *Faustbuch*, found in the Wolfenbüttel library, Ellinger remarks : ' To this hitherto unknown version high

According to the account in the 'Historia' Faust was the son of a peasant at Rod near Weimar, graduated as a doctor of theology at Wittenberg, but soon threw the Holy Scriptures 'behind the door and under the

value is attached because it is undoubtedly older than the printed edition of 1587, from which it also differs outwardly in various ways. First and foremost it has a preface which is entirely different from the preface to the Spires edition, and which has much affinity with Milichius' *Zauber-teufel*. Secondly, the work itself exhibits many noteworthy deviations, and a comparison of these with the printed text leads almost everywhere to instructive conclusions. The numerous smaller variations cannot of course be gone into here ; but we must, at least, point to the two chapters which are contained in the MS. copy, though not in the first printed edition. One of these tells the story of a nobleman languishing in Turkish captivity, supposed to be dead by his wife, who decides on a second marriage, which, however, does not take place, as Faust at the last moment, by his magic act, brings the supposed dead husband safely back again. It is obvious that we have here a narrative akin to the Saga of *Heinrich der Löwe*, or the folksong of the *Edler Moringer* ; only the fertile materials are worked up here in a way which bears throughout the stamp of the coarse-minded sixteenth century. The second of these chapters, omitted in the first printed edition, is of more importance. In this Faust heals the sick Bishop of Salzburg and predicts to him the future of the papacy. It is by no means impossible that we have here to do with a bit of genuine Faust biography, which might perhaps be verified ; we know already that the historical Faust did show himself at the courts of the bishops, and that he was welcomed cordially by them, and prophesied the future to them ; for one such case, at any rate, we have positive evidence, and the prelate in question was one of the most admirable spiritual princes of the sixteenth century, the Bamberg bishop, George Schenk of Limburg. The prophecy we are concerned with does not come from the author of the *Faustbuch*, but is in all probability borrowed from some other source, which remains to be verified as to details. It is, however, in perfect agreement with the anti-Catholic spirit of the *Faustbuch*, and, as is always the case when religion in the sixteenth century is in question, the language shows a quickened pulse-beat, as in the following words : ' Oh, Germany, thou art robbed of thy crown, for the Pope has set himself up above thy crown and rules as Emperor and King ; where he will he flies high, as the eagle, does with you also according to his will, and this fox is lord and master and treats you as monkeys. . . . But, Germany, rejoice once more, for though he has gotten possession of thy money and goods, thou wilt nevertheless be proof against his deceitfulness and his false belief, and in Germany the pure Gospel will arise, and the German princes will turn to it and will deal out a great blow to the papacy.'

bench,' gave himself up to a reckless, godless life, and
set to work to study all sorts of occult and magic arts.
'His plan was to love everything which ought not to
be loved; this course he followed day and night,
took to himself eagle's wings, sought to fathom all
things in heaven and earth, for his curiosity, libertinage
and lightmindedness did in such wise goad and entice
him, that at one time he undertook to construct and
experiment with certain magic names, figures, characters
and conjurations, with which he might bring the devil
into his presence.' By order of Lucifer there appears
to him the high and mighty demon Mephistopheles,
to whom he signs away his soul with his own blood.
'Even in this hour this godless man falls away from
his God and Creator, who has formed him; yea, he becomes a member of the damnable devil, and this fall
came from nothing but his own proud haughtiness,
desperation, audacity and presumption; it was with
him as with those giants of whom the poets write,
that they carried away mountains and dared to fight
against God; yea, like unto the wicked angel, who set
himself up against God, wherefore on account of his
pride and arrogance he was banished by God.' Faust
himself says in his bond to Mephistopheles that he
had given himself up to the latter 'after I had taken
in hand to speculate about the elements; but among
the gifts that had been graciously bestowed on me
from above could not find skill enough for this task in
my own head, and could not learn it from men.' After
having once surrendered himself to the devil he is lost
eternally. For a period of twenty-four years all the
arts of hell are placed at his disposal, and then he
falls a prey to the devil body and soul, in spite of all

wailing and lamentation over his irremediable fate, and in spite of the language, full of penitence and warning, which he addresses to his friends on the evening before his terrible death.

All the deep religious ideas and all the impressive features of the older popular book were completely wiped out by a rearrangement of it which George Rudolf Widman published at Hamburg in 1599, in three parts, under the title : ' Wahrhaftigen Historien von den gräulichen und abscheulichen Sünden und Lastern . . . so Doktor Johannes Faustus . . . getrieben hat ' (' True Stories of the abominable Sins and Vices . . . which Dr. J. Faustus . . . has committed ').[1] This work, which became the dominant ' Faustbuch,' contained nothing but all sorts of farcical stories and extraordinary adventures, and in the ' Erinnerungen ' (' Reflections ') appended to each section it aimed chiefly at incensing the Protestant people against the papacy.[2]

Not only ' the old women and witches, who are daily burnt,' but also the magicians and necromancers ought, says Widman, to be punished in ' body and life

[1] Printed by Scheible, *Kloster*, ii. 275–804.

[2] The titles of the three parts are in Goedeke, *Grundriss*, ii. 567, V. 2. ' The Frankfort Folk-book had indeed quenched for the moment the thirst for the history of Faust, but it had not at all points satisfied the interest or the needs of Lutheran readers. The narrative was not complete and detailed, not learned and instructive, neither was it, in its Lutheran tendency, sufficiently anti-Catholic and anti-popish. In order to make up thoroughly for these deficiencies, George Rudolf Widman of Schwäbisch Hall produced his massive work in three parts, copiously furnished with long-winded " Reflections," which appeared in Hamburg in 1599, and served as guide to the later Faust-books.' K. Fischer, pp. 134–135. The new and enlarged edition prepared by the doctor of medicine, Ch. Nicholas Pfizer, in 1674 at Nuremberg, and lately published by A. von Keller in the *Bibl. des Stuttgarter Litterar. Vereins*, vol. cxlvi. (Tübingen, 1880).

and exterminated by the ruling authorities.' There
were two different kinds of magic, he said, ' one to the
right, the other to the left.' The first was ' very common in the papacy in benedictions, consecration and
confirmation,' and was just as much as the second the
actual black art, ' a falling away from the Creator to
Moloch, and from God to the creatures.'[1] Altogether,
there were numbers of magicians and necromancers
among the Papists. Gregory VII, for instance, had
' despatched six popes with the help of Venetian soups,'
with the help of an experienced master he had cut the
throats of Clement II, Damasus II, Leo IX, Victor II,
Stephen IX, Nicholas II, notwithstanding that these
were all themselves magicians, so that one devil drove
out another.' ' Against the protests of ecclesiastical
prelates he had secretly handed over Christian children
to the Jews, from whom he required half the blood of
the little victims, with which he compassed the death
of numbers of clergy. When he shook the large sleeve
in his black cowl bright flames and sparks of fire came
out of it,' and so forth. Pope Gregory IX understood
the not very common magic art of ' flying from one
place to another.' When Pope Paul II bound him-

---

[1] J. G. Gödelmann, professor of Law at Rostock, spoke still more
strongly on the subject. ' Verily,' he said, ' the whole papacy is infested
with spiritual magic ' ; ' the true and zealous Papists, especially in the
clerical classes, are plunged as deeply, and even more deeply, in Satan's
power and empire as were the sorcerers themselves.' The blessing of
salt, water, herbs, and so forth, was ' pure devilish, godless and blasphemous
witchcraft,' as that most distinguished Tübingen theologian, James
Heerbrand, had rightly written. ' The Chrism was nothing but pure
devil's work ' ; above all, the transformation of bread and wine in the
Mass was nothing but sorcery (Gödelmann, p. 63 ff., 480–481). Abraham
Scultetus also declared in his sermons on magic (p. 13) that this transformation was a ' devilish abuse,' and ' downright sorcery.'

self in writing to the devil, 'the devil grabbed at the spurting blood.'

Every class and every land had its special devils; the higher sort use heresy and despair, as weapons of attack, such as the devils of the pope and the sects: there is also a special Zwinglian and Calvinistic devil. 'The devil disguises himself in monk's form, to show thereby that the monks in the papacy, the impious Brothers, are his faithful servants and larvae, in which he clothes himself, and that there is no rascality, wickedness or infamy so great which the godless monks and all the sorcerers, as tools of the devil, which the devil rides, could not perpetrate if, God permitting, it came in their way.' The devil also appears as a sea-wonder 'in full episcopal vestments, and walks on the water with his bishop's staff.' That Doctor Faust should have eaten a whole cartload of hay is by no means impossible; for another magician, by name Wildfeuer, had 'eaten a peasant with his horse and cart; likewise Doctor Hedion relates that a Magus who was coming to Kreuznach met a peasant with a horse and cart, taking wood to the market to sell, and that he ate up the peasant, his horse, his cart and his wood. This same Magus also once swallowed a man clad in armour, and afterwards spat him out.' To conjure a devil to oneself in a glass did not seem at all astonishing to Widman, for had not the necromancer Peter Apponus 'had seven thoroughly experienced devils in a glass, each one of which instructed him in one special art out of the seven liberal arts' ? [1]

---

[1] In Scheible, *Kloster*, ii. 277–278, 294, 302, 304, 308, 324, 333, 336, 337, 347, 348–349, 354, 416–417, 486, 491, 536–537, 692, 770 ff., 777, 786. Sigmund Friedrich (Bl. B 4) says: 'Joachim Camerarius writes that he

As a continuation of the ' Faustbuch,' there appeared in the year 1594, at ' Gerapoli, published by Constantine Joseph,' in quarto and octavo volumes, a life of Christopher Wagner, ' sometime Famulus to the world-famed arch-magician John Faust,' who exorcised the devil ' Auerhan ' on the Blocksberg. ' Then the whole earth hopped round, the stars fell from heaven and ran about on earth like flames of fire ; some of them turned into horrible snakes and threatened to stab Wagner with their pointed tongues ; others became flying fire-dragons which struggled and fought in the air with great noise. . . . At last Wagner saw a camel coming forward out of the smoke, and he said to him : " What dost thou want ? "   The camel answered : " That thou should'st appear in the form of a monkey." The monkey appeared at first with four heads, but at Wagner's request he discarded three of the heads and became " a proper monkey."   The monkey jumped up and down, danced galliard and other voluptuous dances, played on the dulcimer and the fife, and blew trumpets as though there were a hundred or more.' With this devil Wagner travelled about, visited the newly discovered countries, and carried on all sorts of tricks in the way of spectral apparitions, until at last, like his master Faust, he was fetched away by the

himself has seen magicians who carried about with them a head through which the devil answered the questions they asked him.   A head of this sort must first be enchanted, in the same way that rings and crystals, in which people can see and discover whatever they want to know, are enchanted ; for in unenchanted crystals and rings nothing can be seen or discovered.'   The Marburg Magister, Philip Louis Elich (1607), rejected the opinion that magicians as such were able to confine the devil in crystals, rings, &c., as though in prison.   ' Daemones enim semper voluntarie adsunt, vel superiorum Daemonum imperio coacti, seque carceri includi sinunt ' (Elich, p. 201).

devil. The author stated that the object of his work was that all people might learn from it to know the devil better, and know better how to protect themselves against him.[1]

How truly ' the heads of all people, high and low, were full of devils' and all conceivable ' devil's feats passed as truly history with high and low ' is markedly shown in the tales which, according to the man's own account, were circulated in numbers of places about the house physician of the Elector of Brandenburg, Thurn von Thurneissen. Once the devil was close to him in the form of an elk, which Thurneissen had received as a present from the Duke of Lithuania. This devil, it was said, he used to take with him ' up and down the lands to collect money.' Then again it was asserted ' in public speeches and writings ' that one day, in a state of intoxication at a banquet, he had given away his horses and carriage, and at the same time ordered his coachman to harness the horses. ' The coachman had answered : " Sir, what are you going to drive in ? Are you so overcome by eating and drinking as not to be aware that you have given away your horses and carriage, and myself also ? " To which I am said to have answered : " Ei, get off with you in the name of 100,000 devils ; you'll find a carriage and horses fast enough." Then as he went from me, not knowing what he should do, there appeared to him four very beautiful and well-formed black horses, and also a well-appointed carriage. Nobody, however, knew or could imagine out of what materials this same carriage had been made. The coachman went up to the horses (neverthe-

[1] In Scheible, *Kloster*, iii. 1–188 ; cf. especially pp. 38–60, 43, 185–186.

less in fear and trembling, because he knew that they
were not natural horses, but that they came from the
devil), harnessed them into the carriage, and told me
that all my orders had been fulfilled. I remained still
some time eating and drinking until I thought that the
right and fitting hour had come to drive off with the
demon horses, when I took leave of my guests and got
into the carriage, while the coachman mounted on horse-
back, and I said to him, " Now drive off in the name
of all the 100,000 devils."   At that instant, and in the
sight of all bystanders, the horses and carriage are
said to have swung into the air, and in twelve hours
I travelled from Basle almost to Halle in Saxony.'
Further, a man who was looked up to in Basle ' knew '
on good authority that Thurneissen had bought a
house and paid ready money for it, and that this money
had afterwards turned into coals.   When the vendor of
the house sent these coals to the Elector of Brandenburg, Thurneissen, ' so as not to incur disgrace and
danger of death, paid the purchase sum in current
thalers and added an extra honorarium, and also made
many promises to the Elector to induce him to keep
the matter secret, and not spread the devilish tale of
sorcery among the people.'

Still further wonderful stories followed. Thurneissen had built on to his house a little tower for
observing the stars, and it was ' reliably ' asserted
that this tower was meant for the devil, who took
shelter there at night, in order that he might hold undisturbed converse with his pupil. According to other
reports, however, the devil did not only occupy this
tower, but also sat on the roof of the house in the shape
of a horned owl : Thurneissen had conjured him up

there in order to learn from him whether his wife was faithful to him.   Already in his youth, when he was learning the goldsmith's trade, this devil's artist had been wont to spend the whole day in eating and drinking, while he devoted his nights to performing all sorts of beautiful and cunning works with a number of devils in human form.   And not content with this, writes Thurneissen, ' several of the Basle people have declared that they have seen the devil incarnate sitting with me on the roof of my house.   Others also, who set up for being respectable inhabitants of Basle, have shamelessly asserted that they have seen the devil in my house behind the oven, and that when I was at my table writing he dictated to me, and spoke into my pen what I was to write.'   Other good people of Basle ' boasted publicly of having found in my house a mirror, in which they saw the devil bodily as a protector and guardian of my belongings, and that he had also talked with certain members of the council.'   At the table of his father-in-law Herbrot, Thurneissen is said to have ' bewitched three spiders which were not real spiders but devils ; when the heathen cross was made over them they vanished, leaving a stench behind them.'   ' I am further accused of having three wives in Basle and one in Berlin, and of carrying on with them, through the devil's arts, things not to be spoken or written of.   Also, by day and night, it is said, strange unknown birds fly round about my house, and make such a piteous screaming and lamentation that there is no other conclusion to arrive at than that it is my own spirit, and that in a short time it will carry me away from hence and take me to the abyss of hell.   A ghost, that I am supposed to have bewitched in my house,

screams day and night with a small voice like a young
child.' 'Always when I am writing I am said to have
two great black dogs, which are devils, lying by me.
The devil also makes calendars for me.' [1]

On the other hand it was also reported that the devils
were not always at the command of Thurneissen, that
only lately indeed they had almost struck him a death-
blow. He had begged the Elector of Brandenburg to
let him have every Friday as a free day on which he
would not ask about him or send for him, for on Friday
he wanted to give himself up to his ' sorcery and devil's
evocations.' Once, however, on a Friday, something
exceptional had happened at court, and he was very
much wanted, and the Elector had sent a page to
summon the doctor to his presence. But when the
page reached his dwelling-house, the grey cloister,
he found there three devils in the form of enormous
black monks, who were eating and drinking with
Thurneissen : as the lad was about to turn back, terrified,
the monks seized hold of him and treated him in such a
manner that he instantly turned pale in death. Thereupon the Elector had sent a halberdier to find out why
neither the page nor Thurneissen came. This halberdier
had also been seriously wounded by the devils, but not
quite killed. When he gave information at court of
what had befallen himself and the page, the Elector
had had the cloister surrounded by a number of people
and his physician taken prisoner. ' When this happened, the devils were still sitting by me, but when I
was seized they hurried away like flying spirits, and

---

[1] *Ein durch Nothgedrungenes Aussschreiben*, i. 84 ff.   ** Concerning
this remarkable piece of writing, cf. Janssen's statements in his article
'Zur Sittengeschichte des sechzehnten Jahrhunderts,' *Katholik* (1889),
i. 41 ff.

left me in the lurch.' Finally, Thurneissen goes on,
' they bound me hand and foot with iron chains, put
me on my trial, and sentenced me to death by fire as
a sorcerer.' ' When the day appointed for carrying
out the sentence came, there arose such a boisterous,
tempestuous and terrible wind that everybody thought
the Day of the Lord was at hand, and that the town of
Berlin with the whole compass of the globe would
fall in a heap and go to ruin. And I, so report said,
before being consigned to the flames, was carried away
by the devils who had served me so long, and visibly
lifted up into the air and torn to pieces.' Reports of
this kind were ' not only circulated by the common
people from whom one might expect such credulity,
but also by the most distinguished persons.' [1]

Moreover, Thurn von Thurneissen himself had not
the slightest doubt that the devil frequently appeared
to him in a bodily form, and that ' everything in the
world was full of devilry and devil's arts.' In a pamphlet of 1575 he pointed out plainly how Satan, not
very long before, had carried on his work in person in
Rottweil, Basle, Baden, and elsewhere :

> Certain it is that in Norway we find,
> In Iceland also, spirits who mankind
> Will wait upon and serve,
> Who show themselves and let themselves be heard,
> Who call men by their names . . . [2]

There were also ' all at once devils ' :

> Who in glass and crystal clear
> Are conjured to our sight down here,
> Who point out mines and treasures rare—
> Who show us all the places where

---

[1] *Ein durch Nothgedrungenes Aussschreiben*, i. 92–94.
[2] Εὐπορα δήλωσις, Bl. 40 ff. 45[b].

> Copper, silver, iron, lead,
> Gold, tin, and precious stones lie hid ;
> Who have the knowledge of all arts,
> Who know the properties and parts
> Of herb-roots, and also of metals ;
> Who by their wisdom make men wise ;
> Who appear in mirrors, water and crystals
> When we command them and exorcise.[1]

Endless reports about ' the devil himself,' about bodily apparitions of the devil, kept the people in an incessant state of anxiety and terror. ' Scarcely a single year goes by,' lamented a writer in 1563, ' without the most appalling news from numbers of principalities, towns, and villages of the shameless and horrible ways in which the prince of hell, by bodily apparition in all sorts of forms, is trying to extinguish the new and shining light of holy evangel, and plaguing and martyring poor Christianity.'[2] At the Augsburg Diet of 1530 a superintendent gave information of six devils in the form of monks, so that there was justification for ' painting the devil in a monk's cowl.'[3]

When on Easter Eve of the year 1533 the little town of Schiltach in the Black Forest was on fire, the wicked spirit appeared in bodily form, and was heard in the town playing on a timbal ;[4] a newspaper telling the story was to have been circulated in Strassburg, but the council forbade its being printed, because ' they did not want to have anything to do with the devil.'[5] At Rottweil, where the council ' had long been hostile to the Gospel, and had banished several God-fearing people from the town,' the devil, according to the report

---

[1] Bl. 30ᵇ.   [2] Von Höllenzwängen, p. 7.

[3] Weber, Historische Predigten, pp. 109–110.

[4] Scheible, Schaltjahr, iv. 96–97 ; Bücherschatz, p. 128, No. 1926 ; cf. Fincelius, i. Bl. E 7ᵇ.

[5] Reuss, La Justice criminelle . . . à Strasbourg, pp. 266–267.

of Job Fincelius, ' went visibly about the town in 1545,
sometimes in the form of a hare, sometimes like a
weasel, sometimes like a goose, talked in a distinct
voice, and threatened to burn down the town.' [1]   Elsewhere the devil was seen in the forms of a bear, a dog,
a cat.[2] Very remarkable was the ' truthful story '
told by Fincelius in 1557, ' which had happened a few
years before in the Mark ' : the devil appeared bodily
in a law court, in a blue hat, as counsel for a Landsknecht, ' argued soundly about justice,' and finally
carried a tavern-keeper, the accuser of the Landsknecht, ' over the market away in the air, as everybody saw, but nobody has yet discovered where he took
him.' [3] In Saxony, where he had already been seen
before, ' he changed himself into horrible shapes, ran
about the streets naked, and knocked at the doors of
the houses ; he frightened everybody with his bawling
and howling.' [4]

In 1559 the people learnt from a ' gruesome, alarming, and wonderful, but true newspaper,' that the devil
had appeared at Platten, two miles from Joachimsthal,
' in the form of a cuckoo, a raven, and a bumblebee,
and had imitated the sounds of these birds and in-
sects.' When the preacher of Schlackenwald asked him :
' How is it that you who have been one of the most
beautiful creatures can change yourself into such
forms, sometimes into that of a sow, sometimes some

---

[1] Fincelius, i. Bl. K 3 ; Scheible, *Schaltjahr*, iv. 340 ; Gross, *Magica*,
i. 48ᵇ.

[2] Scheible, *Kloster*, ii. 299, 300, 314.

[3] Fincelius, Bl. O 5ᵇ–7ᵇ.

[4] Herold, p. 529.   Fincelius also (Bl. P 7ᵇ) complained that in 1551
' the devil at many hours of the night was seen walking about the streets
and knocking at doors ; frequently he wore white clothes, frequently
also he accompanied funerals and looked very sad.'

other beast,' the devil answered : ' Dear parson, I often
become a hare ; oh, the rich swells delight in eating
me.'[1] At Erfurt he recited a verse from the Psalms
in the form of a raven ;[2] from Copenhagen, through the
medium of a preacher, there came ' true and reliable
information that at several different times he had
appeared as a large black bird on the roof and had
begun to pipe a hymn, which several people had distinctly heard.'[3] On the stage also, ' where the devil
was almost always acted,'[4] ' the black, horrible Satan
showed himself several times in bodily form to the
people in the plays.' Speaking of the English comedians
Hans Stern says : ' It must have been a horrible sight
when once, as they were performing " Doctor Faust,"
among the stage devils who were to carry him off
there appeared suddenly a real live devil in bodily
form, and, as everybody saw, drove the comedians off
the stage.'[5]

In the parish church at Weimar the devil, according
to the statements of the Lutheran controversialists,
Wigand and Hesshus, appeared bodily, before the eyes
of the faithful, at the side of the Elector of Saxony's

[1] ' Die Zeitung ' in Scheible, *Schaltjahr*, ii. 466–474.

[2] Gross, *Magica*, i. 59ᵇ.

[3] ' Wider den Teufel als Gottesfeind, Menschenmörder und listigen
Betrüger,' sermon by M. K. Sauerborn (1559), p. 2.

[4] See above, pp. 131–137.

[5] Evenius, *Dedikation*, Bl. 4. In the *Simplicissimus* it says : ' What is
there that people are more fond of acting and seeing performed than the
history of the arch-sorcerer, Doctor John Faust, and only because a heap
of devils are always introduced into it, and are represented in all sorts of
horrible forms. Although it is well known how frequently at these devilish
masquerade dances and Faust comedies, by the judgment of God, real
devils appear among the fictitious ones, and nobody knows where this
fourth, or seventh, or twelfth extra devil (as the case may be) comes from.'
See Meissner, p. 91.

preacher Mirus in a horrible and abominable form, and
' his likeness was taken by several people and afterwards
printed.' [1]   Other ' veritable apparitions of the devil,'
connected with the confessional dissensions between
Lutherans and Calvinists, were made known in 1606
by the Lutheran preacher Nicholas Blum. ' Five
years ago,' he said in his ' Historische Erzählung,'
the devil appeared repeatedly to a young lady of the
nobility in the Lausitz in the form of a woman, and gave
her a gold chain in the name of a great lord, and also a
' Calvinistic book on divine Providence.'   ' He told her
that she had not been properly christened, and that she
could not be saved.   When her father wrote to me in
great distress, and begged and prayed me to help her
in virtue of my office, I visited the young lady, comforted her and instructed her from God's Word, after
which the devil with his golden chain, golden trinkets,
and Calvinistic book on Providence, kept away.' ' Every
year and a little oftener the devil comes in the form of a
black man to Müglen, in the parish of Dohna, and visits
the dear and pious daughter of a Christian couple ;
three times he has seized hold of her in the house or in
front of the door ; the first time he took her to a stream
of running water with the intention of drowning her in
it ; a second time he took her to an open field, and a
third time into a barn and up into the loft, intending
to throw her down.   When the young girl asked the
fellow why he dragged her about like this, he answered :
" Because you are not properly baptised ; you are mine
in body and soul ; you shall not escape me." ' [2]

As in this instance the devil was twice conquered

[1] Wilkens, *Tilemann Hesshusius* (Leipzig, 1860), pp. 191–192.
[2] *Historische Erzählung* ;. see above, p. 336, note 1.

by the Word of God according to Lutheran faith, so on two other occasions he was obliged to succumb to the archangel Gabriel. A 'terrible newspaper' of 1594 announced that 'the devil had come in the form of a man to a herdsman named Gabriel Kummer at Spandau.' Simultaneously, however, there appeared the archangel Gabriel. The latter 'blew very hard at the devil, so that it was like a rushing wind, and a naked, glancing sword went forth from the angel's mouth, at which the devil then yielded.' Thereupon the archangel, who had on his head a beautiful crown of rue bound round with gold, gave the herdsman a sprig of rue to eat, and he heard instantly 'a heavenly chant, Latin and German, one chorus after another, most beautiful and lovely ; but loveliest of all was a distant voice heard among the others, so clear and beautiful, words cannot describe it.' Gabriel ordered the fellow to inform the superintendent at Spandau that he ought to admonish the people with stronger language. In the church also the herdsman saw the devil in wolf's skin dancing and jumping over several possessed persons and other people ; he threw a cord 'round the herdsman's neck and would have strangled him, had not Gabriel appeared again and saved him. On a second appearance the archangel was furnished with a scythe, and he threatened 'to mow down the pious people with this scythe' unless at Spandau and throughout the whole land daily prayer was offered up every evening at seven o'clock.[1]

In this same year it was reported by the Berlin provost doctor James Coler, that on September 28 an

[1] In Scheible, *Schaltjahr*, iv. 462-467. Recorded in Weller, *Zeitungen*, No. 795.

archangel and a devil appeared simultaneously at the
bedside of a young girl, Ursula Seger, the daughter of
a brewer ; the archangel shone resplendently, and had
a drawn sword in his hand; the devil was a black
man with fiery eyes ; instead of ears he had long,
straight horns, and a crumpled horn on his forehead.
The archangel drove the devil to flight with his sword
and then swung the sword three times round in a
circle, crying out each time : ' Woe, woe to Germany ! '
Thereupon he withdrew from the young girl's sight, but
promised her that he would often come again.[1]   Another
victim, an innocent, five-year-old child, fared much
worse : according to an ' Erbärmliche und erschröckliche neue Zeitung' (Görlitz, 1579) it was set on fire by
the hellish apparition.[2]

The devil, according to all sorts of current reports,
busied himself especially with the new theologians,
who quarrelled with one another, and, after the pattern
of Luther, saw in each of their opponents an instrument of Satan, a being either spiritually or physi-
cally possessed by the devil.   When the theologian
Andrew Osiander died in 1552, it was spread about by
his opponents that the devil had twisted his neck round
and torn his body to pieces ;[3] ' as had happened before
to the theologian Carlstadt,' the people were told in
sermons.[4]   Of the Dresden court preacher David Steinbach, who suffered imprisonment as a friend of Nicholas
Krell, it was stated in an official document of 1592 that,

---

[1] From Coler's report in Wolfius, *Lectiones*, ii. 1021–1022.

[2] Weller, *Zeitungen*, No. 514.

[3] *Erläutertes Preussen*, ii. 69, 71.

[4] See how Sebastian Artomedes, pastor and consistorial assessor at
Königsberg, speaks on the subject in his sermons published in 1590.
Schenk, pp. 34–35.

by his own confession, ' he had attempted to free himself from custody with the help of the wicked fiend,
and had passed through three locked doors which had
remained intact ; the devil had often visited him at
night in his prison, and had bathed in his hand-basin
and turned over the leaves of his books ; in the castle
yard the evil spirit had actually been seen and heard.' [1]
The Mark superintendent-general Andrew Musculus
was incessantly plagued by the devil in bodily form,[2]
and the renowned Saxon court preacher, Matthew Hoe,
did not conceal the fact that the devil had blown out the
light in his study, had made an uproar, and thrown
books at him.[3] In the case of the superintendent
Bugenhagen the devil, it seems, devoted himself less
to plaguing the master of the house than the mistress.
Bugenhagen, however, as the Wittenberg preacher
Sebastian Fröschel informed his congregation in 1563,
knew a way for driving off the devil, which though not
exactly gentle was effectual.[4]

The devil also appeared frequently in person to
princes and distinguished statesmen.   For instance, the
military general Claus Berner, in 1551, informed Duke
Albert of Prussia that the devil had appeared in visible
form to three princes, the Margrave Albert of Branden-
burg-Culmbach, the Elector Moritz and Duke Augustus
of Saxony, at a banquet. On further inquiries which
Duke Albert made into the matter, he learnt from
Count George Ernest of Henneberg that the prince
of hell had appeared ' in the form of a young woman,

[1] See our statements, vol. ix. pp. 153–155,

[2] Spieker, *Musculus*, ii. 15.

[3] See Tholuck, *Akademisches Leben*, i. 131.

[4] ** In his sermon : ' Von den heiligen Engeln. Vom Teuffel und des
Menschen Seele.'   Wittenberg, 1563.   K. 8[b] ; cf. Schenk, p. 23.

of beautiful countenance, dressed in a green gown, and having long claws.'[1] Eight years later a preacher told the following tale : 'A few years ago I knew a prince of high lineage, whom out of respect I forbear to name, who told me himself that because he, as a lover of the holy evangel, had swept out of his land every vestige of Popish filth and idolatry, the devil had become so fierce and hostile towards him that he had appeared to him at different times in the most horrible shapes : once when he was at a meal Satan had come like a ferocious dog, or rather a wolf, and had eaten up at one gulp all that was on the table ; another time he came in the form of his servant, only several feet taller, threw him on the ground and beat him, till he bled. A third time he came in the shape of a large black cat, which had a human voice, and which scratched him, and left such a stench behind that all the inmates of the castle were greatly astonished. In this same cat form he strangled a little son of the Prince, and finally he changed into a gigantic and terrible man, and sent forth such an awful howl that, among other persons, the Prince himself fell on the ground in a fainting fit.' 'All this,' the preacher declared, 'I have verily heard from the mouth of the Prince, and it all happened in the course of three or four years.' 'In such wise does the enemy of God and the murderer of men attack, in bodily presence, even those in the highest positions in life. And, said the Prince, it was well known that he was not the only one in his position to whom such a terrible thing had happened': the devil had once appeared, dressed as a huntsman, to a popish prince, just as he was going to Communion, and

---

[1] See our statements, vol. vi. p. 439.

had tried to stick a burning Host made of pitch in his mouth.[1]

The disgraced chancellor Krell, it says, was visited by the devil ' several times in his prison in the form of a black bird, and the devil talked to him, as the keepers heard,' but they could not understand the language in which the two talked.[2]

' As a horrible and deterrent example, from which all might see what followed when people did not resist the visits of the devils, but rather encouraged them and bound themselves by writing to the devil,' an ' Erschröckliche Zeitung ' of 1606 related for the people's benefit the account of the fate of the jurist Henning Brabant, town prefect of Brunswick.   During a lawsuit, in which Brabant was involved with the Lutheran clergy of the district, it was rumoured about, in May 1604, that Brabant had been visited by the devil in the shape of a raven, and that the servants had complained of the suspicious visit.   When further several other evil deeds were charged against the town prefect by a man on the rack, Brabant himself was put on the rack three times, for several hours each time.   In order to escape from the most excruciating tortures he declared that to all questions that were put to him he would answer ' Yes.'   He then confessed to the charge of having intended, with the help of the devil, to betray the town of Brunswick to the Duke of Brunswick, who

[1] In the sermon quoted at p. 374, n. 3. Forner, *Panoplia*, p. 13, quotes a ' confession ' of the witches : at their gatherings a devil offers up a sacrifice, generally under a gallows tree, in mockery of the Mass, to the chief of the devils, and administers to the witches, instead of the Eucharist, a burning pitch-host and a chalice with a brimstone drink, which burns like hell-fire through all their entrails.

[2] See our remarks, vol. ix. pp. 153–154.

claimed sovereign territorial rights over this town and its district. At first, so his ' confession ' ran, ' Satan had appeared to him in his large room, in the form of a tall, lanky, black fellow, with a high hat and a tuft of feathers, and had seized him violently by the right arm, at which he had been alarmed and had said " Satan, begone from me ! " Then the devil had vanished, banging the door loudly to.' The next day the devil had come again, and had appeared under the foliage in the form of a tall youngster, with a pointed hat and feather, but he (Brabant) had not made any contract with him. Further, ' On the Church of St. Giles there had sat a raven which had shot straight at him and floated over his head.' ' After this, on a Sunday, when the food was being brought to table, a raven had flown in, seated itself on the table, and nodded as if it meant to join in the meal. Brabant had said : " Satan, get away from me ! " whereupon the raven had flown off.' Eight days later the raven had again shown itself, and had cried out, ' Raf ! Raf ! ' but still even then no agreement had been concluded. Finally, however, he had made an agreement for six years, when the devil had said to him : ' he would help him in all his affairs, and that he must set himself against the ruling authorities and every- body ; he should have freedom in all things, sin and crime would be made easy to him ; he must only defy the authorities and stir up rebellion ; he must be bold and intrepid. He, the devil, would stand by him and make him into a great lord.' On the other hand, Brabant had promised, ' by his share in heaven, that he would be the devil's servant with body and soul.' This bond had been signed and cemented with an oath, ' the raven had stretched out a great, rough hand with crooked fingers, and had pressed his hand very hard.'

So ran the confession extracted on the rack. The magistrates, with the burgomaster Haverland at their head, indulged so freely in wine whilst Brabant was undergoing torture that all of them, and the town bailiff as well, were dead drunk.

This ' bondsman of the devil and traitor' was sentenced to a terrible death. On the day of execution, September 16, 1604, one of the preachers delivered a sermon, in which he set forth, first, how a Christian magistracy ought to proceed against a public criminal and evildoer, and secondly, how pious Christians ought to be present at such punishments and lay them to heart as warnings. On September 17 Brabant, already wofully lacerated by the tortures he had undergone, was taken to the place of execution. First of all two fingers of his right hand were chopped off. Then red-hot tongs were applied to his arms and his breast, and he was emasculated. His body was cut up in five pieces and hung on five gates of the town. The five young children of the unhappy man were deprived of all their inheritance; they lived and died in poverty and need.[1]

' With like punishment,' said the ' Erschröckliche Zeitung ' at the end of its account of the execution of

---

[1] All further details from the original documents concerning the lawsuit are in F. K. von Strombeck's *Henning Brabant, Bürgerhauptmann der Stadt Braunschweig, und seine Zeitgenossen* (' A contribution to the history of the condition of German towns and German justice at the beginning of the sixteenth century' : Brunswick, 1829). Andrew Lonner, one of an enormous crowd who witnessed the execution, speaking before the honourable and learned gentlemen of the university of Giessen, expressed the wish that the Jesuits, as ' devilish criminals,' and ' bedevilled sorcerers,' might be punished in the same way as Brabant. See our statements, vol. x. pp. 366, 367.

Brabant, ' must all devil's allies and mischievous agi-
tators against spiritual or secular authority be visited.'
' Therefore let each one guard himself against the
pitfalls of the devil into which Brabant has rushed,
and live in fear and terror of the apparitions of
Satan, who if he has shown himself to persons of such
high standing and esteem as Brabant, and appeared
to them in so many different forms, will still more
easily practise his arts on the common people.' ' Do
we not hear of how many thousands of times he appears
to the witches and sorceresses, who enter into alliance
with him, and who are then punished in thousands
with death by fire ? How many of these have said
under torture that, since once for all they have entered
into league with the devil, they would rather be carried
away alive by him than undergo such martyrdom.
Not a few, moreover, of these unhappy creatures
(according to the documents of the lawsuits) have
been carried away so far in the air by the devil that
nobody has known what has become of them. Many
other evil-doers also are carried away alive by the
devil, as is made known to you, dear Christian reader,
in truthful newspapers.' [1]

'Truthful' newspapers and songs of this sort on
the carrying off of living people by the devil were
frequently circulated, especially after the second half
of the sixteenth century. ' Cases were known,' said a
preacher in 1559, ' and could be counted in hundreds,
of men and women of all ages.' [2] In the year 1550
Henry Wirry of Solothurn wrote ' in rhyme a wonder-

----

[1] *Erschröckliche Zeitung,* ' giving an account of the proceedings against
Hennig Brabant at Brunswick, devil's ally and traitor,' &c. (Lauingen,
1606).   [2] In the passage cited above at p. 374, n. 3.

ful true and strange history of how, before his own
eyes, a priest and his cook were carried off by the
devil.' [1] In the following year there appeared at Leipzig 'Erschreckliche neue Zeitung' of a woman who
was carried away by the devil in the Meckelburg district : ' he was seen to strangle the woman in the air,
and finally he dropped her down on the earth.' [2] Still
more horrible was his treatment of another woman,
concerning whom John Hermann, preacher at Oster
in Mecklenburg, published a newspaper account,[3]
while the preacher Erasmus Winter held her up as a
warning to his audience : ' on June 24, not far from the
Neue Brandenburg, in the village of Oster, at a wedding,
the devil took a swearing woman away from table,
carried her up into the air, tore her in four pieces, and
threw one piece into each street, but placed the entrails
on the table before the magistrate in the presence of
all the company, and said that as he would not desist
from his extortion and blasphemy, and also would not
punish such vices in others, the same fate, and no other,
would soon befall him.' [4] In Vienna, as is seen from a
sermon of the Jesuit George Scherer, the firm belief
prevailed that in 1570 a baker in the town, who had
mocked at the Corpus Christi procession, had been
carried round by the devil during the ceremony, and

[1] Weller, *Annalen*, i. 227, No. 139.
[2] Weller, *Zeitungen*, No. 195. In an old death-register of the parish
of Culmbach there is the following entry : ' Anno 1564, on the night of
Fabian and Sebastian, the wicked spirit seized and cruelly injured several
people on the Plassenburg ; two of them, the chief cook and the quarter-
master of the Margrave George Frederic, he actually strangled.' Spiess,
Archivische Nebenarbeiten, i. 62.
[3] Lisch, *Jahrbücher des Vereins für mecklenburgische Geschichte*, xxii.
267.
[4] Winter, *Encaenia*, p. 182.

afterwards let fall on a nut tree, 'with the result that people had thought an earthquake had taken place.' [1] From Dresden, in 1582, there went out two 'veritable and terrible accounts, the one of a young woman who had given herself up to the devil for six years, and had been carried off by him before the time had elapsed ; the other of a student whom the devil in like manner had driven into horrible sins and then strangled.' [2] According to a Cologne paper of 1584, the devil carried off a proud wench of Antwerp and caused a dog to jump out of her coffin.[3] From Prague 'a terrible wonder-story was related in verse' of how a peasant 'in this year 1586 was set fire to by the devils on account of his manifold blasphemy of God.' [4] In Königsberg the devil carried off a shoemaker's apprentice ; at Willisau, in Switzerland, a gambler ; at a wedding, once, three musicians.[5] It was spread about by the Protestants as a well-known fact that, once at Forchheim, Satan had carried off from the pulpit, right up into the air in

---

[1] Scherer, *Postille*, Sermon on the first Sunday in Lent.

[2] Weller, *Zeitungen*, No. 557. The author of the pamphlet, *Von Höllenzwängen und Teufelsbeschwörungen*, p. 8, complains in 1563 that 'the young people have become so wicked, godless, and devil-seeking, that even before they go to the universities, when they are only boys at gymnasia, they have already often entered into leagues with the devil incarnate.' A Danzig school regulation of 1568 decrees : ' Abstineant Scolastici ab execrationibus, iuramentis, *magia* . . . Nemo faciat *pacta cum Diabolis*, callidius aetati imbecilliori insidiantibus ' (Löschke, p. 147).

[3] Weller, *Zeitungen*, No. 594.

[4] Weller, *Annalen*, ii. 438, No. 611.

[5] Cf. Weller, *Annalen*, ii. 440, No. 628 ; 441, No. 633 ; Schopper, pp. 240–241. 'In the open street,' wrote the Protestant theologian Saubert to a friend, ' a man was torn to pieces by the devil and all the parts of his body scattered about, here a leg, there an arm, here the lungs, there the liver : a dreadful sight ; some of my colleagues were eye-witnesses.' Tholuck, *Das kirchliche Leben*, p. 76.

the sight of the whole congregation, a Catholic priest who was disputing the Protestant doctrines.[1]

On the soil of such universally prevalent belief in the marvels of occultism, magic and devilry, amid the coarsening and deterioration of intellectual, moral, and religious life which is so plainly apparent in the art and the popular literature of the period, there was abundant scope for the prolific growth of one of the most terrible episodes in the whole history of mankind—namely, the belief in witches, and the persecution of witches.

[1] Cf. Döllinger, ii. 420. Von Liliencron (*Mitteilungen*, pp. 138–139) rightly sees in the whole range of this literature of horrors ' nothing but a dark picture of the coarseness and superstition of a decadent age.' ** Charles H. Herford (*Studies in the Literary Relations of England and Germany in the Sixteenth Century*, Cambridge, 1891) points out that Germany in the sixteenth century was only known in England as the land of wonder-tales of necromancy, sorcerers, witches, devils, and so on, and that the ' wonderful strange news from Germany' formed a complete body of pamphlet literature.

SUPPLEMENTARY

To vol. xi. p. 22, n. 1. The relation of the late Gothic to the Renaissance has lately led to a lively controversy, not yet concluded, which cannot be entered into in detail here. Against Haenel and Schmarsow's 'Reformvorschläge zur Geschichte der deutschen Renaissance' (in the 'Bericht über die Verhandl. der sächs. Gesellsch. der Wissensch. zu Leipzig, Phil.-hist. Kl.' Bd. li. 1899) Dehio has expressed his opinion in Zimmermann's 'Kunstchronik,' N.F. Jahrg. xi. Nos. 18 and 20. Schmarsow answered him in the 'Kunstchronik,' 1900, No. 27, and in the article 'Zur Beurteilung der Spätgotik' in the 'Repert. für Kunstwissenschaft' xxiii. (1900), 290 ff. Of late also H. A. Schmid has expressed his views in an essay on the use of the term Renaissance. 'Über den Gebrauch des Wortes Renaissance' ('Kunstchronik,' 1900, No. 30). The reasons which are here brought forward against the use of the word 'Renaissance' appear to me highly noteworthy. To this connexion belongs also the article of A. Schröder, 'Spätgotik und Protestantismus' in Schnütgen's 'Zeitschr. für christl. Kunst' (1900), 150 ff. Haenel's discovery of the Protestant character of the late Gothic is so admirably and conclusively refuted here, that this hypothesis may be considered as demolished.

To vol. xi. p. 123 f. Cf. Bezold, 'Baukunst der Renaissance,' p. 132 ff., who pronounces the following judgment: 'In comparison with the artistic sense which even the

later Catholic church-buildings display, all that was
achieved on the Protestant side was, with few exceptions, inferior.   The attempt to evolve a suitable form of
church building out of the requirements of Protestant
worship did not succeed.   Greater originality is all that
can be claimed by the Reformed Church.   It broke more
decisively with the Lutheran Church, which at first only
slightly modified the forms of Catholic worship.   The
present-day rationalistic form of the Lutheran Church
service must not be put back to the sixteenth century;
it was only developed in the course of the eighteenth and
nineteenth centuries.   The order of divine service was
determined in 1536 by Luther's pamphlet, " Die deutsche
Messe und Gottesdienstordnung zu Wittenberg für
genommen."   In accordance with this, preaching, it is
true, formed the most important feature of the service,
but besides the opening and closing congregational singing, parts of the Mass were retained in a German translation.   The second part of the service consisted of the
Lord's Supper.   This was the rule.   Here and there,
however, still more of the old form was retained ; the
service of the altar also always had a large share, and the
Church service had two central points instead of one.
This circumstance introduced into the architectural
organism an anomaly which even to-day has not been
fully overcome ; the respective positions of pulpit and
altar have never been definitely settled.   The sixteenth
century by no means hit on a satisfactory architectonic
solution of this question.   The position of the altar
remained the same, and either the pulpit was moved
nearer to the altar in order that both might be in sight
of the whole congregation, or else the pulpit was left
in the nave, and the seats so placed as to attain the

desired object. In view of the increased importance of the sermon it was necessary as far as possible to enable all the members of the congregation to understand the preacher, and the seats must, therefore, not be too far removed from the pulpit. The architectonic solution of this question would have been the adoption of round buildings as the normal form of Protestant churches. The Reformed party, to which the importance of the altar was a slighter consideration, did not scruple to resort to this solution, and there is no lack, in Holland especially, of interesting attempts in this direction. On the part of the Lutherans also this consideration has not prevailed against tradition, and with them recourse was had to galleries as a way out of the difficulty, and these adjuncts soon came to be regarded as an indispensable feature of Protestant churches. They were constructed either without any close dependence on the structural conditions, or else they were brought into connexion with the organism of the building by providing the aisles with upper stories, opening on the nave through arcades. This form is not exclusively Protestant. The first is the more widespread. If the round building was to be avoided, the next best arrangement for Protestant services was an oblong, one-naved hall. But in such interiors the raised seats could only be introduced as galleries supported by pillars or consoles. Thus the Protestantism of the sixteenth and seventeenth centuries represents a distinct architectural loss. The impressive spaciousness and the symbolism of Catholic church building had almost entirely disappeared or become superfluous, while from no other quarter had adequate compensation presented itself.'

INDEX OF PLACES

INDEX OF PERSONS

97, 186 (*n.* 2), 190 (*n.* 1), 220 (*n.* 1), 360 (*n.* 1)

Schertlin, Leonard (poet), 216 (*n.* 2)

Schlayss, John (dean and comedy-writer), 22, 26 ff., 35, 160 (*n.* 2)

Schlutterbäurin, Anna (a woman possessed by a devil), 336

Schmarson, Aug. (art historian), 387

Schmeltzl, Wolfg. (schoolmaster), 12 f.

Schmid, Eric (historian of literature), 75 (*n.* 1), 88 (*n.* 1), 91 (*n.* 1), 152 (*n.* 1), 190 (*n.* 1)

Schmid, H. A. (art writer), 387

Schmid, Thom. (stonemason), 133

Schmidt, Hans (smith's apprentice), 337

Schmitt, Karl (historian of literature), 172 (*n.* 3)

Schoppius, Andr. (theologian), 208 (*n.* 2)

Schröder, A. (historian), 387

Schultze, Karl Allwin (printer), 275 (*n.* 2)

Schumann, Valentine (poet), 182 (*n.* 2), 190

Schütz, John (preacher), 324

Schwartz, Christopher (Court painter), 14 (*n.* 1)

Schwenkfeld, Caspar v. (theologian), 112 f., 255

Scultetus, Abraham (preacher), 364 (*n.* 1)

Sebisch, Melch. (physician), 290 (*n.* 1)

Seger, John (poet laureate), 33

Seger, Ursula, 377

Selnekker, Nich. (theologian), 253

Seneca, 147

Seydel, Maurice, 258

Shakespeare, W., 142

Sickingen, Franz, 5

Sigfridus, Thom. (author), 355

Sigmund (Archduke of Austria), 218

Sigwart, John George (theologian) 261

Silberschlag, George (pastor), 334 (*n.* 1)

Sixtus V (Pope), 184 (*n.* 1)

Sommer, John (pastor), 150, 206, 216 (*n.* 2)

Sophia of Kursachsen (electorate of

Saxony), later Duchess of Pomerania), 28

Spahn, M. (historian), 67 (*n.* 1)

Spalatin (Burckhart), George (theologian), 70 ; his wife Gutta, 70

Spangenberg, Cyriacus (chemist), 189, 206 (*n.* 1), 323

Spencer, John (stage director), 165

Spengler, F. (historian of literature), 13 (*n.* 1), 49 (*n.* 1)

Sperber, Jul. (house physician), 284

Spiers, John (bookseller), 358 (*n.* 1)

Sprengel, Karl (physician and botanist), 284 (*n.* 1), 290 (*n.* 1)

Stein, Marquard v. (author), 218

Stein, William (pastor), 3

Steinbach, David (court preacher), 377

Steinhart, Henry (dean), 71

Steudlin, Helias (notary), 300

Stifel, Esais (' prophet '), 267

Stimmer, Tob. (painter and moulder), 182 (*n.* 2)

Stöcker, James (theologian), 206 (*n.* 1)

Strauch, Ph. (historian of literature), 71 (*n.* 3)

Strauss, Dav. Frederic (author), 113 (*n.* 1)

Streuber, Pet. (superintendent), 114

Stricerius, John (preacher), 158

Stymmel, Christopher (poet), 155 (*n.* 1)

Taurer, Ambrose (author), 245

Terence, 51

Tetzel, John, 104–109, 118

Tholuck, Fred. Aug. Gottren (theologian), 385 (*n.* 5)

Thurn von Thurneissen, Leon (house physician), 297 f., 352, 367

Tittmann, J. (historian of literature), 42 (*n.* 2), 53 (*n.* 1), 163 (*n.* 1)

Trautmann, Karl (historian), 14 (*n.* 1), 161 (*n.* 3)

Trithemius (abbot), 346 (*n.* 1)

Tyrolf, John (poet), 83

Ulrich III (abbot of Einsiedeln), 6 (*n.* 5)

END OF THE TWELFTH VOLUME

PRINTED BY
SPOTTISWOODE AND CO. LTD., NEW-STREET SQUARE
LONDON

DATE DUE